Date Due

BRODART, CO.   Cat. No. 23-233-003   Printed in U.S.A.

THE

TANTE MARIE'S COOKING SCHOOL COOKBOOK

More Than 250 Recipes for the Passionate Home Cook

MARY RISLEY

SIMON & SCHUSTER
New York   London   Toronto   Sydney

SIMON & SCHUSTER
Rockefeller Center
1230 Avenue of the Americas
New York, NY 10020

For information about special discounts for bulk purchases,
please contact Simon & Schuster Special Sales:
1-800-456-6798 or business@simonandschuster.com

Designed by Katy Riegel

Manufactured in the United States of America

3   5   7   9   10   8   6   4

Library of Congress Cataloging-in-Publication Data
Risley, Mary.
The Tante Marie's Cooking School cookbook : more than 250 recipes for the
passionate home cook / Mary Risley.
p.   cm.
Includes index.
1. Cookery, French.   I. Tante Marie School of Cookery.   II. Title.
TX719.R545   2003
641.5944—dc21
2003042567
ISBN 0-7432-1491-9

To Julia Child

ACKNOWLEDGMENTS

THE GREAT THING about being involved in cooking is having so many friends around the world. Everyone in the food world is generous and warm of spirit. The other great thing about having a cooking school in San Francisco is being able to bring so many wonderful students here to learn cooking. All this wouldn't be possible without the hard work and dedication of all the teachers at Tante Marie's, great teachers like Diane Dexter, Kathleen Volkman, Jim Dodge, Pam Farrell, Carolyn Dille, Cindy Mushet, Heidi Krahling, Cathy Burgett, Alice Medrich, Linda Sullivan, Catherine Pantsios, Joanne Weir, Giuliano Bugialli, Farina Achuck, Jessica Lasky, Nick Malgieri, and Jodi Liano. None of this would have been possible without Peggy Lynch, the administrative director of Tante Marie's. Thank you, Peggy!

Thanks also to Jane Dystel, my agent; Sydny Miner, my editor; Jonathon Brodman, production editor; and Virginia McRae, copy editor.

A very special thanks to Jodi Liano, for testing and typing all the recipes in this book; as well as Amanda Haas, for re-testing.

The San Francisco Bay Area is the home to an amazing number of people who love food and cooking and enjoy sharing their knowledge. With much gratitude, I acknowledge just some of the people who have helped me verify the information in this book: Mats and Dafne Engstrom of Tsar Nicoulai Caviar; Peggy Smith of Tomales Bay Cheese Co.; Maggie Klein of Oliveto, in Oakland; Tom Worthington of Monterey Fish Co.; Gerald Asher, formerly of *Gourmet* magazine; Karen Techeira of Freed, Teller, and Freed; and the inimitable Flo Braker, who knows all about chocolate. I am also truly grateful to Heidi Krahling, Tori Ritchie, and Nick Malgieri for their help.

CONTENTS

INTRODUCTION

COOKING IS FUN! When I started teaching cooking in 1973 in my San Francisco flat, there was a common expression: "If you can read, you can cook." That was an era when we were all falling in love with cooking. We were coming out of an era when "gourmet cooking" included casseroles made with cream of mushroom soup; we were moving into an era of beef Wellington and Grand Marnier soufflé. Some of us taught ourselves how to cook by reading *The Joy of Cooking*; others by reading *Mastering the Art of French Cooking,* volumes one and two. We read, and cooked, and talked about food. It was a very exciting time.

In those days, Julia Child taught us on television. There were cooking demonstrations by people such as Marcella Hazan and Richard Olney at the Sutter Street store of Williams-Sonoma; Jacques Pépin was teaching at a cooking school in Palo Alto. Not long after, James Beard started giving classes at the Stanford Court Hotel. I was lucky enough to watch Julia's shows, memorize her books, and take classes from these great cooks. I also took a short course at Le Cordon Bleu in London.

With very little formal training, I began teaching people how to cook. Two or three evenings a week eight people would come to my flat to cook together. I would read the book the night before, buy the groceries, and hand out the recipes. It was just plain fun.

Very soon after, I began giving demonstrations at stores such as Design Research and Williams-Sonoma. I also taught regularly on local morning television shows. Although I was teaching in my home, I called my school Tante Marie's Cooking School after an old French cookbook. (Tante Marie means Aunt Mary.)

After five years of this, I started to think about getting serious about my career. One day I told a friend I simply wasn't making enough money and I didn't have any resources—what if I broke my leg? Two days later I slipped on first base and did break my leg! That was when I raised some capital and started a full-time cooking school in April 1979 on a residential block between Telegraph Hill and Fisherman's Wharf. About that time I was able to go back to Europe for another short course at the London Cordon Bleu and at La Varenne in Paris, a mecca in those days for anyone wanting to learn French cooking.

Tante Marie's Cooking School in San Francisco didn't exactly take off. Yes, we had an assured business of young people coming after work to cook together, but I had only one full-time student the first summer. His teachers each week were Jeremiah Tower, Carlo Middione, and Ken Hom. The next summer I had three full-time students. You might say it was a slow start, but we kept going.

Five years later I went back to Europe, this time to learn sauces from Madeleine Kamman in her home in Lake Annecy and to learn pastry, again at La Varenne. I spent some weeks in three consecutive years with Lorenza de Medici at her home, Badia a Coltibuono, learning Italian cooking. At other times I took groups to cook with Darina Allen at Ballymaloe Cookery School in Cork; to Bordeaux with Jean-Pierre Moulle; to Mexico with Diana Kennedy; to Provence with Lydie Marshall; and to Sicily with Anna Tasca Lanza.

Now Tante Marie's is busy every day and every night of the week. In the same storefront where we started in 1979, fourteen students cook every weekday with a chef/instructor for the Six-Month Full-Time Culinary Course. Another fourteen students cook every Monday and Wednesday evening and every other Saturday with their chef/instructor for the Six-Month Part-Time Pastry Course. On the other weekends, people come from places such as Portland, Reno, and Los Angeles for Weekend Participation Courses, for classes on subjects such as Mediterranean cooking or California Asian cooking. Once a week for six evenings, students come to the Evening Participation Courses. Between terms we offer Cooking Vacations for students from around the world. Finally, whenever the school is free, we have Party Classes for groups who take over the school for the whole evening. On these evenings, between twenty and thirty people cook a meal together for such events as a party for summer associates of a law firm or perhaps for a birthday party. At Tante Marie's the teachers specialize in getting everyone to cook. That's what makes it fun.

A good cooking teacher needs to read new cookbooks, food magazines, and newspaper food sections to be up on what's current in cooking. However, the best way to learn is to eat in good restaurants. Chefs are the innovators. A good cooking teacher eats a dish in a restaurant, tries it at home or with her students, and writes it up in her own words, giving credit to the chef. The recipes in this book are from many sources. We have been cooking with them over the years, making changes, adapting, and enjoying. I have tried my best to credit sources.

How to Cook

The first thing to learn about cooking is not to worry! When you offer to cook for others, it is one of the nicest things you can do for them. So what if the food doesn't come out exactly as you'd like? The fact that you have shared yourself with others by giving them food is all that counts.

In this book I've tried to supply explanations and hints to give you the confidence to cook, to risk making mistakes, and to figure out how to correct them. For instance, if you understand what it means to deglaze, or what flour does when exercised, it will help you to see how simple cooking really is. Most cookbooks are basically recipe collections that tell you exactly how to execute the recipes. What I am trying to do here is teach you how to cook so that you can start cooking without recipes. Each chapter starts with simpler recipes and moves to the more complicated. If you really cook your way through this book, you will have learned every technique that an accomplished home cook needs. You may, however, prefer to try recipes randomly. Hopefully this will be a learning experience as well. The concept of this book is to teach cooking through recipes, with additional information supplied throughout so that you will begin to understand cooking in its entirety. Although we teach much more in the full-time culinary kitchen of Tante Marie's Cooking School—how to cook sweetbreads and how to make aspic, for example— I have included only recipes in this book that I would serve in my own home.

When approaching a recipe, keep in mind that recipes are just guidelines; they do not have to be followed to the letter. However, it is a good idea not to start drastically changing a recipe until you've tried it first as it is written. The top of the recipe lists what ingredients to get out and what needs to be prepared ahead. Read through this to note when things like toasted nuts or melted butter are called for. What good cooks do when following a recipe is read through the recipe first to get clear in their minds the steps to be followed. They may refer back to the recipe once in a while, but not constantly. Keep in mind that when it says "chopped," "minced," "sifted," or "melted" before the ingredient, you do those things before measuring. When it says, for example, "1 cup chopped walnuts," chop them before measuring them.

KNIVES

It is very important to learn how to use a knife properly. You should hold your 8- or 9-inch French chef's knife firmly, grasping the blade as well as the handle. Slice in one downward motion forward onto a wooden board. Do not lean or slide the knife over to get the food off. It will come off in the next slice. Your other hand should be curled so that the thumb is behind the fingers, which are curled so that the knife will glide off the knuckles if it gets too close. I find lifting the elbow helps to keep the noncutting hand in place. It takes about three weeks to develop a new habit. Now is the time to start the habit of slicing, chopping, and mincing correctly. When chopping, try not to have the knife going toward your hand or body. When mincing, keep both hands on the knife. Always clean the knife and put it away when you are through with it. Do not grab for a falling knife; rather, jump away. Remember that a French chef's knife is not suitable for cutting everything. Meat should be sliced with a thin knife, while cakes and bread should be cut with a serrated knife. Paring knives are fine for many small tasks.

INGREDIENTS

The professional cook chops and minces everything ahead of time. Since most cooking in restaurants now is done "to order," or "à la minute," the professional doesn't start cooking until the order comes in. Getting everything ready is called doing the "mise en place." However, to save time a home cook is more likely to prepare the onions and put them on to cook, while mincing the garlic and then peeling, seeding, and chopping the tomatoes to add after that. The idea for both the professional and the accomplished home cook is to plan time so there is no waiting for something to cook.

In the Tante Marie kitchens and in this book, sugar is always granulated unless specified otherwise; flour is always unbleached all-purpose; butter is unsalted; olive oil is virgin or extra virgin; lemon juice is always freshly squeezed; eggs are large; and onions are always yellow unless specified otherwise.

The assumption in this book is that you will wash all ingredients except mushrooms and berries such as strawberries and raspberries—these should be wiped with a damp cloth, so that they don't absorb excess moisture.

MEASURING

Glass measuring cups are for measuring liquids. Metal measuring cups are for measuring dry ingredients, flour in particular. You will look silly trying to measure vinegar in a little metal cup or packing flour into a glass measuring cup. In fact, you would look silly trying to grind pepper into little measuring spoons. These are for baking. If you aren't sure what a teaspoon of something looks like in your hand, measure a teaspoon of salt and put it into your hand, so that you can start using your hand to measure while cooking. It is very important that you measure baking soda and baking powder exactly, but everything else you can guess at. You never see restaurant cooks using little spoons that are all tied together to measure a tablespoon of brandy; they just pour it in. Think of this too: there are about four cups of wine in a bottle, so when a recipe calls for a cup of wine, use about one-quarter of a bottle. This is what I mean about taking risks. There is no harm done if you add too much brandy one time and too little the next, or salt or butter, for that matter. Just do it!

However, ingredients are usually purchased by weight—an ounce of this, or a pound of that. That is why many books give conversion charts: a pound of flour has a much larger volume than a pound of butter. Don't confuse weight and volume. When a recipe calls for something like 2½ pounds of potatoes, remember that generally a potato, an apple, and a tomato each weighs about half a pound. So 2½ pounds of potatoes is five large potatoes.

UNDERSTANDING HEAT

Moderating the flame is something no one can teach you. After a while you just get a feel for it. Don't be afraid to cook over high heat—for most cooking it is better than low heat. Always turn the handle of a pot on the stove so that it is not sticking out where someone might knock it.

It is important to stir mixtures when they are coming to a boil to prevent them from sticking and burning. Once the mixture boils and the heat is lowered to a simmer, the movement of the simmer will help to keep the mixture from sticking on the bottom of the pan.

A low oven (250 degrees) is for baking meringues and warming plates. A moderate oven (350 degrees) is for reheating food, baking, and general cooking. A hot oven (450 to 500 degrees) is for roasting. After a while, you will be able to stick your arm in an oven and tell about what temperature it is. With the cost and scarcity of energy, it makes no sense to always preheat the oven. The truth is that the only time you need a preheated oven is for baking and for soufflés.

All these recipes have been tested in regular home ovens. When using convection ovens, the cooking times recommended here must be shortened.

SEASONING

You should know what absolutely every ingredient you put into a dish tastes like. Good cooks taste all the time when they are cooking to see how the dish is progressing and to know what's happening. You can't leave taste to random guessing or blind following of recipes. I can't emphasize this enough! The more you taste the food you are making, the more control you will have over the final dish. Never, never serve food without tasting it to make sure it is seasoned the way you want.

SERVING

Put hot food on heated plates. When serving individual plates, food that is mounded is more attractive than food that is flat. I do not mean food that is layered one course on top of another; just mound it a little. All the food should be in the middle of the plate; there should be no bare spots showing in the middle. There should also be no food on the rim of the plate—the rim should rather be like a frame of a picture. Don't waste time making the plate look perfect. If the food gets cold while you are arranging it, stick it in a hot oven to warm it up.

Recommended List of Equipment

8- or 9-inch chef's knife
bread knife
paring knife
boning knife
carving knife
sharpening steel
1-, 2-, and 4-quart saucepans (copper or
    All-Clad)
10-inch sauté pan (stainless steel–lined
    copper or All-Clad)
nonstick frying pan (SilverStone)
pasta pot (stainless steel)
10 by 16-inch roasting pan (Le Creuset)
10 by 16 by 5-inch oval deep enamel
    covered pot (Le Creuset) (sometimes
    called Dutch or French oven)
6 baking sheets (half sheet pans)
kitchen scissors
measuring spoons
dry measuring cups
pastry cutter and scraper
rolling pin
4- and 9-inch metal tart tins with removable
    bottoms; 4-inch flan rings
8 or 9 by 3-inch cake pans
large flat plates for serving tarts or cakes
pie server
cooling racks
1-, 2-, and 4-cup Pyrex measuring cups
3-inch Pyrex custard cups
9 by 13-inch Pyrex glass baking pans
stainless steel bowls in various sizes
vegetable peeler
wine opener

ladle
tongs
wooden spoons and spatulas
bulb baster
meat pounder
sauce and balloon whisk
juicer
scales
sieve
grater
3-inch individual ring molds
2-inch individual ramekins
4-inch individual gratin dishes
1-inch cookie cutter
3-inch cookie cutter
string
skewers
potato ricer
food mill
immersion blender
Cuisinart food processor
Kitchen Aid mixer
large salad bowl and servers
pizza peel and stone
grill pan with ridges
cold smoker
charcoal grill with chimney starter
blowtorch
ice cream machine

Methods of Cooking

If someone brings you a whole salmon, or a wild turkey, or a piece of venison, the first thing you should say to yourself is "How am I going to cook this?" It is very important that you know whether the fish, poultry, or meat is tough or tender before you decide what method of cooking to use. Generally, all fish is tender whether caught in the wild or farmed, but falls apart easily as soon as it is cooked through. Most chickens, ducks, and rabbits for sale in the markets are slaughtered when they are young and tender. Meat can range from tough to tender, depending on what part of the animal it comes from. Most of the pork, lamb, and beef offered for sale in upscale markets is tender and lean. Sometimes you can purchase the tough cuts of meat only by special order.

When a hunter brings you a bird or a piece of venison, you need to know how old it is to determine how tender it is. The size of the turkey or deer will usually tell you its approximate age. You can roast a young bird but must marinate an older one.

With any purchased meat, it is not only a question of age but of cut. If the cut is from the forequarters, it is probably tough. If it is from the hindquarters, it may be tender. The farther the meat from the center of the back, the tougher it can be. More tender cuts of meat have white streaks of fat, called marbling, throughout. Tougher cuts of meat have no marbling. When in doubt, it's best to ask the butcher. Don't try to grill or roast tough meats unless they have been marinated—it is

the tough cuts of meat that make the delicious braises and stews.

The following cooking methods should be reviewed before you begin to cook any fish, poultry, or meat without a recipe.

Moist heat	poach	fish, eggs, pears
	steam	fish, green vegetables
	boil	pasta, green vegetables
Dry heat	roast/bake	fish, chicken, tender cuts of meat
	grill/broil	fish, chicken, tender cuts of meat
In fat	pan-fry, stir-fry, sauté	fish, chicken, tender cuts of meat
	deep-fry	fish, chicken, tender cuts of meat
Combination	braise	fish, chicken, tender cuts of meat to flavor, tough cuts of meat to flavor and tenderize
	stew	tough cuts of meat to tenderize
Encased	in parchment	fish and other tender foods
	in pastry	fish and other tender foods
Miscellaneous	marinate	fish
	cure, pickle, and/or smoke	fish, poultry, meats

MOIST HEAT

The principal reason to cook food in moist heat is to keep it from drying out. Poaching means to keep the liquid below a boil so that it barely moves. If a fish boils vigorously, it will fall apart when fully cooked. Boil food that you want to cook evenly, such as pasta and vegetables, and use plenty of water.

DRY HEAT

Food must already be tender before being roasted, baked, or broiled in an oven, or grilled over a wood, charcoal, or gas grill. Care must be taken with fish so that it doesn't dry out in the oven or on the grill. A protective skin or layer of fat on poultry or meat will help to keep it from drying out. Food can be tenderized by marinating before roasting, baking, grilling, or broiling.

IN FAT

Cooking in a hot pan in a small amount of fat is called pan-frying, stir-frying, or sautéing. The difference is that generally sautéing is at a lower heat; pan-frying is at a higher heat; and stir-frying is still higher. The French word *sauter* means to jump; in other words, the pan is so hot that the food seems to jump around in it. New cooks often use the word sauté when they really mean cook. You don't really sauté onions until they are soft; you sauté food over high heat to give it a brown crust.

Deep-fry means to submerge food in a large amount of hot oil. Deep-fried properly, the food cooks so quickly at such a high heat that there is a minimum of fat absorption. Deep-fried food should have a golden brown, crisp crust. Tender food can be sautéed or deep-fried.

COMBINATION

To cook food by a combination of cooking methods usually means to brown (sauté) it first in fat, then cook it in a flavorful liquid (boil gently or simmer). Tender foods such as fish and chicken and tender cuts of meat may be braised simply to add flavor. Usually, however, meat is first browned in butter and/or oil, then cooked in a small amount of stock flavored with wine, aromatic vegetables (mirepoix), and fresh herbs (bouquet garni). Stewing is similar to braising, but there is considerably more liquid. Both braising and stewing are preferable for tough cuts of meat. When you brown meat, the sugar in the juices from the meat caramelizes on the bottom of the pan and these juices are dissolved by deglazing or simmering. When the meat is submitted to long, slow cooking, the juices from the meat go into the cooking liquid, and the flavors and liquid go into the meat, essentially making a sauce.

ENCASED

Encased in either parchment or pastry, food loses no juices to the cooking liquid as in the case of poaching or boiling, and the food does not dry out as in roasting or grilling because it essentially cooks in its own juices. This is particularly attractive for fish. In old-fashioned cooking, pastry gave fish, poultry, or meat the appearance of elegance.

MISCELLANEOUS

If you have leftover uncooked fish, you can cure it and/or smoke it to preserve it. You can also marinate poultry or meat to preserve it. Fish is sometimes "cooked" by marination.

A few methods of cooking are unique to certain food. If the fish is less than an inch or two in thickness, it does not have to be submerged in liquid but is put in a baking pan with ½ inch of liquid and covered with buttered parchment. In other words, it is simply poached in a small amount of liquid.

Although stews are always made with tough poultry or meat, some fish stews from coastal fishing towns are made with fish and seafood left over from the day's catch. These, of course, cannot be cooked a long time.

A chicken sauté, made with cut-up chicken, is similar to a stew. The chicken is browned well in a sauté pan, then returned to the pan to cook in its own juices.

Often a pork roast is browned on all sides in a deep casserole, then returned to the pan and roasted, covered, in its own juices to keep it moist. This cooking in a covered pot is similar to roasting.

Kinds of Sauces

If you roast a whole fish, a chicken, or a standing rib roast of beef on the bone, it will have more flavor than if you take it off the bone, yet sometimes the fish, chicken, or meat is more appealing served boneless. How do you capture the flavor from the bones and return it to the dish? You make a sauce from the bones. In classical French cooking, sauces start with making stock. The bones are cooked with aromatic vegetables and fresh herbs. For fish stock, the bones are cooked with 30 to 50 percent dry white wine and bouquet garni for no more than 30 minutes. For light chicken stock, the bones are cooked with the vegetables and bouquet garni for 3 to 4 hours. For dark veal stock, the bones and vegetables are first browned, then simmered with water, the bouquet garni, mushrooms, and tomatoes for 4 to 6 hours. Each of these stocks is a neutral liquid that can be used as an ingredient in soups, sauces, and stews. A good stock adds depth of flavor to a dish.

In classical French cooking, stock can be made into a mother sauce for meat by being cooked with such ingredients as carrots, onion, celery, bay leaf, parsley, thyme, and equal amounts of flour and butter. After the meat is cooked, all the fat is removed from the pan—it is degreased—and then the glaze (or sediment) on the bottom of the pan is dissolved in cold liquid, usually wine—this is called deglazing. The resulting pan juices can be strained into the demi-glace sauce or the demi-glace sauce added to the pan juices. Either way, the sauce needs to be simmered, flavored, and finished with butter or cream.

The purpose of a sauce is to enhance the dish, to make the dish taste better than it would without the sauce. A good sauce should have a coating consistency; it should appeal to the eye; and it should taste delicious. Classical cooks say there should be only 2 tablespoons of sauce in a dish and no more than one sauce in a meal. It is traditional to serve warm sauces with warm food and cold sauces with cold food. However, although it is not traditional to serve a hot artichoke with a mayonnaise or a cold artichoke with melted butter, go ahead and do it if it suits you—I believe it's okay to break the rules as long as you know them. The reason French cooking has become so important to understanding Western cooking is that the French have organized cooking, especially saucemaking, into a system. Whether one is cooking in Normandy with butter, in Provence with olive oil, or in Gascony with duck fat, the procedures are the same. Other cuisines such as Greek and Italian are still regional; that is, cooks not only cook differently in each region but they call the same thing by different names.

The five families of sauces in French cooking are

Béchamel	roux (flour and butter) plus milk
Velouté	roux plus fish or chicken stock
Demi-glace	browned roux plus brown stock (sometimes called espagnole)
Mayonnaise	cold egg and oil emulsion
Hollandaise	warm egg and butter emulsion

From each mother sauce, many smaller sauces can be derived simply by addition of other ingredients. For instance, when you add cheese to a béchamel sauce it becomes a Mornay sauce, a demi-glace with tomatoes and mustard is called sauce Robert, and an orange-flavored hollandaise is called sauce maltaise. These derivative sauces are called "petites sauces" by the French.

Important French sauces that are not really mother sauces are tomato, vinaigrette, and warm butter.

Dessert sauces include crème anglaise (stirred custard sauce), sabayon (warm egg and fortified wine sauce), fruit puree, chocolate, and caramel.

Many sauces can be classified as miscellaneous. These include mint sauce, horseradish sauce, pesto, and red pepper and peanut sauces, not to mention salsas and chutneys.

What is *glace de viande?* The flour-based mother sauces are made with stock. Although *demi-glace* sounds as if it means half glaze, it is really a basic brown sauce (mother sauce), according to me, the stock being cooked with roux, mirepoix, and bouquet garni. *Glace de viande* is an ingredient kept in classic French kitchens, a dark veal stock that has been reduced and reduced until it becomes a thick, dark gel. It can be kept in the refrigerator and added to stews and sauces to enrich them. You don't really need to keep *glace de viande* on hand if you do a good job of browning meat.

A BRIEF HISTORY OF SAUCES

When these sauces were codified at the end of the nineteenth and the beginning of the twentieth century, it was the cook's habit to mask the food with a sauce. Often food such as fresh fish had traveled a long distance, and although it wasn't spoiled, it didn't look appealing.

In the first half of the twentieth century the food in very fine restaurants was plated by the waiter. The waiters would wheel carts of warm food into the dining room and carve the meat, or fillet the fish, or cut up the game bird and serve it to the diner on warm plates accompanied by the sauce and vegetables.

In the early '70s, there was a revolution in how food was served, called nouvelle cuisine. Many changes were made in the traditional haute cuisine, which originated as the cooking of the aristocrats before the French Revolution and became the cooking of the fine dining restaurants after the revolution. The most important changes at that time were that the chef rather than the waiters designed and assembled the plates in the kitchen, and sauces were often served under the food rather than over it. Although béchamel was sometimes used for casserole-type dishes such as lasagna, the flour-based sauces using stock (fish velouté, chicken velouté, and demi-glace) were replaced in the repertoire of sauces by reduction sauces. Instead of hollandaise, beurre blanc became popular. In California, aïoli replaced mayonnaise as a mother sauce. At well-known restaurants, you saw menu items such as wild mushroom aïoli and red pepper aïoli.

A good reduction sauce for meat is made according to the same three steps described above for demi-glace sauce: (1) degrease and deglaze the pan with wine and boil; (2) add reduced stock (or essence) instead of demi-glace sauce, and add flavorings; and (3) finish with cream or butter. It is important to remember these three steps when making a French sauce from fish, chicken, or meat.

After the fad of nouvelle cuisine faded, many of the well-known chefs in California started looking beyond French cooking to see how to make food more flavorful. They traveled to India, Thailand, and Mexico to learn how to use exotic ingredients such as ginger, lemongrass, a variety of chiles, and spices that are now common. While consumers and home cooks became obsessed with taking fat out of food, restaurant chefs were adding more foreign ingredients and making towers of food. Sauces became simpler and simpler.

Now food in restaurants is often served without a sauce or with simple pan juices. If there is a sauce, it might be a flavored warm vinaigrette for fish, chicken, and meats, or an infused oil. One of the reasons for this change in attitude toward sauces is that both restaurant and home cooks now have access to such excellent ingredients. There is no need to cover fresh fish with sauce; a little butter or oil and a sprinkling of fresh herbs are all that is needed to make it look and taste delicious. Nevertheless, a knowledge of saucemaking is important for every good cook. Inevitably, the fashion will change and sauces will become popular once again. Throughout this book I have interspersed recipes for all the sauces I think a modern cook should know.

STOCKS

In French cooking, a stock is called the *fond de cuisine,* the foundation of cooking. Sometimes cooks in a professional kitchen make eight or ten different kinds of stock. A good home cook should be able to make fish, light chicken, and maybe dark veal stock. Stocks are generally the fresh bones of fish, poultry, or meat cooked in water with aromatic vegetables, herbs, and a bouquet garni long enough to extract the flavor from the bones.

Since fish stock takes so little time to make, it can be made the same day it is needed. Fish stock should not be confused with court bouillon, which is simply an acidulated liquid for poaching fish or shellfish. Concentrated fish stock is called fumet. (See page 376 for how to make fish stock.) A fish stock should not boil too vigorously or too long—20 to 30 minutes is long enough. For a neutral stock to be used with any fish or shellfish dish, make a stock from bones from any fish except salmon. Stock made from salmon will give a salmon taste to other fish dishes.

When you cook a lot, you invariably have chicken bones in the refrigerator or freezer. It's easy to cook them up with onions, carrots, and celery with parsley, thyme, and bay leaf for 3 to 4 hours to make a neutral ingredient to use in many ways. (See page 377 for how to make light chicken stock.) Chicken livers should not go in stock; save them for another use.

Very good meat sauces depend on very good meat stock. Generally, you can use dark veal stock with duck, veal, lamb, beef, and pork because it is a neutral ingredient that acts as a base for the flavors of these meats. It's worth finding a source for veal bones and taking the time to make dark veal stock if you love cooking meat. (See page 378 for how to make dark veal stock.)

All stocks should be simmered slowly and skimmed from time to time to prevent them from becoming cloudy.

CORRECTING SAUCES

No recipe can tell you exactly how to give your sauce the perfect texture and taste. This is because each fish, chicken, or meat dish cooks at a slightly different temperature and releases a different amount of juices. However, here are the steps to be followed to achieve a good sauce. When you have a simmering saucepan of strained sauce, the first thing to do is get the texture the way you want it—it should lightly coat the back of a metal spoon—and then proceed to correct the flavor.

CORRECTING TEXTURE

There are four options for achieving the correct texture, and they should be considered in this order:

1) *Reduction*—Let the sauce simmer until it is the right consistency. Remember that when you are reducing liquid, although the water is evaporating, the salt remains and, therefore, seems to intensify. Keep tasting; when the sauce becomes salty, stop reducing it.

2) *Adding starch in the form of beurre manié* (kneaded butter)—Mix together equal amounts of flour and butter by weight until the mixture resembles cookie dough. Whisk pea-size bits of this mixture into the boiling

sauce and wait to see how much the sauce thickens. Add more until the desired consistency is reached. A sauce thickened with beurre manié should not boil more than 10 minutes because it is not as stable as a sauce thickened with a cooked roux. Both beurre manié and roux are made of equal amounts of butter and flour. The difference is that roux is cooked before liquid is added, which makes it more stable, and beurre manié is whisked into boiling liquid.

3) *Adding starch in the form of a slurry*— Mixing a tablespoon or more of arrowroot, cornstarch, or potato starch with 3 or more tablespoons of cold water makes a slurry of pure starch. This can be whisked into the boiling sauce until the desired consistency is reached. A sauce thickened with a slurry should not boil more than 10 minutes. The difference between thickening with flour as in beurre manié and with pure starch as in a slurry is that flour makes the sauce somewhat pasty. Arrowroot, cornstarch, or potato starch makes the sauce gelatinous. You can remember the difference if you think of turkey gravy (pasty) and lemon meringue pie (gelatinous). The choice is up to the cook.

4) *Adding fat*—In the old days, a *liaison* of egg yolks mixed with cream was added to dishes such as white veal stew, a fricassee of chicken, or a vegetable soup to enrich the dish. Once a liaison is added, the mixture must not boil or the eggs will curdle. Sometimes, cream is added or cream mixed with arrowroot. Occasionally, a small amount of soft butter is added to thicken and enrich the sauce.

5) *Adding blood*—Sometimes classical dishes such as duck à l'orange or civet of rabbit are thickened with the blood of the recently killed animal. The most famous dish of this type still being served is the duck à l'orange at La Tour d'Argent in Paris. Sometimes a little foie gras or chicken liver can be added to get a similar effect. These obscure methods of thickening are never used at Tante Marie's.

The idea is that first you try reducing the sauce. When it becomes salty or you are running out of sauce, you can then decide whether to thicken with a beurre manié or a slurry. Whisk in the starch until the desired consistency is reached. At this point, correct the taste and add any flavorings or flourishes, such as Madeira for a Madeira sauce or cooked sliced mushrooms for a forestière sauce. You finish the sauce by swirling in a little butter or cream.

In modern reduction sauces, the starch is omitted and the sauce is thickened simply by reducing the stock. Nevertheless, the flour-based sauces are important to learn.

CORRECTING TASTE

When you taste a sauce and think, "This needs something," the chances are it needs salt. However, when salt isn't necessarily the answer, here are some considerations and remedies. It is important to remember that a good sauce should have a balance of salt (from the meat itself or from added salt); sweet (usually from onions and carrots); acid or sour (from wine); and bitter (often from browning the meat).

Lacks salt	Add salt
Too much salt	Add softened butter or crème fraîche
Lacks depth of flavor	Fish—add anchovy
	Meat—add *glace de viande* (meat glaze)
	Vegetable—add soy sauce
Lacks sweetness	Add butter (never sugar)
Too sweet	Add lemon juice (never vinegar)
Lacks acid	Add brandy or lemon juice (never vinegar)
Too much acid	Add reduced cream (cream boiled until it is reduced by half)
Lacks bitterness	Some cooks add Angostura bitters or unsweetened cocoa
Too bitter	Add softened butter or reduced cream

There is really nothing you can do when a sauce is extremely salty except to increase the proportions of everything else in the sauce (or stew, for that matter). That is why it is so important not to guess at how much salt is needed; rather, add some and taste again, and then keep adding and tasting. If the sauce is really bitter, it probably means that it is burned. There is no correcting this, either; you just have to start over.

The most important thing about making any sauce is to get some of the cooking juices of the dish into the sauce. A mint sauce for lamb will taste much better if it has some lamb juices in it. A vinaigrette for mussels will taste much better if it has some of the cooking liquid of the mussels in it.

In Summary

I am hoping to build your confidence in the kitchen by teaching you the techniques you need and giving you the necessary knowledge to be a good cook. People with a passion for cooking really do make better food than people who are just going through the motions. Cooking is a skill—you really will become better and better at cooking the more you practice. There are a few people who are born with a talent to cook, and the rest of us can get really, really good through learning, concentrating, and practicing.

I like to compare cooking to an opera. In an opera, the impresario can bring together the best singers, the best designer, the best orchestra, and the best directors. All the elements can be the very best, yet somehow the opera just doesn't have that special something. It is the same with a dish or a meal. The final outcome cannot always be determined—there's always that special something. It's a kind of magic. In the long run, it's what makes cooking appealing and it's what makes life appealing—the unpredictability. The most important thing is to have fun doing it, share it with people you care about, and hope for that special something!

Now get going and start having fun cooking!

HORS D'OEUVRES

IT IS SAID THAT hors d'oeuvres should stimulate conversation as well as appetite. Nothing would dull both more than soggy, tasteless hors d'oeuvres! What I have assembled here is a collection of hors d'oeuvres that are delicious served with a drink before dinner or served to a group of friends at a cocktail party. What I call an hors d'oeuvre is something eaten with fingers; often they are called appetizers.

The word hors d'oeuvre is really old French for something "outside the work"—in other words, a little something that is not part of the planned menu. In France hors d'oeuvres are not necessarily finger food; they are often served on plates. Canapé is a French term for an hors d'oeuvre or appetizer served on cracker, bread, or toast. Crostini is an Italian term for an hors d'oeuvre served on a little toasted slice of bread. A large grilled slice of bread served on a plate and eaten with a knife and fork is called bruschetta in Italy.

When guests arrive, it is customary to offer them a drink or a glass of wine with a little something to eat. This could be as simple as a bowl of marinated olives or roasted almonds, or more elaborate, like hot goat's cheese canapés. It's important not to offer too many hors d'oeuvres or the guests will be full by the time dinner is served.

SERVING HORS D'OEUVRES

I like to serve hors d'oeuvres on round platters with cocktail napkins nearby as well as a saucer for discards like olive pits, artichoke leaves, or shrimp tails. I put an olive pit, artichoke leaf, or shrimp tail in it to show what it's for. I cut into things like goat's cheese or chicken liver mousse to show people they can too. If something looks too perfect, no one will eat it. Please don't serve a block of cheese, or worse still, little squares of cheese before dinner—it's too heavy. Use cheese as an ingredient in hors d'oeuvres, rather than by itself. On the other hand, a cheese course at the end of the meal can be sublime when served with good bread and a glass of wine.

COCKTAIL PARTIES

Cocktail parties are another story; here you can go all out with a large array of finger food. In the old days, a host or hostess would plan on four hors d'oeuvres per person because invariably guests would be going on to dinner somewhere else. Nowadays people may "graze" at your cocktail party instead of eating dinner, so plan to serve twelve hors d'oeuvres per person. People may even serve coffee and dessert at the end of a cocktail party.

A well-planned cocktail buffet should have a variety of food. Serve some fish, poultry, meat, dairy, vegetable, and something salty and something vinegary. Plan to have a variety of hors d'oeuvres, using bread, pastry, and vegetables. It's best not to serve too many dips or things that people have to spread or spoon themselves. It is also important not to serve sweets on the same table as savories. Putting what you thought was a cheese biscuit in your mouth but turns out to be a sugar cookie is an unpleasant surprise. At a proper cocktail buffet, the cold food is displayed beautifully, and two kinds of warm hors d'oeuvres are passed to the guests. You can make a cocktail buffet look great by crowding and raising the platters of food. I keep a collection of wooden wine boxes for putting on the table or counter. I cover these with white tablecloths and then arrange platters or baskets of food close together on top of the tiers. It is also good to mound the food on the platters so that people won't feel they are ruining the display by taking, say, one of the shrimp.

The Big Problem

The big problem with hors d'oeuvres is that so often they need to be heated, assembled, and served at the last minute. If you are the host, you want to enjoy your guests, not be preparing the hors d'oeuvres in the kitchen. That is why most of the hors d'oeuvres in this chapter are simple and can be made ahead. If you are having a cocktail party, the best idea is to hire someone to heat and pass the hors d'oeuvres, restock the buffet table, and clean up. That way, you can enjoy the party.

How to Make Hors d'Oeuvres Without a Recipe

When you need a quick hors d'oeuvre, mix equal amounts of soft butter and grated Parmesan with a little minced garlic and fresh herbs. Spread the mixture on lightly toasted, thin slices of baguette and then reheat in the oven. You can top the cheese mixture with such things as halved cherry tomatoes or cooked asparagus tips and warm briefly before serving. Don't forget always to taste the first hors d'oeuvres.

CAVIAR

FOR VERY SPECIAL OCCASIONS you may want to serve caviar. Caviar is the preserved roe (as yet unlaid eggs) of various species of sturgeon found around the world; it is classified as beluga, osetra, and sevruga. In the past, the best was said to be from the Caspian Sea. Overfishing has been a problem for many years, which is why sturgeon found in many American rivers is now a protected fish. However, caviar from farmed fish is in good markets. Look for Tsar Nicoulai California Estate Osetra. One of the reasons it is so expensive is that special handling is required to harvest the roe and pack it. It is also very perishable.

Always buy caviar from a reputable dealer. Look for caviar that is light or dark gray in color, with eggs intact. Keep it well chilled and do not open it until ready to serve. Good-quality caviar should always be served on white toast (preferably buttered) with just a drop of lemon and a glass of vodka or Champagne. I recommend serving it in a glass bowl over a larger bowl of ice with mother-of-pearl spoons (never silver). Although it is acceptable to serve good-quality caviar with crème fraîche or on blini (little yeast pancakes), it should never be served with chopped onions and chopped eggs—save these for lesser-quality caviar.

SMOKED SALMON

ANOTHER ELEGANT WAY to start a meal is to serve good-quality smoked salmon. The best-quality smoked salmon is considered to be wild salmon from Scotland, Ireland, or the Pacific Northwest. It should be translucent in appearance and have a light smoky taste.

Before smoking salmon, it is always put in a salt solution (brine) for a few days, which essentially pickles it. It is then smoked in such a way that it does not cook; in other words, cold smoked. See page 379 for how to cold-smoke your own salmon. If smoked salmon has an opaque look and falls apart easily, it has been hot smoked, which means it was cooked at the same time it was smoked. Hot-smoked salmon usually has a stronger taste.

It is best to purchase smoked salmon where it is sliced to order. Good-quality smoked salmon should be served on brown bread (preferably buttered) with a squeeze of lemon and a few grindings of pepper. The tradition of serving smoked salmon with cream cheese on bagels is okay when the salmon is quite salty. And if the smoked salmon is of lesser quality, it can be served with such things as sliced onions, capers, and olive oil. Smoked salmon should not be confused with gravlax, which is salmon that has been simply cured and not smoked. Gravlax should always be served with a sauce.

Marinated Olives

My favorite snacks before dinner are a bowl of marinated olives and a bowl of freshly roasted almonds. They go well with cocktails, red or white wine, or my favorite sparkling Normandy apple cider and are not so filling that they ruin one's appetite for dinner.

*1 pound good-quality olives, such as
    Picholine or Niçoise*
1 orange
4 bay leaves
4 sprigs thyme
6 garlic cloves, peeled
2 cups olive oil

Remove the zest of the orange with a vegetable peeler. Drain the olives and put them in a bowl. Add the orange zest, bay leaves, thyme, garlic, and olive oil. Let marinate for at least 48 hours before draining and serving.

SERVES 8 TO 12

Roasted Almonds

2 cups whole almonds, unblanched
2 to 4 dashes Tabasco sauce
2 tablespoons melted butter
Coarse salt
Freshly ground black pepper

Spread the almonds on a baking sheet. Add Tabasco to the melted butter and pour over the almonds. Sprinkle lots of salt and pepper over the nuts. Roast the almonds in a 350-degree oven for 15 minutes, or until light brown, stirring from time to time. Serve warm.

SERVES 8 TO 12

The first person to eat an olive must have been very hungry, because in their raw state olives taste terrible. Raw olives are cured by soaking them in water, salt, oil, or lye. At Tante Marie's, we have never been successful in curing our own olives. That is why I recommend buying them already cured and marinating them yourself.

Citrus rind is composed of the zest (the yellow or orange outer skin) and the pith (the white layer underneath). The zest is preferred in cooking because it contains the favorful oil of the fruit. The pith is avoided because it can turn bitter in cooking. When a recipe calls for a strip (or more) of the zest of an orange (lemon or grapefruit), remove the zest in strips with a vegetable peeler. When grated zest is called for, grate the orange or other citrus on a fine grater, or microplane, being careful not to remove the white pith, or use a citrus zester, which removes the zest in thin strips. Often cooks chop these little strips to make the zest finer.

Goat's Cheese Platter with Sun-Dried Tomatoes and Basil

This is an easy, attractive presentation that you can put together quickly as guests are arriving. I first learned it from my friend Rosemary Barron, who taught at Tante Marie's many years ago and is an expert on Greek cooking. In this dish, a soft creamy goat's cheese is surrounded by red, black, and green: sun-dried tomatoes, Niçoise olives, and shredded basil. The guest covers the bread with oil-soaked cheese and covers that with basil and/or sun-dried tomatoes. Be sure to warn your guests about olive pits!

4 ounces fresh goat's cheese in one large round or 3 small rounds
2 ounces sun-dried tomatoes, in oil
¼ cup Niçoise olives
½ bunch (2 ounces) fresh basil
3 tablespoons extra-virgin olive oil
Freshly ground black pepper
1 baguette, sliced

Place the goat's cheese in the middle of a round serving platter. Cut the tomatoes into ¼-inch lengths and place in three "spokes" around the cheese. Cut the basil leaves into chiffonade (shreds) and place them between the tomatoes. Scatter olives around the platter. Pour the oil from the tomatoes over the cheese with the olive oil. Grind plenty of black pepper over the cheese. Serve with sliced bread.

MAKES 2 PLATTERS, SERVES 8

To make basil chiffonade, place clean basil leaves, stems removed, crosswise on a board and roll them up like a cigar. With a sharp knife, cut thin shreds. (You can keep rolling in more leaves to cut.) Unfortunately, basil will turn black if cut more than an hour ahead.

Thanks to some dedicated cheesemakers in the United States, very interesting cheeses can be found made from goat's, sheep's, and cow's milk. Good-quality aged cheeses are best served at room temperature with good bread or crackers and should not be covered in olive oil and other flavorings.

Portobello Mushroom Sandwich with Grilled Red Onions and Fresh Mozzarella

Portobello mushrooms are all the rage now. They are really little cremini (Italian field) mushrooms, allowed to grow to giant size. Although they are delicious grilled just with olive oil, salt, and pepper, the addition of grilled onions and fresh mozzarella makes them even better. I cut the sandwiches in quarters to make a rustic hors d'oeuvre.

1 medium-size red onion
Coarse salt
Freshly ground black pepper
½ cup extra-virgin olive oil
4 portobello mushrooms, stems removed
3 tablespoons minced fresh herbs, such as parsley, thyme, chives, and savory
Four 1-ounce slices fresh mozzarella
4 soft hamburger-size buns

To grill the onions, preheat an unoiled 9- or 10-inch iron grill pan with ridges over high heat for about 10 minutes. Cut the onion in 8 wedges about ½ inch wide, making sure each wedge has a little of the root end attached to it. Rub each of these with 2 tablespoons olive oil and season with salt and pepper. Grill in the hot pan until wilted, moving them around to get them to cook evenly, 2 to 3 minutes.

To grill the mushrooms, rub them generously with the olive oil, herbs, and salt and pepper. Grill them in the same pan until they are slightly wilted, about 3 minutes on each side.

To serve, cut the buns in half crosswise, lay a slice of mozzarella on each, and cover with a mushroom and two pieces each of grilled red onion. Press the top part of the bun down firmly on the sandwich, cut in quarters, and serve warm. SERVES 8

Generally, red onions kept in storage are stronger in taste than freshly picked ones. Freshly picked onions tend to be lighter in color.

❧

Choose mushrooms that are lighter in color and firm to the touch with no soft spots. Mushrooms should always be stored in brown paper bags because they sweat in plastic bags.

Fava Bean Crostini with Pecorino

When driving through wine country, you can often see rows of green plants with little white flowers growing between the grapevines. These are fava beans, which have been planted to put nitrogen back into the soil. How fortunate we are that these harbingers of spring are so good to eat. They do, however, take work; fava beans need to be cooked twice. Making a fava bean spread to coat little toasts makes the hard work worth it. Fava beans and pecorino are a classic pairing.

1 pound fresh fava beans in their pods
1 garlic clove, minced
2 tablespoons olive oil
Coarse salt
Freshly ground white pepper
1 baguette
¼ pound medium-soft pecorino, cut into ½- by ¼-inch strips

To prepare the fava beans, first remove the beans from the pods. Drop the beans in a pot of boiling water for 30 seconds. Drain and, using your fingers, remove the tough shell from each bean.

In the same pot, cook the garlic in the olive oil with a sprinkling of salt over medium-high heat until the garlic is soft. Add the fava beans with ⅓ cup warm water and cook until the beans are tender. Mash the beans with a fork and add salt and pepper to taste.

To grill or toast the bread, cut the bread as thin as possible and place on a baking pan under a broiler, until the bread is golden on both sides. Rub a cut clove of garlic three or four times across the bread, and drizzle with olive oil.

To serve, rewarm the bread and the fava bean mixture. Spread each piece of toast with a tablespoonful of the fava bean puree, and top with four or five pieces of cheese. Serve immediately. (The toasts and the puree can be made ahead but should be reheated before serving.)   SERVES 8

In Italy, it is common to eat young fava beans directly from the pods with fresh pecorino cheese—a delicious combination.

❧

Pecorino is a local sheep's cheese in Italy—use the soft pecorino for this recipe, not the hard grating kind. (There is no substitute for pecorino.)

White Bean Crostini with Wilted Greens

Every once in a while it is a good idea to eat something really good for you, and this is it; a healthful hors d'oeuvre that is delicious too: Little toasts with a light coating of olive oil, spread with white bean puree and covered with cooked winter greens, go perfectly with a glass of chilled white wine.

½ onion, chopped
4 tablespoons extra-virgin olive oil
Coarse salt
2 garlic cloves, minced
1 cup cooked white beans, such as cannellini or Great Northern
¼ cup chicken or vegetable stock
1 tablespoon tomato paste
Cayenne pepper
½ teaspoon finely chopped fresh rosemary
Freshly ground black pepper
1 baguette
½ pound Red Russian kale or other mild winter green, washed but not dried, stemmed, and cut in 1-inch lengths

To make the bean puree, cook the onion with 2 tablespoons olive oil and ½ teaspoon salt in a medium-size saucepan over medium-high heat, stirring constantly, until the onion is soft, about 5 minutes. Add half the garlic and cook for a minute longer. Add the cooked beans, chicken stock, tomato paste, a few grains of cayenne, and rosemary and cook over medium-low heat until most of the liquid has evaporated. Remove from the heat and mash with a potato masher in the pot. Add salt and pepper to taste.

To toast the bread, slice it as thin as possible and lay in one layer on a baking sheet. Broil until golden on both sides, watching carefully so that they don't burn. Remove from the oven but leave the toasts on the pan.

To cook the greens, put 2 tablespoons olive oil and the remaining garlic with a sprinkling of salt in a medium-size sauté pan and cook over medium-high heat. When the garlic is soft, add the greens, cover, and cook for a minute. Remove the cover and turn the greens over on themselves with wooden spoons until they are wilted. Turn off the heat.

To assemble, spread a teaspoonful of the bean puree on each toast, top with a little of the wilted greens, and serve. (The toasts, bean puree, and wilted greens can all be made ahead. They should be reheated slightly before serving.)   SERVES 8

When cooking dried beans or legumes, always sort through them carefully and discard any small rocks you find. To do this, put the beans on a baking sheet and go over them systematically. To cook dried beans, soak the beans overnight in plenty of cold water. The next day, cook the beans, covered in fresh water with half an onion and a dried red chile pepper, until the beans are tender. This may take anywhere from 30 minutes to 1½ hours, depending on the age of the beans. Drain and proceed with the recipe.

Alternatively, the quick-soak method for cooking dried beans is to put the beans in a heavy pot, cover generously with water, bring to a boil, turn off the heat, cover, and let sit for an hour. Drain the beans, return them to the pan, and proceed as above, cooking them with half an onion, a dried red chile pepper, and plenty of fresh water until they are tender. This may take anywhere from 30 minutes to 1½ hours, depending on the age of the beans. Drain and proceed with the recipe.

If using canned beans, place the beans in a sieve and rinse well to remove the canned taste.

Charred Eggplant Dip with Pita Triangles

Heidi Krahling, the luscious chef-owner of Insalata's in San Anselmo, graduated from Tante Marie's almost twenty years ago and now teaches at Tante Marie's. Her food is full of the flavors of the Mediterranean and is very gutsy and lively, like her personality. Here is an old favorite of hers, her customers, and her students. Hopefully, it will be your favorite too.

> *1 head garlic*
> *⅓ cup extra-virgin olive oil plus some for drizzling*
> *Coarse salt*
> *Freshly ground pepper*
> *8 Asian eggplants*
> *1 red bell pepper*
> *2 tablespoons capers, rinsed and coarsely chopped*
> *8 Kalamata olives, pitted and coarsely chopped*
> *2 tablespoons minced fresh cilantro leaves*
> *2 tablespoons minced fresh mint leaves*
> *1½ teaspoons toasted and ground cumin seeds (see page 25)*
> *2 tablespoons balsamic or sherry vinegar*
> *2 teaspoons lime juice*
> *6 whole pita breads*

To roast the garlic, cut off the top quarter of the head of garlic. Place the garlic, cut side up, in its skin on a small piece of foil. Drizzle with olive oil and sprinkle with salt and pepper. Wrap the garlic tightly in the foil and roast in a 400-degree oven for about 30 minutes, until the garlic is completely soft. When the head is cool enough to handle, squeeze all the pulp into a large bowl and discard the skin. Mash the pulp with a fork.

To roast the eggplants, place them directly over a high flame on a gas burner, a few at a time. Cook about 2 minutes per side, turning with tongs to char evenly. Remove the eggplants when the skins are blackened and blistering and place them in a bowl tightly covered with plastic wrap. (It's important not to overcook the eggplants or they will taste like an ashtray.) Keep the eggplants covered tightly for 10 to 15 minutes, allowing them to steam. Remove the eggplants, one at a time, keeping the bowl covered, and peel off the skin, using your fingers. Chop the eggplants coarsely and add to the mashed garlic.

To roast the red peppers, hold each pepper on end and cut downward, not through the center but slightly off center, from one dent to another, resulting in four flat pieces. Throw away the seeds and ribs. Place the four pieces skin side up on a baking pan and leave under a broiler until they are literally black. Remove the pan from the oven and, using tongs, place the hot pieces of pepper in the bowl covered with plastic wrap or a brown paper bag or plastic bag to steam them. After 10 minutes, the skins can easily be removed with your fingers. (Some people char the whole red pepper directly over a flame. You can try that technique, but the charred peppers should not be held under running water to remove the black because water dilutes the flavor.) Cut the pepper into ¼-inch dice in the bowl.

To make the dip, stir the capers, olives,

cilantro, mint, cumin, vinegar, and lime juice into the bowl of roasted garlic, eggplant, and red pepper, and mix well. Season with salt, pepper, and additional lime juice to taste. Serve the dip in a bowl in the center of a larger plate of pita triangles. (The dip will keep for a week in the refrigerator.)

To make the pita triangles, split open whole rounds of pita bread to form two rounds. Cut each round into 4 or 6 triangles. Place the triangles rough side up on a baking sheet and toast in a 450-degree oven for about 5 minutes until lightly colored.

SERVES 8 TO 10

To toast whole spices such as cumin seeds, place the dried spice in a small dry frying pan over medium-high heat. Toast for about 2 minutes or until fragrant and lightly brown, shaking the pan often to prevent burning. If the spice needs to be ground, place the cooled spice in a coffee grinder used just for spices. Grind the toasted spice to a fine powder. Ground spices are always more flavorful than those that are purchased already ground. Toasting intensifies the flavor.

Capers are buds from bushes that grow in Mediterranean countries. They are pickled in an elaborate process. Salt capers are considered to have the most authentic taste. Whether brined in salt or liquid, capers should always be rinsed before using.

To pit olives, simply hit them with a flat meat pounder and remove the pits with your fingers.

Homemade Flour Tortillas with Avocado Salsa

*M*aria Balcazar has been washing dishes *and keeping the kitchens clean at Tante Marie's for over twelve years. One of the best-kept secrets at the school is what a good cook Maria is. She's the absolute best. She taught us that we never have to buy packaged tortillas again—they are so easy to make. Here is a great summertime party recipe from Maria!*

1½ tablespoons granular or active dry yeast
Sugar
6 to 7 cups flour
¾ cup lard or butter, melted and cooled
Coarse salt
3 avocados, diced, plus one whole avocado
*   for decorating the dish*
6 fresh tomatoes, coarsely diced
3 jalapeños, finely minced
4 bunches scallions, equal parts white and
*   green, coarsely chopped*
1 bunch cilantro, minced
Juice of 4 limes, plus one whole lime,
*   cut into wedges for decorating*
*   the dish*
Freshly ground black pepper

To make the tortilla dough, warm a glass measuring cup with hot water from the tap. Measure a cup of hot water and stir in the yeast with a pinch of sugar. Let the mixture proof until it is bubbly. Meanwhile, measure the flour into the bowl of an electric mixer. To the flour add ⅛ teaspoon salt. Make a well in the center and pour into it 2 cups warm water with the lard. Pour the yeast mixture into the warm water. Mix the liquid into the dry ingredients with a wooden spoon. Then mix with the dough hook for about 10 minutes. The dough should be soft, smooth, and slightly sticky. Put it in a bowl, cover with a towel, and place it in a warm place to rise, about an hour.

To make the salsa, combine the 3 avocados, the tomatoes, scallions, jalapeños, cilantro, and lime juice in a bowl with a sprinkling of salt and pepper. Stir until just combined. (If you stir too much, the avocado will become mushy and your mixture will resemble guacamole instead of salsa.)

To cook the tortillas, punch down the dough, using your fist to punch the middle of the dough, and bring it together into a ball on the counter. Roll the dough with your hands into a log shape about 3 inches in diameter. Cut 1½-inch lengths from the dough. Cover the dough you are not using with a dry towel. With floured hands, pat each piece into a rough round. Roll each piece with a rolling pin as thin as possible on a floured surface. Heat a nonstick pan without oil over medium-high heat. Place a round of dough in it and cook until light brown on the bottom. Turn quickly with your fingers to cook the other side. Turning over several times will help the tortillas to cook evenly, 15 to 20 seconds on each side. They should be cooked through with brown spots. If the dough puffs up while cooking, press it down with a clean towel, balled up. Let the tortillas cool, then cut into rough triangles.

To serve, put the salsa in a decorative bowl in the center of a round platter. Arrange the triangles of tortillas around the bowl. Decorate the top of the salsa with slices of avocado in a wheel pattern and wedges of lime.

SERVES 12

To dice a tomato, place the tomato on end, and with a knife cut down one side, not through the center but slightly off center, removing the thick flesh and skin, resulting in four pieces of tomato. Throw away the seeds and the center of the tomato. Place each side of tomato on a cutting board, and cut the tomato into dice. The skin does not have to be removed for uncooked tomato dishes.

Finding a ripe avocado is hard because so many people in the store have already pressed each avocado to see if it's ripe. It is best to buy avocados when they are firm, wrap them in newspaper or a brown paper bag, and store them in a drawer until they are ripe.

To mince a jalapeño, cut off the ends, then cut lengthwise into the flesh. With your knife cut around the seeds and ribs. Throw the seeds and ribs away. Lay the jalapeño flat and cut into thin lengths, then crosswise into fine dice. You never need to add all the jalapeño that a recipe calls for—it's a matter of how hot you want your food.

To dice an avocado, cut into the avocado around the seed to twist and separate the two halves. Holding the half with the seed in one hand, hit the seed with the knife before twisting

to remove it. Holding the half avocado in one hand, make slits about ¼ inch apart in one direction through the flesh, then make cuts in the other direction. Scoop the little dice of avocado from the skin with a big metal spoon.

Roasted Red Pepper Focaccia

One of the best things to eat on Saturday mornings at the San Francisco Ferry Plaza Farmer's Market is from the Noe Valley Bakery booth—a big square of thick focaccia covered with a compote of red peppers and scattered with Kalamata olives. Here is my interpretation of this delicious snack. For an hors d'oeuvre, cut the focaccia into 2 by 1-inch rectangles and serve at room temperature.

2 tablespoons granular or active dry yeast
Sugar
6 cups flour
Coarse salt
2 tablespoons olive oil plus ½ cup for pan
2 medium-size red onions, cut in half and thinly sliced
4 red bell peppers, cored, seeded, and cut into ½-inch strips
3 tablespoons good-quality balsamic vinegar
Freshly ground black pepper
20 Kalamata olives, pitted

To proof the yeast, warm a glass measuring cup with hot water. Measure ½ cup very hot water (115 to 120 degrees). (You can barely hold your finger in water this hot.) Stir in the yeast with a pinch of sugar. Let rest 10 minutes. (The yeast mixture should foam like a freshly poured beer. If it doesn't, discard and try again.)

To make the dough, in a large bowl mix 5 cups of the flour with a tablespoon of salt. Make a well in the center and pour in 2 cups warm water. Pour the yeast mixture into the warm water. With a wooden spoon mix the yeast into the water and then start to bring in the flour. When the mixture comes away from the edges of the bowl and begins to hold together, turn it out onto a clean table or counter, keeping the remaining cup of flour nearby. Knead for 10 to 15 minutes, adding more of the flour as needed until you have a smooth, soft dough. Form the dough into a ball. Put the ball into a deep plastic container or bowl generously coated with olive oil. Turn the dough over so all sides are coated with oil. Cover the bowl with a dry towel and set in a warm place, free of drafts, to rise until doubled in size, about an hour.

To make the topping, put the onions with the 2 tablespoons oil and ½ teaspoon salt in a medium-size sauté or frying pan over medium-high heat. Cook 5 minutes, stirring from time to time, until the onions begin to soften. Add the bell peppers and cook 10 more minutes, until soft. Add the vinegar and cook 5 more minutes. Add salt and pepper to taste. (The topping should be very well seasoned.)

To assemble, generously coat a 12 by 17-inch baking sheet with the ½ cup oil. Punch down the dough. With the heel of your hand, spread the dough on the oiled pan, trying not to work it too much or it will become elastic. Let it rest about 10 minutes. Spread the bell pepper mixture over the dough and scatter with the olives. Turn the oven to 400 degrees and place the pan on the top rack. Bake for 20 to 30 minutes, or until the dough is golden on the bottom, about 40 minutes.

MAKES 24 PIECES

Yeast is an important kind of leavener—it is actually a bacterium that needs warmth, moisture, and food to grow. Warmth comes from a warm place to rise in, moisture comes from the liquid in the dough, and food comes from starch—sugar or flour. The more moisture there is in dough, the happier the yeast is. Generally you knead dough so that the protein in the flour changes to gluten, which makes the dough elastic. The more you knead dough, the drier it becomes. The trick is to add just enough flour to keep the dough from sticking to your hands but not so much that the final dough is dry. As you knead the dough, throw a light coating of flour on the board, but try to add as little as possible. The final result should be smooth, elastic dough that doesn't stick—it should feel like a baby's bottom. If you leave dough exposed to the air, it will form a dry crust; that is why it is important to cover all dough that you are not working with.

To slice onions, cut the onion in half, cutting through the roots. Lay each half on a board cut side down and remove the peel. With the fingers of one hand curled so that the knuckles are forward, cut down and forward with the knife in the other hand. Don't try to get the slices off the knife; they will fall off with the next slice.

Focaccia is one of the few foods that has remained relatively unchanged since the Middle Ages. In those days in what is now Italy, people drank a nutritious heavy beer. This bread was cooked on hot stones as a stomach-filler. The dough was cooked sprinkled with a little olive oil and salt or maybe a little tomato—never with all the fancy toppings we use today. Of course, focaccia can be made with other toppings such as caramelized onions or wild mushroom ragout. At the school we often top focaccia with olive oil, chopped rosemary, and coarse salt.

Red bell peppers are green peppers that have been left on the vine to ripen. Roasting them enhances their flavor. They should not be roasted if they are to be cooked again—on top of focaccia or pizza, for instance.

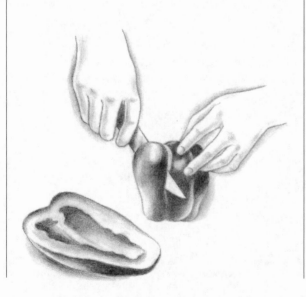

Asparagus-Fontina Pizza with Truffle Oil

After relishing a pizza like this one at Mazzini, a small, friendly restaurant in Berkeley, California, I couldn't wait to try to make it myself. It turned out to be almost as delicious! Asparagus tastes best when cooked and enjoyed in the spring. You can substitute any soft melting cheese, like Teleme, for the fontina. A sprinkling of truffle oil brings the flavors together—it's fantastic! These pizzas are great for casual get-togethers, when your guests can gather in the kitchen, lend a hand, and enjoy the finished pizzas hot from the oven.

1 tablespoon granular or active dry yeast
Sugar
4½ to 5 cups flour
Coarse salt
3 tablespoons olive oil plus some for coating the bowl
1 pound fresh asparagus, tough ends removed
Cornmeal for dusting
½ pound thinly sliced fontina, rind removed
½ cup freshly grated Parmesan
2 tablespoons truffle oil

To proof the yeast, pour ½ cup very hot water (115 to 120 degrees) in a warmed measuring cup. Add the yeast with a pinch of sugar and mix to dissolve. Stir in ½ cup of the flour, cover, and set in a warm place for 10 minutes until bubbles form on the surface.

To make the dough, mix the 4 cups flour and 1½ teaspoons salt in a large bowl. Make a well in the center and pour in 2 cups warm water, the olive oil, and the yeast mixture. Using a wooden spoon, stir the liquids together and bring in the flour. Mix until all the ingredients begin to hold together. If the dough seems sticky, add additional flour. When you have a moist, elastic dough that holds its shape, transfer it to a lightly floured work surface and knead until the dough is smooth, kneading in a bit more flour if necessary. The dough is ready when it feels smooth like a baby's bottom and is slightly springy when pressed gently with your finger. Form the dough into a ball and place in a lightly oiled bowl, turning the dough over to coat evenly with oil. Cover the bowl with a clean towel and set in a warm draft-free place until the dough doubles in size, at least 1½ hours.

Preheat the oven to 450 degrees for at least 30 minutes before baking. Place a pizza stone or four quarry tiles on the lower rack of the oven.

To make the topping, fill a medium-size saucepan with water and bring to a boil over high heat. Cut the asparagus on the diagonal into 1-inch lengths. Drop the asparagus into the boiling water with ½ teaspoon salt. Boil the asparagus for 5 minutes or until it is tender when pierced with a fork. Drain in a colander and run under cold running water to cool. Set aside.

To shape and bake the pizza, punch down the dough, put it on a table or counter, and roll it into a log. Cut the dough into six equal pieces. Roll each piece into a round with your hands as thin as you can, always rolling away from you and keeping the dough moving so that it doesn't stick to the counter. Shape each piece into a 6- or 7-inch round. Keep the pieces of dough covered with a dry towel or inverted bowl when not working with them to prevent them from drying out. Sprinkle a pizza peel with cornmeal. Place a round of dough on the peel and stretch it with your fingers into a thin round. Cover the dough with one-sixth of the fontina, one-sixth of the asparagus, and one-sixth of the Parmesan. Slide the pizza directly onto the pizza stone and bake for 15 minutes, until the edges are puffy and the bottom golden brown. Remove from the oven, drizzle with truffle oil, and serve.

MAKES 6 PIZZAS

The trick to sliding a pizza onto a stone or tiles is to shake it occasionally when putting on the topping to make sure it doesn't stick to the peel and give it a firm jerk to get the pizza off the peel and onto the pizza stone. The cornmeal acts as tiny ball bearings, enabling the pizza to roll off the peel.

What gives pizza and bread a nice crisp crust is baking it directly on tiles or bricks, which absorbs the steam produced by the baking dough. When a pizza is baked in a metal pan, the steam has nowhere to go, so the crust is not likely to be as dry and crisp.

Wild Mushroom Pizza with Ricotta

We all owe a huge debt of gratitude to Alice Waters, who, twenty years ago, built a wood-burning oven upstairs at her renowned Berkeley restaurant, Chez Panisse. Before that, pizza was invariably made with tomato sauce. Now we know we can make pizzas with a variety of interesting and delicious toppings. When using wild mushrooms as a topping, first cook them in butter or oil with herbs and brandy to bring out their earthy flavors.

1 tablespoon granular or active dry yeast
Sugar
4½ to 5 cups flour
Coarse salt
3 tablespoons olive oil
2 shallots, minced
3 tablespoons butter
2 garlic cloves, minced
½ pound wild mushrooms, such as shiitake, chanterelle, and/or portobello, sliced
½ pound fresh domestic mushrooms, sliced
1 tablespoon brandy
2 tablespoons heavy cream
1 tablespoon minced fresh Italian parsley
½ tablespoon minced fresh thyme
Freshly ground black pepper
Cornmeal for dusting
1 cup fresh ricotta
Truffle oil (optional)

To proof the yeast, pour ½ cup very hot water (115 to 120 degrees) in a warmed measuring cup. Add the yeast with a pinch of sugar and stir to dissolve. Stir in the yeast and ½ cup of the flour, cover, and set in a warm place for 10 minutes until bubbles form on the surface. If the mixture does not bubble, throw it away and start over.

To make the dough, combine 4 cups of the flour and 1½ teaspoons salt in a large bowl. Make a well in the center and pour in 2 cups warm water, olive oil, and the yeast mixture. Using a wooden spoon, stir the liquids together and then bring in the flour. Mix until all the ingredients begin to hold together. If the dough seems particularly wet and sticky, add more flour. When you have moist dough that holds its shape, transfer it to a table or a counter. Place a cup of flour on the side. With clean, dry hands knead the dough until it is smooth and feels like a baby's bottom, 10 to 15 minutes, adding only enough flour to keep it from sticking. Form the dough into a ball and place in a lightly oiled bowl, turning it over to coat evenly with the oil. Cover the bowl with a dry towel and set it in a warm place, free from drafts, until it doubles in size, at least 1½ hours.

Place a pizza stone or four quarry tiles on the lower rack of the oven. Preheat the oven to 450 degrees at least 30 minutes before baking.

To prepare the topping, cook the shallots in the butter with a sprinkling of salt over medium-high heat, stirring, until the shallots are soft and translucent, 3 to 4 minutes. Stir in the garlic and cook for a minute more. Toss in the mushrooms and cook until they begin to soften, 3 to 4 minutes. Stir in the brandy, the cream, the parsley, thyme, and salt and pepper to taste. Remove the mushrooms from the pan as soon as they are half wilted.

To shape and bake the pizza, punch down the dough, put it on a table or counter, and roll it into a log. Cut the log into six equal pieces. Pat each piece into a round with your hands, then roll it out as thin as you can, always rolling away from you and keeping the dough moving so it doesn't stick to the counter. Shape each piece into a 6- or 7-inch round. Keep the pieces of dough covered with a dry towel or inverted bowl when not working with them to prevent them from drying out. Sprinkle a pizza peel with cornmeal. Place a round of dough on the peel, and stretch it with your fingers, being careful not to make holes, into a thin round. Slide the pizza directly onto the pizza stone and bake for 15 minutes, until the edges are puffy and golden brown. Since there is no topping on this pizza, check it after 10 minutes; if it has risen in the center, push it flat with a large fork or metal spatula.

Remove the pizza from the oven, spread with one-sixth of the ricotta, and cover the entire pizza with the mushroom mixture, leaving a 1-inch rim. Return the pizza to the oven to reheat the mushroom mixture. Remove it from the oven, brush the rim with olive or truffle oil, and serve immediately. Repeat with the other rounds of dough.

MAKES 6 PIZZAS

Mushrooms are like sponges. If you wash them, they absorb water, which is released during cooking and dilutes the flavor of the final dish.

That is why it is best to brush off any dirt on mushrooms with a wet cloth, or cut it off with a knife, rather than wash them.

Since the stems of wild mushrooms are tougher than the caps, it is best to cut the stems into thin lengths before cooking them with the larger slices of mushrooms.

To mince fresh herbs, remove the leaves from the stems. With the fingers of one hand curled over the point of the blade and the other hand on the handle of the knife and leaving the tip on the board, rock the knife up and down on the board, going back and forth in a circular pattern. From time to time use the blade to reposition the mound of herbs and repeat. When a recipe calls for more than one herb, you can save time by mincing them together rather than separately.

Cooked Vegetable Platter with Shrimp and Aïoli

*I*n the South of France, it is a tradition to make a big display of cooked vegetables served with aïoli for celebrations. Here is my version of this Provençal tradition, which I call La Grande Aïoli. You can use any vegetables— the best are cold new potatoes dipped in this garlicky mayonnaise. Peel the potatoes if you like; I prefer them unpeeled.

When you make a beautiful platter of cooked vegetables and shrimp to be dipped in aïoli, you can be sure that the first people at the party will eat all the shrimp, no matter how many you cooked. That is why it is best to put the shrimp on top of the vegetables so that when the shrimp are all eaten, it isn't obvious.

4 to 6 garlic cloves, peeled
Coarse salt
Freshly ground black pepper
2 egg yolks, at room temperature
2 cups oil (half olive oil and half safflower
*   or other vegetable oil)*
¼ teaspoon freshly ground white pepper
1½ pounds medium-size large shrimp
2 slices onion
2 slices lemon
1 celery stalk, cut in 3 or 4 pieces
6 whole peppercorns
12 (1½ pounds) small new potatoes
8 carrots (1 pound) peeled, cut into
*   2 by ½-inch pieces*
1 pound green beans, trimmed
½ medium-size cauliflower (1 pound),
*   cut into ½-inch florets*

8 medium-size zucchini (2 pounds),
*   cut into 2 by ½-inch pieces*
4 eggs
4 tomatoes (2 pounds), cut into wedges

To make the aïoli, put the garlic cloves and ½ teaspoon of salt in a mortar or small bowl. Using a pestle or a wooden spoon, crush the garlic with the salt until it forms a paste. Add the egg yolks. Whisk in the oil drop by drop until the mixture appears creamy. Transfer the mixture to a medium-size bowl and start whisking in the oil in a slow, steady stream. If the mixture gets too thick, add a tablespoon of warm water. Continue whisking until sauce is thick. Season to taste with salt and white pepper.

To cook the shrimp, combine a quart of water, the onion, lemon, celery, and peppercorns in a medium-size saucepan. Bring to a boil over high heat, reduce the heat to medium, and simmer for 5 minutes. Add the shrimp and poach gently until barely pink. (The shrimp are overcooked if they curl up.) Drain and cool. Remove the shells, leaving on the tails.

To cook the vegetables, put the potatoes in a large saucepan, add 1 tablespoon salt, and cover with plenty of cold water. Bring the potatoes to a boil over high heat and cook until just tender when pierced with a fork, about 15 minutes. Drain the potatoes in a colander and shake well to evaporate excess moisture.

Meanwhile, bring another large saucepan of water to a boil. Add a teaspoon of the salt with the carrots and cook until just tender, about 5 minutes. Remove the carrots with a slotted spoon and place in a colander under cold running water to stop the cooking. Bring the water back to a boil and drop in the green beans. Cook until just tender, about 8 minutes. Remove the beans with a slotted spoon and repeat with the cauliflower. Bring the water back to a boil, adding more water if necessary, and cook about 5 minutes. Remove cauliflower florets and drain and refresh as before. Bring the water back to a boil and drop in the zucchini. Cook until just tender, 2 to 3 minutes. Remove the zucchini, and drain and refresh.

To hard cook the eggs, place the eggs in a small saucepan with enough cold water to cover by an inch. Place over high heat and bring to a boil. When the water reaches a vigorous boil, turn off the heat, cover the pot, and set a timer for 14 minutes. When the timer goes off, immediately hold the eggs under cold running water to stop the cooking. Crack and peel the eggs.

When ready to serve, arrange the cooked vegetables in wedge fashion around a basket or platter, mounding the vegetables to look plentiful. Arrange the shrimp over the vegetables. Decorate the edge of the basket or platter with the halves of egg and tomato wedges. Serve the aïoli in a mortar or small bowl near the basket.   SERVES 10 TO 15

Mayonnaise is one of the important families of sauces in French cooking. Aïoli is a garlic-flavored mayonnaise. The most important thing about making a mayonnaise-type sauce is to make sure all the ingredients are at room temperature and the oil is added slowly at first to start the emulsion. Although a mayon-naise can be made in a machine, aïoli must always be made by hand. The reason is that garlic overworked in a blender or food processor tastes too acidic.

If the eggs and oil are not at room temperature, or if the oil is added too quickly to the aïoli, it will separate or curdle. To correct this, start over with a clean bowl and another egg yolk at room temperature. Slowly start whisking in the curdled sauce and the remaining oil. Add another ½ cup olive oil.

An acidulated liquid for poaching fish or shell-fish is called court bouillon. Always cook the court bouillon for a few minutes before adding the seafood, and be careful not to boil the seafood rapidly because it is delicate. In the case of shrimp or scallops, the seafood will shrink and harden if overcooked, while fish will fall apart. Cooked seafood will keep in the refrigerator for 3 days.

Dropping green vegetables into boiling water is called blanching. The vegetables are perfectly cooked when tender when pierced with a fork. If they are chilled right away under cold running water or in a bowl of ice water and then drained, they can be stored in a plastic bag in the refrigerator and reheated, if desired, by being dropped briefly in boiling water again, or simply stirred over medium-high heat with butter. Cooked vegetables will keep in the refrigerator for up to 3 days. Never put potatoes in cold water to stop the cooking, because potatoes are the one vegetable that will absorb water and become soggy.

❧

To peel shrimp, hold a shrimp in one hand, grasp the legs of the shrimp between the thumb and forefinger of the other hand lengthwise, and open the shell with the help of the thumb from the first hand, leaving a little covering of shell on the tail to use as a handle when dipping the shrimp in sauce.

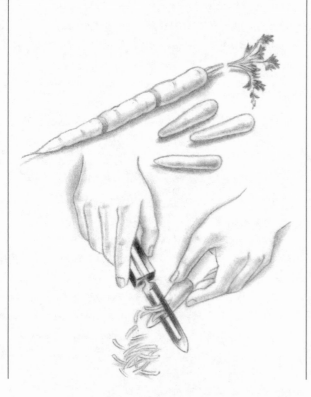

Hot Goat's Cheese Canapés

*L*ittle toasts run under the broiler with a fla-vorful mayonnaise have been popular for years. Here two favorites, goat's cheese and pro-sciutto, add pizazz to this old-fashioned recipe. It is perfectly acceptable to use store-bought mayonnaise for this recipe; however, Best Foods (Hellmann's in the east) is the only kind to use. Any leftover cheese can be substituted here for goat's cheese, except blue cheese.

> *One 1-pound loaf sliced white bread,*
> *   such as Orowheat, Northridge, Arnold's,*
> *   or Pepperidge Farm brand*
> *1 cup mayonnaise, store-bought or*
> *   homemade (page 112)*
> *½ cup grated aged goat's cheese*
> *½ bunch scallions, equal amounts of*
> *   white and green parts, chopped*
> *1 slice prosciutto, ¼ inch thick, cut in*
> *   ¼-inch dice*
> *Coarse salt*
> *Freshly ground black pepper*

To make the toast rounds, cut circles from the bread slices with a 1-inch round cutter. Place the circles on a baking sheet. Broil in the oven until golden on one side.

To make the filling, mix the mayonnaise, goat's cheese, scallions, and prosciutto in a bowl. Add salt and pepper to taste, remembering that the mixture needs to be flavorful because the toast is neutral in taste.

When ready to serve, preheat the broiler and mound a tablespoonful of the goat's cheese mixture on the untoasted side of the rounds. Place on a baking sheet and heat under the broiler until golden brown and puffy, 3 to 5 minutes. Serve immediately.

SERVES 10

Although fresh goat's cheese is available at many good grocery stores, aged goat's cheese is less common. Nevertheless, the more intense flavor of aged goat's cheese is appealing for many dishes. It is worth seeking out.

The people behind the counter at most stores that carry prosciutto are used to slicing it very thinly. For this recipe, you need to show the server exactly how thick you want the slice of prosciutto; that is, ¼ inch thick.

Parmesan Cheese Twists

These spiral cheese pastries look great placed across a bowl of soup or in a bread basket on a buffet. You can use any tired old ends of cheese, Parmesan or other aged cheese, but not blue. These cheese twists can be kept in a tin for two weeks but taste best if reheated before serving.

4 ounces Parmesan, grated
1 cup flour
7 tablespoons sour cream
4 tablespoons (½ stick) butter
Coarse salt
½ teaspoon paprika

To grate the cheese in a food processor, cut the cheese into 1-inch pieces. Start with two pieces in the processor with the blade. Process the cheese; as it is chopped, add more cheese a piece at a time through the hole in the top until you have about a cup.

To make the cheese dough, remove the top of the food processor and add the flour, sour cream, butter, salt, and paprika. Process until the dough comes into a ball. Wrap the dough in waxed paper and chill for 30 minutes.

Preheat the oven to 350 degrees.

To shape the cheese twists, roll the dough on a lightly floured surface until it is ¼ inch thick. With a pastry wheel, preferably with a crinkly edge, cut the dough into strips about ½ inch wide and 6 to 8 inches long. Twist each strip into a spiral by placing one end on a baking sheet, pressing it with your finger, twisting the dough, and continuing this pressing and twisting to the end of the strip.

Place the twists on an ungreased baking sheet and gently press the edges into the sheet to keep them from untwisting. Sprinkle the twists with coarse salt. Chill the pan of twists for 10 minutes before baking until the edges of the twists are golden, about 15 minutes.

MAKES 36 TWISTS

See page 41 for how to roll out dough. You don't have to be very careful with the dough when it contains sour cream or cream cheese, which make dough flaky anyway.

Pepper-Gruyère Cheese Puffs
(*Petites Gougères*)

In Burgundy, it is traditional to eat this cheese pastry shaped in a ring and served cold with red wine. I prefer the pastry as warm little puffs flavored with lots of cheese and pepper. They go well with red wine or other apéritifs.

> ¼ pound (1 stick) butter, cut into
> ½-inch pieces
> 1 cup flour
> 4 eggs, or more if needed
> 1 teaspoon Dijon-style mustard
> ½ teaspoon dry mustard
> 1½ cups grated Gruyère, plus 2 tablespoons
> for topping
> ½ teaspoon coarse salt
> ½ teaspoon freshly ground black
> pepper

Preheat the oven to 400 degrees and line a baking sheet with parchment paper.

To make the pastry, put the butter and a cup of water in a heavy-bottom saucepan, over low heat, swirling from time to time. (It is important that the water doesn't boil before the butter melts.) When the butter is melted, increase the heat and bring the mixture to a vigorous boil. Remove the pan from the heat and dump in the flour all at once. Beat vigorously with a wooden spoon until the mixture comes together in a mass. Continue to beat for another minute, slapping the dough against the sides of the pan. Let the mixture cool for 10 minutes.

In a small bowl, beat the eggs together with a fork until you can't distinguish the yellow from the white of the eggs. Add the eggs, a little at a time, beating vigorously after each addition. The more you beat after each addition of egg, the better the dough will rise in the oven. When all the egg is incorporated, the mixture should be difficult to beat and stick to the sides of the pan. If the dough has not reached this stage, beat up another egg, and continue adding egg until the dough is very sticky. Stir in the mustards, cheese, salt, and pepper. Spoon 1-inch rounds of this dough on the prepared baking sheet, about 1 inch apart. Sprinkle the 2 tablespoons grated cheese over the tops of the rounds. Place the pan on the top rack of the oven, and turn up the temperature of the oven to 425 degrees. Bake until the choux are puffed and light brown in color, about 30 minutes. Serve warm. (The dough can be made ahead and stored in a plastic bag in the refrigerator for 3 or 4 days, or you can make and shape the "petits choux" and keep the baking pan in the refrigerator for 3 or 4 hours. Either way it is best to serve them warm from the oven in a basket lined with a napkin.)

MAKES 32 CHEESE PUFFS

Choux pastry is one of the important kinds of pastry in French cooking. (The translation of the word choux *is cabbages. Actually, "my little cabbage" is a term of endearment in France.) With choux, you make not only gougères but also many savory and sweet pastries such as éclairs, cream puffs (profiteroles), croquembouche, and Saint-Honoré cake. The basic dough is always made the same way with the same proportions—¼ pound butter, 1 cup water, 1 cup flour, and 4 eggs—and should become hollow when baked.*

CHEESE

CHEESE IS PRESERVED MILK. It was originally a method of preserving excess milk for another time of the year. Wherever people milked animals, they probably made cheese.

All fresh and aged cheese is made the same way—the milk is heated to kill unwanted enzymes, then a coagulant is added that breaks down the milk into curds and whey. The coagulant can be a culture (bacteria), acid (vinegar or lemon juice), or rennet. Although vegetable rennet is available, traditional rennet is an enzyme from a calf's stomach.

For fresh cheese, the curd is lightly salted and the cheese is served within a few days. These include cottage, pot, farmer, and cream cheese. Mozzarella is fresh curd that has been heated slightly, stretched, shaped, and stored in liquid. Ricotta is fresh cheese that has traditionally been made by reheating the whey and collecting the resulting curds.

All aged cheese starts the same way—the milk is changed into curds and whey. But the curds are handled in many different manners. For most aged cheese the curds are put into a mold. Sometimes the cheese is sprayed with an ammonia-like mixture—as in Brie or Camembert—or bacteria is activated in the cheese with skewers, as in Roquefort or Stilton. To make Cheddar, the curd is cut in a special way before being placed in the molds. In good-quality Gruyère, the curd is usually pressed into a mold lined with burlap. As cheese ages, it becomes drier and more intense in flavor. A real Parmesan is aged fourteen months before it goes to market.

Aged cheese is not hard to make; however, it is hard to make a consistent product. The equipment and utensils must be very clean so that no unfavorable bacteria flavor the cheese. The aging is so important that often cheese stores in France and restaurants in the United States age their own cheese to get the best flavor. They keep the cheese in a cool, airy place and turn it from time to time until it's ready to serve.

It is best to buy cheese from a purveyor who lets you taste it, hopefully at room temperature, and cuts it according to your instructions. Of course, this is not always possible. Regardless, you can ask knowledgeable salespeople to teach you about the wide variety of cheese. Each time you buy cheese, try to purchase cheese that is made by hand rather than in a factory, and try to get familiar with a cheese that is new to you. It is best to keep cheese in the paper it comes in, or wrap it in fresh plastic wrap or waxed paper each time you use it. The two cheeses we keep on hand at the cooking school are Parmesan, a hard grating cheese, and Gruyère, a firm melting cheese.

Miniature Shrimp Quiches

This cream cheese dough is a remarkable "cheater" dough; it can be overhandled and reworked but still it bakes light and flaky. It is suitable only for savory tarts, not sweet. These miniature quiches can be made ahead and frozen on a tray. When they are totally frozen, put them in plastic bags and store them in the freezer. To serve, simply reheat in a 350-degree oven for about 15 minutes.

> 1½ cups flour
> ¼ pound (1 stick) butter, cut in
>   1-inch pieces
> 8 ounces cream cheese, cut in 1-inch pieces
> 1 egg plus 1 egg yolk
> 1 cup heavy cream
> Dash of Tabasco
> ¼ pound fresh bay shrimp or crabmeat
> ½ teaspoon coarse salt
> ¼ teaspoon freshly ground black pepper

To make the dough, place the flour, butter, and cream cheese in the bowl of a food processor and process until the dough forms a smooth ball. Wrap the dough in waxed paper and chill for 20 minutes.

To make the custard, put the eggs, cream, Tabasco, salt, and pepper in a large glass measuring cup. Mix with a fork until you can't distinguish the yellow from the white of the eggs.

Preheat the oven to 400 degrees.

To make the little quiches, roll out the dough on a lightly floured work surface to ¼ inch thick and cut rounds from it, using a 3-inch cutter or drinking glass. Line miniature muffin tins with each round. Place 2 to 3 shrimp or ½ teaspoon crab in each dough-lined muffin tin. Pour the cream mixture into each cup, making it about two-thirds full. Put the tins on the top rack of the oven and bake until the pastry is golden brown and the filling is lightly puffed, about 20 to 30 minutes. Let the quiches rest for 10 minutes before turning the pans over to release the little quiches.

MAKES 36 MINIATURE QUICHES

To roll out the dough, pound it first to soften. Make sure to have a light coating of flour on the board, the rolling pin, and the dough. Roll from the center up, not so much pressing down as pressing forward. Do not roll off the edge of the dough. After each roll, move the dough one-quarter turn. Often students can roll out the dough perfectly but it sticks to the surface. That is why it is important to keep moving the dough. When rolling out any dough, it is best to work quickly in a cool kitchen. The dough is ready to cut when it is ⅛ inch thick.

Quiches were first made in Lorraine, in eastern France, where there was plenty of butter, cream, and eggs, but other sources of protein were not so plentiful. The original quiches may have had only a piece of ham or a couple of pieces of bacon for an 8- or 10-inch tart. Of course, once quiche caught on in America, we started adding "the works"—lots of onion, parsley, cheese, and whatever else. A real French quiche has more custard than other ingredients.

Mushroom Turnovers

*H*ere is an old faithful, made modern with addition of dried wild mushrooms. These easy-to-make turnovers can be assembled and frozen ready to bake, or baked and frozen, ready to reheat. Either way, bake them until lightly browned. What brings out the flavor of mushrooms is butter or oil, brandy, cream, and fresh herbs.

½ ounce dried porcini (cèpe) mushrooms
1½ cups flour
¼ pound (1 stick) butter, cut in 1-inch
  pieces, plus 2 tablespoons butter
8 ounces cream cheese, cut in 1-inch pieces
2 shallots, minced
½ pound fresh mushrooms, finely chopped
1 tablespoon brandy
3 tablespoons heavy cream
3 tablespoons each minced fresh Italian
  parsley, chives, and thyme
Coarse salt
Freshly ground black pepper

To reconstitute the dried mushrooms, put them in a glass measuring cup and barely cover with hot water. Let sit until softened, about 20 minutes.

To make the dough, place the flour, 1 stick butter, and cream cheese in the bowl of a food processor and process until a smooth ball forms. Wrap the dough in waxed paper and chill for 20 minutes.

Drain the porcini, saving the liquid, and finely chop.

To make the mushroom filling (duxelles),

cook the shallots in the 2 tablespoons butter in a frying or sauté pan over medium-high heat for 2 to 3 minutes until soft. Add the dried and fresh mushrooms and cook, stirring, until they release their liquid and the liquid evaporates. Stir in the reserved mushroom liquid, being careful not to add the last tablespoon, because it may be sandy. Add the brandy and cook for a minute. Add the cream and herbs and cook for a minute. Remove from the heat. Season well with salt and pepper.

Preheat the oven to 400 degrees.

To assemble, roll out the dough on a lightly floured work surface to ⅛ inch thick. Cut rounds from the dough with a 3-inch cutter or drinking glass. Place half a teaspoon mushroom mixture on each round; do not overfill. Fold the round of dough in half over the filling and press the edges together firmly with the tines of a fork. Prick the top of the turnover with the fork and transfer to an unlined baking sheet. Bake on the top rack of the oven until the pastry is golden, about 25 minutes.

MAKES 36 TURNOVERS

For any mushroom recipe—soup, sauce, pasta, risotto—you can enhance the flavor of the dish by using chopped, reconstituted dried mushrooms with their soaking liquid. However, it is important to always finely chop the dried mushrooms because they have a rubbery texture.

Mushroom stems are removed only when the mushrooms are to be stuffed. If the mushrooms are to be cooked as part of a dish, the stems

should be cut off flush with the caps, so that the mushrooms do not shrink when cooked. If the mushrooms are to be sliced, I like to trim off only the coarse ends. In large kitchens the stems of mushrooms are finely chopped and cooked with shallots in butter to make a filling called duxelles. The rough trimmings and peelings go into dark stock.

❧

To chop an onion or shallot, cut it in half, cutting through the root. Lay cut side down on a board or counter. Peel each half. With the tip of a chef's knife, cut three or four slits parallel to the board toward but not through the roots. Without turning the onion, with the point of the knife cut three or four slits down through the onion toward the board but not through the root end. Finally, cut in a third direction down and forward. In the first two directions, the onion will hold together because you don't cut all the way through and the root will hold it together. In the third direction the onion will fall apart.

Spinach Triangles

Here is a delicious package of taste for a do-ahead hors d'oeuvre. For a great presentation, offer all three recipes that use the cream cheese dough together—half moons, rounds, and triangles—all vegetarian, or nearly vegetarian.

1½ cups flour
¼ pound (1 stick) butter, cut in 1-inch
  pieces, plus 3 tablespoons butter
8 ounces cream cheese, cut in 1-inch pieces
½ pound spinach, stems removed and leaves
  washed but not dried
1 small onion, chopped
Coarse salt
1 garlic clove, minced
¼ pound mild feta cheese, crumbled
¼ pound Monterey Jack (or other mild
  white cheese), shredded
1 egg, beaten
Freshly ground black pepper

To make the dough, place the flour, 1 stick butter, and cream cheese in the container of a food processor and process until a smooth ball forms. Wrap the dough in waxed paper and chill for 20 minutes.

To cook the spinach, put half the wet spinach along with a sprinkling of salt in a medium-size frying or sauté pan over medium-high heat. Cover and cook for 2 to 3 minutes, until the spinach begins to wilt. Remove the cover and begin adding the rest of the spinach, turning the wilted spinach over onto the fresh using two wooden spoons. Repeat until all the spinach is wilted.

Put the wilted spinach in a potato ricer, squeeze out the liquid, then chop coarsely.

To make the filling, put the 3 tablespoons butter with the onion and ½ teaspoon salt into a pan over medium-high heat. Cook, stirring frequently, for about 5 minutes until the onion is soft. Stir in the garlic and cook for a minute. Add the chopped spinach and cook for a minute. Place the mixture in a bowl to cool to room temperature, 10 to 15 minutes. Mix in the cheeses, egg, pepper, and salt to taste.

Preheat the oven to 400 degrees.

To make the triangles, roll out the dough on a lightly floured table or counter to ⅛ inch thick. Cut the dough into 2-inch squares. Place a tablespoon of filling at the bottom corner of each square. Fold the top corner over the bottom and crimp the open edges firmly with the tines of a fork. Using the fork, pierce each triangle and place it on a parchment-lined baking pan. Repeat with the remaining squares of dough and filling.

Place the baking pan on the top rack of the oven and bake for 15 to 20 minutes, until the triangles are golden brown, about 25 minutes. Serve warm.

MAKES ABOUT 36 TRIANGLES

Although some cooks blanch spinach by dropping it into boiling water, I like this method of cooking wet spinach in a dry pan. The traditional way to remove liquid from spinach is to press it between two plates.

Feta is a fresh cheese that is stored—actually, pickled—in brine, a salt solution. It can be made from sheep's or goat's milk or both.

Caviar in Beggar's Purses

To celebrate a special occasion like New Year's Eve or an anniversary, buy the best caviar you can find and make these little packages of exquisite flavors. The saltiness of the caviar perfectly balances the richness of the cream and the slight onion flavor of the scallion. Although you can see adaptations of these crêpe purses all over, the best is the original presentation, which I first sampled at The Quilted Giraffe in New York many years ago. Although the recipe calls for dipping the purses in melted butter before serving, I often skip this step.

(I like to serve these Caviar Purses on a glass cake stand with a tomato rose in the middle.)

1 cup milk
4 eggs
½ teaspoon salt
2 cups flour
4 tablespoons (½ stick) melted butter, plus
  ½ teaspoon for cooking crêpes
1 bunch scallions
½ cup crème fraîche
4 ounces good-quality caviar
Half a lemon
2 tablespoons melted butter (optional)

To make the crêpe batter, combine 1 cup cold water, milk, eggs, salt, flour, and 4 tablespoons butter in the container of a blender in the listed order. Blend for a minute and scrape down the sides. Blend for another minute or so, until no lumps of flour remain. Cover and refrigerate for at least 20 minutes. When ready to prepare the crêpes, thin the batter with cold water or milk, a little at a time, until you have the consistency of light cream.

To blanch the scallions, bring a small saucepan of water to a boil over high heat. Trim the white ends from each scallion. Drop the green scallion leaves into the boiling water and simmer for 2 minutes until wilted. Remove and place on paper towels to drain. Cut the leaves into strips about ¼ inch wide and as long as possible.

To make the crêpes, heat a miniature crêpe pan (4 inches) over medium-high heat with the ½ teaspoon butter. When the butter has stopped bubbling and is still, pour in about 2 tablespoons of the batter, swirling the pan immediately to be sure it is evenly coated; pour any excess batter back into the container. Cook the crêpe over medium-high heat until it is lightly browned on the bottom. Lift the edge of the crêpe with a fork and quickly turn over the crêpe with your fingertips. Cook for 30 seconds, until just cooked through. Remove the crêpe from pan and place it, browned side (the first side you cooked) down on waxed paper. Repeat until you have used all the crêpe batter. (If you do not have a 4-inch crêpe pan, you can make crêpes in a 6-inch pan. Proceed with the instructions for making purses, then trim the excess crêpe with scissors after the purse is assembled.)

To assemble, line up the crêpes, crème fraîche, caviar, lemon, and scallions. On the first crêpe, put a scant teaspoon crème fraîche, a teaspoon of caviar, and 2 drops of lemon juice, and bring the edges of the crêpe together in the center to form a little bundle resembling a change purse. Tie the bundle with a strand of the blanched scallion. Trim the ends of the scallion. Refrigerate the bundles until ready to serve, up to 2 hours. You can dip the purses in additional melted butter just before serving.

MAKES 24 BUNDLES

When I taught cooking in my home, I hid my crêpe pan under my sweaters in my closet so that students or guests wouldn't use it for other things. Crêpe pans should be used only for crêpes. They should be cleaned out with paper towels and, if necessary, salt if they are crusty, and stored with a light coating of butter or oil. This way the crêpes never stick to the pan.

A crêpe is a very thin nonabsorbent pancake used to envelop food. Crêpes should be as thin as possible—that is why you get the pan as hot as possible and swirl in the batter, pouring out the excess. If you hold a crêpe up to the light, it should look like lace. You can store crêpes, stacked and wrapped in plastic wrap, for up to 4 days in the refrigerator. You can freeze them, wrapped in plastic wrap and with waxed paper between each crêpe, for up to a year.

To make a tomato rose, remove a 1-inch round from the end of the tomato opposite the stem with a small sharp knife, preferably serrated. This will be the base of the tomato rose. Holding the tomato in one hand with your thumb out of the way, start removing the skin of the tomato in a 1-inch horizontal strip all around the tomato. If the strip breaks, don't worry. When you have most of the skin of the tomato removed, stop. The wrong way to make a tomato rose is to roll up the strip of skin like a rug. The correct way is to start with the end that you first removed and curl the rest of the strip inside, pulling it around in a circle. Work quickly without fussing too much. When you have a coil of tomato skin, slide a knife under it and transfer it to the round. If there is a hole in the middle of the tomato rose, cut a small strip of tomato and insert it in the center, using the small knife to position it. The rose can be kept for a day or two in the refrigerator covered in plastic wrap.

Crème fraîche is a slightly acidic thickened cream commonly used in France. If you cannot find a source for it, you can make an imitation crème fraîche by mixing 3 tablespoons cultured buttermilk into 1 cup good-quality heavy cream, warmed, storing it in a glass jar in a warm place for 24 hours before chilling it.

FIRST COURSES

Accoding to an old French cookbook called *La Véritable Cuisine de Tante Marie,* or *The Complete Tante Marie's French Kitchen,* "The French cuisine, despite its reputation for quality and artistry, is basically simple." Nowhere is this truth exemplified more than in the first course. A well-executed first course should appeal to the eye, taste delicious, and be of the utmost quality without weighing down or overpowering the courses to come. In other words, it should be simple and look beautiful. Of course, a soup or a salad can be served as a first course, but it is much more interesting to serve something unusual and healthful, lively, and fun!

The Big Problem

The big problem with serving a first course is getting it to the table. If the first course is to be served at room temperature, you can put the plates directly on the table and call the guests to the table. It generally takes people 10 minutes to come to the table. During that time, you can make sure that the wine glasses are filled, the candles are lit, and the music is on. However, if the first course is to be served warm, you must insist that your guests sit at the table before you bring out the warmed first course. Always ask them to begin eating and not wait until everyone is served. When it comes time to clear the first course dishes, I always insist that no one get up to clear except me because it ruins the flow of conversation if half the table gets up to clear.

How to Make First Courses Without Recipes

When envisioning a first course, think vegetables, think vinaigrette, and most important think about what's in season. For a French effect, trim and cut vegetables such as carrots, cauliflower, broccoli, or mushrooms and cook them until tender in a liquid of part wine, part chicken (or vegetable) stock and herbs, such as bay leaf; spices like whole coriander and white pepper; and salt. Cook each vegetable separately, and when each is barely cooked

47

through transfer it to a platter and let it marinate in some of the cooking liquid. When ready to serve, arrange the vegetables attractively on individual plates. Called vegetables à la Grecque by the French, they used to be part of a crudité cart offered as a first course in French restaurants.

For an Italian effect, make plates that may include preserved meats like prosciutto or coppa, and slices of grilled eggplant and red peppers. You can also include preserved fish, such as thin slices of swordfish marinated in lemon oil and salt, with a vegetable salad of shaved fennel with shaved Parmesan. Decorate the plates with a variety of good olives and breadsticks. Sprinkle plenty of olive oil over the dishes.

For a Mediterranean effect, arrange Charred Eggplant Dip (page 24) with pieces of lahvosh or other cracker bread, mounds of store-bought hummus, grated carrot salad with a cumin dressing, feta cheese, Kalamata olives, and/or roasted almonds (page 19). Individual salad plates can be made hours ahead and kept at room temperature.

Fresh Salmon Tartare

Steak tartare is a popular chopped or ground raw beef dish in France, and carpaccio is a popular raw beef dish from Italy. While both are delicious, we like to use fresh salmon instead of beef. You can make either dish with the trimmings or ends of the salmon. Both are easy to make. I recommend using wild salmon, not farmed.

¼ pound fresh salmon fillet
1 shallot, finely chopped
1 tablespoon capers, rinsed
Juice of 1 lime
Coarse salt
Freshly ground black pepper
Thinly sliced brown bread
1 lime, cut in wedges

Mince the salmon and put it in a small bowl. Stir in the shallot, capers, lime juice, and salt and pepper to taste and stir. Let the mixture sit 10 minutes and stir again. To serve, pack into a lightly oiled 2-inch ramekin and invert onto salad plates. Arrange slices of brown bread and lime wedges around the salmon.

SERVES 2

To make wedges of lemons or limes, first cut each end flat, then cut into wedges. This makes it easier to squeeze the wedge.

Fresh Salmon Carpaccio

½ pound fresh salmon fillet
2 shallots, finely chopped
2 tablespoons capers, rinsed
⅓ cup extra-virgin olive oil
Coarse salt
Freshly ground black pepper

Remove any bones and skin from the salmon. Cut the salmon, using a thin knife, into ¼-inch-wide slices, as wide as possible. Place each slice of salmon on a board and pound as thin as possible with the flat side of a meat pounder. Lay the slices evenly over four salad plates. Top the salmon slices with a sprinkling of shallots and capers. Drizzle the olive oil over the top and sprinkle with salt and pepper. SERVES 4

Potato Cakes with Smoked Salmon and Crème Fraîche

*A*lthough this first course takes some last-minute cooking, it is well worth the effort, especially to showcase your own smoked salmon (see page 379).

3 large baking potatoes, peeled
3 tablespoons chopped scallions
  (equal amounts of white and green)
1 egg, beaten
3½ tablespoons flour
1 tablespoon coarse salt
1 teaspoon freshly ground black pepper
6 tablespoons butter
1 cup crème fraîche
½ pound good-quality cold smoked salmon
1 lemon

To make the potato mixture, grate the potatoes on the large holes of a box grater. (Hold the potato lengthwise for longer pieces and thus crisper cakes.) Wrap the potatoes in a clean kitchen towel and squeeze out as much excess liquid as possible. Mix the potatoes in a bowl with the scallions, egg, flour, and salt and pepper.

To make the cakes, melt enough butter to coat the bottom of a large nonstick frying pan over moderately high heat. Shape the potato mixture into 3-inch cakes. When the bubbles of hot butter subside, add the potato mixture, gently flattening each cake with the back of a spoon. Cook until nicely browned, about 2 minutes, turn the cakes over, and cook for about 2 more minutes. Transfer the cakes to paper towels and keep warm. Repeat the process with the remaining potato mixture, adding butter as needed.

To serve, place the potato cakes on warmed salad plates, spread with a tablespoon of crème fraîche, and cover with thinly sliced smoked salmon. Squeeze a few drops of lemon juice on each and grind a bit of pepper over each cake. Serve warm.

SERVES 6

It's unnecessary to keep peeled potatoes in cold water before cooking if you're going to brown the potatoes anyway.

If using home-smoked salmon, you may find it does not slice as evenly as you'd like. Don't worry; it will still taste delicious.

Antipasti Platter of Eggplant-Zucchini Sauté, Cauliflower with Salsa Verde, and Red Bell Peppers with Anchovies

A big platter piled high with red, white, and green vegetables is the perfect start to a meal of grilled meats cooked outdoors, or before a main-course pasta such as Fettuccine with Seafood (page 142).

EGGPLANT-ZUCCHINI SAUTÉ

Olive oil
4 Asian eggplants, trimmed and sliced lengthwise in ¼-inch-wide slices
4 large zucchini or 6 small, trimmed and sliced lengthwise in ¼-inch-wide slices
Coarse salt
1 large onion, sliced
¼ cup good-quality balsamic vinegar
Cayenne pepper

To sauté the vegetables, heat a tablespoon of olive oil in a large, wide frying or sauté pan (preferably nonstick) over medium-high heat. Sauté a layer of eggplant on both sides until lightly golden on each side; remove from the pan. Continue cooking all the eggplant and zucchini in the same way, using as little oil as possible. It's important not to add too much oil when sautéing eggplant, because eggplant will absorb all the oil and

the final dish will be too oily. Sprinkle the vegetables with salt as they cook.

In another large sauté pan over medium-high heat, cook the onion in 2 tablespoons olive oil with ½ teaspoon salt, stirring from time to time until the onion is soft, about 5 minutes. Stir in the sautéed eggplant and zucchini, along with the vinegar and a few grains of cayenne. Add salt and pepper to taste. Remove from the heat.

CAULIFLOWER
WITH SALSA VERDE

1 large head cauliflower, cut into 1-inch
* florets*
Coarse salt
2 tablespoons capers, rinsed, and chopped if
* large*
4 tablespoons minced fresh Italian parsley
1 large shallot, finely chopped
2 tablespoons sherry vinegar
½ cup olive oil
Freshly ground black pepper

To prepare the cauliflower, bring a large pot of water to a boil over high heat and add a tablespoon of salt and the cauliflower. Cook until the cauliflower is tender when pierced with a fork, about 8 minutes. Drain and run under cold water to stop the cooking.

To make the salsa verde, mix together the capers, parsley, shallot, vinegar, and olive oil in a small bowl with salt and pepper to taste. Although you can make salsa verde in a processor, it has a better texture when made by hand.

GRILLED
RED BELL PEPPERS
WITH ANCHOVIES

6 red bell peppers
6 anchovy fillets (rinsed if salted), coarsely
* chopped*
2 large garlic cloves, minced
4 tablespoons minced fresh Italian parsley
1½ tablespoons white wine vinegar
⅓ cup extra-virgin olive oil
Coarse salt
Freshly ground black pepper

To roast the peppers, stand each pepper on end and cut down, not through the center but slightly off center, from one dent to the next. You should have four flat pieces. Discard the ribs and seeds. Lay the peppers skin side up on a baking sheet. Place the baking sheet on the top rack of the oven and broil the peppers until they are black. With tongs, put the peppers in a bowl, covered with plastic wrap, or in a brown paper bag for 5 minutes to steam. Remove the skins, lay two or three peppers on top of each other, and cut them in ½-inch-wide lengths.

To make the sauce, combine the anchovies, garlic, parsley, vinegar, and olive oil in a small bowl. Add salt and pepper to taste.

To assemble the antipasti platter, pile the eggplant and zucchini mixture crosswise on one-third of a large oval platter; lay the cauliflower down the middle; and pile the red peppers on the remaining third of the platter. (This platter can be stored in the refrigerator for 3 days covered in plastic wrap.) To serve, spoon the salsa verde decoratively across the cauliflower.   SERVES 6 TO 8

Anchovies are little fish preserved in salt or oil. At the cooking school we buy large cans of salted anchovies because we like the taste better. Salted anchovies should be rinsed of their salt and each fillet removed from the bones with your fingers. At home, I always use little cans of anchovies packed in oil because it would take me years to use up a large can. Once the cans have been opened, the anchovies go bad quickly, so I use what I want and throw the rest away.

Mushrooms Filled with Garlic Butter

T he best thing about eating escargots, the famous dish of snails from Burgundy, is sopping up the bubbly garlic butter with French bread and devouring it with a glass of red wine. Why not use mushroom caps rather than snail shells, leave out the escargots altogether, and add some chopped walnuts for texture? The important thing is to make sure these mushrooms are overflowing with garlic butter. They must be served on a plate and eaten with a knife and fork—definitely not finger food. Enjoy!

*20 medium-size to large fresh white
    mushrooms
¾ pound (3 sticks) butter
2 large shallots, finely chopped
3 garlic cloves, minced
4 tablespoons minced fresh parsley
¼ cup walnuts, coarsely chopped
Coarse salt
Freshly ground black pepper
Parsley for garnish*

To prepare the mushrooms, flip out the mushroom stems and lay the mushroom caps rounded side down on a glass or ceramic baking dish. Save the stems for another use. If the mushrooms are large, bake them at 375 degrees for 8 to 10 minutes to soften. To make the garlic butter, work the butter in a bowl with a wooden spoon until malleable.

Stir in the shallots, garlic, parsley, and walnuts. Add salt and pepper to taste.

To assemble, fill each mushroom cap generously with the garlic butter. These can be made a day or two ahead and stored in the refrigerator.

When ready to serve, place the dish of filled mushrooms under the broiler until very bubbly, about 5 minutes. Serve on warmed plates with plenty of butter poured over the mushrooms. Place the parsley in the center of the plate. Serve with plenty of French bread.

SERVES 4

Mushrooms have a meatlike feel in the mouth and are a natural source of monosodium glutamate, a flavor enhancer. They should always be stored in a brown paper bag in the refrigerator because they become slimy when stored in plastic bags.

Shallots are expensive but are favored by cooks because they combine the flavors of onion and garlic in a delicate way. If they are unavailable, you can substitute the white part of scallions (also called green onions).

To make a compound butter, always soften the butter by beating it in a bowl with a wooden spoon until it is light and fluffy. Then stir in flavorings such as parsley, lemon, salt, and pepper. Compound butter can be formed into a log and wrapped in plastic to store in the refrigerator for up to 3 weeks or in the freezer for up to 9 months. It is a good way to store fresh herbs that can be thawed and put on fish, chicken, or meat as it comes off the grill.

To mince a clove of garlic, separate the clove from the head and lay it on a board. Hit it firmly with the side of a knife, remove and discard the peel, and cut off the little rough end. With the fingers of one hand curled holding the garlic, cut down and forward with the other hand on the knife until garlic clove is sliced. With both hands on the knife, chop in a semicircular motion until the garlic is finely minced.

It is important to mince garlic when it is to be cooked. Garlic put through a press does not give the same flavor.

Asparagus Maltaise

*F*resh asparagus have an affinity for egg sauces, especially for an orange-flavored hollandaise. Maltaise sauce is a "petite sauce" in the hollandaise family of French sauces. Traditionally, Maltaise sauce was made with the juice and zest of blood oranges, producing a rose-colored sauce. Whether made with blood or common oranges, this is an elegant first course. If the asparagus are young and thin, there is no need to peel them. Thick asparagus should be peeled so that they cook evenly.

2 pounds green asparagus
1 orange
½ pound (2 sticks) butter, melted and
  cooled
3 egg yolks
Coarse salt
1 teaspoon lemon juice

To prepare the asparagus, cut them into a size that will fit comfortably on salad plates. Place them on the bottom of a sauté pan until ready to cook.

To prepare the orange, bring a small saucepan of water to a boil. With a citrus stripper, remove 12 strips of orange zest and add them to the boiling water. Turn off the heat, and let sit for 5 minutes. Place on paper towels to drain. Remove the remaining zest from the orange with a zester or fine grater. Juice the orange.

To make clarified butter, remove the top crusty layer from the melted butter. Pour the clear layer of butter into a glass measuring cup and add the milky-looking solids to the first layer and save for another use, such as cooking vegetables.

To make the orange-flavored hollandaise, put the egg yolks, a tablespoon of water, and a few grains of salt in the top of a boiler or a medium-size bowl. Whisk the mixture vigorously off the heat until it is creamy looking. Place the pan with the yolk mixture over a pot of gently simmering water. (The bottom of the top half of the double boiler or the bowl should not touch the hot water.) You should always be able to hold your finger on the bottom of the egg yolk pan. Whisking vigorously, start adding the clarified butter by the tablespoonful. As one spoonful emulsifies, add another. Whisk the sauce over gentle heat so that it cooks slightly while fluffing with air. If the mixture begins to bubble around the edge of the pan, remove it from the pan of water and continue whisking. Return it to the heat, and continue adding spoonfuls of the melted butter and whisking until all the butter has been absorbed and the sauce resembles slightly whipped cream. Remove from the heat and whisk in the lemon juice and orange zest. Add 2 tablespoons of the orange juice with salt and pepper to taste.

To keep the sauce warm, put the top of the double boiler, or bowl with a metal top, on a shelf 12 inches above gently simmering water. If this is not possible, simply keep it covered off the heat. It is impossible to reheat a hollandaise-type sauce. It is much better to serve it over warm food on warm plates.

When ready to serve, pour an inch of boiling water over the asparagus with a sprinkling of salt. Cover the pan and steam the asparagus over moderately high heat until the asparagus have a slight bow when lifted with tongs, or are tender when pierced with a fork, about 8 minutes. Place the asparagus on warmed salad plates, spoon some Maltaise sauce across the middle of the asparagus, and decorate with strips of orange zest.

SERVES 6

To make this sauce as a hollandaise rather than Maltaise, simply follow the procedure described, leaving out the orange juice and orange zest. Hollandaise is a lemon-flavored egg-and-butter emulsion sauce. Add lemon juice with salt and pepper to taste.

The thing to remember when making a hollandaise-type sauce is that eggs thicken at 180 degrees and curdle at 190 degrees. This is 20 degrees below boiling; therefore, care should be taken that the sauce does not come anywhere close to boiling. A hollandaise is a warm *egg and butter emulsion sauce—not hot.*

If the hollandaise-type sauce gets too hot, it will separate (curdle). To bring back a curdled sauce, start over with a clean bowl and a tablespoon of heavy cream. Start whisking the curdled sauce slowly into the cream over gentle heat and continue as before. The resulting sauce will never have the smooth consistency of the uncurdled sauce, but it will taste fine.

It is best to steam asparagus rather than blanch them and reheat it as with other vegetables because the tips are delicate and may be damaged in the blanching process.

Whole Artichoke Filled with Roasted Garlic Soufflé

A wonderful, creative way to serve a soufflé is in a cooked artichoke. The slightly undercooked soufflé becomes the sauce as the diner removes the outer leaves of the artichoke and dips them in the soft garlicky cheesy soufflé. This is my adaptation of a recipe developed years ago by Maurice Moore-Betty, a New York cooking teacher.

1 head garlic
2 tablespoons olive oil
Coarse salt
Freshly ground black pepper
6 large artichokes, trimmed of stem and
    tough outer leaves
1 tablespoon lemon juice
2 tablespoons butter
2 tablespoons flour
⅔ cup milk
3 egg yolks
3 ounces Gruyère, grated
4 egg whites

To roast the garlic, cut off the top quarter of the head (the end opposite the stem) and place it cut side up on a piece of foil. Drizzle the cut garlic with a tablespoon of the olive oil, a sprinkling of salt, and a grinding of pepper. Wrap the foil tightly around the garlic and bake at 400 degrees for 30 to 45 minutes, until the garlic cloves are completely soft. Remove the garlic from the oven and when it is cool enough to handle, squeeze the pulp from the skin into a small bowl. If necessary, use a small knife or spoon to get out all the garlic. Mash the pulp with a fork.

To prepare the artichokes, place them in a pan large enough to hold them in one layer with a tablespoon of salt, a tablespoon of the olive oil, the lemon juice, and enough water to cover the artichokes. Bring to a boil over high heat and cook the artichokes for 35 to 40 minutes, until the bottoms are tender when pierced with a fork. Remove the artichokes from the water and drain upside down on paper towels.

To make the soufflé, melt the butter in a small saucepan over medium heat. Remove the pan from the heat and mix in the flour. Return the pan to the heat and stir with a wooden spoon until the mixture looks greasy. Remove the pan from the heat again and whisk in the milk. Return to the heat and cook 5 more minutes, whisking constantly, until the mixture boils. Remove the pan from the heat and whisk in the egg yolks one at a time, mixing well after each addition. Let cool for a minute, then stir in the roasted garlic, ½ teaspoon salt, a grinding of pepper, and the cheese. (The soufflé base can be made ahead up to this point and covered with plastic wrap.)

Carefully open the leaves of the artichokes to expose an opening about 3 inches in diameter. With a teaspoon, remove the fuzzy choke from the center of each artichoke. Place each artichoke on a lightly oiled square of foil and bring up the edges of the foil to protect the leaves in the oven. Place the artichokes on a baking pan.

Preheat the oven to 400 degrees.

Twenty minutes before serving, beat the

egg whites with a few grains of salt in a clean bowl, preferably copper, with a balloon whisk until stiff but not dry. Gently fold one-third of the egg whites into the cheese mixture, then fold that mixture back into the remaining egg whites. Spoon one-sixth of the soufflé mixture into the center of each artichoke. Bake the artichokes on the top rack of the oven for 15 minutes, until puffed and lightly browned. Serve immediately.

SERVES 6

The best way to beat egg whites is to put the yolk-free egg whites in a clean copper bowl. Tip the bowl toward you and use a balloon whisk to lift the whites out of the bowl, twisting your wrist and holding the whisk slightly. The idea is to keep the hand holding the whisk lowered, while lifting the egg whites to incorporate air into the mixture. As the whites begin to foam, run the whisk around the inside edge of the bowl from time to time. It is always best to whisk egg whites in a copper bowl with a balloon whisk for soufflés because electric mixers can easily overwhip egg whites. Instead of being smooth and shiny, they become dry and chunky.

❦

Whenever you are folding egg whites into a soufflé mixture, always stir one-quarter of the mixture into the soufflé base to lighten the texture of the base, then quickly fold that mixture back into the remaining egg whites. Folding is best done with a large rubber spatula. To fold properly, what you do is cut down the middle of the mixtures with the spatula, lift what is on the bottom up over the mixture on the top, letting it fall back over the mixture, and turn the bowl a quarter turn. Don't forget to turn the bowl each time you fold. Continue doing this until you have only a few streaks of egg whites.

❦

The big problem my students have with soufflés is, first, overbeating the egg whites—it is hard to overbeat them in a copper bowl—and then overfolding. By beating the egg whites, you have created a mass of little bubbles, and the more you fold (or stir), the more you break down these air bubbles. It is the air in the bubbles of egg whites that expand in the oven, making the soufflé rise.

Vegetable Mélange of Leeks, Artichokes, and Shiitakes

All too often, people think the only way to serve artichokes is to boil or steam them and serve them with a sauce. Here is an elegant way to serve artichokes: the artichokes are trimmed and cooked in a compote of leeks and wild mushrooms. It is always important that every element in this dish have the flavor of the vinaigrette.

*4 large leeks, white part only, halved,
    washed, and cut in 1-inch lengths
Coarse salt
¼ cup plus 2 tablespoons plus ¾ cup
    olive oil
6 fresh artichokes, trimmed and cut in
    ¼-inch slices (see page 58)
1 pound shiitake mushroom caps, wiped
    clean and cut in ¼-inch slices
¼ cup white wine vinegar
1 tablespoon lemon juice
Freshly ground black pepper
3 tablespoons minced fresh Italian parsley
1 fresh tomato, cut in tiny dice*

To make the vegetable mixture, put the leeks in a large sauté pan with ½ teaspoon salt and ¼ cup olive oil over medium-high heat. Add enough water to barely cover the leeks. Cook for 10 minutes, stirring occasionally. Add the artichokes and continue to cook until the artichokes are tender, 10 to 15 minutes. Transfer the artichoke mixture to a bowl.

Meanwhile, in a medium-size frying pan, heat 2 tablespoons olive oil over medium-high heat. Toss in the mushrooms all at once with a sprinkling of salt and continue to cook over high heat, stirring, until the mushrooms are half wilted. Add the mushrooms to the cooked leeks and artichokes. Stir to combine and remove from the heat.

To make the vinaigrette, dissolve ¼ teaspoon salt in the vinegar and lemon juice in a small bowl or measuring cup. Add ½ cup of the olive oil, along with ¼ teaspoon pepper.

To serve, add 2 tablespoons of the vinaigrette to the vegetables and reheat over medium-high heat, stirring constantly. The mixture can be made ahead up to this point. To serve, gently reheat the mélange. Spoon one-eighth of the vegetable mixture into a custard cup, press gently, and turn over onto the center of a warm salad plate. Ladle one-eighth of the vinaigrette around the mélange and decorate the plate with alternating little mounds of parsley and tomato. Repeat with the same custard cup and the remaining vegetables.   SERVES 8

Since leeks grow up through the ground collecting dirt, you must always cut them in half and wash them thoroughly. Before washing, cut off and throw away the root, but leave the dark green leaves to use as a handle when slicing the leeks. When all the white and light green of the leeks is sliced, you can throw away the dark green leaves.

❧

To trim a whole artichoke, first cut off the stem. Holding the artichoke in one hand, remove the coarse outer leaves. Rotating the artichoke, break back each leaf in such a way that the edi-

ble part of each leaf stays on the bottom. Do this all the way around, breaking back and removing the inedible part of each leaf until you have only light green leaves on the artichoke. Cut off these leaves about an inch from the base. Remove any dark green parts from the bottom with a vegetable peeler, so that all that remains is a round of edible artichoke. Rub with half a cut lemon. To remove the choke, cut the artichoke bottoms in half. With a smaller knife, cut out the choke or fuzzy leaves in the center of each half. Slice the artichokes in ¼-inch slices and keep in a bowl of lemon water.

Heirloom Tomato Galettes

*W*hat every recipe should do is bring out the flavor of the ingredients, and these flat, slightly sweet open tarts are the perfect way to enhance the marvelous taste of fresh summer tomatoes. This is a recipe from Catherine Pantsios, who was the well-respected chef-instructor of the Six-Month Full-Time Culinary Course at Tante Marie's. Thank you, Catherine!

1½ tablespoons active dry yeast
Sugar
2 cups flour
Salt
6 tablespoons cold butter, cut into
   1-inch pieces
2 eggs
Cornmeal for dusting
8 medium-size, ripe heirloom tomatoes
   (a variety of colors, if available),
   cut into ¼-inch-thick rounds
Extra-virgin olive oil
Freshly ground black pepper
¼ cup chopped fresh herbs, such as oregano,
   marjoram, chives, and/or parsley

To proof the yeast, warm a glass measuring cup and add ⅓ cup very hot water. Mix in the yeast with a pinch of sugar. Let rest until the mixture bubbles, about 5 to 10 minutes.

To make the dough, put the flour, a teaspoon of the salt, and the butter in the bowl of a food processor. Pulse the mixture until the dough is blended but pieces of butter are still visible in small flakes. Add the yeast mixture and the eggs. Process for a few seconds, just until the mixture forms a ball, scraping down the sides of the bowl if necessary. Remove the dough from the food processor and briefly knead it with the palm of your hand. The dough is ready when it is smooth and slightly springy when pressed gently with your finger. Divide the dough into 8 portions, rolling each into a ball. Place the balls of dough on a parchment-lined baking sheet and cover with a cloth. Let the dough rise in a warm place until doubled in bulk, 45 to 60 minutes.

While the dough is rising, line the lower rack of the oven with a pizza stone or quarry tiles. Preheat the oven to 450 degrees.

To make the galettes, roll each portion of the risen dough into a 6-inch circle by first patting it into a round shape with your hands, then rolling it with a rolling pin. Transfer the circle of dough to the pizza peel or the back of a baking sheet that has been lightly sprinkled with cornmeal. Cover each circle with tomato slices and drizzle with a tablespoon or so of the olive oil. Sprinkle with fresh herbs and salt and pepper. Slide the dough onto the pizza stone or tiles in the oven. Bake until the dough is golden and tomatoes are hot, 6 to 8 minutes. Serve the galettes warm from the oven.

SERVES 8

Heirloom tomatoes are the beautiful red, yellow, orange, green, burgundy, and striped tomatoes you find in farmers' markets at the end of summer. They should never be cooked very long and are best served with good olive oil, coarse salt, and a sprinkling of fresh herbs.

Grilled Vegetable Tart

*T*his summer tart of purple, green, and red vegetables sitting in a flavorful custard would make an attractive first course for a dinner outdoors. You can double the quantity of pastry and make individual tarts. Either way the tart can be made ahead and served at room temperature.

2 cups flour
Salt
12 tablespoons cold butter, cut into
  1-inch pieces
1 egg yolk
Olive oil for coating the pan
2 to 3 Asian eggplants (about ½ pound),
  cut into ¼-inch rounds
2 zucchini (about ½ pound), cut into
  ¼-inch rounds
1 large onion, thinly sliced
2 garlic cloves, minced
1 cup cherry tomatoes, stemmed
1 egg yolk
4 tablespoons minced fresh Italian parsley
½ cup heavy cream
Freshly ground black pepper

To make the tart shell, put the flour and 1 teaspoon salt in a bowl. With a pastry cutter or two knives, cut in the cold butter until it is the size of oatmeal flakes. Combine ¼ cup cold water in a measuring cup with the egg yolk, stirring well with a fork. Make a well in the flour mixture and pour the egg-water mixture in the middle. With the fork straight up and down, mix together the dry and liq-uid ingredients. Bring the mixture together with the fingers of one hand. When a rough mass is formed, turn the dough onto a board and knead two or three times with the heel of your hand. To do this, smear the dough across the table and scrape it back together into a rough ball. Repeat. When the dough is together, in a loose mass, wrap it in waxed paper, press into a patty, and chill for about 30 minutes.

To cook the vegetables, pour enough olive oil in a wide sauté pan to coat the bottom of the pan by ¼ inch and put the pan over medium-high heat. When the oil is hot, sauté the eggplant and zucchini slices, one layer at a time, until golden on each side. Remove from the pan and drain on paper towels. When all of the vegetables are cooked, add another tablespoon of oil to the pan and add the onion and ½ teaspoon salt. Cook, stirring from time to time, until the onion is soft, about 5 minutes. Add the garlic and cook for a minute, stirring. Turn off the heat.

To form the tart shell, remove the dough from the waxed paper and place it on a lightly floured work surface. Lightly flour the dough and a rolling pin and roll the dough away from you, turning it after each roll. If it sticks to the surface, add a little flour to the counter or the rolling pin. It is important to keep moving the dough so it doesn't stick to the board. When you have a dough roughly 10 inches round and ⅛ inch thick, fold it in half and in half again. Place the inside corner of the dough in the center of a 9-inch tart pan. Unfold the dough and lay it into the corners of the tart pan. Cut off excess dough around the edge, leaving an extra inch from the edge of the pan. Working at the opposite side of the pan, bring the dough toward you and fold back the extra dough to form a double-thick edge. Press this firmly into the pan, turning the pan continuously so that you are always working on the side farthest away from you. Decorate the top edge of the tart with the prongs of a fork or the heel of a knife, or by making twists with your fingers. Prick the tart shell two or three times with a fork. Line the unbaked shell with a piece of parchment paper. Fill the paper with pie weights, raw beans, or rice kept for this purpose. Bake the shell for 18 to 20 minutes, until it is lightly golden around the edges. (This is called baking blind.) Remove the paper and pie weights. Return the tart shell to the oven and cook it for another 5 to 7 minutes. Remove it from the oven and chill in the refrigerator.

Preheat the oven to 375 degrees.

To assemble the tart, combine the yolk, parsley, cream, ¼ teaspoon salt, and ⅛ teaspoon pepper in a small bowl. Spread the onion mixture evenly over the bottom of the cooled crust. Pour the cream mixture over the onion mixture and arrange the eggplant, zucchini, and cherry tomatoes in concentric circles on top, pressing gently. Bake the tart until the cream mixture is no longer runny, 25 to 30 minutes. Serve at room temperature.   SERVES 6

This is an example of a tart made with basic pastry called pâte brisée in French. The idea is that the butter is cut into the flour in such a way that it becomes little flakes of cold butter surrounded by a paste of flour and liquid. These flakes of butter create steam in a hot oven, making the pastry flaky and light.

The best pans for making tarts are metal with removable bottoms. The tarts should be unmolded over a container like a box of salt and, if possible, the tart slid off the bottom onto a flat serving plate.

Pastry will always bake better when it is cold. First you make the dough, then you chill it. You roll it out and chill it again if it gets too soft. After the tart shell is baked blind, it must be chilled again before the filling is added; otherwise, the filling will leak through.

When a recipe calls for baking a tart shell blind, it means to pre-bake it with a false filling to prevent the final tart from becoming soggy. This is a step that can be skipped if you are an experienced baker and haven't got the time.

Spreading a thin layer of Parmesan or bread crumbs on the bottom of an unbaked tart shell will also help to prevent the bottom of the tart from becoming soggy when cooked.

Buy Japanese or Chinese eggplants that are firm and not too large; large eggplants can be spongy in the middle. In the past, cooks salted eggplant to remove bitterness, but these days eggplants are usually grown so they lack bitterness. The only reason to salt eggplant before cooking is to remove excess water before deep-frying.

Classic Onion Tart
(Tarte à l'Oignon)

In this very traditional onion tart, the onions cook so long that they become sweet and succulent, complemented perfectly by the custard that binds them together. This tart could be served with a simple green salad for a Sunday-night supper in the winter or taken in a basket to a picnic accompanied by a fresh tomato salad in the summer when tomatoes are full of flavor. Either way, you will love this very French tart!

2 cups plus 2 tablespoons flour
Salt
12 tablespoons cold butter plus
   3 tablespoons butter
1 egg yolk
6 medium-size onions, thinly sliced
   (about 8 cups)
2 cups milk
3 eggs
Freshly ground white pepper
½ cup freshly grated Parmesan

To make the tart shell, put the 2 cups flour and 1 teaspoon salt in a bowl. With a pastry cutter or two knives, cut in the cold butter until it is the size of oatmeal flakes. Combine ¼ cup cold water in a measuring cup with the egg yolk, stirring well with a fork. Make a well in the flour mixture and pour the egg-water mixture in the middle. Holding the fork straight up and down, mix together the dry and liquid ingredients. Bring the mixture together with the fingers of one hand. When a rough mass is formed, turn the dough onto a board and knead two or three times with the heel of your hand. To do this, smear the dough across the table and scrape it back together into a rough ball. Repeat. When the dough is together in a loose mass, wrap it in waxed paper, press into a patty, and chill about 30 minutes.

To make the filling, put the 3 tablespoons butter and the onions in a large frying or sauté pan over medium-high heat with ½ teaspoon salt. Cook, stirring from time to time, until the onions are soft and translucent, about 25 minutes. Remove from the heat and sprinkle the 2 tablespoons flour over the mixture. Return to the heat and cook, stirring constantly, for 2 more minutes. Stir in a cup of the milk and bring the mixture to a boil over medium-high heat, stirring constantly. Remove the pan from the heat and let cool for 10 minutes. Pour the remaining 1 cup milk in a measuring cup, add the eggs, ¼ teaspoon salt, and ⅛ teaspoon pepper and mix with a fork until the mixture is thoroughly blended.

Preheat the oven to 375 degrees.

To form the tart shell, remove the dough from the waxed paper and place it on a lightly floured work surface. Lightly flour the dough and the rolling pin and roll the dough away from you, turning after each roll. If it sticks, add a little flour to the counter or the rolling pin. It is important to keep the dough from sticking to the board. When you have dough roughly 10 inches round and ⅛ inch thick, fold it in half and in half again, and place the inside corner of the dough in the center of a 9-inch tart pan. Unfold the dough into the corners of the tart pan. Cut off excess dough around the edge, leaving an extra inch from the edge of the pan. Working at the opposite side of the pan, bring the dough toward you and fold back the extra dough to form a double-thick edge. Press this firmly into the pan, turning the pan continuously so you are always working on the side farthest away from you. Decorate the top edge of the tart with the prongs of a fork or the heel of a knife, or by making twists with your fingers. Prick the shell two or three times with a fork. Chill until firm.

To assemble the tart, spread the Parmesan over the bottom of the unbaked tart shell. Spoon the onion mixture evenly into the shell and pour the egg mixture into the tart. Bake on the top rack of the oven until the liquid in the middle of the tart appears set, about 25 minutes. Cool the tart on a rack.

SERVES 6 TO 8

The sugar in onions is released when they are cooked in butter or oil for about 25 minutes. To cook them any longer would cause the sugar to caramelize; in other words, to become brown in color.

Mussels Ravigote

resh, plump mussels are delicious, especially with this mustard-flavored vinaigrette called ravigote. Although the whole dish can be made a day or two ahead, it is best to serve it at room temperature. As I always repeat, a dish will taste much better if you can get some of the cooking liquid into the sauce. I always tell my students this trick alone is a thousand dollars' worth of information.

2 pounds fresh mussels
4 shallots, finely chopped
1 cup dry white wine
Bouquet garni composed of 4 sprigs parsley,
*   2 sprigs thyme, and 1 bay leaf*
2 celery stalks, cut in ¼-inch dice
1 tablespoon each minced fresh Italian
*   parsley, tarragon, and chives*
¼ cup tarragon vinegar
2 tablespoons Dijon-style mustard
1 cup olive oil
Coarse salt
Freshly ground black pepper

To steam the mussels, put them in a heavy, stainless steel or enameled saucepan with the shallots, wine, and bouquet garni. Cover the pan and turn the heat to moderately high, shaking the pan or stirring the mussels with a wooden spoon once or twice, until they open. With a slotted spoon, transfer the mussels to a large bowl. Add the celery and fresh herbs.

To make the vinaigrette, pour the mussel cooking liquid into a smaller saucepan without pouring out the last tablespoon of liquid, which may be sandy, and reduce the mussel "liquor" to about a cup. Transfer the mussel liquor to a small bowl. Mix in the vinegar, mustard, olive oil, and salt and pepper to taste. Toss the vinaigrette with the mussels. Serve at room temperature with plenty of French bread.   SERVES 6

Whenever a recipe calls for three different kinds of minced herbs, just put a handful of herbs on the board and chop them all together with a large chef's knife.

Before mussels were grown by aquaculture, they grew on rocks and piers along the seacoast. They produced little plastic-like threads to keep them fast to the rocks. Recipes often called for "debearding" the mussels, which meant to rip out these little strings. Nowadays, most mussels are grown in net bags and do not produce beards.

If you don't have tarragon vinegar, you can substitute white wine vinegar. Or you can make your own tarragon vinegar by putting 4 to 6 sprigs of fresh clean tarragon into a 1-liter bottle and filling the bottle with white wine vinegar. In a week you will have tarragon vinegar.

Since mussels are delicate in flavor, they are always steamed in white wine with shallots. Clams should always be steamed in water because they have such a strong taste and are so salty. Salt and wine don't go well together.

Mussels with Mashed Potatoes Gratinée

The students at Tante Marie's absolutely love this dish! I first went crazy for it at a restaurant called Plouf in San Francisco's financial district. It was presented as a first course on a round metal platter on a stand, which is how shellfish is served in France. The mussels, bubbly with butter, are served on a bed of mashed potatoes. The diner can scoop up the mashed potatoes with a mussel shell and enjoy the garlicky mussel in one delicious mouthful.

*2 pounds Yukon Gold or Yellow Finn
   potatoes, cut in halves or quarters if large
6 garlic cloves, unpeeled, plus 3 garlic cloves,
   minced
Coarse salt
⅓ cup heavy cream
½ pound (2 sticks) plus ¼ pound
   (1 stick) butter
2½ pounds (about 60) fresh mussels
3 large shallots, finely chopped
1 cup dry white wine
1 tablespoon minced fresh parsley
Freshly ground black pepper*

To make the mashed potatoes, put the potatoes, 6 garlic cloves, and ½ teaspoon salt in a large pot of cold water over high heat. Boil until the potatoes are tender when pierced with a fork, about 25 minutes. Immediately drain the potatoes and garlic in a colander, shaking the colander to evaporate any excess moisture. Peel the potatoes and spoon them and the garlic into a ricer and press them

through the ricer back into the pot. (Remove the garlic skins from the ricer from time to time.) While the mashed potatoes are still warm, stir in the cream and ½ pound butter. Add salt and pepper to taste.

To prepare the mussels, put the mussels, two-thirds of the shallots, and the wine in a stainless steel or enameled saucepan, covered, over medium-high heat. Steam the mussels until they open, about 5 minutes. (You may need to shake the pan once or twice.)

To make the compound butter, put the ¼ pound butter in a small bowl and mash with a wooden spoon until soft. Stir in the remaining shallots, minced garlic, and parsley. Add enough salt and pepper to make the butter flavorful.

Spread one-fourth of the mashed potatoes on each of four ovenproof serving plates. Open each mussel, remove half the shell, and use the empty shell to loosen the mussel from the other half. Discard the empty half and lay the mussel in the other shell with the rounded side out. Arrange 12 shells on each

plate. Put a generous teaspoon of garlic butter on each mussel in its shell. (If making ahead, cover each plate with plastic wrap and chill until ready to broil.)

When ready to serve, preheat the broiler. Broil each plate 2 inches from the flame until the butter is very bubbly, about 5 minutes. Serve immediately.   SERVES 4

To purchase mussels, look for mussels that are fresh smelling and heavy, and hold themselves closed. Mussels that do not stay closed when pressed should be thrown away because this means they are dead and may have begun to deteriorate.

Scallops in Beurre Blanc with Julienne of Carrots and Zucchini

Almost nothing is more sublime than fresh sea scallops cooked and served in a buttery sauce made from their poaching liquid and decorated with little orange and green vegetables. This scallop dish is so '70s, with beurre blanc and julienne of vegetables, but it's still a great way to present scallops.

2 large shallots, finely chopped
1 cup white wine
1 cup fresh or bottled clam juice
2 pounds sea scallops
1 tablespoon white wine vinegar
¾ pound (1½ sticks) butter, between
  refrigerator and room temperature
Coarse salt
Freshly ground white pepper
½ pound carrots, peeled and julienned
½ pound zucchini, green part only,
  julienned

To poach the scallops, put the shallots, white wine, and clam juice in a stainless steel or enameled saucepan. Bring to a simmer and let simmer gently for 3 minutes. Meanwhile, look over each scallop and remove any little tough bits on the edge of each scallop (the foot). Drop the scallops into the poaching liquid and cook below a boil, until the scallops are opaque throughout and firm to the touch, about 3 minutes. Remove the scallops from the pan and keep warm.

To make the sauce, add the vinegar to the cooking liquid and reduce the mixture over moderately high heat until 1 tablespoon of liquid remains. Meanwhile, cut the butter into about 18 pieces. Remove the pan from the heat and whisk in two pieces of the butter. Whisk vigorously until the mixture appears creamy. Return the pan to low heat and continue whisking in the butter, one piece at a time, adding one as the other emulsifies. If the mixture begins to boil around the edge of the pan, take the pan off the heat again and continue whisking. Return the pan to the heat and continue whisking and adding butter until all the butter is incorporated. (It is best to whisk vigorously without watching the butter because when you watch, you slow down.) Remove the pan from the heat and add salt and pepper to taste. Keep covered with a metal lid until ready to serve.

To cook the vegetables, put the carrots in a small frying pan with ¼ inch water and the zucchini in another pan with no water. Sprinkle with salt and pepper and steam the two vegetables until cooked through, 3 minutes for the carrots and a minute for the zucchini.

To serve, divide the scallops among eight warmed 4-inch gratin dishes, spoon the beurre blanc sauce over the scallops, and scatter the carrots and zucchini on top. Serve immediately. SERVES 8

Beurre blanc is a warm emulsion sauce often served with fish or shellfish. It can be kept warm but will separate if reheated.

❧

When a recipe calls for fish stock and it is hard to find fish frames (fish bones and heads) or you don't have time to make it, substitute freshly made clam juice: Steam some clams in water and use the resulting juice with equal amounts of dry white wine and water. (A substitute for this would be bottled Atlantic clam juice—never canned.)

To cut carrots into julienne, first remove a sliver of carrot from the bottom of a round peeled carrot so that it will lay flat on a board. Cut the carrot into 1½-inch-long strips. Cut these into ¼-inch-wide strips. Layer these strips on top of each other and cut into ¼-inch-long strips roughly the size of paper matches.

To cut zucchini into julienne, cut off both ends and cut each zucchini into 1½-inch-long strips. Remove a ¼-inch slice from the side of each piece. (Save the white parts for soups or throw them away.) Cut each green zucchini piece into ¼-inch-long slices roughly the size of paper matchsticks. This way, all the zucchini julienne are partly green.

French Potato Salad with Bacon Vinaigrette on Arugula

In this country we think of potato salad as a summer picnic dish made with mayonnaise and/or sour cream. More often in France, the potatoes are dressed with stock, oil, and vinegar. Here is a modern presentation of French potato salad with a flavorful vinaigrette.

> 3 strips thick-cut bacon
> 2 pounds Yukon Gold or Yellow Finn potatoes
> Coarse salt
> 5 tablespoons extra-virgin olive oil
> 3 tablespoons Champagne or white wine vinegar
> Freshly ground black pepper
> 1 cup light chicken or vegetable stock
> 3 ounces baby arugula or spinach

To cook the bacon, fry it in a heavy skillet over medium-high heat, turning it occasionally, until crisp, about 6 minutes. Transfer the bacon to a paper towel and reserve the bacon fat. Finely chop the bacon.

To cook the potatoes, put them in a saucepan with plenty of cold water and ½ teaspoon salt and bring to a boil over medium-high heat. Boil until the potatoes are tender when pierced with a fork, about 25 minutes. Drain the potatoes in a colander and shake them to evaporate any excess moisture.

To make the vinaigrette, in a measuring cup mix together 1 tablespoon of the bacon fat, the olive oil, vinegar, and salt and pepper to taste. Stir in the bacon.

When the potatoes are cool enough to handle, peel off the skins, slice the potatoes into ¼-inch rounds, and toss with the stock and half the vinaigrette.

To assemble, arrange flat circles of clean, dry arugula leaves in the centers of six salad plates. Pack one-sixth of the potato salad into a 3-inch custard cup. Invert this onto one of the plates and repeat with the remaining potato salad. Surround each potato salad with one-sixth of the remaining vinaigrette.

SERVES 6

New potatoes are usually boiled until just tender. Because potatoes will absorb excess moisture and become soggy, it is important to dry them after they are cooked. We used to return the potatoes to the hot pan and shake them over high heat. Now I find that shaking them in a colander does just as well. Whatever you do, don't put them in cold water to stop the cooking!

Whenever you are making a salad of potatoes, rice, pasta, or other starch, it will taste much better if you add the stock, oil, and/or vinegar to the starch when it is still warm. Because these starches absorb the flavors, it is important to taste them and adjust the seasoning before serving.

Potato Galettes with Smoked Mackerel and Mesclun Salad

Here is a really sophisticated rendition of fish and chips. A flat cake of mashed potato soufflé is the bed for smoked fish, which is topped with a peppery salad. Upscale grocery stores now carry delicious peppered smoked mackerel, which are smoked soon after coming out of the ocean so that they don't have that oily taste we usually associate with mackerel. The adventurous will be delighted with the result, and the less adventurous will choose smoked trout or salmon—either way, this is a delicious first course! These potato galettes can be made ahead and reheated.

*1 pound Yukon Gold or Yellow Finn
   potatoes, cut in half or quarters if large
Coarse salt
4 scallions, equal amounts of white and
   green parts, thinly sliced
6 tablespoons butter
½ cup milk
2 eggs, separated
Freshly ground white pepper
8 ounces smoked mackerel, trout, or
   salmon
4 ounces baby arugula or watercress leaves,
   washed and dried
4 tablespoons Meyer lemon–flavored
   olive oil*

To prepare the potatoes, put them with ½ teaspoon salt and plenty of water in a large pot over medium-high heat. Boil the potatoes until tender when pierced with a fork, about 25 minutes.

Meanwhile, cook the scallions in 2 tablespoons of the butter until wilted, 3 to 4 minutes. Lay eight 4-inch flan rings on a cookie sheet. Butter the rings and the cookie sheet. Preheat the oven to 425 degrees.

When the potatoes are cooked, immediately drain them in a colander and shake to evaporate any excess moisture. Remove the potato skins. Spoon the potatoes into a potato ricer and press them back into the pot. Add the milk, the remaining 4 tablespoons butter, and the cooked scallions. Beat in one egg yolk at a time; beat well after each one. Add salt and pepper to taste.

Beat the egg whites with a few grains of salt in a clean, preferably copper bowl, until stiff but not dry. Fold one-quarter of the beaten egg whites into the mashed potato mixture, then fold the potato mixture back into the remaining egg whites. Fill each ring with the mixture, using a spatula to smooth the top. Bake on the lower rack of the oven until the potato soufflés are lightly brown and puffy, about 20 minutes. If making these ahead, remove the cookie sheet from the oven and with a small knife loosen and remove the rings. With a metal spatula, loosen the soufflés from the cookie sheet. Cover with plastic wrap and chill until ready to reheat.

When ready to serve, place the cookie sheet of galettes in a 375-degree oven for 10 to 15 minutes. Place the smoked fish on a piece of foil and heat for 2 minutes in the same oven until just warmed through, about 2 minutes. Place the greens in a large bowl.

Spoon the oil over the greens. Toss just to coat.

Warm the salad plates. Remove the galettes from the oven and with a metal spatula place each one in the middle of a plate. With your fingers, remove the skin from the fish, sprinkle the fish with additional oil, and lay the fish on the galettes. Top with the greens and sprinkle with salt and pepper. Serve immediately.

MAKES 8 SERVINGS

This recipe would be fabulous made with home-smoked salmon. See page 379 for instructions on smoking your own fish.

Smoked trout and smoked mackerel are usually hot smoked. A hot smoker cooks and smokes at the same time.

HERBS

HERBS ARE MEANT to enhance the flavor of food, not overpower it. Culinary herbs are green, leafy plants that generally grow in temperate climates. Growing your own is easy; just plant them in well-drained, sandy soil in an area that receives plenty of sunshine. Herbs don't need much water and, except for basil and cilantro, will grow year after year, especially if you keep trimming the growth.

Herbs have maximum flavor if harvested just before they are about to flower. It is better to buy fresh herbs in bunches rather than in plastic containers. Whether they are harvested or purchased, the best way to store herbs is in a plastic bag in the refrigerator.

New cooks always think there is some magic formula for cooking with fresh herbs. In fact, they often use the word "spice" when they are talking about herbs. Although there are some great combinations like tomatoes and basil, the addition of fresh herbs to food really depends on the desire and taste of the cook. I really recommend trying different herbs to see what you like; use a light hand at first so the flavor of the herbs doesn't overpower the food.

When cooking with herbs, you can try many combinations; herbs like parsley, chives, thyme, and marjoram work well together. The two herbs that do not mix well with others are rosemary and dill; they are best used alone.

It is always better to cook with fresh herbs rather than dried. If a recipe calls for dried herbs, use three times as much fresh. If fresh herbs are not available, tie the dried herbs in a bit of cheesecloth for cooking, and then remove them after the dish has cooked. This way, diners do not get little flakes of dried herbs in their mouths. Fresh herbs add maximum flavor to a dish if thrown in a few minutes before the cooking is finished.

A great way to store leftover herbs is to chop them and mix them with softened butter, salt, and pepper to taste. You can roll this compound butter into a log shape, wrap it in waxed paper or plastic wrap, and store in the refrigerator for 2 to 3 weeks or in the freezer for 6 to 9 months. A round of soft compound butter is delicious on a piece of grilled fish, chicken, or meat.

Whenever a recipe calls for a bouquet garni, simply tie together 4 sprigs of parsley with 2 sprigs of thyme and a bay leaf. Sometimes cooks tie these to a piece of celery stalk or leek so they hold together in cooking. The size of the bouquet garni depends on how much soup or stew it is going into.

SPICES

Spices are things like the bark, root, seeds, pods, and buds of plants that almost always grow in the tropics. I recommend buying spices whole whenever possible and grinding them yourself in a coffee grinder reserved for that purpose. Whole spices keep for about a year if stored in a cool, dark place. If you can cook freshly ground spices, they will add a much better flavor to food. In other words, cooking the ground spices in onions and oil or butter before adding the other ingredients to a soup or a stew will give the final dish better flavor than adding uncooked ground spices toward the end of the cooking. When a recipe calls for cooking whole spices in oil, it is to change the flavor, usually making it more intense.

PEPPER

The most universal spice is pepper, a dried berry of a tropical vine. When preserved fresh in brine, the berries are called green peppercorns. When allowed to dry, the skin turns black. Sometimes this skin is removed before drying to make white peppercorns. (What are commonly called pink peppercorns come from a different plant.) Green peppercorns go well in rich dishes like duck or beef. Black and white pepper should be freshly ground whenever possible. Traditionally, white pepper is used when a less pungent taste is desired or when the cook doesn't want black flecks in the food. Some cooks put equal amounts of black peppercorns, white peppercorns, and whole allspice berries in their pepper grinders; others like to use peppercorn mixtures.

Creamy Polenta with Red Bell Peppers and Winter Greens

*T*his is a recipe adapted from Georgeanne Brennan, who writes so lovingly about growing and cooking vegetables near Sacramento and in Provence. Her book *Potager* is a favorite of mine. This easy and delicious dish never fails to please people—cheesy, creamy polenta, covered with vivid greens and red bell peppers.

1 cup polenta-type cornmeal
Coarse salt
2 tablespoons butter
8 ounces (about 2 cups) grated sharp
  Cheddar
2 tablespoons olive oil
4 garlic cloves, minced
3 red bell peppers, cut into ¼-inch julienne
1 bunch (about 10 ounces) Swiss chard,
  stems removed, cut into ½-inch-wide
  strips
1 bunch (about 10 ounces) chicory or
  dandelion greens, stems removed, cut into
  ½-inch-wide strips
1 bunch (about 10 ounces) spinach, tough
  stems removed, cut into ½-inch-wide
  strips
Freshly ground black pepper

To make the polenta, bring a large saucepan filled with 1 quart water to a boil over high heat. Add ½ teaspoon salt and whisk in the cornmeal. Return the mixture to a boil, while stirring constantly with a wooden spoon. Reduce the heat to low and cook, stirring constantly, until the wooden spoon will stand up in the cooked polenta, about 15 minutes. (The longer it takes to cook polenta, the smoother it will be.) When it is done, remove the pan from the heat and stir in the butter, cheese, and salt and pepper to taste. Cover and set aside.

To prepare the greens, heat the olive oil in a 10- or 12-inch sauté pan over medium-high heat. Add the garlic and bell peppers and cook for 2 to 3 minutes, stirring. Add the greens and a generous sprinkling of salt. Reduce the heat to medium-low and cover. Cook for 3 to 4 minutes to steam the greens. Remove the cover and continue cooking for 2 to 3 minutes, until the greens begin to wilt but still retain their color. Add salt and pepper to taste. To serve, spoon the warm polenta on four warmed salad plates and cover with the greens.   SERVES 4

Polenta is easy to make. It is always made in a ratio of 1 cup polenta-style cornmeal to 4 cups water. Some cooks prefer to substitute milk and/or stock for water. Other types of meal made from corn are grits and yellow and white cornmeal. Cornmeal for polenta is usually more coarsely ground than the others. Grits or regular cornmeal work fine in this recipe.

To remove tough stems from greens, simply hold the stem firmly in one hand and the leaves in another. Pull hard so the stem pulls out.

Pesto-Filled Polenta Roulade with Fresh Tomato Sauce

This is an absolutely splendid first course to serve on a vegetarian night! It makes ordinary polenta seem special—a pinwheel of polenta filled with pesto-flavored ricotta served in a fresh tomato sauce. The trick is to roll the polenta while it is still warm. The entire dish can be totally made ahead and reheated.

FOR THE PESTO
4 ounces Parmesan, cut in 1-inch cubes
2 garlic cloves
⅓ cup pine nuts
3 cups basil leaves
½ cup olive oil

FOR THE ROULADE
Coarse salt
1 cup polenta-type cornmeal
4 tablespoons (½ stick) butter
½ cup freshly grated Parmesan
2 cups ricotta cheese
Freshly ground black pepper
1 medium-size onion, chopped
½ cup olive oil
3 garlic cloves, minced
6 large red, ripe tomatoes, peeled, seeded, and chopped
8 to 10 fresh basil leaves for garnish

To make the pesto, put two pieces of the cheese in the container of a food processor fitted with the blade. Process until fine, drop in the remaining cheese, one by one, and continue processing until fine. Add the garlic,

pine nuts, and basil leaves. With the machine running, quickly pour in the oil. Stop when all the oil is incorporated. Set the pesto aside.

To make the polenta, bring 6 cups water to a boil in a large saucepan over high heat. Meanwhile, butter an 18 by 11-inch baking sheet and line it with foil so that there is a 1-inch edge of foil around the pan. Generously butter the foil. When the water boils, add a teaspoon of salt and whisk in the cornmeal. Return the water to the boil, turn down the heat, and simmer, stirring from time to time with a wooden spoon. The polenta is done when it is thick enough for a spoon to stand up in it without falling over, about 20 minutes. Stir in the butter and 4 tablespoons of the grated Parmesan and spread the polenta evenly on the prepared pan. Let cool for 10 minutes, until slightly firm to the touch.

To make the filling, mix the ricotta with the pesto.

To make the roulade, remove the polenta from the pan by lifting it in its foil and lay it lengthwise on a counter. Quickly spread the ricotta mixture over the polenta. Using the foil, lift the *long side* of the polenta closest to you and, using your hands, start rolling the polenta away from you in a long round roll. Wrap the roll in the foil, being careful not to enclose any of the foil. Chill.

To make the fresh tomato sauce, cook the onion in the oil with ½ teaspoon salt in a medium saucepan over medium-high heat, stirring from time to time, until the onion is soft, about 5 minutes. Add the garlic and cook another 2 minutes. Add the tomatoes and remaining 2 tablespoons fresh herbs.

Continue cooking and stirring from time to time for another 5 minutes. Add salt and pepper to taste.

When ready to serve, cut the polenta roulade into 1-inch pinwheels and lay the slices cut side down on a lightly buttered baking sheet. Place in a 350-degree oven for 12 minutes to warm through. Reheat the tomato sauce, stirring occasionally. Place large spoonfuls of the tomato sauce on eight salad plates, top with a slice of polenta roulade, and garnish with fresh basil leaves.

SERVES 4 TO 6

The technique of rolling can be used for soufflés, omelettes, and polenta. The trick is not to let the mixture cool to the point that it stiffens and then cracks when rolled. It may take practice to get the roulade round.

In Italian households, cooks make creamy polenta for dinner to serve with such dishes as sausages and stews, and they purposely make extra to be spread on a baking sheet and cooled in the refrigerator. The resulting firm polenta can be sautéed, grilled, or baked and served another day.

If a fresh tomato sauce is too pale and lacks flavor, add a tablespoon of tomato paste.

Molded Vegetable Risotto with Porcini Sauce

I'll never forget the Christmas Eve dinner I had at Corby Kummer's apartment in Boston. He had just returned from Italy with fresh mozzarella stuffed with thick cream. For the main course he served a magnificent molded risotto. I have adapted the idea to make a first course suitable for vegetarians. Everyone at Tante Marie's loves this delicious variation!

Making risotto is common now—but making it into an individually molded first course is special. The risotto can hold for up to 30 minutes in the molds before reheating.

1 ounce dried porcini (cèpe) mushrooms
6 tablespoons butter plus some for the molds
½ cup red wine
1½ cups chicken or vegetable stock
Coarse salt
Freshly ground black pepper
1 cup fresh or frozen peas
4 medium-size fresh mushrooms, sliced
½ medium-size onion, finely chopped
1 celery stalk, finely chopped
1 carrot, peeled and finely chopped
1¾ cups Arborio rice
2 tablespoons tomato paste
1½ quarts (6 cups) chicken or vegetable stock, heated
6 tablespoons freshly grated Parmesan
Fine bread crumbs for the molds

To prepare the dried mushrooms, soak them in ½ cup hot water for 30 minutes. Remove the mushrooms from the soaking liquid, squeeze out the excess liquid, and coarsely chop them. Set the soaking liquid and mushrooms aside.

To make the sauce, put the chopped porcini in a small saucepan with 2 tablespoons of the butter and cook over moderate heat, stirring from time to time, for about 10 minutes. Add half the reserved mushroom liquor, ½ cup of the wine, the stock, and a sprinkling of salt and pepper. Bring to a boil and simmer until the sauce has reduced by one-third, about 15 minutes. Add the peas and fresh mushrooms and simmer another 5 minutes. Add salt and pepper to taste.

To make the risotto, put 2 tablespoons of the butter, ½ teaspoon salt, the onion, celery, and carrot in a medium-size saucepan over moderately high heat. Cook, stirring from time to time, until the vegetables are soft, about 5 minutes. Add the rice and stir to coat. Stir in the tomato paste and the remaining ½ cup wine and bring to a simmer. Start adding the stock one ladleful at a time, stirring slowly after each addition. As the stock is absorbed, add another ladleful. The rice will be done when it becomes creamy in appearance and is no longer crunchy when tasted. It is always better to undercook risotto than to overcook it. Remove from the heat and stir in the remaining 2 tablespoons butter and the Parmesan. Cover and let rest for 5 minutes to allow the rice to absorb the flavors.

Preheat the oven to 375 degrees. Butter the bottom and sides of twelve ½-cup ramekins and coat the insides of these dishes lightly with bread crumbs, shaking off the excess.

Spoon the risotto into the ramekins and

gently press the tops to pack it in slightly. Place the ramekins on a baking pan in the oven for about 15 minutes. Warm salad plates. Unmold the ramekins onto the plates and surround them with the sauce.

SERVES 12

Herb Crêpes with Goat's Cheese Soufflé and Mesclun Salad

This recipe is from Catherine Pantsios, who was the chef-instructor at Tante Marie's for five years. She is a teacher with an immense amount of information to pass on to her students. Here, small crêpes are made with herbs and folded over a goat's cheese soufflé, which puffs up in the oven. Served with mesclun salad on the side, this is a very elegant first course.

½ cup sifted flour plus 3 tablespoons flour
2 eggs
⅔ cup milk
2 tablespoons butter, melted, plus extra for cooking the crêpes
Salt
1 tablespoon minced fresh Italian parsley
1 tablespoon minced fresh tarragon
3 tablespoons butter
¾ cup milk, heated
3 eggs, separated, plus 1 egg white
4 ounces aged goat's cheese, grated
Freshly ground pepper
1 tablespoon lemon juice
1 tablespoon white wine vinegar
¼ cup extra-virgin olive oil
½ pound mesclun (mixed red and green lettuces)

To make the crêpe batter, whisk together the sifted flour and eggs in a bowl. Gradually whisk in the milk and melted butter. Add a pinch of salt. Stir in the chopped herbs. Let the batter rest in the refrigerator for an hour.

To make the crêpes, brush a 5½-inch-diameter crêpe or nonstick pan with a thin layer of melted butter and heat over a medium-high flame. Pour in about 2 tablespoons of the batter, immediately swirling it around the bottom of the pan, and pour off any excess. When lightly browned, turn over the crêpe to cook the other side until lightly browned and spotted. Turn the cooked crêpe onto a plate so that the first side (the nicely browned side) is down. Repeat with the remaining batter until you have a pile of crêpes.

To make the soufflé mixture, melt the 3 tablespoons butter in a medium-size saucepan over moderately high heat. Take the pan off the heat and stir in the 3 tablespoons flour with a wooden spoon. Return to the heat and cook, stirring constantly, until the mixture appears greasy. Whisk in the milk off the heat. Return to the heat and bring to a boil, whisking. Reduce the heat and let simmer for 5 minutes. Off the heat again, whisk in the egg yolks, one at a time, beating well after each addition. Add the cheese with salt and pepper to taste. (This mixture can be made ahead up to this point but must be covered with plastic wrap to prevent a crust from forming.)

In a separate bowl, whisk the egg whites until they are stiff but not dry. Fold one-quarter of the egg whites into the egg yolk mixture, then fold the mixture back into the remaining egg whites.

To prepare the soufflé, preheat the oven to 375 degrees.

To assemble the crêpes, lightly butter a baking sheet. Place each crêpe on the sheet and put a heaping tablespoonful of the soufflé mixture slightly below the center of each crêpe. Fold over the top halves of the crêpes and bake until puffed, about 8 minutes.

To make the vinaigrette, mix the lemon juice, vinegar, ¼ teaspoon salt, and oil in the bottom of a large bowl and toss with the mesclun. When the crêpes are ready, place them on twelve warmed salad plates and put a handful of dressed salad next to each.

SERVES 12

If the soufflé base is warm when the egg whites are incorporated, the crêpes may be filled and held for up to an hour before being baked in the oven.

Egg whites without a trace of yolk may be stored in a container in the refrigerator for 3 weeks. One egg white is about 2 tablespoons. There are a generous 8 egg whites in a cup.

SOUPS

SCOFFIER, the great French teacher of cooks of the early twentieth century, said that you must pay strict attention to the preparation of soup because it gives your guests an impression of the meal to come. However, in modern times we may not sit down to a dinner in which the soup precedes the meal; rather, soup may *be* the meal. Either way, as an appetite stimulator or as a complete meal, a good soup should satisfy our need for nourishment and comfort, and above all, it should taste great.

Historically, soups have been classified as clear, cream, or family (whole-meal) soups. An example of a clear soup is a consommé, which is made of clarified meat stock, flavored and sometimes garnished. A cream soup or velouté is thickened with a roux—butter and flour cooked together before liquid is added. It may have stock, vegetable puree, and cream or an enrichment of egg yolk and cream, a *liaison,* added at the end. The family or whole-meal soup is neither clear nor a smooth puree. Rather, it may include ingredients such as pasta, beans, sausage, and a variety of vegetables, all of which provide texture and taste. Often, the whole-meal soup uses up odds and ends of leftovers in a delicious way. All you need to complete the meal is a piece of good cheese, a chunk of crusty country bread, and a glass of red wine.

Should you use water or stock for making soup? The choice is yours. French cooks prefer water because they want the vegetables to taste like themselves. I like to think of cooking with stock like painting with oil paints—it gives depth of flavor, whereas cooking with water is like painting with watercolors, clean, bright, and uncomplicated. Americans prefer more depth of flavor, so we are more likely to use stock as the base for soups.

To puree soups

There are three ways to puree a soup to make it smooth. You can use an electric blender or food processor and pulse on and off until you get the desired consistency. You can also leave it in the pot on the stove and puree it with an electric immersion blender. Another way is to put it through a hand-cranked food mill. Elegant soups should have a very smooth texture. If this is desired, the soup should be put through a fine sieve after pureeing.

To garnish soup

It's best to garnish soup with the principal ingredient—asparagus tips in asparagus soup or sliced mushrooms in mushroom soup. You can also sprinkle soup with minced, snipped, or chiffonade of (shredded) fresh herbs such as parsley, chives, or basil. Another appealing soup garnish is croutons, pieces of bread sautéed in butter and/or oil or coated in butter or oil and baked in the oven.

Serving soup

Hot soup should be served in warmed bowls with a larger plate underneath each bowl. A soup that is to be served cold needs extra salt and less butter. Just as heat enhances flavor, chilling deadens it. No food should be served on chilled plates or in chilled bowls.

Storing soup

If you cover a hot soup in the refrigerator, it can turn sour quickly. This happens because when the hot soup cools, condensation forms on the top and drops back into the soup. That is why it is important to cover the soup but leave room for the steam to escape. It is always best to chill soup as quickly as possible. Small amounts can go into the refrigerator immediately. If the amount of soup is so large that it will bring down the temperature of the refrigerator, chill it in a sink of ice water before refrigerating it. A soup with a base of chicken, veal, or beef stock will keep in the refrigerator for 5 days. If you still have soup or stock after 5 days, put it in a pot, bring it to a boil, and boil it for 5 minutes. Pour it into a clean container and chill, partially covered until it is cold, in the refrigerator, where it will keep for another 5 days. A soup with a water, milk, or vegetable base will keep in the refrigerator for a week. Most soups and all stocks freeze well.

The Big Problem

The big problem people have when cooking soup is letting it reduce to a porridge-like consistency. If this happens, don't be afraid to add water and cook the soup another ten minutes to meld the flavors again. Another problem is that if a soup is reduced or cooked down too much it becomes salty, because when water evaporates, the salt is left. That is why when you order soup late in the evening at a cheap restaurant it is often salty. A good restaurant heats and seasons the soup for each customer when it is ordered.

How to Make Soup Without a Recipe

To make a puree of vegetable soup, cook half an onion with half a teaspoon salt in half a stick butter or olive oil until soft. Off the heat, stir in an equal amount of flour, then return to the heat, stirring to make a roux. Off the heat again, add a couple of cups of stock, then return to the heat. Bring to a boil, stirring, drop in a pound of one or more green vegetables cut in 1-inch pieces and blanched, and cook about ten minutes. Puree, add half a cup of cream with salt and pepper to taste, and garnish with additional vegetables.

If you prefer a more rustic soup, just trim and clean whatever vegetables you have on hand. Sauté some onions in butter or oil until soft, add minced garlic, and cook for a minute. Add some peeled, seeded, and chopped tomatoes and continue to cook for another 2 to 3 minutes. Add liquid (chicken or vegetable stock or water) and then add cleaned, trimmed vegetables such as carrots, cauliflower, or other hard vegetables. If the hard vegetables are about ½ inch thick, cook them for about 20 minutes.

Add softer vegetables such as spinach, zucchini, or corn and cook another 2 minutes. Cooked rice, pasta, or beans can be added with the soft vegetables along with pieces of cooked meat such as chicken or sausage. Remember, potatoes absorb flavor and root vegetables such as onions, carrots, and celery give flavor. The soup is ready when the vegetables are just tender when pierced with a fork. Take a look at the texture. If it is too thick, add water and cook 10 more minutes before tasting. If the soup is too thin, remove the vegetables and other ingredients with a slotted spoon and boil, stirring constantly, until the excess liquid has evaporated and the soup base is reduced. Taste the liquid to make sure it is not getting too salty; if it is, stop reducing it. Add the vegetables back in to rewarm them.

Once you have the desired consistency, taste the soup. If it is a vegetable soup and lacks depth of flavor, add a splash of Kikkoman soy sauce. If you would like a more peppery taste, try a dash of Tabasco (hot pepper) sauce. (These are the two secret ingredients I always have on hand for correcting taste.) If the soup needs acid, add a teaspoon of lemon juice or brandy. Of course, you should make sure the soup is well seasoned with salt and pepper.

I recommend underseasoning soup so the diner can add salt and pepper to suit his or her taste.

SALT

SALT, A MINERAL THAT COMES FROM THE SEA, is very valuable to the cook because it enhances the flavor of almost every food. These days it is fashionable to cook with such salts as gray salt from Brittany, red salt from Hawaii, or flaky salt from England. However, my favorite is still kosher salt. It is coarse in texture and mild in flavor and has no additives. Regular (plain) table salt has to have additives to make it pourable. Iodized salt is intended to prevent thyroid disease. People who eat fresh vegetables and fish don't need added iodine. In my opinion, iodized salt has an unpleasant metallic taste.

Occasionally you see salt in pepper-like grinders. I haven't found that freshly ground salt tastes better than salt out of a box. The bottom line in cooking is that whenever you taste a dish and think, "This needs something," it's probably more salt.

When a recipe says "add salt and pepper to taste," I always recommend using a light hand because people's tolerance for salt varies so much. The diner can always add salt at the table.

In fact, you can now find little bowls of coarse salt on tables in fashionable restaurants so customers can sprinkle it on whatever they want. The idea is that the little crystals of salt touch the tongue first for an added flavor dimension.

Fresh Corn Soup with Basil Butter

All year we wait to taste freshly picked corn. To bring out the fresh taste of corn, grate it, cook it briefly, and serve it with fresh basil butter—a quick and easy taste of summer! An interesting alternative to basil butter would be butter mixed with a puree of roasted red bell pepper. Either way, butter and corn are very good together.

1 bunch fresh basil
¼ pound (1 stick) butter, softened,
  plus 4 tablespoons butter
Coarse salt
Freshly ground white pepper
6 ears fresh yellow corn
1 medium-size onion, chopped
4 cups milk

To make the basil butter, wash and dry the basil leaves, roll them up, and cut them into fine shreds (called chiffonade) with a sharp knife. In a small bowl, cream the ¼ pound butter with a wooden spoon. Mix in the basil with salt and pepper to taste. Place the basil butter on a square of waxed paper and, using the paper, roll up into a log about an inch in diameter.

To prepare the corn, remove and discard the husks. With a sharp knife, remove the outer two-thirds of the kernels from each ear. Using the back of the knife, scrape down the cobs to remove any remaining juices. This is called milking an ear of corn. You can also place a large box grater on its side in a glass baking dish and grate the corn off the cob horizontally.

To make the soup, cook the onion in the 4 tablespoons butter with a sprinkling of salt in a saucepan over medium-high heat, stirring from time to time, for about 5 minutes, or until the onion is soft. Add the corn kernels and milk from the cob as well as the milk. Bring to a boil, stirring, and simmer for 5 minutes.

Puree the soup on the stove using an immersion blender if it is too chunky. The soup does not have to be perfectly smooth. Reheat the soup and add salt and pepper to taste.

To serve, ladle the soup into warmed bowls and top each with a tablespoon of basil butter.

SERVES 4

Fresh Pea Soup
with Cilantro

This recipe comes from my friend Darina Allen, who runs an exceptional school in Ireland called Ballymaloe Cookery School. The freshness of the peas, accented by the freshness of the cilantro (called coriander in Ireland), would make this a perfect start to a dinner of salmon or other fish.

1 medium-size onion, finely chopped
4 tablespoons (½ stick) butter
Coarse salt
2 garlic cloves, minced
½ jalapeño, seeds and ribs removed, minced
1 pound fresh green peas (about 4 cups)
5 cups chicken or vegetable stock
¼ cup chopped fresh cilantro leaves plus
   ½ cup whole leaves for garnish
Sugar
Freshly ground black pepper
½ cup heavy cream

To make the soup, cook the onion in the butter with a sprinkling of salt in a large saucepan over medium-high heat, stirring from time to time, for 5 minutes, or until the onion is soft. Stir in the garlic and jalapeño and continue cooking for another 2 to 3 minutes. Add the peas and the stock. Bring to a boil, stirring, and simmer for 10 to 15 minutes, until the peas are soft. Stir in the chopped cilantro.

Puree the soup in a blender, a food processor, or a food mill, and return the soup to the pan. (It is fine if some small pieces of pea remain in the soup.) Add a pinch of sugar with salt and pepper to taste.

To serve, lightly whip the cream in a small bowl with a small whisk. Serve the soup in warmed bowls with a dollop of whipped cream in the center of each, topped with the whole cilantro leaves.   SERVES 4

Whenever I buy fresh peas in the market, I always taste them first. If the fresh peas seem starchy, it is quite acceptable to use frozen peas in this recipe.

Cream of Beet Soup with Cucumbers and Goat's Cheese

This beet soup is a refreshing cold soup for summer and is beautiful to behold. It is decorated with spoonfuls of goat's cheese and finely diced cucumbers.

2 red onions, chopped
3 tablespoons olive oil plus 1 tablespoon for the cucumbers
Coarse salt
¼ cup red wine
3 pounds beets, peeled and cut into ½-inch dice
1½ quarts chicken or vegetable stock
1 cup crème fraîche or sour cream
3 to 5 tablespoons balsamic vinegar
Freshly ground black pepper
½ English cucumber
2 ounces fresh goat's cheese

To prepare the soup, put the onions and the olive oil with ½ teaspoon salt in a saucepan over medium-high heat. Cook, stirring from time to time, until the onions are soft, about 5 minutes. Stir in the wine and let boil a few minutes to cook off the alcohol. Stir in the beets with the stock. Bring to a simmer and continue cooking until the beets are soft, about 20 minutes. Puree in a blender or food processor, or with an immersion blender. Stir in the cream. Season to taste with vinegar and salt and pepper. Transfer the soup to a bowl and chill.

To prepare the garnish, cut the cucumbers (with both peel and seeds) into tiny dice. Coat the cucumbers with olive oil and season with salt and pepper.

To serve, ladle the soup into bowls, place a generous spoonful of the diced cucumbers in the middle of each bowl, and arrange three small spoonfuls of the goat's cheese around the cucumbers.   SERVES 6

It's worth investing in an immersion blender. These blenders are designed so that you don't have to move the pot from the top of the stove. Don't lift the blade out of the soup while the blender is running, or you will get soup all over the kitchen.

Roasted Eggplant Soup with Tomato

With its shiny, dark purple skin, eggplant is one of nature's most beautiful vegetables. However, because the taste of eggplant by itself is somewhat bland the vegetable adapts well to different flavors. In this soup, puree of eggplant is the vehicle for the cumin. It is always better to use freshly ground spices for maximum flavor and to make sure the ground cumin is cooked in the onion mixture before adding the other ingredients. Whenever you add more cumin, you need to add more salt to balance the taste.

2 large eggplants, about 1 pound each
2 medium-size onions, chopped
    (about 2 cups)
Coarse salt
4 tablespoons olive oil
2 garlic cloves, minced
1 teaspoon cumin seed, freshly ground
½ cup gray (not French) lentils
3 to 4 cups chicken or vegetable stock
2 tablespoons minced fresh cilantro
Freshly ground pepper
1 teaspoon lemon juice
⅓ cup heavy cream
2 red, ripe tomatoes, cut in ¼-inch dice for
    garnish

To prepare the eggplants, slice them in half lengthwise and place them cut side down on a lightly oiled roasting pan. Bake in a 400-degree oven until completely soft, about 20 minutes. When the eggplants are cool enough to handle, peel off and discard the skin. Squeeze the eggplants to release as much water as possible and chop coarsely.

To make the soup, cook the onions with ½ teaspoon salt in the olive oil in a large saucepan over medium-high heat. Cook, stirring, until the onions are soft, about 5 minutes. Add the garlic and cook another minute. Stir in the cumin and cook for 2 more minutes. Stir in the eggplant, lentils, and stock. Simmer until the lentils are soft, about 15 minutes. Puree the soup with an immersion blender. Add enough water to make a pourable consistency. Add half the cilantro, the lemon juice, and salt and pepper to taste. Lightly whip the cream in a small bowl with a small whisk until it just holds its shape when the whisk is lifted. Serve the soup in warm bowls garnished with a dollop of the whipped cream, the diced tomatoes, and the remaining cilantro. SERVES 6

Generally, when vegetables such as winter squash, carrots, or parsnips are roasted, the sugars are released and caramelized, which adds flavor. This is not the case with eggplant; the roasting here is to soften the vegetable without adding moisture.

When buying eggplants, look for those that are firm and small. Larger ones are sometimes spongy in the middle.

Potato-Garlic Soup with Croutons

Good French mothers will often make leek and potato soup for their sick children. At the beginning of the twentieth century, the chef of the Ritz-Carlton Hotel in New York, Louis Diat, pureed his native leek and potato soup, added cream, and served it chilled. Voilà! Vichyssoise! Jacques Pépin, one of the best cooking teachers I know, made his version of this French classic with many cloves of garlic. We have been savoring it ever since at Tante Marie's!

In this recipe, sneaking in too much leek greens will result in a green soup.

> 2 medium leeks, white part only,
>   halved and thinly sliced
>   (about 1½ cups)
> 4 tablespoons (½ stick) butter
> 1 head garlic, cloves separated and peeled
>   (12 to 15 cloves)
> 8 cups chicken or vegetable stock
> 2 pounds (4 large) baking potatoes, peeled
>   and cut into 1-inch pieces
> Coarse salt
> Freshly ground black pepper
> 1 cup heavy cream
> Croutons for garnish

To make the soup, put the leeks and butter in a large saucepan over medium-high heat and cook, stirring from time to time, until the leeks are soft, about 5 minutes. Add the garlic, stock, potatoes, and ½ teaspoon salt. Bring to a boil, stirring, then lower the heat. Simmer for 30 to 45 minutes, until the garlic and potatoes are completely tender.

Puree the soup until completely smooth in a food mill or an electric blender, or with an immersion blender. (Do not use a food processor, because the potatoes will become gummy.) Return the soup to the saucepan and add the cream. Bring the soup to a boil, stirring constantly. Add salt and pepper to taste. Serve with croutons and/or snipped chives.

SERVES 8

To make croutons, lay 4 or 5 slices of thin sliced white bread on a cutting board or a counter. Trim off the crusts. Cut the bread into ¼-inch squares. In a 10-inch sauté or frying pan, heat 2 tablespoons butter with 2 tablespoons olive oil over medium-high heat. When the bubbles have subsided, toss in the bread squares all at once and toss quickly to coat the bread in the hot butter-oil mixture. Continue cooking and tossing until the croutons are golden. Place them on paper towels and sprinkle with coarse salt. They will keep fresh in a tin for 10 days.

An efficient way to peel potatoes is to scrape off the ends of the potatoes with a vegetable peeler, then remove the skin in long strips with the peeler, cutting toward yourself.

Butternut Squash Soup

Autumn is the best time of year for butter-nut squash soup. In this recipe, the squash has a slightly Asian appeal because the soup is flavored with Chinese five-spice blend and coconut milk. Homemade Chinese five-spice blend is seductive.

4 pounds butternut squash or other winter squash, such as Kabocha, Preservation, or Hubbard
1 medium-size onion, thinly sliced
3 tablespoons vegetable oil
Coarse salt
1 to 2 garlic cloves, finely minced
1 tablespoon grated fresh ginger
6 cups chicken or vegetable stock
1½ teaspoons Chinese five-spice powder, storebought or homemade
Freshly ground black pepper
One 8-ounce can unsweetened coconut milk

To prepare the squash, trim both ends. Cut the squash in half. Cut off all the skin. Cut the rounded part in half and remove the seeds with a metal spoon. Cut the squash into 1-inch dice, put them on a lightly oiled baking dish, and sprinkle with ½ teaspoon salt and the Chinese five-spice blend. Bake in a 400-degree oven until soft when pierced with a fork, about 30 minutes.

To roast the seeds, spread them on a baking sheet, lightly coat with oil, and sprinkle with salt and pepper. Roast along with the squash for 10 minutes.

To make the soup, cook the onion with a sprinkling of salt in the oil in a large saucepan over medium-high heat until soft, about 5 minutes. Add the garlic and the ginger and cook another 2 minutes. Add the squash and stock and bring to a boil over medium-high heat, stirring occasionally.

Puree the soup in a food processor or with an immersion blender and return to the saucepan. Stir in the coconut milk. Add salt and pepper to taste. Garnish with roasted seeds. MAKES 10 CUPS

An alternative way to cook all winter squashes—whether for soups, vegetable dishes, or pies—is to cut them in half, remove the seeds, and bake them in the oven until soft. The squash can then be pureed in a food processor or through a food mill. Cooked pumpkin or other winter squash will keep for a week in the refrigerator.

To make your own Chinese five-spice blend, put in a spice blender equal amounts of cinnamon stick, fennel seeds, cloves, star anise, and white pepper. Blend to a fine powder.

Yellow Gazpacho

Gazpacho is a summertime vegetable soup that has come a long way from the days when it was taken out to peasants working in the fields of Spain. It is still a delicious and refreshing start to a meal on a hot summer day or evening.

FOR THE GAZPACHO
12 large yellow tomatoes, peeled, seeded, and coarsely chopped
1 large onion, coarsely chopped
2 garlic cloves
Coarse salt
1 jalapeño, minced
1 large red bell pepper, roasted and coarsely chopped
1 cucumber, peeled, seeded, and coarsely chopped
6 tablespoons fresh cilantro, coarsely chopped
2 tablespoons lemon juice
2 tablespoons apple cider vinegar
1 teaspoon balsamic vinegar
1 teaspoon toasted ground cumin seeds
1 teaspoon toasted ground coriander seeds
Freshly ground black pepper
½ cup extra-virgin olive oil

FOR THE GARNISH
1 small cucumber, peeled, seeded, and cut into ¼-inch dice
2 medium-size red tomatoes, cut into ¼-inch dice
½ red onion, cut into ¼-inch dice
¼ cup chopped cilantro
2 tablespoons fresh oregano or marjoram, finely minced

To make the gazpacho, combine the tomatoes, onion, garlic, ½ teaspoon salt, jalapeño, bell pepper, cucumber, cilantro, lemon juice, cider vinegar, balsamic vinegar, cumin, coriander, and a few grindings of pepper in a large stainless steel bowl and set aside for two to three hours to combine flavors. Puree the soup in a blender. Add additional lemon juice with salt and pepper to taste. Stir in the olive oil. Thin with water to reach a pourable consistency. Chill until ready to serve.

Serve the soup in bowls garnished with cucumber, tomato, red onion, cilantro, and oregano. SERVES 8

Since gazpacho is traditionally made with red tomatoes, you can substitute red tomatoes in this recipe. The important thing is always to use the very flavorful tomatoes of late summer and early fall.

❧

Red bell peppers are green peppers that have been left on the vine to ripen. Yellow peppers also start out as green peppers; however, they are a special variety. Purple peppers are simply ornamental because they turn green when cooked.

❧

When using a regular cucumber, it is best to remove all the green peel with a vegetable peeler, cut the cucumber in half lengthwise, and scoop out and discard the seeds with a teaspoon before cutting into dice. The reason to remove the skin is that often it is waxed and sometimes it tastes bitter. English cucumbers do not need to have their skin and seeds removed.

French Onion Soup Gratinée

For decades, truckers brought fresh produce, fish, and meat to the market area called Les Halles in the center of Paris. If you went there at three or four in the morning, you would see elegant revelers having a late-night supper next to truckers just finishing up their day's work. The class distinctions disappeared in the early morning hours, when everyone shared this rich and delicious soup. I would serve French onion soup with a green salad and a glass of wine as a simple supper. The soup can be kept in the refrigerator for five days and also freezes well.

¼ pound (1 stick) butter
5 medium-size onions, thinly sliced
Coarse salt
1 garlic clove, finely minced
2 tablespoons flour
1 cup dry white wine
2 quarts beef or chicken stock
Freshly ground black pepper
¼ cup dry sherry
12 thin slices dry French bread
½ cup freshly grated Parmesan
½ cup freshly grated Gruyère

Put the butter and the onions in a deep pot over medium-high heat with a half teaspoon of salt. Cook the onions, stirring from time to time, for 40 minutes. After about 30 minutes, the onions will begin to caramelize; that is, the sugar will come out of the onions and begin to brown. At this point, keep stirring so that the pan doesn't burn. When the onions are a nice, rich brown, stir in the garlic and cook for a minute more. Sprinkle in the flour and continue to cook, stirring constantly, until the flour begins to brown. Stir in the white wine and cook another minute. Add the stock, ½ teaspoon salt, and several grindings of pepper, and bring to a boil. Lower the heat and simmer for 30 minutes, stirring from time to time. Stir in the sherry. Add salt and pepper to taste. (It is better if the soup is slightly undersalted because the cheese will add salt as well.)

To serve, preheat the broiler. Ladle the soup into ovenproof bowls and cover each bowl of soup with bread, pushing it down into the soup to moisten. Cover the bread generously with the cheeses (each bowl should be entirely covered with bread and cheese) and place the bowls under the broiler until the cheese has just melted. (If the cheese cooks too long, it will all come off in one piece when the diner takes the first spoonful.)

SERVES 6

When slicing any round fruit or vegetable, always cut it in half and lay the cut sides on the board. That way it won't roll when you are trying to cut it.

If the bread is cut too thick, it will absorb all the soup.

Since Parmesan is a hard grating cheese, it has to be grated on a grater with small holes to release maximum flavor. Gruyère or other semi-firm melting cheeses should be grated on larger holes on the grater.

Wild Mushroom Soup

What gives mushrooms their meaty flavor is the fact that they are a natural source of monosodium glutamate; in other words, they have naturally great taste. In this soup the mushroom flavor is foremost.

½ ounce dried morels
½ ounce dried porcini (cèpe) mushrooms
Coarse salt
1 medium-size onion, chopped
4 tablespoons (½ stick) butter
1 garlic clove, minced
1 tablespoon flour
*½ pound fresh mushrooms and ½ pound
    wild mushrooms such as morels or
    shiitakes, coarsely chopped*
*Bouquet garni composed of 4 parsley stalks,
    1 sprig thyme, and 1 bay leaf*
4 cups chicken or vegetable stock
¼ cup brandy or Madeira
½ cup heavy cream
*3 tablespoons minced fresh herbs such as
    parsley, chives, and thyme*
Freshly ground black pepper

To reconstitute the dried mushrooms, place them in a measuring cup and cover with ¾ cup very hot water. Let sit for 30 minutes.

To make the soup, cook the onion in the butter with ½ teaspoon salt in a large saucepan over medium-high heat, stirring from time to time, for about 5 minutes, until the onion is soft. Stir in the garlic and continue cooking for another minute. Sprinkle on the flour and cook for another minute.

Add the mushrooms and continue cooking and stirring until the mushrooms release their liquid. Add the brandy.

Remove the dried mushrooms from the soaking liquid and chop finely. Add to the saucepan with the bouquet garni. Add all but the last tablespoon of the soaking liquid to the soup pot with the chicken stock. Mix well, bring to a boil, and simmer for 20 to 30 minutes. Discard the bouquet garni. Add the cream and herbs. Simmer for 5 more minutes. Add salt and pepper to taste.

SERVES 6

Cream of Artichoke and Hazelnut Soup

When an elegant cream soup is called for in a menu, this is the soup! Although trimming the artichokes takes time, it is worth it. What you want is a perfect balance of the taste of artichoke and hazelnut, so don't be stingy with the artichokes or add too much liquid. In restaurants, cooks pare the artichokes down much more than I do here, but I like to leave some of the leaves—the restaurant technique seems wasteful to me. This soup was made famous twenty years ago in a restaurant called Fournou's Ovens in the Stanford Court Hotel in San Francisco, back in the days when all the famous cooks used to stay there.

1 quart milk
1 small onion, sliced
Coarse salt
1 sprig thyme
8 fresh medium-size artichokes
1 lemon
¼ pound (1 stick) butter
4 tablespoons flour
¼ cup hazelnuts, skinned and coarsely chopped
2 cups chicken or vegetable stock
½ cup heavy cream
Freshly ground black pepper

To infuse the milk for the soup, put the milk, onion, and thyme in a saucepan over medium-high heat. When bubbles form around the top of the milk, turn off the heat, cover, and set aside for 10 minutes.

To prepare the artichokes, fill a large saucepan with water and the juice of half the lemon. Cut the stem off each artichoke and remove the coarse outer leaves. Tear each leaf, leaving the small edible part on the artichoke bottom. When you get to the light-colored leaves, and they start breaking off in such a way that the edible part is removed, stop. Cut the top off the artichoke, leaving about half an inch of light green. With a vegetable peeler, remove all the dark green from the artichoke bottom. Rub the lemon over the artichoke where it was cut and put it into the pot of acidulated water. When all the artichokes have been trimmed, bring the pan of artichokes to a boil over high heat. Reduce the heat to a simmer and cook for 10 to 15 minutes, or until the bottoms of the artichokes are tender when pierced with a fork. Remove from the heat and drain the artichokes on paper towels.

To prepare the soup, in a large saucepan, melt the 4 tablespoons of the butter over medium heat. When the butter is bubbly, remove the pan from the heat and sprinkle on the flour, stirring with the back of a wooden spoon. Return the pan to the heat and cook until the mixture looks greasy. Off the heat again, strain in the milk, whisking with a wire whisk. Discard the onion. Bring the soup to a boil, stirring constantly. Reduce the heat and simmer gently for 10 minutes, stirring from time to time.

Remove the fuzzy choke from each artichoke with a metal spoon and slice the artichoke bottoms in ¼-inch slices. Heat the remaining 4 tablespoons butter in a medium sauté pan over medium-high heat. Add the sliced artichokes and the skinned hazelnuts. Cook for 5 to 7 minutes, until lightly browned.

Stir the artichoke-hazelnut mixture and stock into the soup base. Cook over medium-low heat for 10 minutes. Puree the soup in a blender or food processor or with an immersion blender until smooth. (If using a blender or food processor, puree the soup in batches, filling the blender no more than half full for each batch.) Then return the soup to the saucepan, place over medium-low heat, and stir in the cream. Bring to a boil and add salt and pepper to taste. SERVES 6

To skin the hazelnuts, place them on a baking sheet in a 350-degree oven for about 15 minutes. Place the nuts in a towel and rub gently to remove the skins, or place them in a small colander and do the same thing. Don't worry if you can't get off all the dark brown skins.

Equal amounts (by weight) of fat (butter) and flour cooked together are called a roux. It is used as a base for sauces in old-fashioned cooking. With the addition of milk, it becomes béchamel sauce. In this case the roux plus milk becomes the soup base.

Cream of Root Vegetable Soup with Black Truffles

Make this soup when you are given a special gift of a truffle, or when you really want to know what the true taste of truffle is. The whole idea of the soup is to highlight the earthy, very appealing flavor of black truffles. This recipe was created by Paul Bertolli, the truly talented chef of Oliveto in Berkeley.

Since this soup is so special, it's best to follow the directions for pureeing and then straining the soup. A less elegant soup can be pureed with an immersion blender.

2 tablespoons butter
½ cup finely chopped, peeled celery root (8 ounces)
½ cup thinly sliced leek, white part only (4 ounces)
½ cup finely chopped, peeled parsnip (4 ounces)
4 small red potatoes, peeled and finely chopped (4 ounces)
1 sprig thyme
Coarse salt
4 cups chicken or vegetable stock
1 black truffle (1½ ounces)
½ cup heavy cream
Freshly ground pepper

To prepare the soup base, melt the butter in a large, heavy saucepan over medium heat. Stir in the celery root, leek, parsnip, potatoes, thyme, and a large pinch of salt. Simmer the mixture, covered, for 10 to 15 minutes. Stir until the vegetables are softened. Stir in the stock and remove the thyme. Using a blender, puree the soup until smooth. Be sure to puree the soup in batches, filling the blender no more than half full for each batch. Strain through a fine sieve and return to a clean saucepan.

To prepare the truffle, brush or scrape any dirt off. Slice the truffle in very thin slices. In a mortar with a pestle, grind the truffle slices until they form a coarse paste. Stir the paste into the pureed soup with the cream and salt and pepper to taste. Heat over medium heat for 5 to 10 minutes, until just heated through. Serve the soup in warmed soup bowls.　　　SERVES 4

Black truffles come from France around the first of the year. They are a kind of elusive fungi that grow under oak trees in very rich soil. Truffle hunters keep the locations of their finds very secret, and the market for black truffles is tightly controlled. Generally, black truffles need to be cooked so as to bring out their earthy flavor. Italian white truffles are much more delicate in taste and don't need to be cooked. They are usually grated fresh over mild, creamy mixtures such as pasta and risotto.

Spring Vegetable Soup with Pecorino

*I**f you're a gardener, you can't wait for the artichokes, fava beans, and peas of spring, not to mention wonderful new potatoes. If you're not a gardener, you can take delight in finding these harbingers of spring at a local farmers' market. Either way, with this recipe you'll put them all together in a truly memorable springtime soup. If you have no interest in trimming fresh artichokes, just leave them out—canned or frozen are no substitutes.*

1 medium-size onion, chopped

2 medium-size leeks, equal amounts of white and green parts, halved and sliced

Coarse salt

4 tablespoons (½ stick) butter

2 bunches scallions, equal amounts of white and green parts, sliced

1 medium-size fennel bulb, trimmed, cored, and cut into ½-inch dice

4 medium-size artichoke bottoms, trimmed and cut into ½-inch dice (page 58)

6 medium-size new potatoes, such as Yukon Gold or Yellow Finn, peeled and cut into 1-inch pieces

1 quart chicken or vegetable stock

1 pound fresh fava beans, shelled

½ pound peas, shelled

Juice of half a lemon

Freshly ground pepper

½ cup freshly grated soft pecorino

To make the soup base, in a large pot, cook the onion and leeks with ½ teaspoon salt in the butter over medium-high heat, stirring from time to time, until the onion and leeks are soft, about 15 minutes. Add the scallions and cook 5 more minutes. Add the fennel, artichokes, potatoes, stock, a quart of water, and ½ teaspoon salt. Bring to a boil and simmer for 30 to 40 minutes, or until the vegetables are tender when pierced with a fork, about 30 minutes.

Meanwhile, to prepare the fava beans, fill a saucepan with water and bring to a boil over high heat. Remove the fava beans from their pods. Drop the shelled fava beans in the boiling water for 30 seconds. Drain in a colander and run under cold water. Peel the coarse skin from each fava bean.

Add the fava beans and peas to the soup and bring to a boil. Simmer for 5 more minutes and add the lemon juice and salt and pepper to taste. Serve the soup in warmed bowls with plenty of grated pecorino cheese.

Serves 8

To trim a fennel bulb, discard the stems and fronds as well as the coarse bottom. Cut the fennel bulb in half and then, with a large knife, cut ½-inch pieces from around the core of the bulb.

Artichokes, corn, and peas are similar in that their sugars start to change to starch as soon as they are picked. Thus, the longer they sit at the market, the more starchy they will taste. That is why I have no hesitation in using frozen peas in this recipe—the frozen food companies blanch and freeze vegetables very quickly after they are picked. (If you can't find fava beans, just leave them out.)

Winter Vegetable Soup with Prosciutto

Here is a hearty, rustic soup perfect for a cold winter's evening after a day of skiing. When the vegetables are cooked, the sweet potatoes melt, becoming a natural thickener for this soup. I like the saltiness of the prosciutto, which cuts the sweetness of the cooked vegetables. You could substitute freshly grated Parmesan and sprinkle it on top of each bowl.

1 medium-size onion, chopped
2 medium-size carrots, peeled and chopped
1 celery stalk, chopped
Coarse salt
3 tablespoons butter
2 garlic cloves, minced
3 pounds tomatoes, peeled, seeded, and chopped, or one 28-ounce can Italian plum tomatoes, coarsely chopped
1 quart chicken or vegetable stock
1 pound winter squash, such as butternut, Hubbard, or banana, peeled and cut into ½-inch dice (about 1 cup)
1 medium-size rutabaga, peeled and cut into ½-inch dice (about 1 cup)
1 medium-size parsnip, peeled and cut into ½-inch dice (about 1 cup)
1 sweet potato or yam, peeled and cut into ½-inch dice (about 1 cup)
1 slice of prosciutto, ¼ inch thick, or country ham, cut into ¼-inch dice
½ cup fresh Italian parsley, coarsely chopped
Freshly ground black pepper

In a large deep pot, cook the onion, carrots, and celery with ½ teaspoon salt in the butter over medium-high heat, stirring frequently, until the vegetables are soft, about 8 minutes. Stir in the garlic and cook another minute. Stir in the tomatoes and continue cooking, stirring, for another 2 minutes. Add the stock, the winter squash, rutabaga, parsnip, and sweet potato, and bring to a boil. Simmer until the vegetables are tender when pierced with a fork, about 30 minutes. (You may need to add water at this point to make a pourable consistency.) Add the prosciutto and parsley and cook for a minute. Add salt and pepper to taste. SERVES 6

To peel, seed, and chop a tomato, drop the tomato into boiling water for exactly 10 seconds. With a slotted spoon, transfer the tomato to a bowl of cold water. With a paring knife, peel off the skin and remove the core. Cut the tomato in half as you would a grapefruit. Insert your fingers into the cut half and squeeze out the seeds. It is best to do this into a small strainer over a measuring cup to capture the juices. Chop the tomato coarsely. It is best to remove the peel and seeds when tomatoes are to be cooked, because the skin curls and the seeds are likely to burn.

To chop carrots, cut a slice off one side of the carrot so it will lie flat. With a chef's knife, cut slices lengthwise down the carrot about ¼ inch wide. Line up the slices and make ¼-inch-wide crosswise cuts in the other direction.

To chop celery, make cuts lengthwise down the celery and crosswise as with the carrots.

Pacific Coast Bouillabaisse

*French legend has it that bouillabaisse was
created by Venus to woo her lover Vulcan. It
is the only food in France said to be created by a
god. It is also said that real bouillabaisse can be
made only with fish from the Mediterranean—
that is why I call my version Pacific Coast Bouillabaisse. Bouillabaisse should be a boiling
emulsion of onions, leeks, and olive oil in which
bits of fish and other shellfish are cooked. It is traditionally served with little bowls of rouille, a red
pepper–garlic mixture (recipe follows), teaspoonfuls of which the diner adds to suit his or her taste.
This version is a robust fisherman's stew.*

24 littleneck clams, scrubbed
1 large onion, chopped
2 leeks, cut in ½-inch lengths
½ cup olive oil
Coarse salt
4 garlic cloves, minced
3 pounds fresh tomatoes, peeled, seeded,
*   and chopped, or one 28-ounce can*
*   Italian plum tomatoes, coarsely chopped*
1 tablespoon tomato paste
1 cup dry white wine
4 cups fish stock
Bouquet garni composed of 4 sprigs parsley,
*   1 sprig thyme, 1 bay leaf, and 1 strip*
*   orange zest*
¼ teaspoon saffron threads
¼ cup Pernod (or Chartreuse)
3 pounds firm fish fillets, such as halibut,
*   cod, or bass*
Freshly ground black pepper
1 pound sea scallops or peeled shrimp
Rouille

To steam the clams, put them in a small
saucepan with one inch of water, cover, and
steam until the clams open. Put the clams in a
bowl and cover with plastic wrap. Pour off all
but the last tablespoon of clam juice (which
may be sandy) and add to the fish stock.

To make the soup base, put the onion and
leek in the oil with a sprinkling of salt in a
large saucepan over medium-high heat. Cook
for 5 minutes, stirring from time to time,
until the onion is soft. Stir in the garlic and
cook for another 3 minutes, stirring. Add the
tomatoes, tomato paste, wine, stock, bouquet
garni, saffron, and Pernod. Simmer for 20
minutes, then discard the bouquet garni.
(This soup base can be made ahead and kept
in the refrigerator for up to 3 days.)

Twenty minutes before serving, bring the
soup base to a boil, stirring from time to
time. Meanwhile, cut the fish into 1½-inch
pieces, coat the fish with olive oil, and season
with salt and pepper. Add the fish to the soup
base and let boil for 5 minutes. Add the scallops or shrimp with the clams. Bring to a boil

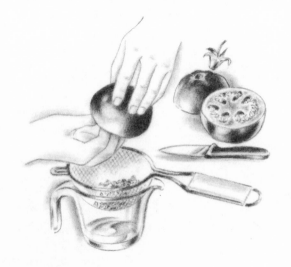

and let cook for another 3 minutes. Turn off the heat, cover, and let sit for 5 minutes. Add salt and pepper to taste.

Serve the bouillabaisse with plenty of French bread and the rouille passed separately. (Some cooks prefer to serve aïoli rather than rouille, or rouille mixed with aïoli.)

SERVES 8

ROUILLE

½ cup soft bread crumbs
2 to 3 garlic cloves
½ teaspoon red pepper flakes
2 tablespoons extra-virgin olive oil
1 teaspoon tomato paste
Coarse salt

Put the bread crumbs in a small bowl with enough warm water to barely cover. With your hands squeeze out the excess liquid from the bread crumbs and put them in a mortar. Add the garlic, red pepper flakes, olive oil, tomato paste, and a few grains of salt. Crush and work the pestle until the rouille is creamy, the texture of mayonnaise. Mix in 2 tablespoons of the soup base.

If you are unable to make fresh fish stock from fish bones, you can substitute what I call mock stock in this recipe. Mock stock is made of equal amounts of bottled clam juice (Atlantic is best), dry white wine, and water.

It's best to use only saltwater white fish in this recipe and not to include salmon, tuna, or freshwater fish.

New England Seafood Chowder

*T*he late Richard Sax, a wonderful friend and cook, created this chowder, using puree of potato in place of the large quantities of heavy cream usually found in New England chowder. You can use any selection of fish—whatever is the freshest at the market. This soup would be delicious in the summer with the addition of kernels of yellow corn.

1 pound littleneck clams, scrubbed
4 slices thick-cut bacon, cut in
   1-inch squares
3 medium-size onions, chopped
2 celery stalks, coarsely chopped
Coarse salt
3 pounds boiling potatoes, peeled and
   cut into ½-inch dice
1 cup dry white wine
Bouquet garni composed of 3 sprigs parsley,
   1 sprig thyme, and 1 bay leaf
3 cups milk plus additional for thinning
½ cup heavy cream
Dash of Tabasco sauce
Freshly ground black pepper
1½ pounds fillet of halibut, sea bass, or cod,
   cut into 1-inch cubes
1 medium-size tomato, cut in tiny dice
2 tablespoons finely minced fresh Italian
   parsley

To steam open the clams, put them in a small saucepan with one inch of water. Cover and cook over high heat until they open, stirring or shaking vigorously from time to time. Discard any clams that do not open. When cool enough to handle, remove the clams from their shells and discard the shells. Reserve the clams and the liquid separately.

Cook the bacon in a large pot over medium-high heat, turning from time to time, until golden, about 8 minutes. Transfer to paper towels, using a slotted spoon. Discard all but 3 tablespoons of the bacon fat. Add onions and celery with ½ teaspoon salt to the pot. Cook over medium heat, stirring occasionally until soft, about 10 minutes. Add the potatoes, wine, clam juice, bouquet garni, and enough water just to cover the potatoes, about a cup. Bring to a boil and simmer until the potatoes are tender, about 15 minutes.

Transfer half the potatoes to a food mill and puree until smooth. Return the potato puree to the soup. (Alternatively, puree about half the potatoes with an immersion blender in the pot on top of the stove.) Add the milk, cream, Tabasco, and salt and pepper to taste. Bring the soup to a boil, stirring until mixed. Thin with more milk to reach a pourable consistency. (This soup base can be made ahead and kept in the refrigerator for up to 3 days.)

When ready to serve, bring the soup base to a boil. Meanwhile, season the fish generously with salt and pepper. Add the fish to the soup base and simmer for 8 minutes, or until the fish is opaque. Discard the bouquet garni. Add the clams, bacon, tomatoes, and parsley to soup. Cover and let sit for 5 minutes. Add salt, pepper, and/or Tabasco to taste. MAKES ABOUT 8 CUPS

Generally, you can expect to cook fish for 8 to 10 minutes per inch of thickness, no matter what the method of cooking. Fish is cooked when it flakes easily when prodded with a fork or when it is opaque all the way through.

Before you add tomatoes to soups or stews, you need to peel, seed, and chop them, but when adding them to a dish as garnish, I recommend the following: cut off the skin with a thick layer of tomato flesh in four large pieces and discard the seeds and pulp, or save for another use. Lay the tomato skin side down on a board and cut into ¼-inch dice.

A bouquet garni is made with sprigs of parsley (Italian or curly) tied together with a sprig of thyme and a bay leaf. Some cooks tie the bouquet garni on a string to the handle of the pot so it can be easily retrieved. The leaves of parsley are minced and added to dishes at the end of the cooking time for fresh flavor or used to garnish dishes.

Cabbage and Potato Soup with Duck Confit
(Garbure)

One of the best cooks I know is Jean-Pierre Moullé, who for years was the chef of Chez Panisse in Berkeley. Here is the recipe for a wonderful, hearty peasant soup that he taught us many years ago at Tante Marie's. In Toulouse, where the thick soup called garbure is famous, a good cook might have bits of duck confit and a few sausages on hand to add to a soup of winter vegetables. You could even make this soup with a ham hock. After all, it's just soup, and soup is usually made with what the cook has on hand.

½ pound thick-cut country bacon (or pork belly, if available), cut into ½-inch pieces
2 medium-size onions, chopped
2 leeks, trimmed, halved, and cut into 1-inch lengths
2 tablespoons rendered duck fat or olive oil
Coarse salt
3 garlic cloves, minced
1 pound dried white beans (cannellini or Great Northern), soaked overnight in 2 quarts water
3 quarts chicken stock
Bouquet garni composed of 4 sprigs parsley, 1 sprig thyme, and 1 bay leaf
Freshly ground pepper
6 pieces Duck Confit, legs and/or thighs (see page 381)

1 small savoy cabbage, cored and shredded
3 turnips, peeled and cut into ½-inch dice
2 pounds small new potatoes, peeled and cut into ½-inch dice

To remove the smoky taste from the bacon, bring a saucepan of water to a boil. Toss in the bacon, turn off the heat, and let sit for 10 minutes. Drain the bacon and discard the liquid.

To make the soup, cook the onions and leeks in the duck fat with ½ teaspoon salt in a large pot over medium-high heat, stirring until the onions are soft, about 5 minutes. Stir in the garlic and continue cooking for 1 minute, stirring. Drain the beans, discarding the soaking liquid. Add the beans, stock, bouquet garni, with a sprinkling of salt and pepper. Bring to a boil, stirring, and simmer for 45 to 60 minutes, until the beans are barely tender. (The cooking time may vary tremendously; add more water as needed.)

To prepare the duck confit, remove the meat from the bones. With your fingers or a knife cut the meat into 1 by ½-inch pieces.

When the beans are cooked through, discard the bouquet garni and add the cabbage, turnips, potatoes, duck, and bacon to the soup. Simmer until the potatoes are tender when pierced with a fork, about 15 minutes. Add salt and pepper to taste. You can serve this soup with a few drops of sherry in each bowl.

SERVES 8

The quick-soak method for beans is good to know when you forget to soak the beans overnight. Put the beans in a large pot, cover *generously with water, and place over high heat. When the water is boiling vigorously, cover the pan, turn off the heat, and let sit for an hour. Discard the water and proceed with the recipe. The reason for soaking (or quick-soaking) the beans is so that they look better when cooked; the skins of soaked beans are less likely to shrivel or break.*

For this recipe it is acceptable to use canned beans (Progresso brand is the best). They need to be put in a sieve and rinsed under cold running water to remove the canned taste before being added to the recipe. Because canned beans are already cooked, proceed with the recipe by adding all the vegetables and meat with the beans.

If substituting a ham hock for the duck confit, add the hock with the potatoes and other vegetables. When the soup is cooked, remove the hock, cut what meat there is into ½-inch pieces, and return the meat to the soup.

Country Soup of White Beans and Sausage

*W*hether you make your own sausage or buy good-quality sausage, here is a hearty minestrone-type soup for a cold winter's evening. You could add leftover vegetables such as broccoli, cauliflower, or green beans, and a cup of cooked pasta as well. You can layer leftover soup with thickly cut bread and grated cheese for a casserole to serve another day. In Tuscany, this is called ribollita.

1 pound dried white beans such as
   cannellini or Great Northern, soaked
   overnight in two quarts of water
2 large onions, chopped, plus half an onion
1 dried red chile pepper
Coarse salt
3 tablespoons olive oil
4 garlic cloves, minced
½ teaspoon minced jalapeño
4 celery stalks, cut into ½-inch dice
4 carrots, peeled and cut into ½-inch dice
2 red bell peppers, stems, seeds, and ribs
   removed, and cut into ½-inch dice
3 pounds tomatoes, peeled, seeded, and
   coarsely chopped, or one 28-ounce can
   Italian plum tomatoes, coarsely chopped
2 quarts chicken stock
Bouquet garni composed of 4 sprigs parsley,
   1 sprig thyme, and 1 bay leaf
2 pounds pork sausages, store-bought or
   homemade (see page 382)
½ pound andouille sausage, preferably
   Aidells

½ cup dry white wine
Freshly ground black pepper
2 tablespoons minced fresh herbs such as
    oregano, thyme, and/or parsley
Freshly grated Parmesan for serving
    (optional)

To prepare the beans, drain them, discarding the soaking liquid. Put the beans in a big pot and cover with plenty of cold water. Add the half an onion and the dried red chile pepper. Bring to a boil and cook until the beans are tender when tasted. Drain. Discard the onion and chile.

To prepare the soup, put the onion, olive oil, and ½ teaspoon salt in a large pot over medium-high heat and cook for 5 minutes, or until the onions are soft. Stir in the garlic and jalapeño and continue to cook for a minute. Stir in the celery, carrots, and bell pepper and cook 10 minutes more, or until the vegetables are soft. Add the beans to the soup with the tomatoes, stock, and bouquet garni. Bring to a boil, reduce the heat to a simmer, and cook uncovered for 10 to 15 more minutes, stirring from time to time.

To prepare the sausage, prick each sausage in two or three places and put in a 10-inch frying or sauté pan with ¼ inch water. Cook the sausages over medium heat until their fat begins to melt and the sausages brown, turning them from time to time, about 15 minutes. Deglaze the pan with the wine and add to the soup. Slice all the sausage into ¾-inch-wide slices and add to the soup with the fresh herbs. Discard the bouquet garni.

Add salt and pepper to taste. Simmer 5 minutes more. Serve with freshly grated Parmesan if desired. MAKES 16 CUPS

For this recipe it is acceptable to use canned beans. (Progresso is a good brand.) Before adding them to the soup, put them in a sieve and rinse them in cold water to get rid of the canned taste and proceed wih the recipe. See page 23 for the various ways to cook dried beans.

The subject of chiles and peppers is confusing. The truth is that except for sweet bell peppers, the only real pepper is the spice from the tropics. Most vegetables called peppers are really chiles, often called chile peppers by manufacturers.

When using canned Italian plum tomatoes, you can just crush them in your hand as you put them in the pot rather than taking the time to chop them.

Learning the differences among chiles is a study in itself. Chiles have different names, depending on where they are grown and whether they're fresh or dried. Some say the smaller they are, the hotter they are; or that red ones are hotter than green; or that pointed ones are hotter than rounded. Experts can tell how hot a chile is by touching the cut end to their tongues, not their lips. I recommend using a light hand with chiles until you learn what you like.

SALADS

AN OLD SAYING GOES: "It takes a miser for vinegar, a spend-thrift for oil, a counselor for salt, and a madman to stir it all up." That is, to make the perfect vinaigrette for a salad—and it's true! Nothing is better than wonderfully fresh, clean lettuces lightly coated in plenty of good-quality oil with a little vinegar and a sprinkling of salt and pepper.

Serving salads in the French manner would be to serve a simple green salad after the main course to cleanse the palate and aid the digestion.

Serving salads California style would be to serve them at the beginning of the meal. As a first course, the salad is much more interesting with elements such as cooked vegetables, meat, cheese, or fish. In French cooking, this kind of salad is called a composed salad. A composed salad could also be served as the main course for a luncheon or light supper.

A vinaigrette is the only dressing you will find in French cooking. The basic vinaigrette is 1 part acid (vinegar or lemon) to 3 or 4 parts olive or other vegetable oil. It is considered a temporary emulsion, which is why you need to mix it just before serving. You can add one of four ingredients to help bind a vinaigrette; namely, a spoonful of mayonnaise, heavy cream, prepared mustard, or meat juices. This gives it a more creamy consistency. I recommend mayonnaise or cream with delicate greens such as butter or leaf lettuce and mustard with stronger greens such as watercress or spinach.

Whether you serve salad at the beginning of the meal or after the main course, don't ever think of serving dressing separately—a good salad should always be tossed with the dressing.

Mesclun is a word from Provence that refers to a mixture of green and red lettuces. Nowadays, you can buy mixtures of baby lettuces at many grocery stores. It's a good idea to wash the greens again even though they may have been washed by the grower many times.

When buying salad greens, look for the crispiest lettuces with no brown edges and nice dark leaves. Store the lettuces in the plastic bag from the grocery store until the day you are going to serve them. Wash each leaf under cold running water, tear it into 1- or 2-inch pieces, and spin the leaves dry in a salad spinner. Store them in a clean dry towel in the refrigerator until ready to serve.

The Big Problem

The big problem people have when making salads is tossing the greens with the dressing long before it is to be eaten and then using too much dressing. When a salad is made properly, it should be tossed just before serving, and there should be no extra dressing on the plate or in the bowl. If you are served a salad dripping with dressing in a restaurant, complain to the server.

How to Make Salads Without a Recipe

For a simple green salad, put enough greens in a large glass, ceramic, or plastic bowl for each person. Put the vinegar in the bowl of a wooden spoon with a large pinch of coarse salt; dissolve the salt into the vinegar right in the spoon, stirring it with the fork. (The reason it is good to dissolve the salt in the vinegar is that salt takes a long time to dissolve in oil.) Spoon this over the salad greens and then spoon over 3 spoonfuls of olive oil. Grind black pepper and toss the greens with the wooden spoon and fork, bringing the lettuces on the bottom up and over those on the top. Taste a lettuce leaf, add more vinegar, oil, salt, or pepper, and serve.

Some cooks like to mix the vinegar with salt and perhaps minced shallots in the bottom of the salad bowl and then whisk in the oil just before serving. Others place the oil, vinegar, salt, and pepper in a little glass bottle and shake just before serving. A Dijon mustard bottle works well for this.

If you want to compose a salad with interesting ingredients, think about ingredients that complement each other and have different textures. Three different flavors with three different textures is ideal. Too many ingredients confuse the diner. Combinations that work well include poached chicken breast with avocado and mango; warm sausage with cooked potatoes and red bell peppers; smoked trout with shaved fennel and preserved lemons.

Whenever you cook potatoes, rice, pasta, or beans for a salad, be sure to flavor these with oil and vinegar while they are still warm so they absorb the flavor. Be sure to taste and adjust the seasoning before serving such a salad, as the flavors change when they are absorbed.

It is best to leave tomatoes out of a tossed salad; rather, serve them on their own—as in a tomato and mozzarella salad with basil or with sliced red onions in vinaigrette. Olives, prosciutto, or sun-dried tomatoes are great additions for salt and texture, but not all together.

OLIVE OILS

LEARNING ABOUT OLIVE OILS is fascinating. When olives are harvested young, they are green. When they are allowed to ripen, they turn black. To extract the oil from the olives, the whole green olives with their pits are first crushed; the olive mash is then pressed to extract the oil. This is usually what is meant by the term "cold pressed." This first pressing is then tasted and rated. It may be called extra-virgin, depending on the amount of acidity. Often the mash is pressed again, and again, sometimes with heat and sometimes with added chemicals. That is why cold pressed and extra-virgin are considered higher quality than other grades of olive oil.

What you want to do is save your extra-virgin olive oils for salads and use virgin or other vegetable oil for cooking, because you want the fresh wonderful taste of extra-virgin for salads but you don't want to use expensive oil just for cooking onions or zucchini. The reason you never deep-fry in olive oil is that it begins to smoke at a lower temperature than other oils. In other words, olive oil has a lower smoking point. Generally, when you are buying olive oils, the price is no indication of quality. I recommend buying small quantities of good-quality oils and tasting them carefully to see what you like. We keep both French (Puget) and Italian (Celio) oils in Tante Marie's kitchen. French oils are more delicate; Italian oils are stronger and slightly peppery. Sometimes we mix a less distinctive olive oil with the extra-virgin for a milder taste, in a two-thirds to one-third ratio. Sometimes we mix hazelnut or walnut oil with olive oil for a milder nut flavor. Once a container of a nut oil is opened, it must be refrigerated to prevent it from going rancid. Other oils that are good for you include canola, safflower, corn, and peanut. These too can be mixed with olive oil. Always read the label when buying a generic oil to make sure it doesn't contain a cheap oil like coconut or cottonseed, which is not as healthful.

Asparagus Salad with Fava Bean Sauce

One of my favorite cooks in San Francisco is Loretta Keller, the chef/owner of Bizou, a warm, comfortable bistro at the corner of Fourth and Brannan streets. Here is my adaptation of a dish I was served at Bizou—cooked asparagus with a sauce of fava beans mixed with pecorino, accompanied by a green salad with cherry tomatoes. This is a very suitable first course to serve in the spring, the season of asparagus and fava beans.

1 pound thin, green asparagus
½ pound young fava beans in their pods
1 garlic clove
7 tablespoons extra-virgin olive oil
¼ pound soft pecorino, freshly grated
Coarse salt
Freshly ground black pepper
2 tablespoons white wine vinegar
1 head red or leaf lettuce
Half pint cherry tomatoes

To prepare the asparagus, trim the asparagus at the point where the stems get tough, discarding the tough ends. Place the asparagus in a stainless steel sauté pan and pour in an inch of boiling water. Sprinkle with salt, cover, and steam over high heat until the asparagus are tender when pierced with a fork or they bends like a bow when lifted with tongs, about 7 minutes.

To peel the fava beans, first place a saucepan filled with water over high heat. Take the fava beans out of their pods and drop the beans into the boiling water. Simmer for 30 seconds, drain, and let rest until cool enough to handle. Remove the tough shell from each bean.

To make the fava bean sauce, cook the garlic in 3 tablespoons of the olive oil in a small saucepan over medium-high heat until soft but not colored, about 2 minutes. Add the fava beans with ½ cup water and continue to cook over low heat for 3 more minutes. Mash the fava beans with a potato masher or a fork. Turn off the heat and stir in half the cheese. Add enough warm water to make a sauce, about ½ cup more. Add salt and pepper to taste.

To assemble the salad, combine the vinegar with ½ teaspoon salt in the bottom of a large bowl. Stir to dissolve the salt. Mix in 4 tablespoons of the olive oil and pepper to taste. Toss in the lettuce and the cherry tomatoes. Add salt and pepper to taste. Put the asparagus on one side of eight warmed salad plates, spoon the fava bean sauce across the asparagus, and sprinkle with the additional cheese. Arrange the salad on the other side of the plate.   SERVES 8

Artichoke and Goat's Cheese Salad

I *believe it was M. F. K. Fisher who said arti-* *chokes are the one food you have more of* *when you finish eating than when you start.* *For this recipe the inedible part of the artichokes* *is trimmed before they are cooked. Although this* *is an absolutely wonderful salad to serve in the* *spring or fall, when artichokes are in season, it* *would also be great in the winter, made with* *roasted beets instead of artichokes.*

⅓ cup red wine vinegar
⅓ cup extra-virgin olive oil
⅓ cup walnut oil
1 tablespoon minced fresh herbs, such as
  parsley, chives, and/or chervil
Coarse salt
Freshly ground black pepper
Juice of half a lemon
6 medium-size artichokes, trimmed of
  all inedible pieces and quartered
  (see page 58), or 8 red beets, roasted
2 heads butter or leaf lettuce, or equal
  amounts of mixed green and red lettuces,
  washed, dried, and torn into 1-inch
  pieces
8 ounces fresh goat's cheese
½ cup walnut pieces, toasted
  (see page 109)

To make the vinaigrette, mix together the vinegar, olive oil, walnut oil, herbs, and salt and pepper to taste.

To prepare the artichokes, bring a large pan of water to a boil. Add the lemon juice and the artichoke bottoms. Bring to a boil again, reduce the heat, and simmer until the artichoke bottoms are tender when pierced with a fork, about 20 minutes. Drain the artichokes upside down on paper towels. When cool enough to handle, remove the fuzzy choke from each artichoke bottom with a small metal spoon and cut the artichokes into quarters. Toss the artichoke in the prepared vinaigrette and marinate, at room temperature, for at least an hour.

To assemble the salad, remove the artichokes from the vinaigrette. Save one-third of the vinaigrette in a small bowl for the cheese. Add the lettuces to the bowl and toss until each leaf is coated with the vinaigrette. Arrange the lettuces on salad plates. Place a round of goat's cheese in the middle of each plate. Arrange the artichoke quarters and the walnut halves around the cheese. Drizzle the remaining dressing over the cheese.

SERVES 8

Professionals cut soft cheeses with a string and *harder cheeses with a wire. In this recipe, a* *knife is fine.*

❧

To roast beets, cut off the stems and leaves, leaving an inch of stem. Coat with oil, wrap individually in foil, and bake in a 350-degree oven until tender, about an hour. Peel when cool enough to handle, put in the marinade, and proceed with the recipe.

Fig, Mozzarella, and Mizuna Salad with Basil

This sensuous salad was first served to me at the River Cafe in London in July, when figs are in season. When made correctly, it displays a beautiful contrast in green, white, and purple as well as a taste sensation of sweet, soft, and peppery. It is important to tear open the figs gently to expose their colorful interiors.

6 fresh figs, preferably Turkey or Black Mission
12 small balls fresh mozzarella
1 bunch mizuna or arugula, coarse stems removed
1 bunch Thai basil or purple mint, coarse stems removed
⅓ cup fruity extra-virgin olive oil
Half a lemon
Coarse salt

Remove the little stem from each fig with a paring knife. Remove the cheese from its liquid.

Combine the mizuna with the basil in a large salad bowl. Spoon the olive oil over it and toss gently to coat. Pile the greens in the middle of four salad plates. With your thumbs, gently pull each fig in half and lay the halves open side up on the greens. Scatter the cheese over the greens and drizzle the cheese and figs with a little olive oil. Squeeze a few drops of lemon juice over and sprinkle with coarse salt.   SERVES 4

Pear, Gorgonzola, and Walnut Salad

Pears, Gorgonzola, and walnuts make a per-fect combination for a salad to begin a meal in the fall when the pears and walnuts are fresh in the markets and Gorgonzola is nearly at its best. This salad is a contrast in color and texture: the pears are sweet and soft, the cheese is soft and salty, and the walnuts are hard and strongly flavored when toasted. To decide whether or not to peel the pears, taste the skin to see if it is acceptable. The best pears for this salad are French Butter pear, d'Anjou, or Comice. Bosc pears are best for cooking, and Bartlett pears are best eaten right away.

2 heads butter or leaf lettuce, or a mixture of red and green lettuces, washed, dried, and torn into 1-inch pieces
4 pears, such as French Butter, d'Anjou, or Comice, peeled, and cut into ¼-inch-wide slices
½ pound Gorgonzola, broken into ½-inch chunks
½ cup walnut pieces, lightly toasted
3 tablespoons red wine vinegar
1 teaspoon Dijon-style prepared mustard
½ cup extra-virgin olive oil
Coarse salt
Freshly ground pepper

Put the lettuces in a large salad bowl. Add the pears, cheese, and walnuts.

To make the vinaigrette, combine the vinegar, mustard, and salt in a measuring cup. Stir to dissolve the salt. Mix in the olive oil. Add salt and pepper to taste. Mix well with a small spoon.

To serve, mix the vinaigrette again and pour over the salad, tossing gently with your hands. Add salt and pepper to taste. Mound the lettuces in the centers of salad plates. With your hands, arrange the pears, Gorgonzola, and walnuts on top. Serve with French bread.   SERVES 6

To peel pears, use a vegetable peeler and peel from the stem to the bottom in long strokes. With a small knife cut each pear in half, and with a pear corer or knife, remove the core and the fiber that runs the length of the pear. Place the pear, cut side down, on a board and cut into ¼-inch-wide slices.

To toast the walnuts, place them in a small fry-ing pan with no oil or butter on medium-high heat. Shake the pan and toss the nuts until they are lightly browned. If the walnuts burn, throw them away and start again.

Pears are the one fruit that doesn't fully ripen until after it is picked. Even though pears can be kept for months in storage, they are best eaten in the fall.

Gorgonzola is a delicious cheese from Italy that is both creamy and blue. When young, it has a mild, delicious flavor.

Pear, Persimmon, and Pomegranate Salad with Pecans

Here is an absolutely beautiful and delicious salad of autumn colors to serve during the holidays!

4 bunches watercress or arugula, washed, dried, and coarse stems removed

4 pears, such as French Butter, Comice, or d'Anjou, peeled and cut into ¼-inch-wide slices

4 Fuyu persimmons, cut into ¼-inch-wide slices

½ cup pomegranate seeds

½ cup fresh pecans

1 shallot, finely chopped

3 tablespoons sherry vinegar

1 teaspoon Dijon-style mustard

⅓ cup extra-virgin olive oil

Coarse salt

Freshly ground black pepper

Put the watercress in a large salad bowl with the pears, persimmons, pomegranate seeds, and pecans.

To make the dressing, combine the shallot, vinegar, mustard, olive oil, and salt and pepper to taste in a measuring cup. Mix well.

When ready to serve, pour the dressing over the salad, and toss. Pile the greens on salad plates. With your hands, arrange the fruit on top and scatter nuts and seeds over it.

SERVES 6

Nuts have a much better flavor when purchased fresh from a farmers' market or in bulk from a good grocery store. By the time they are sold in little packages in supermarkets, they can be pretty old and stale.

At Tante Marie's we keep almonds, walnuts, and hazelnuts in the freezer and always buy pecans fresh when needed.

To remove the seeds from a pomegranate, simply cut into the pomegranate and remove the seeds, discarding the white membrane and the skin. In professional kitchens, this can be done in a bowl of cold water to prevent the juice from getting all over everything.

There are generally two kinds of persimmons in the market. The larger, dark orange, pointed ones should be ripened until they are very soft; the pulp is usually used in baking. The small, hard, light orange ones are usually used raw in salads such as this.

Avocado and Grapefruit Salad

Avocado and grapefruit salad keeps coming back into fashion because it is so good—a perfect combination of textures and tastes. This California salad makes a refreshing first course.

4 grapefruits, preferably pink
4 avocados
Coarse salt
1 teaspoon good-quality balsamic vinegar
2 teaspoons lemon juice
½ cup extra-virgin olive oil
Freshly ground white pepper
2 heads butter or leaf lettuce, washed and
*   dried, cut or torn into 1-inch lengths*
1 bunch chives (optional)

Peel and section the grapefruit over a bowl to capture any grapefruit juices. There should be no white membrane around any of the sections.

Cut each avocado in half, remove the pit and peel, and lay the halves cut side down on a board. Cut into ½-inch-long slices and coat lightly with olive oil to keep them from turning brown.

To make the vinaigrette, put ½ teaspoon salt in the bottom of a large bowl. Stir in the vinegar and lemon and grapefruit juices. Mix to dissolve the salt. Stir in the olive oil. Add salt and pepper to taste. Reserve ¼ cup of the vinaigrette in a measuring cup.

When ready to serve, toss the lettuce in a big bowl with the vinaigrette and arrange the lettuce on salad plates. On top of the lettuce arrange alternating slices of grapefruit and avocado in a fan shape. Spoon the remaining vinaigrette on top and sprinkle with snipped fresh chives if desired.   SERVES 8

For perfectly sectioned grapefruit or oranges, cut off both ends of each grapefruit so that the flesh of the fruit can be seen. Stand the fruit on one of the cut ends. With a sharp knife, remove all the rind of the citrus by cutting down onto the board, cutting off 1- to 1½-inch pieces all the way around. Pick the fruit up in one hand and, with a small knife, cut down one side of a membrane and then the other to remove a triangular section of fruit. With the remaining sections, run your knife in the inside of the upper membrane, and turn the knife to follow the lower membrane, always cutting away from yourself.

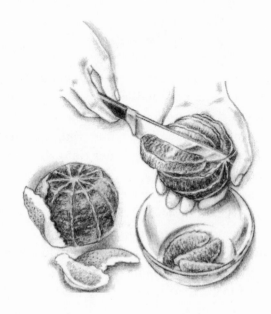

Celery Root, Endive, and Watercress Salad

When I first started teaching cooking thirty years ago, my students were regulars at a restaurant called Trader Vic's. They always wanted to know how to make the restaurant's watercress and endive salad. Here is my version of that popular salad with the addition of celery root, a delicious winter vegetable.

Coarse salt
Juice of half a lemon
1 medium-size celery root
6 Belgian endives
2 bunches watercress
2 small or 1 large shallot, minced
2 tablespoons white wine vinegar
1 tablespoon Dijon-style mustard
2 tablespoons mayonnaise (store-bought is fine; recipe for homemade follows)
½ cup extra-virgin olive oil
Freshly ground black pepper

To prepare the vegetables, bring a large pan of water to a boil, add ½ teaspoon salt, and squeeze in the lemon juice. Remove all the brown skin of the celery root with a sharp knife. Slice the celery root into ¼-inch rounds. Pile up the rounds and cut them into 1-inch widths. Cut these into ¼ by 1-inch julienne and drop into the boiling water for 30 seconds. Refresh under cold water. Cut the endives into 1-inch-wide slices. Remove the tough stems from the watercress.

To make the dressing, combine the shallots, vinegar, mustard, mayonnaise, olive oil, and salt and pepper to taste in the bottom of a large salad bowl.

When ready to serve, add the celery root, endive, and watercress to the bowl and toss to coat the greens evenly with the dressing. Serve on individual salad plates.

SERVES 6

Since raw celery root turns gray when exposed to the air for any length of time, the method described here is a good one to follow for any celery root salad.

The best store-bought mayonnaise is Hellmann's or Best Foods, which still tastes great with canned tuna and a tomato sandwich. Here is a recipe for homemade mayonnaise, a must for crab or lobster salad.

MAYONNAISE

1 egg yolk, at room temperature
2 teaspoons lemon juice
½ teaspoon dry mustard
¼ teaspoon coarse salt
⅛ teaspoon freshly ground white pepper
¾ to 1 cup olive and/or other vegetable oil, at room temperature

Combine the egg yolks in a small bowl with the lemon juice, mustard, salt, and pepper. Beat vigorously with a wire whisk and while mixing, start adding the oil, drop by drop at first. When the mixture begins to look creamy, add the oil faster. If the mixture gets very thick, whisk in a tablespoon of warm water. When all the oil has been incorporated, add lemon juice, salt, and pepper to taste. (The mayonnaise can be kept for up to a week in the refrigerator.)

To bring eggs to room temperature, place them in a glass measuring cup with slightly warm water for 15 minutes.

If your mayonnaise curdles (breaks), do not throw it away. Simply start over with a room-temperature egg yolk. Whisk in the curdled mayonnaise alternately with the oil until you have a smooth emulsion. Add ½ cup additional oil to make up for the extra yolk.

Mayonnaise can be made in a mixer as described or in a food processor, using a whole egg and adding the oil in a thin, steady stream.

Classic Caesar Salad

*T*his famous salad, which used to be served tableside in fancy restaurants in the '60s, faded out of fashion in the '70s and came back in the '80s. Whether in or out of fashion, Caesar salad is easy and fun to make for a supper by itself or to precede a light dish like New England Seafood Chowder (page 98). You can toast the bread rather than make croutons, but be sure to rub a cut clove of garlic over the bread. If you don't like anchovies, you can substitute a teaspoon of bottled Worcestershire sauce. Be sure to grate additional cheese on each salad.*

Romaine lettuce is a must for this salad because it can withstand being tossed with dressing three times.

> *3 garlic cloves*
> *½ cup olive oil plus ¼ cup extra-virgin olive oil*
> *Coarse salt*
> *½ pound crusty country bread, sliced and broken into 1 to 2-inch cubes*
> *6 to 10 anchovy fillets*
> *1 teaspoon dry mustard*
> *1 large egg*
> *1 lemon*
> *2 heads Romaine lettuce, washed, dried, and cut into 2-inch lengths*
> *¾ cup freshly grated Parmesan*
> *Freshly ground black pepper*

To make the croutons, slice two of the garlic cloves and put them in a large bowl with the ½ cup olive oil and ½ teaspoon salt. Toss in the bread and coat with the oil. Place the bread on a baking sheet in a 350-degree oven, and stir from time to time, until the bread is golden brown, about 15 minutes. Return the croutons to the bowl and throw away the garlic slices.

To make the salad, finely mince the remaining garlic clove with the anchovy fillets. Put these in the bottom of a large salad bowl with the dry mustard and mash with a fork. Mix in the ¼ cup olive oil. Break the egg into the center of the mixture. Squeeze the lemon juice directly onto the uncooked egg. Mix together the lemon juice and egg with a fork before incorporating the other ingredients. Put the lettuce on top of the dressing and toss with salad servers until the lettuce is coated with the dressing. Add the Parmesan and lots of freshly ground black pepper and toss again. Add the croutons and toss a third time. Add lemon juice, salt, and pepper to taste. Serve on salad plates.

SERVES 6

The best way to wash lettuce is to separate each leaf, run it under cold water, tear it into pieces, dry it in a salad spinner, and store it in a towel until ready to use. You must look at each piece to check for browning, dirt, or bugs.

Some people prefer to cook the egg for a minute before proceeding with the recipe. I find this an unnecessary extra step because I think the lemon juice essentially "cooks" the egg. However, it is very important that a recipe calling for raw eggs be served only at home. In professional kitchens, pasteurized eggs must be used to prevent any chance of contamination.

Salade Niçoise

Although the editors of Saveur magazine claim that the real salade Niçoise has no lettuce, no cooked vegetables, and no vinegar, I prefer my rendition of this favorite luncheon dish. This is a great way to use leftover cooked vegetables. Tomatoes, peppers, and olives are the traditional French garnish called Niçoise. For the tuna, I recommend buying a Portuguese canned tuna called Idamar—it's great right out of the can. You can also gently poach a piece of well-seasoned tuna in olive oil until it is cooked through. Seared fresh tuna has no place in this salad.

1½ pounds new potatoes
Coarse salt
1 pound small green beans
1 head butter or leaf lettuce,
  washed, dried, and torn into
  1-inch pieces
6 ounces good-quality canned tuna fish,
  packed in olive oil
6 anchovy fillets
2 medium-size red tomatoes, cut into
  ½-inch wedges
2 hard-cooked eggs, peeled and quartered
  (see page 35)
½ small red onion, peeled and cut into thin
  rings
½ small green pepper, cored and cut into
  thin rings
½ cup Niçoise olives, pitted
2 tablespoons Champagne or white wine
  vinegar
2 teaspoons Dijon-style mustard

⅔ cup extra-virgin olive oil plus some for
    sprinkling
1 tablespoon capers, rinsed and coarsely
    chopped if large
3 tablespoons minced fresh herbs such as
    parsley, chives, tarragon, thyme, and/or
    marjoram
Freshly ground black pepper

To prepare the potatoes, put the potatoes in a medium-size saucepan with ½ teaspoon salt and cover generously with cold water. Bring to a boil and boil until the potatoes are just tender when pierced with a fork, about 20 minutes. Drain in a colander and shake over the sink to evaporate any excess moisture. When the potatoes are cool enough to handle, peel them, put them in a nice wide bowl, and toss with olive oil, salt, and pepper while they are still warm.

To prepare the green beans, bring another pot of water to a boil. Trim both ends of the green beans and slice lengthwise in half if large. Add ½ teaspoon salt to the water and drop in the beans. Continue boiling the beans until they are tender when pierced with a fork, about 7 minutes. Drain and refresh under cold running water.

To assemble the salad, put the lettuce in a nice bowl, mound the tuna in the center, and arrange a grid of anchovies on top of the tuna. Make two piles each of potatoes and green beans around the tuna. Decorate the edge of the salad with tomatoes and hard-cooked eggs, and arrange rings of red onion and green pepper over all ingredients. Scatter the olives over the salad.

To make the dressing, in a small bowl or measuring cup, mix the vinegar, mustard, the ⅔ cup olive oil, capers, fresh herbs, and salt and pepper to taste.

When ready to serve, make sure everyone sees the beautiful presentation. Pour the herb dressing over the salad and toss. Serve on six salad plates.   SERVES 6

All green vegetables should be dropped in boiling salted water and cooked uncovered until they are tender. This is called blanching. Refreshing them under cold water stops the cooking and restores the green color. New potatoes, however, should never be put in cold water to stop the cooking because they are porous and will absorb liquid. Always shake them after cooking to evaporate excess moisture.

VINEGAR

WINE VINEGARS ARE CULTURED from wine—that means a healthy bacterium called mother has been added to wine to change it to vinegar. The quality of vinegars on the grocery shelf varies tremendously, which is why you always need to taste vinegar to judge its strength before following a recipe exactly. You will need less of a strong vinegar and more of a weak vinegar, so use your own judgment. Lesser-quality vinegars are diluted with water. We keep red wine, white wine, and sherry vinegar on the shelves of Tante Marie's—all by Kimberly, a California vinegar maker. Any vinegar that becomes cloudy should be discarded.

Balsamic vinegar is really more like a condiment such as Worcestershire sauce than a vinegar. If you like a sweet-tasting vinaigrette, you can mix balsamic vinegar with red or white vinegar. Good-quality balsamic vinegar is much too sweet and strong in flavor to use in place of regular vinegar in a salad. Good-quality balsamic vinegar is made directly from grape juice in an elaborate process that includes adding more grape juice each year and aging the vinegar in a succession of wooden casks. It should take at least ten years to make a good balsamic vinegar, which deserves to be expensive. A really good bottle of balsamic vinegar might be signed and dated by the maker. There are many terrible imitations in the markets now, so be careful when selecting one.

Panzanella
(Tuscan Bread Salad) with Tuna

Here is a recipe I learned from Lorenza de' Medici, who still offers one-week cooking vacations in her home in the hills of Chianti in a converted monastery called Badia a Coltibuono. Because there is always leftover stale (saltless) bread in Tuscany, cooks never have to make the bread stale or make croutons as described here. They simply moisten bread and mix it with the vinegar and oil and the tomatoes and basil of summer. Lorenza's idea of adding canned tuna makes it a perfect luncheon dish for a hot summer's day! Instead of tuna you can add grilled scallops or strips of grilled chicken.

2 garlic cloves, sliced
½ cup virgin olive oil plus ½ cup extra-virgin olive oil
1 loaf crusty country bread (1 pound), sliced and torn into 1-inch pieces
Coarse salt
1 large red onion, chopped
1 tablespoon white wine vinegar
4 large tomatoes
1 bunch basil
6 ounces good-quality tuna, packed in olive oil
⅓ cup Niçoise olives, pitted
Freshly ground black pepper
3 tablespoons red wine vinegar

To make the croutons, mix the garlic and ½ cup olive oil with ½ teaspoon salt in a large bowl and toss in the bread. Place the bread mixture on a baking sheet in a 350-degree oven, stirring from time to time, until the bread is golden brown, about 15 minutes. Return the croutons to the bowl and discard the garlic slices.

To prepare the onions, put the onions in a bowl with cold water to cover and add the white wine vinegar.

To prepare the tomatoes, hold the tomatoes over the bread and with a small serrated knife cut approximately 1-inch pieces of tomato skin and flesh and allow them to fall into the salad.

To make the salad, drain the onions and add to the salad. Tear the basil leaves into ½-inch pieces and add them along with the tuna, olives, and plenty of salt and pepper. Mix the red wine vinegar with 3 tablespoons water and sprinkle over the salad. Sprinkle over the ½ cup extra-virgin olive oil and toss, preferably with your hands. Add vinegar, olive oil, salt, and pepper to taste. Serve on individual salad plates.   SERVES 6

Soaking onions in water and vinegar removes some of the strong taste.

Fattoush
(Middle Eastern
Bread Salad with Feta)

I am very proud of Heidi Insalata Krahling, the chef-owner of Insalata's in San Anselmo. She is full of talent, passion, and personality, and she was my student almost twenty years ago. This refreshing salad is so popular at her Mediterranean-style restaurant that she can't take it off the menu! It is a great beginning to a meal, or you can add a grilled chicken breast to make it a main course for lunch or supper.

1 pint (2 cups) cherry tomatoes, halved

1 medium-size cucumber (2 cups), diced

1 medium-size red onion, halved and thinly sliced (1 cup)

½ cup chopped fresh cilantro

½ cup chopped fresh mint

1 large head Romaine lettuce, washed, dried, and torn in 1-inch pieces

4 pita pockets, each cut into 2 discs, toasted, and broken into 1-inch pieces

8 ounces (1 cup) Feta cheese, crumbled

1 cup Kalamata olives, pitted

1 garlic clove, minced

¾ cup lemon juice

2 tablespoons rice vinegar

1 teaspoon sugar

½ teaspoon cumin seeds, toasted and ground

Coarse salt

Freshly ground pepper

1½ cups olive oil

To make the salad, mix the tomatoes, cucumber, onion, cilantro, mint, lettuce, pita, feta, and olives in a large salad bowl.

To make the dressing, combine the garlic, lemon juice, vinegar, sugar, and cumin in a measuring cup with ½ teaspoon salt and a generous grinding of pepper. Stir to dissolve the sugar and salt and mix in the olive oil. Add salt and pepper to taste.

When ready to serve, pour the dressing over the salad, toss, and serve on individual salad plates. SERVES 4 TO 6

Raw onions—white, yellow, or red—will turn gray when exposed to air over time. If you are chopping or slicing onions ahead of time, simply put them in a sieve and run cold water over them to prevent discoloring.

Mexican Chicken Salad

*D*onna and Frank Katzl have run the Café for All Seasons in San Francisco for years. It is a neighborhood restaurant serving very fresh, wholesome food. Their Mexican chicken salad can't be beat for a summertime whole-meal salad! Since this salad requires extra effort, it is best made in a large quantity for a party.

3 heads Romaine lettuce, torn into 1-inch strips
4 poached half chicken breasts, cut into ½-inch dice (see page 120)
4 cups cooked black beans or two 8-ounce cans black beans, rinsed
2 cups fresh corn, cut from the cob (4 small ears)
2 cups chopped ripe tomatoes (4 medium tomatoes)
2 cups chopped red onion (2 medium-size onions)
4 small avocados, peeled and chopped
3 cups grated mild Cheddar cheese (12 ounces)
4 cups broken-up tortilla chips
1 cup cumin dressing (recipe follows)
1 cup spicy sour cream (recipe follows)
1 bunch thinly sliced scallions, equal amounts white and green

To make the salad, put the lettuce, chicken, beans, corn, tomatoes, onion, avocado, cheese, and chips in a large bowl and carefully toss together with cumin dressing. Serve mounded on individual plates topped with a dollop of spicy sour cream and a sprinkle of scallions.

CUMIN DRESSING

¾ cup apple cider vinegar
¼ cup coarse salt
4 teaspoons freshly ground black pepper
4 tablespoons Worcestershire sauce
2 teaspoons dry mustard
¼ cup sugar
¼ cup lemon juice
4 garlic cloves, minced
½ cup tomato paste
1 teaspoon red pepper flakes
¾ cup olive oil
1 cup safflower oil
¼ cup toasted and ground cumin seeds

To make the cumin dressing, mix together ¾ cup water with the vinegar, salt, pepper, Worcestershire sauce, mustard, sugar, lemon juice, garlic, tomato paste, red pepper flakes, olive oil, safflower oil, and cumin seeds.

SPICY SOUR CREAM

1 cup sour cream
1 tablespoon minced jalapeño
2 tablespoons chopped fresh cilantro
¾ teaspoon coarse salt

Combine all the ingredients in a blender or food processor. Blend until smooth and refrigerate for at least an hour before using.

SERVES 4

To poach a chicken breast, put a large half breast on the bone in a small pan and cover with chicken stock. Add half an onion, a bay leaf, a garlic clove, and a sprinkling of salt and pepper. Bring to a boil, turn the heat to low, cover, and cook at a bare simmer until the chicken is opaque down to the bone, about 15 minutes. Remove the chicken, saving the liquid for soup. When cool enough to handle, remove the chicken from the bone and the skin from the chicken.

When increasing quantities in a recipe, all you have to do is double, triple, or otherwise multiply the ingredients. The exceptions are when cooking with liquid, as in a soup or a stew, or when using yeast or other leaveners. When you increase the amount of meat for a stew, you will need only half again as much more liquid, not double. The same is true of leaveners, such as baking powder or yeast.

Bistro Salad
(with Country Bacon, Garlic Croutons, and Soft-Cooked Egg)

What makes this French bistro salad taste so delicious is the soft-cooked egg yolk combined with the red wine vinegar, which coat the bitter salad greens and are set off by crisp bacon and the strong garlic croutons. It is so good when made properly—a satisfying dish for a light supper at home.

4 thick slices crusty country bread
1 garlic clove, cut in half
6 slices thick-cut bacon
3 tablespoons red wine vinegar
5 tablespoons extra-virgin olive oil
Coarse salt
Freshly ground black pepper
2 heads frisee lettuce or mesclun, washed, dried, and torn into 1-inch pieces
4 eggs

To make the garlic croutons, put the bread on a baking sheet under the broiler and broil until lightly browned. Turn the bread over and broil the other side. Remove from the oven and run the cut side of the garlic clove over one side of each piece of bread a few times. Break the toasted bread into 1-inch pieces.

To cook the bacon, cook the bacon slices on both sides in a frying pan over medium-high heat until crisp; drain on paper towels. Put a tablespoon of the bacon fat into the bottom of a large metal bowl. When the bacon is cool enough to handle, break it into ½-inch pieces.

To finish the salad, mix the vinegar, olive oil, ½ teaspoon salt, and several grindings of pepper to the bacon fat. Warm the bowl over direct heat. Add the lettuce, garlic croutons, and bacon. Toss with salad servers or your hands, add salt, pepper, and vinegar to taste, and arrange the salad equally on four warmed plates.

Meanwhile, gently fry the eggs in a non-stick pan until the white is cooked through. Carefully transfer an egg to the top of each salad and serve. (Tell the diners to cut right into the egg yolk and toss the salad on their plate so that the egg mixes with the dressing.)

SERVES 4

Although this dish is usually served with poached eggs, I prefer seeing the egg yolk. However, care must be taken to fry the eggs over very low heat so they do not become rubbery.

Warm Red Cabbage Salad with Smoked Chicken and Walnuts

In the early '80s a handsome and charming man named Jeremiah Tower became the consulting chef for the Balboa Café in San Francisco. Overnight this second-rate bar became a mecca for food enthusiasts eager to eat Jeremiah's food. This salad of slightly cooked red cabbage with walnuts and smoked chicken was a favorite there and is still a favorite quick supper dish for students from Tante Marie's. Whether you buy a smoked chicken or smoke one yourself, the idea is to get some of the chicken flavor into the salad dressing—just a little chicken fat, walnut oil, and red wine vinegar makes this warm red cabbage salad come to life.

1 whole smoked chicken (about 1 pound smoked chicken off the bone)
⅓ cup olive oil
½ cup walnuts
1 medium-size red cabbage, shredded
Coarse salt
⅓ to ½ cup red wine vinegar
¼ cup walnut oil
Freshly ground black pepper

To render the chicken fat, remove the skin from the chicken with your hands. Cut the fatty skin into 1-inch pieces and put in a small saucepan, along with any fat from the chicken and 2 tablespoons water over low heat. Let melt gently for 8 to 10 minutes and strain the resulting fat into a measuring cup. Throw away the skin. If necessary, add enough olive oil to the chicken fat to equal ¼ cup.

To prepare the chicken, with your hands, remove the chicken from the bones and cut into 1 by ½-inch strips.

To toast the walnuts, put them in a small, dry frying pan over medium-high heat and shake the pan, tossing the nuts until they are lightly colored and taste toasted. Transfer them into a bowl to cool.

To prepare the salad, stand the cabbage on end and cut ½-inch shreds all around until only the core remains. Throw away the core. Put the cabbage in a 10-inch frying or sauté pan with a sprinkling of salt and the chicken fat and/or olive oil over medium-high heat. Cover and let cook for a minute to release the moisture in the cabbage. Uncover and continue cooking, stirring from time to time, until the cabbage begins to soften. Add the vinegar and cook for 2 minutes more, stirring occasionally. Mix in the chicken, toasted walnuts, and walnut oil. Add salt, pepper, and vinegar to taste. Serve on warm salad plates.

SERVES 8

It is impossible to give an exact measurement for red wine vinegar because the intensity differs so much from one producer to another. As a general guide, darker red wine vinegar is usually stronger than light colored.

Warm Farro Salad with Prosciutto

Everyone loves Giuliano Bugialli's cooking classes. He has come once a year to teach at Tante Marie's for over fifteen years. It's a great teacher who can take groups to cook in Florence in the spring and summer, teach across the United States in the winter, and publish a new cookbook every year. Here is one of our favorite recipes of his. Farro is an old variety of wheat— it is delicious cooked with green beans, carrots, and prosciutto. (Substitute sun-dried tomatoes for prosciutto for guests who don't eat meat.)

½ pound dried white beans (cannellini or Great Northern), soaked overnight in plenty of cold water
½ pound farro, spelt, or wheat berries, soaked for two hours in cold water
6 ounces prosciutto or pancetta, sliced ¼ inch thick
10 tablespoons extra-virgin olive oil
Coarse salt
Freshly ground black pepper
¾ pound very thin green beans, trimmed and cut into 2-inch lengths
¾ pound thin baby carrots, peeled and julienned the same size as the green beans
4 garlic cloves, minced
¼ teaspoon red pepper flakes
Juice and zest of 1 lemon
20 large fresh basil leaves, cut in chiffonade, plus 5 whole leaves for garnish

To cook the beans, drain them and put them in a large pan with 4 quarts fresh water, one-third (2 ounces) of the prosciutto, and 2 tablespoons of the olive oil. Place the pot over medium heat, bring to a boil, stirring, and reduce the heat to a simmer. Simmer until the beans are tender, about 45 minutes.

When the beans are cooked, strain the cooking liquid into a large pot and discard the cooked prosciutto. While the beans are still warm, put them in a large bowl, toss with 2 tablespoons of the olive oil, and season well with salt and pepper.

Put the pot of bean-cooking liquid over medium-high heat. Drain the farro and add. Bring to a boil, stirring constantly, and reduce the heat to a simmer. Cook until the farro is tender, about 30 minutes. Drain well. Put the farro in the bowl with the beans, drizzle with 2 tablespoons of the olive oil, and season well with salt and pepper.

To prepare the vegetables, place a large pot of water over high heat and bring to a boil. When the water boils, add ½ teaspoon salt and drop in the green beans. When the beans are tender when pierced with a fork, 5 to 7 minutes, remove them with a slotted spoon, and run them under cold water. Do the same with the carrots. Add the vegetables to the beans and farro.

To prepare the sauce, process the remaining two-thirds prosciutto with the garlic in a food processor until finely chopped. Put this mixture with the remaining 4 tablespoons olive oil in a small frying pan and cook over medium-high heat until the mixture is crisp and lightly browned, about 10 minutes. Season with salt, pepper, and red pepper flakes. Remove the pan from the heat and stir in the lemon juice and zest, and basil. Pour this

mixture over the bean mixture. Toss to coat, and add salt and pepper to taste. Serve warm.

SERVES 10 TO 12

Whenever a recipe calls for citrus zest, be sure to wash the lemon, orange, or grapefruit in soap and water because it may have been sprayed with chemicals. Whenever a recipe calls for lemon juice, roll the lemon on a counter or board, pressing hard to loosen the juices before juicing.

Prosciutto is the back leg of a hog that has been salt cured and air dried. Italian and French hams are often air dried, in contrast to German and American hams, which are cured and then smoked.

Pancetta is bacon that has also been cured and air dried. If you can't find a source for pancetta, you can blanch American bacon and proceed with the recipe.

Warm Chicken Liver Salad with Cherry Tomatoes and Arugula

People either love chicken livers or hate them. This is a recipe for the chicken liver lovers you know. I order it every time I go to my friend Carole Peck's restaurant in South Woodbury, Connecticut, which is called The Good News Café—Carole is a great cook and will make this salad for me whether or not it is on the menu. Thank you, Carole!

1 pound chicken livers
1 cup milk
6 tablespoons olive oil
1 large shallot, minced
Half pint cherry tomatoes, stemmed
1 teaspoon minced fresh thyme
1 tablespoon good-quality balsamic vinegar
1 tablespoon red wine vinegar
2 bunches (about 6 cups) arugula, washed
    and dried
Coarse salt
Freshly ground pepper

To prepare the chicken livers, remove any excess fat or veins from the livers, put them in a small bowl with the milk, and let stand, covered, for 30 to 60 minutes. Drain the livers and pat dry with paper towels.

To prepare the tomatoes, cook the shallot in 2 tablespoons of the oil with a sprinkling of salt in a small frying pan over medium-high heat until it is soft, about 4 minutes.

Toss in the tomatoes and thyme and cook until the tomatoes are warmed through, about 2 minutes. Season the tomatoes with salt and pepper.

To cook the chicken livers, get a nonstick frying pot as hot as you can; it should be covered with a light coating of olive oil. Put the livers an inch apart and cook over high heat until they are crusty on the outside and slightly pink on the inside, about 1 minute on each side.

To make the salad, mix together the vinegars and the remaining 2 tablespoons of olive oil in the bottom of a large stainless steel bowl. Put the bowl directly over medium-high heat to warm it. Remove from the heat, and add the tomatoes, chicken livers, and arugula with plenty of salt and pepper. Taste and adjust the seasoning. To serve, arrange the greens on warmed salad plates with the chicken livers and tomatoes on top.

SERVES 4

Most organ meat needs to be cooked quickly over high heat for maximum flavor. Liver in particular develops an unpleasant taste when overcooked.

Every time you cook a chicken, save the liver in a plastic bag in the freezer. When you have a pound of livers, make this recipe.

Warm French Lentil and Sausage Salad

Little French green lentils are far more desirable than ordinary gray ones because they keep their shape when cooking and are a much more attractive color. In this recipe, the lentils will have a slight taste of the sausages and are well complemented by the peppery taste of arugula.

2 cups French green lentils

6 sprigs fresh Italian parsley

3 garlic cloves, lightly crushed

1¼ cups olive oil

2 pounds pork sausages, store-bought or homemade (see page 382), preferably lightly smoked

½ cup red wine

2 tablespoons red wine vinegar

2 tablespoons Dijon-style mustard

Coarse salt

Freshly ground black pepper

6 cups arugula or watercress, stemmed

To cook the lentils, put them in a saucepan with enough water to cover by an inch. Add 1 teaspoon salt, the parsley sprigs, and the garlic. Bring the mixture to a boil over high heat, stirring, reduce the heat, and simmer until the lentils are barely tender, about 25 minutes. If necessary, add hot water while the lentils are cooking to keep them from drying out or sticking to the bottom of the pan. There should be very little liquid left when the lentils are cooked. Discard the parsley and garlic. Immediately toss the lentils with ¼ cup olive oil and cover to keep warm.

To cook the sausages, prick them two or three times with a fork and put them in one layer in a sauté or frying pan with ½ inch water over medium heat. Cook the sausages, turning from time to time, until they are lightly browned on all sides, about 15 minutes. Remove the sausages to a cutting board. Without hesitation, deglaze the pan with the wine and boil up to cook off the alcohol. Strain this mixture into a small bowl. Add the remaining 1 cup olive oil, the vinegar, and mustard, with salt and pepper to taste. Cut the sausages on a diagonal into 1-inch lengths.

To assemble the salad, mix the sausages into the lentils with half the vinaigrette. Toss the remaining half of the vinaigrette with the arugula in another bowl. Mound the lentils and sausages in the middle of eight warmed salad plates and surround with the arugula.

SERVES 8

Store-bought or homemade sausages can be smoked in a cold smoker for 4 hours and then stored in the refrigerator for up to a week or in the freezer for up to 9 months.

Sausages should be pricked before being heated so they do not break open when cooking. The reason you always start off cooking them with a little water is to help the fat to begin to melt out or render. The water will evaporate in the cooking, leaving the sausages to brown.

PASTA AND RISOTTO

Pasta

Whether you call it macaroni, spaghetti, or fettuccine, pasta is easy to make, healthful to eat, and perfect for our modern lifestyle. Although noodles are made the world over, it is the Italians who have made an art out of cooking pasta. In the United States, it is often served as a main course (or entrée) rather than as the smaller second course served in Italy, after antipasto and before fish, poultry, or meat. Furthermore, as with pizza and quiche, we have a tendency to overdo it with pasta, adding too many ingredients to the sauce and too much sauce to the pasta.

WHICH IS BETTER, FRESH PASTA OR DRIED?

They are entirely different. Fresh pasta has a soft texture and goes well with such things as wild mushrooms and seafood. Dried pasta always has more bite to it when it is cooked properly and works well in dishes where texture is called for, such as with asparagus. Often an Italian cook will match the kind of pasta to the kind of sauce: a smooth sauce like tomato would call for small strands of pasta like spaghetti. Wider-cut vegetables, however, would call for wider-cut pasta like fettuccine. Short-cut vegetables like asparagus would call for short-cut pasta like penne. Little shells, ears, and corkscrews are good for catching smaller ingredients like peas and chopped or ground meats.

COOKING PASTA

Pasta, whether fresh or dried, should be dropped in plenty of boiling salted water. It should be stirred with a wooden fork to separate the strands. It should be tested with the teeth or the fingernail to see when it is just al dente, firm but cooked through. It should then be drained, not too thoroughly, and sauced. There is no reason to add olive oil to the cooking liquid, because it will prevent the sauce from sticking to the pasta later. There is also no reason to rinse pasta after it is cooked to remove the starch. After all, pasta *is* starch. When the pasta is perfectly cooked and drained, it should be coated with some of the sauce to prevent the pasta from sticking together when it cools. Additional sauce can be put on top of the serving platter or individual plates.

The Big Problem

The most important thing about serving pasta is keeping it hot. This is why I recommend returning the cooked pasta to the hot pot, tossing it with the warmed sauce, tasting it quickly, adding whatever it needs, and serving it right away on hot plates. If you prefer to serve it family-style in a bowl, be sure the bowl and the plates are hot. The thing is that the pasta continues to dry out after cooking, so it is important to make sure there is plenty of liquid in the sauce.

How to Make Pasta Without a Recipe

Even though Italian cooks have been saucing pasta with tomato sauce and cream sauces for years, what also works is a modern sauce of reduced stock with a little butter and olive oil. This can go on dried pasta of any size with the addition of a couple of complementary ingredients such as broccoli and cherry tomatoes with garlic; sun-dried tomatoes and basil; or smoked ham and peas. You must first make sure the complementary ingredients are cooked or nearly cooked. Reduce the stock if it is not already concentrated. Drop the pasta into boiling salted water. Cook it until it is cooked through but still firm. Drain the pasta, return it to the hot pot, toss

it with the ingredients and the reduced stock. Throw in a spoonful of butter and/or olive oil, and perhaps a little cheese, and serve in warm bowls with plenty of liquid. The trick is to run to the table with the hot plates and make sure people are there ready to eat.

Risotto

Risotto is so special in Italy that it is always served as a separate course. It is served with the main course only when osso bucco is served with saffron risotto. Risotto is short, fat grains of rice (usually Arborio) that are first cooked in butter and onions and then in a flavorful stock. The warmed stock is added by the ladleful and stirred until it is absorbed. The process is then repeated until all the liquid is used. With this method the rice cooks evenly and swells to make a creamy delicious rice dish. Risotto is one dish that is better when made by the home cook rather than in a restaurant. This is because the home cook can spend twenty minutes or more stirring and seeing that the rice is cooked perfectly. Most restaurants can't afford to have a person preparing risotto to order. Often restaurants use a lesser-quality rice and precook it, so that it can be reheated and finished when ordered. It ends up becoming just another rice dish.

If the stock is made from clams, for example, a few cooked clams can be added at the end. If the stock is made from wild mushrooms, cooked wild mushrooms can be added. However, these ingredients should be stirred in for a contrast in texture and to highlight the flavor of the rice. Risotto should not be garnished with layers of embellishments such as clam shells, lemon slices, or sliced mushrooms. It should never be floating in stock either, as we are seeing in trendy restaurants now.

The Big Problem

There are two big problems with risotto. The first is determining when the rice is cooked. Arborio rice is cooked when the last bit of raw starch in the middle of the rice kernel is cooked through and the simmering rice appears creamy. The cook needs to keep tasting the rice; when the risotto is done, quickly turn off the heat and add butter and cheese to stop the cooking. Cover the pot and let it rest for a few minutes to allow the flavors to meld.

The other big problem cooks encounter with risotto is making sure the guests are sitting and are ready to eat it. To do this, it is important to have them eat a first course. What if they are in the dining room, and you have to stir the rice for twenty minutes in the kitchen? In this case, you can have people standing around with you in the kitchen, enjoying a glass of wine, but then you must hand them a warm plate and instruct them to go right to the table and start eating. Everyone loves risotto; it is definitely worth waiting for!

How to Make Risotto Without a Recipe

Perhaps you have some leftovers such as cooked vegetables or sausages in your refrigerator. Choose a combination of ingredients that go well together; two ingredients are fine. Figure out how to get the flavor of those ingredients into the stock and the rice.

Let's say you have decided on risotto with peas and prosciutto. First, heat up a quantity of stock at least twice the volume of the rice. Adding peas or prosciutto to the stock really won't add much flavor. First fry little pieces of prosciutto (to match the size of the rice), in butter or oil before cooking the onions. This way the flavor will get into the cooking fat. Remove the prosciutto from the pan and cook the onions in the butter or oil, adding garlic if you would like its flavor. Stir in the rice and start adding ladlefuls of heated stock. When the risotto is done (each grain of rice is swollen with liquid and is still firm yet cooked through), stir in the cooked prosciutto and the peas with butter and cheese to stop the cooking. Cover and let the rice rest for a few minutes. Serve immediately on warm plates.

Remember, cooking takes practice; you may have to practice a few times to learn when to stop the cooking of the risotto. You can tell when the cooking has gone too far when each grain of rice splits open and releases its liquid. In this case, the rice kernels look like dog bones.

Toasted Pastini
with Artichokes and Hazelnuts

A few years ago, when risotto became popular, many restaurant chefs started experimenting with other grains (and even pasta) that resembled the expensive Arborio rice to find an easier and less expensive substitute. Even though this fad has disappeared, everyone still loves this dish, which uses tiny pasta instead of rice. Artichokes and hazelnuts have a special affinity for each other, but you may prefer to use other combinations such as cooked shrimp and peas or smoked salmon and asparagus.

1 pound pearl pasta, pastini, or orzo
2 medium-size fresh artichokes, trimmed
  (see page 58)
Coarse salt
1 large shallot, finely chopped
3 tablespoons butter
1 tablespoon Pernod or Chartreuse
  (optional)
2 cups chicken or vegetable stock
3 ounces hazelnuts, skinned, toasted, and
  coarsely chopped (see page 93)
⅓ cup freshly grated Parmesan
Freshly ground black pepper

To toast the pastini, put it in a dry frying pan over medium-high heat and toss until lightly browned.

To prepare the artichokes, bring a saucepan of water to a boil over high heat. Cut the artichoke bottoms into ¼-inch dice. Add ½ teaspoon salt to the water and drop in the diced artichoke. Cook the artichokes until they are tender when tasted, about 6 minutes. Drain.

To cook the pasta, put the shallot with a tablespoon of the butter and a sprinkling of salt in a large saucepan over medium-high heat. Cook, stirring, until the shallot is soft, about 5 minutes. Stir in the Pernod and cook another minute to evaporate the alcohol. Mix in the toasted pastini with the stock and 2 cups water, bring to a boil, and simmer until the pasta is tender when tasted, about 6 minutes. Drain any excess liquid from the pasta into a glass measuring cup. Return the pasta to the pot and add the artichokes, hazelnuts, Parmesan, and remaining 2 tablespoons butter with salt and pepper to taste. If the pasta becomes dry before serving, add some of the pasta-cooking liquid. Serve on warm plates.

MAKES 6 SERVINGS

Garganelle
with Asparagus and Morels

Two great harbingers of spring are tender green asparagus and earthy morels. Fortunately for us they go really well together, especially in this dish of pasta with a creamy sauce. If you have no source of fresh morels, you can substitute shiitakes. Dried morels would not work as well in this dish because of their rubbery texture. The truth is that garganelle with asparagus only would be delicious too, as long as it is served with good Parmesan.

½ pound asparagus, trimmed and cut at an
    angle into 1-inch lengths
Coarse salt
3 ounces fresh morels or shiitake
    mushrooms
Vinegar
1 large shallot, finely chopped
2 tablespoons olive oil
1 tablespoon brandy or Madeira
½ cup heavy cream
Freshly ground black pepper
2 cups chicken stock
2 tablespoons butter
1 pound dried garganelle or penne
½ cup freshly grated Parmesan cheese

To cook the asparagus, bring a large pan of water to a boil. Toss in the asparagus and a teaspoon of salt. Boil the asparagus until it is tender when pierced with a fork, 6 to 8 minutes. Drain the asparagus and run it under cold water to stop the cooking.

To prepare the morels, put them in a bowl and cover with cold water. Add a dash of vinegar and let them soak for 10 minutes. Drain the mushrooms, cut off the coarse stems, and cut the morels into ¼-inch-wide slices.

To cook the morels, put the shallot with a sprinkling of salt and the olive oil in a frying pan or sauté over medium-high heat. Cook, stirring from time to time, until the shallot is soft, about 3 minutes. Toss in the morels and continue cooking until the morels are half wilted. Add the brandy and cook for 1 to 2 minutes to evaporate the alcohol. Add the cream and cook, stirring, for another 3 to 4 minutes to thicken the sauce. Season with salt and pepper and transfer the mixture to a bowl to stop cooking.

To make the sauce, put the stock in a small saucepan over high heat and boil until reduced by half, about 10 minutes. Add the butter with salt and pepper to taste.

To cook the pasta, fill a pasta pot or other large pot with water and bring to a boil over high heat. Stir in a tablespoon of salt and the pasta. Return to a boil and cook, stirring from time to time, until the pasta is al dente; in other words, until the pasta is cooked through but is still firm when bitten, about 8 minutes. Drain most of the cooking liquid from the pasta and return it to the pot with the heat turned off. Quickly toss in the asparagus, the morels, the sauce, and the cheese. Add salt and pepper to taste. Serve immediately in warmed bowls with lots of liquid.   SERVES 4

When buying asparagus, look for closed tips, without little seeds showing. The asparagus should be all the same size and green in color all the way to the ends. Otherwise you are paying for thick, white stems, which are inedible. Asparagus has been picked long ago when the ends are dried out and lines appear along the length of the spears.

❧

Although some cooks like to take each asparagus spear in hand and break it where it goes from tender to tough, I recommend lining them up and cutting them cleanly with a knife.

❧

Asparagus should be peeled if it's thick. To do this, lay the asparagus on its side and run a vegetable peeler from the tip to the end, starting at each of the pointed leaves. This allows the asparagus to cook evenly.

❧

When buying morels, choose fresh morels that are firm, not shrunken or slippery.

❧

Although in general you shouldn't soak fresh or wild mushrooms, you always need to soak morels in water with a dash of vinegar to get any bugs that live in the crevices to come out.

❧

A good trick is to pour some of the pasta water into a large measuring cup when draining the pasta. This can be added to the pasta if it dries out before serving.

Orecchiette with Butternut Squash and Red Russian Kale

This wonderful winter pasta takes only a few minutes to prepare and cooks in one pot. These healthful vegetables taste great with pasta and soft pecorino, an Italian sheep's milk cheese. If you don't have a cheese store that sells soft pecorino, it's worth ordering it from a quality mail-order gourmet store such as Dean & DeLuca in New York.

2 cups rich chicken or vegetable stock
1 pound peeled and seeded butternut squash or other winter squash (4 cups), cut in ½-inch dice
Coarse salt
½ pound red Russian kale leaves or other bitter greens (4 cups), cut crosswise in 1-inch pieces
1 pound dried orecchiette or penne pasta
2 tablespoons butter
4 ounces soft pecorino, grated
Freshly ground black pepper

To make the sauce, put the stock in a small saucepan over high heat and boil until reduced by half, about 10 minutes.

To cook the butternut squash, fill a pasta pot or other large pot with water and bring to a boil over high heat. Toss in the squash with a tablespoon of salt and continue boiling until the squash is just tender when pierced with a fork, about 5 minutes. Remove the squash to a colander with a slotted spoon. (If you work quickly, it is not necessary to refresh the squash under cold water.)

To cook the kale, toss it into the same water and boil rapidly over high heat until it has wilted, about 3 minutes. Remove the kale to the colander with the slotted spoon.

To cook the pasta, you may need to add water to the vegetable cooking liquid before bringing it to a boil again. Toss in the pasta, stirring with a wooden fork to separate. Return the pasta to a boil and cook, stirring from time to time, until the pasta is al dente when tasted; in other words, until the pasta is cooked through but is still firm when tasted, about 8 minutes. Drain most of the cooking liquid from the pasta and return the pasta to the pot with the heat turned off. Quickly add the vegetables, the stock, butter, and half the pecorino with salt and pepper to taste. Serve immediately in warmed bowls or plates, sprinkled with the remaining pecorino.

SERVES 4

When cutting leaves of vegetables such as kale or Swiss chard, it's best to line up the washed leaves and cut across them, using the stems as a handle. When all the leaves are cut, discard the stems.

Penne with Swiss Chard and Toasted Bread Crumbs

For several years I took groups of Tante Marie students to study cooking in the hills of Chianti with Lorenza de' Medici. It was she who first taught me that not all pasta dishes have to be served with grated Parmesan. Here the topping of toasted bread crumbs makes a terrific contrast to the peppery pasta and Swiss chard. Buon appetito!

7 tablespoons olive oil
1 cup fresh bread crumbs
Coarse salt
1 pound green Swiss chard, leaves and stems cut crosswise in 1-inch pieces (8 cups)
1 pound dried penne
6 garlic cloves, minced
½ teaspoon red pepper flakes
6 to 8 flat anchovy fillets
Freshly ground black pepper

To make the bread crumb topping, heat 3 tablespoons of the olive oil in a medium sauté or frying pan over medium-high heat. Toss in the bread crumbs and continue stirring or tossing until they are golden brown. Transfer to a paper towel and sprinkle with salt.

To cook the Swiss chard and pasta, fill a pasta pot or other large pot with water and bring to a boil over high heat. Add a tablespoon of salt and stir in the Swiss chard and pasta. Cook, stirring from time to time, until the pasta is al dente; in other words, until the pasta is cooked through but is still firm when tasted, about 8 minutes.

To make the sauce, put the garlic, red pepper flakes, anchovy fillets, and 3 tablespoons of the olive oil in a small frying pan over medium-high heat and cook, stirring, until the garlic is barely colored and the anchovies have dissolved.

Drain the pasta and chard, reserving some of the cooking water. Return the pasta and chard to the pot, toss it with the garlic-anchovy sauce, another tablespoon extra-virgin olive oil and salt and pepper to taste. Serve on warmed plates, sprinkled generously with the toasted bread crumbs.

SERVES 4

To make fresh bread crumbs, put 5 slices white bread, each broken into 4 or 5 pieces, in a food processor and process for 10 minutes until the bread crumbs are very fine. If the bread is very fresh, you may have to put the crumbs through a sieve to make them finer. You can use any bread, with or without crusts, except sourdough bread, which has too strong a flavor.

At Tante Marie's we store bread crumbs in the freezer so that we always have some on hand.

If you use red Swiss chard in this recipe, the whole dish will turn an unappealing color of pink.

Penne with Roasted Eggplant, Tomatoes, and Smoked Mozzarella

This is a simple, easy to prepare dish that's best served before grilled chicken or meat or as a vegetarian main course with good cheese and a green salad. Think eggplant or mushrooms when preparing a vegetarian meal, because both have the texture of meat and adapt well to a variety of dishes.

5 tablespoons olive oil

4 Asian or 1 large eggplant, trimmed but unpeeled, and cut into ½-inch cubes

Coarse salt

Freshly ground black pepper

1 large red onion, chopped

2 garlic cloves, minced

⅛ teaspoon red pepper flakes

6 red, ripe tomatoes, peeled, seeded, and chopped, or one 28-ounce can Italian plum tomatoes, coarsely chopped

1 tablespoon tomato paste

1 pound dried penne or other short tubular pasta

1 cup freshly grated Parmesan

4 ounces smoked mozzarella, cut in ¼-inch cubes

3 tablespoons minced fresh Italian parsley

To cook the eggplant, heat 3 tablespoons of the olive oil in a medium-size sauté pan until very hot. Toss in the eggplant and season generously with salt and pepper. Cook, while stirring over very high heat, until the eggplant looks lightly colored and slightly crispy, about 10 minutes.

To make the sauce, put the onion with another 2 tablespoons of the olive oil and ½ teaspoon salt in a medium-size sauté or frying pan over medium-high heat. Cook, stirring from time to time, until the onion is soft, about 5 minutes. Stir in the garlic and red pepper flakes and cook another minute. Add the tomatoes and tomato paste and continue cooking for 5 minutes to meld the flavors. Stir in the eggplant. Add salt and pepper to taste. (The eggplant sauce can be made ahead and kept in the refrigerator for up to a week.)

To cook the pasta, fill a pasta pot or other large pot with water and bring to a boil over high heat. Add a tablespoon of salt and stir in the pasta. Cook, stirring from time to time, until the pasta is al dente; in other words, until the pasta is cooked through but is still firm when tasted, about 8 minutes.

While the pasta is cooking, gently reheat the sauce, stirring. Drain most of the cooking liquid from the pasta and return the pasta to the pot with the heat turned off. Quickly toss in the pasta with the sauce, smoked mozzarella, half the Parmesan, and the parsley. Add salt and pepper to taste. Serve immediately on warmed plates sprinkled with the remaining Parmesan.

SERVES 6 AS A FIRST COURSE OR 4 AS A MAIN COURSE

To cut the eggplant, trim both ends, cut the eggplant lengthwise into ½-inch-wide slices, stack the slices on a board or counter, and cut into ½-inch-wide strips. Turn these and cut in the opposite direction. This is called dicing.

Fettuccine with Smoked Salmon and Asparagus

Don't make this fettuccine for an Italian—it's definitely not traditional! The sauce is light—reduced stock with a little butter; and it has lots of vegetables and fish compared with the amount of pasta. But do make this for a simple supper at home—it's delicious and easily adaptable to other combinations of ingredients. A light and lively modern pasta for today's lifestyle.

½ pound fresh asparagus, trimmed and cut on the diagonal into 1-inch lengths
Coarse salt
3 cups chicken or vegetable stock
2 tablespoons butter
1 pound fresh fettuccine
½ pound smoked salmon, broken or cut into 1 by ½-inch pieces
1 tablespoon lemon juice and zest of 1 lemon
2 tablespoons extra-virgin olive oil
Freshly ground black pepper

To cook the asparagus, bring a large saucepan of water to a boil. Add ½ teaspoon salt and drop in the asparagus. Cook until it is tender when pierced with a fork, 6 to 8 minutes. Drain and run under cold running water to stop the cooking. Set aside.

To make the sauce, heat the stock in a small saucepan over medium-high heat. Simmer until it is reduced by half, about 10 minutes. Add the butter and turn off the heat.

To cook the pasta, fill a pasta pot or other large pot with water and bring to a boil over high heat. Add a tablespoon of salt and stir in the pasta. Cook, stirring from time to time, until the pasta is al dente; in other words, until the pasta is cooked through but is still firm when tasted, about 2 minutes. Drain most of the cooking liquid from the pasta and return the pasta to the pot with the heat turned off. Quickly add the sauce, asparagus, smoked salmon, lemon juice and zest, olive oil, and salt and pepper to taste. Serve immediately in warmed bowls with plenty of sauce.

SERVES 4

For this recipe it is perfectly acceptable to use store-bought hot- or cold-smoked salmon. See page 379 for how to smoke your own salmon.

Pappardelle with Wild Mushrooms and Truffle Oil

Wild mushrooms cooked with brandy, cream, and herbs deserve soft home-made pasta. If you make your own pasta for this dish, you can cut the noodles the same width as the mushrooms to make a very appealing pre-sentation. You can also buy sheets of fresh pasta and cut wide noodles as well. This pasta would be wonderful followed by a main course of chicken, pork, or beef.

1 ounce dried porcini (cèpe) mushrooms
2 cups chicken or vegetable stock
1 tablespoon butter
1 tablespoon olive oil
Coarse salt
Freshly ground black pepper
1 large shallot, finely chopped
1 pound fresh wild mushrooms, such as shiitakes, or chanterelles, sliced
2 tablespoons brandy
¼ cup heavy cream
2 tablespoons minced fresh herbs, such as thyme, parsley, chives, and/or tarragon
1 pound fresh pappardelle or tagliatelle
Truffle oil (optional)

To reconstitute the dried mushrooms, put them in a measuring cup, barely cover with hot water, and let stand for 20 minutes.

To reduce the stock, put it into a small saucepan over high heat and boil until it has reduced by half, about 10 minutes. Add the butter and oil with salt and pepper to taste.

To make the mushroom sauce, cook the shallot with a sprinkling of salt in a medium-size sauté pan over medium-high heat, stirring from time to time, until it is soft, about 5 minutes. Remove the reconstituted mushrooms from their liquid and finely chop. Reserve the liquid. Stir the chopped mushrooms into the shallot.

Toss in the sliced wild mushrooms and cook until they are half wilted, about 5 minutes. Add the brandy and cook for a minute more. Add the cream, reduced stock, mushroom liquor, and herbs, and cook for 2 minutes. (Be careful not to overcook the mushroom mixture or the mushrooms will shrink too much.) Add salt and pepper to taste.

To cook the pasta, fill a pasta pot or other large pot with water and bring to a boil over high heat. Add a tablespoon of salt and stir in the pasta. Cook, stirring from time to time, until the pasta is al dente, cooked through but still firm when tasted, about 2 minutes. Drain the cooking liquid from the pasta and return the pasta to the pot with the heat turned off. Quickly add the wild mushroom sauce with salt and pepper to taste. Serve immediately on warmed plates drizzled with truffle oil.

SERVES 6 AS A FIRST COURSE

Most mushrooms sold as wild mushrooms are not really foraged in the wild. They are grown domestically. That is why there is an attempt by some marketers to rename them exotic mushrooms.

Spaghetti with Pesto, Potatoes, and Green Beans

Fresh pasta with a sauce of garlic, basil, Parmesan, and olive oil is well loved by all. Here is my interpretation of Viana La Place's idea to add new potatoes and green beans to this classic dish. Viana writes so splendidly about Italian food.

2 garlic cloves, crushed
⅓ cup pine nuts
½ cup freshly grated Parmesan cut into
   ½-inch chunks
3 cups basil leaves
½ cup extra-virgin olive oil
½ pound small red potatoes
½ pound small green beans, trimmed
1 pound fresh spaghetti or fettuccine
Coarse salt
Freshly ground black pepper

To make the pesto, combine the garlic, pine nuts, cheese, and half the basil in a food processor. With the processor running, pour in the olive oil and run until the mixture is smooth. Add the rest of the basil and pulse on and off until the mixture has the consistency of a rough sauce. Put this pesto in a small bowl or jar and cover with a thin layer of olive oil.

To cook the potatoes, put them in a saucepan with ½ teaspoon salt. Cover generously with cold water and bring to a boil over high heat. Cook the potatoes until they are tender when pierced with a fork, about 25 minutes. Drain well in a colander and shake to allow any excess moisture to escape. When cool enough to handle, remove the skins and slice the potatoes into ¼-inch-wide slices.

To cook the beans, bring another medium-size saucepan of water to a boil. Drop in the beans with ½ teaspoon salt and boil them until they are tender when pierced with a fork, about 8 minutes. Drain the beans in a colander.

To cook the pasta, fill a pasta pot or other large pot with water and bring to a boil over high heat. Add a tablespoon of salt and stir in the pasta. Cook until the pasta is al dente; in other words, cooked through but still firm when tasted, about 2 minutes. Drain most of the cooking liquid from the pasta, reserving a cup of it in a glass measuring cup. Return the pasta to the pot with the heat turned off. Stir in half the pesto, the potatoes, green beans, and pasta-cooking liquid. Add salt and pepper to taste. Serve immediately on warmed plates. (You can put a teaspoon of pesto to the top of each plate of pasta and save the rest for another day.)

SERVES 6 AS A FIRST COURSE
OR 4 AS A MAIN COURSE

Pesto needs to be covered with olive oil or it will quickly turn black when exposed to air. It keeps well for weeks in the freezer.

Linguine
with Roasted Peppers
and Sausage

Roasting red, yellow, and orange peppers brings out their flavor. This vibrant sauce of peppers and sausage could be served on creamy polenta, with sautéed new potatoes, on thick slices of grilled country bread, or as a sauce for pasta as here. This is a great supper dish.

2 red bell peppers

2 yellow and/or orange bell peppers

1 pound pork sausages, store-bought or
    homemade (page 382)

½ cup dry white wine

1 large red onion, chopped

4 tablespoons olive oil

Coarse salt

3 garlic cloves, minced

1½ pounds large red, ripe tomatoes, peeled,
    seeded, and chopped, or one 14-ounce
    can Italian plum tomatoes, coarsely
    chopped

¼ teaspoon red pepper flakes

3 tablespoons minced fresh Italian parsley

1 tablespoon minced fresh marjoram or
    oregano

¾ cup freshly grated Parmesan

1 pound dried linguine, tagliatelle, or
    spaghetti

Freshly ground black pepper

To roast the peppers, stand each pepper on end and make four cuts down the pepper, leaving the seeds and ribs. Place the peppers skin side up on a roasting pan, put under the broiler, and roast until the peppers are literally black. Using tongs, put the blackened peppers in a brown paper bag, plastic bag, or bowl covered with plastic wrap for 5 minutes to steam. With your fingers remove the black skins from the peppers, pile three or four pieces of pepper on a board, and cut them lengthwise into ¼-inch strips.

To cook the sausages, prick each sausage two or three times with a fork and put in a medium-size sauté pan or frying pan with ¼ inch water to help render the fat. Brown the sausages over medium heat on all sides until they are cooked through but not shrunken, about 15 minutes. Remove the sausages. Immediately pour off any excess fat and deglaze the pan with white wine.

To make the sauce, add the onion, oil, and ½ teaspoon salt to the pan and put over medium-high heat. Cook the onion, stirring from time to time, until soft, about 5 minutes. Stir in the garlic and cook another minute. Add the tomatoes, the red pepper flakes, and the herbs, and cook another 5 minutes. Cut the sausages into ½-inch rounds. Stir in the roasted peppers, sausages, and herbs. Add salt and pepper to taste.

To cook the pasta, fill a pasta pot or other large pot with water and bring to a boil over high heat. Add a tablespoon of salt and stir in the pasta. Return the pasta to a boil and cook, stirring from time to time, until the pasta is al dente when tasted; in other words, until the pasta is cooked through but is still firm when tasted, about 8 minutes. Drain most of the cooking liquid from the pasta and return the pasta to the pot with the heat turned off. Quickly stir in half the sauce. Add salt and pepper to taste. Serve immediately on warmed plates. Spoon over the remaining sauce and sprinkle with ¼ cup of the cheese. Serve the rest of the cheese separately.

SERVES 4

It is always best to grate Parmesan within 30 minutes of serving or cooking. Freshly grated Parmesan tastes much better than Parmesan purchased already grated.

Recipes always call for cooking the onions before adding the garlic because garlic burns easily. Burned garlic ruins the taste of a dish.

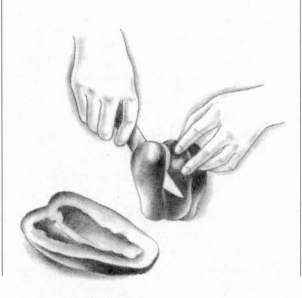

Fettuccine with Spring Vegetables
(Pasta Primavera)

*A*lthough pasta primavera is served every-where now, it was a sensation when it was first served at Le Cirque in New York in the '70s. Here a sauce of cream is combined with a variety of spring vegetables and basil to make what was then considered a modern pasta dish. This can be a spectacular dish, well worth the extra effort to prepare. Of course, you can make this pasta with fewer kinds of vegetables and it will still taste great.

Coarse salt
1 medium-size zucchini, trimmed and
   sliced into ¼-inch rounds
½ small bunch broccoli, trimmed and cut
   into ½-inch florets
⅓ pound snow peas, trimmed
6 stalks asparagus, trimmed and sliced on
   the diagonal into 1-inch lengths
½ pound fresh peas, shelled
2 tablespoons olive oil
10 medium-size fresh mushrooms, trimmed
   and sliced into ¼-inch-long slices
Freshly ground black pepper
½ cup pine nuts, lightly toasted
12 cherry tomatoes, stemmed and halved
2 garlic cloves, minced
1 pound fresh fettuccine
4 tablespoons (½ stick) butter
½ cup freshly grated Parmesan
1½ cups heavy cream
½ cup fresh basil leaves, cut in chiffonade

To cook the vegetables, fill a large pot with water and bring to a boil over high heat. Add a tablespoon of salt and cook each kind of vegetable separately in the following order: zucchini, broccoli, snow peas, asparagus, and peas. When each vegetable is tender when pierced with a fork, remove it with a slotted spoon, put it in a colander, and hold under cold running water to stop the cooking. As each vegetable is finished, put it in a large sauté pan off the stove. After cooking the peas, strain and discard the water.

To cook the mushrooms, put a tablespoon of the olive oil in a small frying pan over medium-high heat. Toss in the mushrooms and cook, stirring or tossing, until they are half wilted. Season with salt and pepper and add them along with the toasted pine nuts to the sauté pan with the other vegetables.

Put the garlic with the remaining tablespoon of olive oil in another small sauté pan over medium heat and cook for a minute. Add the tomatoes and cook, stirring, until they begin to soften, about 2 minutes. Remove from the heat. (The recipe can be made ahead up to this point.)

To cook the pasta, fill a pasta pot or other large pot with water and bring to a boil over high heat. Add a tablespoon of salt and stir in the pasta. Return the water to a boil and cook, stirring from time to time, until the pasta is al dente, cooked through but still firm when tasted, about 2 minutes.

Meanwhile, gently heat the large sauté pan of vegetables and the small pan of tomatoes.

Drain the cooked pasta. Return the pot to the stove and add the butter, Parmesan, and cream. Heat over medium-low heat to melt the butter. Quickly toss in the drained pasta, stirring to coat. Toss the pasta with about one-third of the warmed vegetables, the basil, and salt and pepper to taste. Serve the pasta on warmed plates. Top with the remaining vegetables and cherry tomatoes.

SERVES 6

Whenever a recipe calls for a lot of cream, you can usually substitute chicken stock for part of the cream.

Fettuccine with Seafood (Mussels, Shrimp, and Scallops)

Imagine homemade or store-bought fresh pasta in a flavorful tomato sauce with fresh "fruits from the sea"—mussels, shrimp, and scallops. What could be better! The trick to making a delicious sauce is to add the juices from the cooked seafood to the fresh tomato sauce. All you need to complete the meal is a green salad and a bottle of Italian light red wine.

1½ pounds mussels, scrubbed
1 large shallot, finely chopped
¾ cup dry white wine
3 tablespoons olive oil
1 pound sea scallops, trimmed and halved if large
1 pound large shrimp, peeled
Coarse salt
Freshly ground black pepper
4 large shallots, chopped
2 teaspoons flour
½ cup dry white wine
6 large red, ripe tomatoes, peeled, seeded, and chopped; or one 28-ounce can Italian plum tomatoes, coarsely chopped
1 tablespoon tomato paste
1 pound fresh spaghetti or tagliatelle
1 tablespoon minced fresh Italian parsley

To steam the mussels, put them with the finely chopped shallot and ¾ cup white wine in a small saucepan over high heat. Cover the pan and steam the mussels, shaking from time to time, until the mussels open. Turn off the heat and keep covered.

To prepare the seafood sauce, put 2 tablespoons olive oil in a medium-size sauté pan over medium-high heat. Season the scallops and shrimp with salt and pepper. When the oil is hot, carefully place the scallops in one layer and cook until they are just opaque. Remove and continue the process with the rest of the scallops and shrimp. When all the seafood has been sautéed, add 1 tablespoon olive oil, ½ teaspoon salt, and the 4 large chopped shallots. Cook, stirring, over medium-high heat until the shallots are soft, about 5 minutes. Off the heat, sprinkle the flour into the mixture and return to the heat, stirring until the flour thickens. Add the ½ cup white wine and cook over high heat for 2 to 3 minutes to allow the alcohol to evaporate. Stir in the tomatoes, tomato paste, and mussel-cooking liquid, except for the last tablespoon, which may contain sand. Bring the sauce to a boil, stirring constantly, and

simmer gently for 5 minutes. Add salt and pepper to taste. (The recipe can be made ahead to this point.)

To cook the pasta, fill a pasta pot or other large pot with water and bring to a boil over high heat. Add a tablespoon of salt and stir in the pasta. Return the pasta to a boil and cook, stirring from time to time, until the pasta is cooked through when tasted, about 2 minutes. Drain most of the cooking liquid from the pasta and return the pasta to the pot with the heat turned off.

Meanwhile, reheat the tomato sauce, stir in the cooked scallops, shrimp, mussels in their shells, and parsley. Add salt and pepper to taste. Stir in half the tomato sauce and seafood and toss to coat the pasta. Serve the pasta on warmed plates and top with the remaining seafood. (I do not recommend serving this dish with grated Parmesan.)

SERVES 4

Mezzaluna of Winter Squash with Brown Butter and Sage

A joy of autumn is the abundance and variety of winter squash in the farmers' markets and it's fun to try new and different ones. Pumpkins are a well-known variety of winter squash. Although pumpkins can be absolutely delicious, most in this country are grown for Halloween. When a recipe calls for cooked pumpkin, I recommend substituting another winter squash unless you know the pumpkins are grown for taste rather than decoration. In this recipe the brown butter, sage, and Parmesan offset the sweetness of the winter squash. Although you can buy fresh pasta for many recipes, it's much better to make your own for this impressive pasta course!

> *3 pounds butternut, Kabocha, Preservation, Hubbard, or banana squash; or pumpkin*
> *¼ pound (1 stick) butter, softened*
> *1½ cups freshly grated Parmesan*
> *Coarse salt*
> *Freshly ground black pepper*
> *1½ pounds fresh pasta (see page 383 for how to make)*
> *30 sage leaves*
> *¼ cup olive or vegetable oil*

To cook the winter squash, trim and halve the squash and remove the seeds with a metal spoon. Place the squash halves cut side down on a lightly oiled baking sheet and bake in a 350-degree oven until the flesh is soft, about 45 minutes. When cool enough to handle, remove the skin with a knife and puree the squash in a food processor until smooth. Put the pureed squash in a bowl with 4 table-spoons of butter, ½ cup of the Parmesan, and salt and pepper to taste. The filling should be well seasoned because it will be enclosed in dough.

To make the mezzaluna, lay a length (about 5 inches wide and 24 inches long) of freshly made dough on a board. Using a 3-inch cutter, cut rounds of dough. Fill each with a spoonful of the squash mixture. Fold the dough in half to make half-moon shapes. Press the edges firmly together.

Let the mezzaluna dry on a well-floured wooden board for 15 minutes, then turn over and dry on the other side for 15 minutes more. They are now ready to cook and can be transferred to a baking sheet lined with a floured tea towel for cooking later in the day. Or they can be frozen.

Make the sauce just before cooking the pasta. Heat the remaining 4 tablespoons but-ter in a medium-size frying pan until it turns chestnut brown. Immediately drop in the clean, dry sage leaves. The mixture will bub-ble up, but don't worry. Add a sprinkling of salt.

To cook the pasta, fill a pasta pot or other large pot with water and bring to a boil over high heat. Add a tablespoon of salt and care-fully drop in the filled pasta. Return the water to just below a boil and cook, stirring only to separate the mezzaluna, until they float or you can easily pierce one with your

fingernail. Drain the mezzaluna and spoon quickly onto warmed plates. Spoon the sage brown butter generously over the pasta, put-ting sage leaves in every serving.

SERVES 8

Cappellacci of Herb Ricotta, Soft Egg, and Parmesan

This very special pasta appeals to a lover of eggs, butter, and cheese! Because they're so rich, only one ravioli is served to each person. When the diner cuts into the ravioli with a fork, the soft egg yolk mixes with the melted butter and freshly grated Parmesan to make a splendid sauce for the ricotta-filled pasta.

1 cup ricotta
1 cup freshly grated Parmesan
¼ cup minced fresh Italian parsley
Coarse salt
Freshly ground black pepper
1 pound freshly made pasta sheets
* (see page 383)*
8 eggs
½ pound (2 sticks) melted butter

To make the filling, combine the ricotta, half the Parmesan, and the parsley in a bowl with salt and pepper to taste.

To make the cappellacci, lay a length (about 5 inches wide and 24 inches long) of freshly made pasta on a board. Using your

fingers, make very thin rings of the ricotta mixture right on the dough about 1½ inches across in the center and at 4-inch intervals.

Gently break each egg into your hand, saving or discarding the white, and place each yolk in the center of each ring of ricotta. Cover with another length of freshly made pasta about the same size. Carefully press the top dough onto the lower dough by cupping your hands around the filling and pressing any air bubbles out through the edges. With a 4-inch fluted ring cutter, cut out each egg-filled ravioli and lay it on a floured wooden counter or board. Let the ravioli dry for 15 minutes, turn over, and dry on the other side for another 15 minutes. They are now ready to cook but can be transferred to a baking sheet lined with a floured tea towel for cooking later in the day.

To cook the pasta, fill a pasta pot or other large pot with water and bring to a boil over high heat. Add a tablespoon of salt and carefully drop in the large rounds of filled pasta. Return the water to just below a boil and cook, stirring very gently. Cook the ravioli until they float or you can easily pierce one with your fingernail, about 2 minutes. With a flat slotted spoon or sieve remove each ravioli, one at a time, blot on a towel, and place in the middle of a warmed plate. Sprinkle generously with Parmesan and spoon over plenty of melted butter. SERVES 8

The sheets of fresh pasta should adhere to each other. If they get dry, you can brush a little water around each ring of ricotta. The important thing is not to have any air bubbles or the ravioli will open when cooked in the water.

Parmesan is a hard grating cheese made from the curd of cow's milk after the milk has been broken down into curds and whey. Parmesan usually ages for at least fourteen months. When made in the old-fashioned manner, ricotta is a fresh cheese made by reboiling the whey to get more curds. This fresh cheese is high in protein.

Risotto with Spring Vegetables
(Risotto Primavera)

When making risotto with spring vegetables, it is important to use the best Parmesan you can find because the vegetables have very little flavor to add to the stock as in other kinds of risotto. This risotto primavera makes a simple, light supper served with salad and cheese.

> 6 ounces green beans, cut into ½-inch lengths
> 8 asparagus spears, trimmed and cut at an angle into ½-inch lengths
> 1 medium-size zucchini, cut into ¼-inch dice, each with some of the green skin
> 1 small onion, finely chopped
> ¼ cup olive oil
> Coarse salt
> 1 garlic clove, minced
> 1½ cups Arborio rice
> ½ cup dry white wine
> 6 cups chicken or vegetable stock, heated
> ½ medium-size red bell pepper, peeled, seeded, and cut into ¼-inch dice
> 2 tablespoons butter
> ½ cup freshly grated Parmesan

To precook the vegetables, bring a saucepan of water to a boil and add a tablespoon of salt. Drop in the green beans and cook them until they are tender when pierced with a fork, about 6 minutes. Remove them with a slotted spoon into a strainer and run under cold water until cool. Do the same with the asparagus, cooking for about 7 minutes. Do the same with the zucchini, cooking for about 30 seconds.

To make the risotto, put the onion with ½ teaspoon salt and the olive oil in a saucepan over medium-high heat. Cook, stirring, until the onion is soft, about 5 minutes. Stir in the garlic and cook for another minute. Stir in the rice and coat with the onion mixture. Pour in the wine and cook for another minute. Begin adding the stock, a ladleful at a time, while continuing to stir over medium-high heat. When the liquid is absorbed, stir in another ladleful of stock. Continue doing this until the rice appears creamy and the grains of rice have no uncooked starch inside when tasted. Without hesitation stir in the cooked vegetables with the bell pepper, butter, and Parmesan and cover the rice for a couple of minutes. Serve on warm plates to waiting guests.

SERVES 6

Most people allow all the liquid to be absorbed by the rice before they add more stock. This is not necessary. The constant stirring helps the rice to absorb the stock evenly. Once the rice has swollen with stock, stop the cooking by adding the butter and cheese. It is better to do this earlier rather than later. If you wait too long, the rice will split open and lose some of the liquid.

Inexperienced cooks like to taste and stir seasoning into the finished risotto. This is a mistake because cooked rice will break up when stirred.

Seafood Risotto (with Clams, Shrimp, and Scallops)

The idea of risotto is to add flavorful stock by the ladleful to rice coated with onion and butter. That is why you want to get the flavor of seafood into the stock. This seafood risotto is the ultimate luxury; however, it can easily be made with just clams or shrimp, or any combination of seafood.

*3 pounds clams, scrubbed
4 tablespoons (½ stick) butter
½ pound uncooked small shrimp, peeled
½ pound bay scallops, rinsed
Coarse salt
Freshly ground black pepper
1 small onion, chopped
1 small bulb fennel, finely chopped
2 garlic cloves, minced
1½ cups Arborio rice
½ cup dry white wine
3 cups fish or chicken stock
¼ cup fresh Italian parsley, minced*

To steam the clams, put them in a heavy saucepan with an inch of water. Cover tightly and place over high heat. Steam the clams, shaking once or twice, until they open, about 6 minutes. If one or two clams don't open, discard them. Remove the clams from their shells and keep covered in a bowl.

To cook the shellfish, heat 2 tablespoons of the butter in a large sauté pan over medium heat. Season the shrimp and scallops well on both sides with salt and pepper, place them in one layer in the pan, and cook until the seafood becomes opaque on the bottom. Turn and cook on the other side. Place the cooked shellfish in a dish and repeat with the remaining shellfish. When all the shellfish is cooked, add a tablespoon of butter to the pan with the onion and the fennel. Cook, stirring from time to time, until the vegetables are soft, about 5 minutes. Stir in the garlic and continue cooking another minute. Stir in the rice and cook 2 more minutes. (The recipe can be made ahead up to this point.)

Twenty minutes before serving, return the pan of rice to medium-high heat. Add the wine and cook, stirring for a minute. Add all but the last tablespoon of the clam cooking liquid to the heated stock. Ladle in 1½ cups of the stock. Slowly stir the risotto until most of the liquid is absorbed. Add another ladleful of stock and continue stirring, adding stock and stirring until the rice appears creamy and is not crunchy when tasted. When that point is reached, remove the risotto from the heat and quickly stir in the clams, scallops, and the remaining tablespoon of butter with salt and pepper to taste. Cover and let rest for 5 minutes. Serve on warm plates to waiting guests.

SERVES 6

If you see a black vein down the back of a shrimp, you should devein it. To do this, simply cut down the back of the shell right through the vein with a pair of scissors and hold the shrimp under running water.

Always check scallops and remove any hard attachment called the "foot." It can be added to fish stock or discarded.

Chopped fennel adds a slight anise flavor to this seafood risotto. If you don't have a source for fennel, you can leave it out.

Whenever the amount of stock looks low, add boiling water if you are afraid you don't have enough stock.

The method described here should be followed for all risotto recipes. The idea is that the fat grains of Arborio rice absorb the flavored stock to make a creamy mixture. The stock must be hot so that the cooking of the rice remains constant, and the rice must be eaten immediately so that it doesn't become gummy.

Sweet Potato Risotto with Arugula and Fresh Mozzarella

What are commonly sold as yams are dark-skinned tubers with orange flesh. You will love this orange-colored risotto with bitter greens and soft white cheese.

4 tablespoons butter
1 medium-size onion, finely chopped
Coarse salt
1 garlic clove, finely minced
1½ cups Arborio rice
1 yam or sweet potato, peeled and cut in
   ¼-inch dice
2 quarts chicken or vegetable stock, heated
1 cup fresh mozzarella, cut into ¼-inch dice
2 cups arugula leaves cut in chiffonade
½ cup freshly grated Parmesan
Freshly ground black pepper

To make the risotto, put 2 tablespoons of the butter, the onion, and ½ teaspoon salt in a medium-size saucepan over medium heat and cook, stirring constantly, until the onion is soft, about 5 minutes. Add the garlic and cook for another minute. Stir in the rice and the diced yam. (The recipe can be prepared ahead up to this point.)

Twenty minutes before serving, return the pan of rice to medium-high heat. Ladle in 1½ cups of the hot stock. Slowly stir until most of the liquid is absorbed. Add another ladleful of stock, and continue stirring, adding stock and stirring until the rice

appears creamy and the grains of rice have no uncooked starch on the inside when tasted. When that point is reached, remove from the heat and quickly stir in the mozzarella, arugula, Parmesan, and the remaining 2 tablespoons butter, with salt and pepper to taste. Cover and let rest for 5 minutes. Serve on warmed plates.   SERVES 6

The best way to peel a potato, sweet potato, or yam is to use long strokes the length of the tuber with a vegetable peeler after taking off the skin at the ends. Some cooks prefer removing the skins with knives rather than a peeler.

Yams and sweet potatoes both add sweetness to a dish, but unlike winter squashes, the yams dissolve quickly when cooking to melt into the dish.

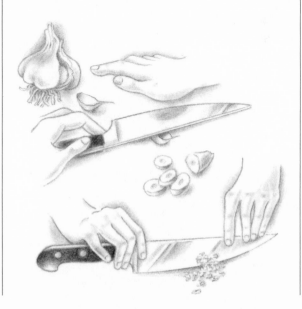

Wild Mushroom Risotto with Hazelnuts

If you keep dried mushrooms, Arborio rice, hazelnuts, and canned stock in your cupboard and a wedge of Parmesan cheese in your refrigerator, you can make this comforting dish without making a special trip to the grocery store. Always use freshly grated Parmesan.

1 ounce dried porcini (cèpe) mushrooms

1 ounce fresh hazelnuts, skinned and toasted (see page 93)

3 cups chicken or vegetable stock

1 large onion, finely chopped

Coarse salt

4 tablespoons (½ stick) butter

1 garlic clove, minced

1 cup Arborio rice

½ cup dry white wine

½ cup freshly grated Parmesan

3 tablespoons chopped chives (or the green part of scallions)

To reconstitute the porcini, put them in a measuring cup and barely cover with hot water. Let them soak for 20 minutes.

To remove the skins from the hazelnuts, place them on a baking sheet in a 350-degree oven for 10 minutes. Remove the pan of nuts from the oven and rub all the nuts with a towel. To toast the nuts, return the nuts to the baking pan in the oven and toast for another 7 to 8 minutes. Coarsely chop the hazelnuts.

To make the stock, remove the mushrooms from the soaking liquid and finely chop them. Pour all but the last tablespoon of liquid into a large saucepan with the chicken stock and heat over medium-high heat.

To make the risotto, put the onion with ½ teaspoon salt and 2 tablespoons of the butter in a medium-size saucepan over medium-high heat. Cook, stirring, until the onion is soft, about 5 minutes. Stir in the garlic and cook for another minute. Stir in the rice to coat with the onion mixture. Stir in the reconstituted mushrooms. Pour in the wine and cook for another minute. Begin to ladle 1½ cups of the stock, slowly stirring the risotto until most of the liquid is absorbed. Add another ladleful of stock and continue stirring, adding stock and stirring until the rice appears creamy and is not crunchy when tasted. When this point is reached, remove the risotto from the heat and quickly stir in the hazelnuts with the remaining 2 tablespoons butter, the Parmesan, and the chives.

SERVES 4

If you prefer to make this dish ahead, try making a wild mushroom pilaf instead of risotto. To do this, cook short- or long-grain rice in onions with garlic, add the chopped mushrooms, the rice, and the mushroom-flavored stock in the ratio of 1 part rice to 2 parts liquid. Cover and simmer over low heat until the liquid is absorbed by the rice, about 25 minutes. This pilaf will hold 30 minutes before serving.

FISH AND SHELLFISH

Fish

Anybody can put salt and pepper on a lamb chop or a steak and grill it over charcoal, and it will taste delicious. But it takes a real understanding of cooking methods as well as kinds of sauces to make fish taste good. This is because most fish, except for fresh salmon and tuna, simply doesn't taste good by itself. Fish is generally referred to as delicate in flavor. Fish needs to be cooked properly and sauced well to be made appealing. Both salmon and tuna have more of a meat texture and a stronger taste, which is why they are sometimes eaten raw, as in carpaccio or tartare.

Fish can be categorized into two groups: roundfish, such as salmon, cod, and sea bass, whose eyes are on either side of the head; and flatfish, such as halibut and sole, whose eyes seem to be on the same side of the head. Actually, flatfish are born with eyes on either side of the head, but because they live on the bottom of the sea, one eye soon rotates so that it is looking upward, while the mouth seems to work sideways.

Cooks also sometimes categorize fish as saltwater or freshwater fish. The difference isn't terribly important except when making a fisherman's stew, where it's better to use one or the other, not a mixture.

The salmon is a fascinating fish because it is usually born in fresh water and migrates to the sea. Atlantic salmon migrate back upstream to lay their eggs perhaps as many as five times in a lifetime; Pacific salmon usually migrate once when three years old, lay their eggs, then die.

How to Buy Fish

What you want to do when you buy fish is look the fishmonger right in the eye and ask, "What is your freshest fish?" He will look away and say, "All our fish is fresh." At which point you want to let him (or her) know that you are serious; you want to know which fish came in that day. That is the fish you want to buy! It doesn't matter whether the recipe calls for sea bass and you use halibut or the recipe calls for salmon and you use sea bass—the important thing is to buy the freshest fish you can buy and then take it home and put it on ice until you cook it. (Put the fish in the package it came in on a rack over ice in a baking pan in the refrigerator. That way if the ice melts, the fish won't soak in the water.)

If you have the opportunity to buy whole fish, the eyes should look alert; sunken eyes tell you the fish is old. The gills should be pink or red, not dark and muddy looking. When you press the fish, you should not see the impression of your finger—the flesh should be resilient. And, as Escoffier is reputed to have said, the fish should smell like the ocean, the lake, or the river it came from. Be wary when the head has been taken off the fish, or the gills removed, or the fish looks damaged. More and more often, fishermen are catching fish by hook and line rather than in nets and cleaning and chilling them on board, rather than dumping them in the hold. Fish that is cleaned and flash-frozen on the boats can be of superior quality. It is important that you can trust the fishmonger to sell you the highest-quality fish in order to alleviate any fears of contamination.

HOW TO COOK FISH

All fish is naturally tender, which means that it will usually cook in a matter of minutes. There is no need for long, slow cooking as there is with tougher cuts of meat, or for hours of marinating. However, care must be taken that fish doesn't dry out when cooking.

Basically, all fish cooks in the same amount of time no matter what method of cooking is used. A good rule of thumb when cooking fish is to start testing for doneness after 8 to 10 minutes per inch, measured at the thickest width, not length.

When fish is uncooked, it appears translucent and does not pull apart easily when prodded with a fork. When fish is cooked, it appears opaque and flakes easily when prodded with a fork. Uncooked fish is soft to the touch. Cooked fish is firm to the touch. You can serve both salmon and tuna undercooked if it is good-quality fish; the amount of doneness is up to you. If pink or white bubbles appear on the surface of the fish, it is totally overcooked. Cooked fish will keep for 3 days in the refrigerator.

POACHING

Poaching is often the first consideration when thinking about how to cook fish. Paupiettes of Sole with Shrimp Sauce (page 163) is an example of poaching in a small amount of liquid. Cold Poached Salmon with Sauce Verte (page 166) is an example of poaching in a large amount of liquid. In this case, the poaching liquid, called court bouillon, is too acidic to turn into a sauce. Concentrated fish stock is called fumet and can be made into a sauce.

When being roasted or baked, fish needs to be protected by its skin, as in Roasted Whole Fish with Brown Butter Vinaigrette (page 156), or have a protective covering, as in Halibut Baked with Warm Shallot Compote (page 157). When being grilled or broiled, fish must be very fresh and slightly undercooked so that it doesn't dry out. Grilled Salmon and Thai Salsa with Basmati Rice (page 171) is an example of grilling. Fish can be marinated 30 minutes before grilling or broiling in a coating of olive oil with salt or pepper or other flavorings. Be careful not to use lemon or lime in marinades because it will start to cook the fish.

Cooking fish in a small amount of fat keeps the fish moist and flavorful, as in Fillet of Salmon with Summer Vegetables and Citrus Oil (page 159). Deep-frying, if done properly, cooks fish at such a high heat that it seals in the natural juices, as in Classic Fish and Chips (page 162).

In fishing communities, fish stews are a universal use for small or broken-up fish. See Pacific Coast Bouillabaisse (page 97).

Fish cooked in parchment or pastry stays moist, as it cooks in its own juices. Fish and scallops are the only protein foods that can be cooked by marination. When they are left to soak in lemon and/or lime juice for four or more hours, they will appear opaque, as if they have been cooked. Seviche is a common example of this. In South America, cooked fish is marinated and may be stored in a vinegar mixture called escabeche.

Fish can also be cured and served with a sauce, as in gravlax, or cured and smoked, as in smoked salmon. Any fish sprinkled with aquavit or vodka, coarse salt, sugar, and perhaps dill and wrapped in foil in the refrigerator for a few days is called gravad. Gravad salmon has come to be called gravlax. Salmon cured in a wet brine for a couple of days and then smoked in a cold smoker will appear translucent—in other words, cold smoked salmon. Salmon cured and smoked in a hot smoker will appear opaque, as in hot smoked salmon.

HOW TO SAUCE FISH

After deciding how to cook the fish, the cook has to figure out what sauce to make. Delicate methods of cooking fish such as poaching and steaming or cooking in pastry or parchment call for a delicate sauce such as beurre blanc, a fish velouté, or a fish reduction sauce. These sauces are often made with fish stock, a liquid made from fish bones.

Methods of cooking such as roasting or grilling call for stronger-tasting sauces such as aïoli, compound butter, warm vinaigrette, or salsa. In a braise or stew, the seafood makes its own sauce.

The Big Problem

The big problem with cooking fish is that there are so many kinds of fish to choose from in the market. Remember that all kinds of fish can be cooked by all methods, and fish never needs to cook for very long. Disregard what a recipe calls for and cook whatever fish is the freshest.

How to Cook Fish Without a Recipe

Put enough butter in a frying pan to generously coat the bottom and place the pan over moderately high heat. When the pan is hot enough that the bubbles subside, dip the fish in flour seasoned with plenty of salt and pepper, lay it in the pan, and cook until it is golden on the bottom. Turn the fish carefully with a metal spatula and cook on the other side until the fish feels firm when pressed with your finger. Remove the fish, place on a warm plate, and squeeze lots of fresh lemon juice over it. Add water to the pan to dissolve the essence of fish left on the bottom, add flavorings like minced parsley, and pour the pan juices over the fish—Voilà! Fillet of sole à la meunière! Seasoning the fish, testing with your finger to see whether it is done, and deglazing the pan to make a simple sauce are all you need to remember when cooking fish. (If the fish is more than ½ inch thick, you may need to cover the pan for a few minutes so that the fish cooks evenly.)

Shellfish

Whereas all finfish, whether round or flat, freshwater or saltwater, can be cooked by the same methods, shellfish are different one from the other. The two categories of shellfish are crustaceans and mollusks. Examples of crustaceans are lobsters, crabs, and shrimp. Examples of mollusks include clams, oysters, and mussels, and cephalopods such as squid and octopus.

HOW TO BUY SHELLFISH

In all cases, shellfish should be purchased as fresh as possible and kept well chilled (preferably over ice) until cooked.

Since lobsters do not eat again after being taken from the ocean, it is best to purchase and cook them close to where they are harvested. If you have the opportunity to buy live lobsters, they should be very lively and flapping their tails.

Live crabs should also be cooked close to the source. Because crabs begin to deteriorate as soon as they come out of the water, they are often boiled where the boats come in. Crabs cooked as soon as they come out of the water are much better than crab that has been held in a tank for any length of time.

Although shrimp (sometimes called prawns in California) can be caught in the wild, many of them are now farmed. When purchasing shrimp, look for those that are firm and white.

Oysters, clams, and mussels should be bought live and should hold themselves closed when pinched. Otherwise, they should be discarded. They should also smell fresh. Do not soak clams or mussels in water or they will die.

Because scallops never hold themselves closed, they are often removed from their shells at sea. The larger ones are called sea scallops, and the smaller ones are called bay scallops. When a restaurant refers to scallops as being "day boat scallops," that means that the scallops are brought in by nets but not necessarily frozen. "Diver scallops" means divers have harvested them from the bottom of the sea.

When shopping, look for scallops and squid that are moist and fresh smelling. The bottom of the display pan should be without liquid. The liquid indicates that they have been frozen and thawed.

How to Cook Shellfish

Oysters, clams, and sometimes very fresh scallops are often eaten raw with a squeeze of lemon. A typical sauce for oysters is mignonette sauce: chopped shallots, wine vinegar, and black pepper.

When cooking clams for Seafood Risotto (page 147) or mussels for Fettuccine with Seafood (page 142), remember that clams should always be steamed open in water, and mussels in white wine with shallots.

Since scallops are very delicate, great care needs to be taken that they do not overcook. That is why Scallops in Beurre Blanc with Julienne of Carrots and Zucchini (page 66) is a great way to cook them.

Shrimp can be stir-fried and deep-fried, among other ways. They are cooked when they turn pink and overcooked when they curl up.

The best way to cook lobsters is to cut them up while they're still alive, baste them with melted butter, and grill them over a charcoal fire. To cut them up, use a large chef's knife to sever the backbone where the tail meets the carapace. Quickly turn the lobster over and cut it right down the middle of the underside through the head. (You can be assured it died quickly.)

Dungeness crab is so sweet and delicate, I can think of no better way to serve it than in its shell, cracked, of course, with the sauce of your choice. I like to flavor a mayonnaise with ketchup, relish, tomato, and Tabasco or make a vinaigrette of oil and vinegar bound by a little of the crab butter, the rich yellow part from inside the shell.

There are many ways to cook fresh squid (calamari). Squid is interesting to cook because it can be deep-fried in thirty seconds or stewed for forty minutes. This is because it goes from tender to tough very quickly and needs long cooking to be tenderized again.

The Big Problem with Shellfish

The big problem with shellfish is freshness. It is essential that you find a reliable purveyor of fresh shellfish. As with fin fish, shellfish should smell fresh and taste sweet, and it is important that you keep it as cold as possible until it is to be eaten or cooked.

How to Cook Shellfish Without a Recipe

Since each kind of shellfish is cooked differently, as described above, here is how to cook shrimp without a recipe. Remove the shells, and the veins if they are dark. Heat a frying pan with a generous layer of butter and oil and toss the shrimp in all at once. Stir or toss until they are just pink through and remove them to a warm serving platter. Add minced garlic and white wine to the pan. Let the mixture boil up, add salt and pepper to taste, and pour the liquid over the shrimp. This is called shrimp cooked in the manner of scampi.

Roasted Whole Fish with Brown Butter Vinaigrette

Traci Des Jardins, the brilliant chef of Jardinière in San Francisco, taught the students of Tante Marie's how to make this brown butter vinaigrette. The trick is to make it at the last moment. Try this sauce on poached eggs or sautéed chicken breasts as well as fish. This fish would go well with roasted new potatoes.

Two 1-pound whole fish, such as trout
6 tablespoons olive oil
Coarse salt
Freshly ground black pepper
4 tablespoons (½ stick) butter
2 tablespoons good-quality balsamic vinegar
3 tablespoons capers, rinsed
4 scallions, equal parts white and green,
    thinly sliced at an angle
2 tablespoons minced fresh Italian parsley

To roast the fish, remove any fins from the fish with scissors and rub the fish generously with 4 tablespoons of the olive oil. Season the fish well with salt and pepper. Place the fish in a small roasting pan and roast on the bottom rack of a 450-degree oven until it's firm to the touch or flakes easily when prodded with a fork, 10 to 15 minutes.

To make the vinaigrette, put the butter in a small saucepan over moderately high heat. The butter will melt and then begin to brown. When it is a deep chestnut color, remove the pan from the heat and let stand for a minute. Stir in the vinegar, capers, and scallions with the remaining 2 tablespoons of olive oil. Immediately pour the sauce over the fish, sprinkle with minced parsley, and serve.

SERVES 2

When cooking whole fish, make sure there is absolutely no blood down the inside of the backbone because it turns very bitter when cooked. The blood must be washed out with running water prior to cooking.

To eat a whole trout, cut down the center of one side of the fish from the gills to the tail. With the knife or fork pull the fish away above the cut from the bones. Do the same with the flesh below the cut. The exposed frame of the fish can then be lifted, again with the knife and the fork, from the tail to the head and put on a plate to be discarded. This is how waiters used to serve whole fish at tableside in fancy restaurants in the old days.

Halibut Baked
with Warm Shallot Compote

*I*n this recipe, halibut is baked in the oven
and smothered in a warm compote of shallots, red bell peppers, and black olives flavored
with sherry vinegar. An alternative would be to
substitute preserved lemons and green olives for
the bell pepper and black olives. This recipe is a
favorite of the students at Tante Marie's. Whenever you can add some of the cooking liquid
from the fish, chicken, or meat to the sauce—it
makes the dish!

½ cup olive oil
2 large onions, chopped
2 large shallots, coarsely chopped,
    plus 1 shallot, finely chopped
Coarse salt
1 large garlic clove, minced
4 tablespoons sherry vinegar
1 large tomato, peeled, seeded, and chopped
½ red bell pepper, diced
1½ teaspoons minced fresh thyme
1 tablespoon minced fresh Italian parsley
6 Kalamata olives, pitted and chopped
Six 4-ounce pieces of Alaskan halibut,
    about 1 inch thick
Freshly ground pepper
½ cup dry white wine
1 cup fish stock (or ½ cup bottled clam juice
    and ½ cup water)

To make the compote, heat 2 tablespoons of
the olive oil with the onions, coarsely
chopped shallots, and ½ teaspoon salt in a
medium-size frying or sauté pan over
medium-high heat. Cook, stirring from time
to time, until the onions are soft. Add the
garlic and continue cooking another minute.
Stir in the vinegar and tomato and cook 5
more minutes. Stir in the bell pepper and
remaining 6 tablespoons olive oil and cook
another 5 minutes. Add the thyme, parsley,
and olives. Remove from the heat and cover
to keep warm.

To prepare the fish, scatter the finely
chopped shallot on the bottom of a buttered
glass baking dish. Season both sides of the
fish with salt and pepper and place the fish in
the baking dish. Pour the wine and fish stock
around the fish. Cover the fillets with a piece
of buttered parchment paper, buttered side
down, and bake in the middle of a 350-
degree oven until the fish is firm to the touch
and flakes easily when prodded with a fork,
10 to 15 minutes.

Transfer the fish to warmed dinner plates.
Quickly pour about ½ cup cooking liquid
from the baking dish into the compote.
Cook the compote, stirring, for 2 to 3 minutes. Add salt and pepper to taste. Spoon the
compote generously over each piece of fish
and serve.   SERVES 6

*The technique for chopping shallots is the same
as it is for onions. (See page 43.)*

Grilled Sea Bass with a Choice of Sauces

*G*rilling can add a lot of flavor to fresh fish. Here is a choice of sauces that will complement the fish. Grilled vegetables and roasted new potatoes would go well with any kind of grilled fish, as would chilled white wine.

Six 4-ounce fillets of sea bass or
    other white fish, about 1 inch thick
Olive oil
Coarse salt
Freshly ground black pepper

FOR THE BASIL BUTTER
8 tablespoons (1 stick) butter, softened
½ cup basil, in chiffonade
Coarse salt
Freshly ground black pepper

FOR THE AÏOLI
2 large garlic cloves
½ teaspoon coarse salt
1 egg yolk, at room temperature
1 cup olive and/or other vegetable oil

FOR THE SALSA VERDE
1 large shallot, minced
2 tablespoons capers, rinsed
2 anchovy fillets
4 tablespoons fresh Italian parsley,
    minced
2 tablespoons sherry vinegar
½ cup olive oil
Coarse salt
Freshly ground black pepper

FOR THE ROASTED TOMATO
    VINAIGRETTE
6 red cherry tomatoes
Coarse salt
2 teaspoons good-quality balsamic vinegar
½ cup olive oil
Freshly ground black pepper

To prepare the fish, remove any bones, cut into uniform shapes, coat with olive oil, and season with salt and pepper. Refrigerate until ready to cook.

To make the basil butter, pound the butter in a bowl with a wooden spoon until soft. Stir in the basil with salt and pepper to taste. Let the mixture sit at room temperature until ready to use.

To make the aïoli, mash the garlic with the salt in a small bowl with a spoon and beat in the egg yolk. Whisk in the oil drop by drop at first until it begins to emulsify, which means it begins to look creamy. Keep adding oil and whisking until all the oil has been absorbed. If the mixture gets too thick, add a tablespoon of warm water. Season well with salt and pepper.

To make the salsa verde, combine the shallot, capers, anchovies, parsley, and vinegar in the container of a food processor or blender. With the machine running, pour in the olive oil. Do not continue to run the machine after all the oil has been incorporated. Transfer to a bowl and season with salt and pepper to taste.

To make the roasted tomato vinaigrette, cut the tomatoes in half, squeeze out the seeds, sprinkle with salt, and place the halves cut side up in a lightly oiled baking pan in a

300-degree oven for an hour. The tomatoes should be slightly wilted and dried out. Put them in the container of a food processor or blender and with the machine running, pour in the vinegar and olive oil in a thin, steady stream. Stop the machine when the oil has been incorporated. Transfer to a bowl and season with salt and pepper.

To grill the fish, bring a charcoal fire to the point where the coals are white. With an old cloth, oil the grill. It should be about 4 inches from the coals. Lay the fish over the grill, leaving about an inch between each piece. When about ½ inch of the edges of the fish are opaque, with a sharp motion use a metal spatula to turn the fish over. The fish is cooked through when it is firm to the touch. Serve immediately on a warm platter or warmed dinner plates, topped with a tablespoon of one of the sauces.   SERVES 6

It is important to remember that a food processor will liquefy everything in it when you run the machine too long. That is why it's not good to use it as a mixer. It is always better to transfer the processed food to a bowl and mix in the flavorings with a spoon.

Fillet of Salmon with Summer Vegetables and Citrus Oil

*W*hat better way to usher in the wild salmon season than to gently cook it and serve it with a confetti of colorful vegetables and warm citrus oil. This presentation requires some last-minute arranging as in a restaurant kitchen, but the final results are well worth the effort. The citrus oil can be made ahead and stored in the refrigerator. Any leftover oil can be served with other fish or even pan-steamed chicken breasts.

1½ cups extra-virgin olive oil
1 orange
2 lemons
1 lime
Coarse salt
2 bunches (about 20 ounces) fresh spinach, stems removed
1 ear yellow corn, kernels removed
1 medium-size zucchini, cut into ¼-inch dice, each with some green skin
Half pint red cherry tomatoes, halved
Freshly ground black pepper
Six 4-ounce pieces of salmon fillet, about ½ inch thick

To make the citrus oil, heat the oil in a small saucepan over low heat until the oil is barely warm to the touch. Meanwhile, use a vegetable peeler to remove the zest from the orange, lemons, and lime in long, thin strips, taking care not to remove any of the white

pith. Make a horizontal pile of the citrus strips and, using a sharp knife, cut crosswise into tiny slivers. Add the slivers to the warm oil along with a sprinkling of salt.

To cook the spinach, bring a large saucepan of water to a boil over high heat. Add ½ teaspoon salt and the spinach and cook for 2 to 3 minutes, until the spinach is half wilted. Remove the spinach with tongs and place in six equal portions on a baking sheet lined with paper towels. (This can be done ahead and the spinach reheated in a warm oven at the last minute.)

To cook the other vegetables, put a tablespoon of the citrus oil in a medium-size frying pan over medium-high heat. Stir in the corn, zucchini, and tomatoes with salt and pepper to taste. Cook until the vegetables are warmed through, about 3 minutes.

To cook the salmon, place a tablespoon of the citrus oil in a wide nonstick frying pan over medium-high heat. Add the fish, light side down. Cook very gently over low heat so the fish does not brown. To ensure that the fish cooks evenly, cover it with a lid that is smaller than the pan so the top of the fish will steam. When the edges of the fish are opaque, carefully turn the pieces over with a spatula. To tell whether the fish is cooked, press it with your finger. It is slightly resilient for medium-rare and firm to the touch for fully cooked.

Meanwhile, place the entire pan with the spinach and paper towels in a 300-degree oven for a few minutes to reheat. Gently reheat the citrus oil and vegetables. Place a mound of spinach in the middle of each of six warmed dinner plates and top with a piece of fish, dark side down. Surround with vegetables and spoon a generous amount of citrus oil and zest over each plate.

SERVES 6

Always wash citrus well with soap and water before grating.

Citrus rind is made up of the zest, with the oils, and the pith, which can turn bitter when heated. When you remove the zest with a vegetable peeler and cut it into thin slivers, this is called julienne of zest. When a recipe calls for zesting a citrus, it usually means to grate it on a fine grater or remove the zest with a utensil called a zester. Either way, you want to avoid getting too much pith.

Because salmon is farmed all over the world, there is now a year-round supply of farmed Atlantic salmon. The wild Pacific salmon (king salmon) season starts mid-April and runs until the middle of October. Wild salmon is leaner and firmer than farmed salmon and has more flavor.

Having all the components of a dish ready before cooking the fish is typical of what is called cooking "à la minute" in restaurants; in other words, cooking to order.

All fish fillets have a light side and a dark side. It is always more attractive to serve the light side up.

Pan-Fried Fish with Ginger, Lime, and Cilantro Sauce

Garlic, ginger, and lime are a typical combination in Thai cooking. Here you add chile and cilantro to give this fish recipe some zip. Serve this pepper-crusted fish with rice and zucchini for a simple supper.

1 tablespoon mixed whole peppercorns, crushed
2 tablespoons flour
Coarse salt
Two 4-ounce pieces of fillet of white fish, such as cod or sea bass
4 tablespoons vegetable oil
1 garlic clove, minced
1 tablespoon grated fresh ginger
1 teaspoon minced jalapeño
Juice of 1 lime
1 tablespoon Thai fish sauce
Pinch of sugar
½ cup fresh cilantro leaves, chopped

To prepare the fish, mix together the peppercorns and flour with a sprinkling of salt on a plate. Remove any skin and bones from the fish. Dredge the fish in the peppercorn mixture. Heat 2 tablespoons of the oil over medium-high heat in a nonstick pan large enough to hold the fish. Place the fish in the pan and cook until the edges of the fish have an opaque rim of about an inch. Turn the fish and cook on the other side until the fish is firm to the touch. Remove the fish and keep

warm. Into the pan, put the garlic, ginger, and jalapeño and cook for a minute, stirring. Add the lime juice, the remaining 2 tablespoons oil, and the fish sauce with the sugar. Add enough water to make a sauce for the fish. Stir in the cilantro and serve over the fish.   SERVES 2

If you can't find mixed peppercorns, you can make your own by mixing together equal amounts of white peppercorns, black peppercorns, and whole allspice.

Serrano chiles are a fine substitute for jalapeños. The difference is that you chop serranos whole and discard the seeds and ribs of jalapeños.

Classic Fish and Chips

F ish and chips are a tradition in England. They used to be cooked in rendered animal fat, wrapped in newspaper, and eaten with a stick. Today, a healthier vegetable oil is used. A fish-and-chips party is a great idea—serve baskets of fish and chips lined with newspaper and plenty of lager or ale for a fun party!

1 cup self-rising flour
Salt
1 tablespoon malt vinegar
One 12-ounce bottle cold beer
Vegetable oil for deep-frying
2 pounds Russet potatoes, peeled and cut
    into ½ by 4-inch sticks
½ cup flour
Freshly ground black pepper
2 pounds fillet of fresh white fish, such as
    cod or haddock

To make the batter, sift the flour and salt into a bowl. Stir in the vinegar. Gradually whisk in the beer until a thick batter forms. Let the batter rest in the refrigerator for 20 minutes before using.

To cook the potatoes the first time, heat the oil in a deep-fryer or wok until a thermometer indicates an oil temperature of 300 degrees. Drop in the potatoes in batches and cook for 3 minutes. (They should not color.) Remove them with a slotted spoon, let the oil from the spoon drop back into the fryer, then drain on paper towels.

To fry the fish, put the ½ cup flour on a plate. Season with salt and pepper. Heat the oil until the thermometer reaches 350 degrees, or until a piece of bread dropped into the oil bounces around and begins to fry. Take the fish by the tail end, dredge it in seasoned flour, and shake off the excess. Dip each piece into the batter, completely coating the fish. Carefully place the batter-coated fish into the oil and fry until the fish is cooked through, 4 to 5 minutes, depending on its size. Remove from the oil and place on paper towels to cool for 3 to 4 minutes before serving.

To fry the potatoes a second time, heat the oil to 350 degrees. Drop the potatoes in in batches and cook until browned, 4 to 5 minutes. Drain on paper towels. Serve the fish and chips in baskets lined with newspaper and, over that, waxed paper, sprinkle with salt, and serve malt vinegar.

SERVES 6

Although it is acceptable to cook chips (French fries) only once, the best kind are cooked twice: the first frying, at a lower temperature, is done to cook the chips through; the second frying, at a higher temperature, is done to crisp and brown the chips.

Paupiettes of Sole with Shrimp Sauce

This dish of sole with shrimp sauce is an example of an old style of coating the fish with the sauce. In the old days fillet of sole à la Normande meant several kinds of seafood from the Normandy coast. Now it has come to mean sole with shrimp. You can roll halves of fillet of sole to make paupiettes, or make triangles of each piece of sole by folding it in half with the dark side on the inside. Either way, the fish is coated with a beautiful velvety seafood-flavored sauce. Serve with boiled new potatoes or rice pilaf.

4 tablespoons (½ stick) butter
¼ cup flour
3¾ cups fish stock, heated, plus more if needed
2 shallots, finely chopped
Six 8-ounce fillets of sole
Coarse salt
Freshly ground black pepper
¾ cup white wine
1 tablespoon tomato paste
¼ cup heavy cream
1¼ pounds cooked baby shrimp

To make the velouté sauce, in a medium-size saucepan melt the butter over medium-high heat until it is bubbly. Take the pan off the heat and sprinkle in the flour, pressing it down with the back of a wooden spoon. Return the pan to the heat and cook this flour and butter mixture (roux) until it appears greasy. Off the heat, whisk in a cup of the fish stock. Return to the heat and whisk until the sauce is smooth and then whisk in another cup of the stock. Bring the sauce to a boil, stirring, turn down the heat, and simmer gently for 30 minutes, adding more stock if necessary to keep a sauce consistency. From time to time skim and discard the impurities that rise to the top. (If the sauce is made ahead, be sure to cover it with waxed paper or plastic wrap pressed right down on top of the sauce to prevent a skin from forming.)

To prepare the fish, lightly butter a glass baking dish and sprinkle it with the shallots. Lay the fish on a board and season both sides with salt and pepper. Turn the fish dark side up and cut each piece lengthwise in half. Starting at the thick end of each half, roll each half into a roll, tucking the thin edge underneath while standing it up in the prepared baking dish. When all the fish have been rolled into "paupiettes," surround the fish with the wine and ¾ cup fish stock. Cover the fish with a piece of buttered parchment and bake on the top rack of a 350-degree oven until the fish flakes easily when prodded with a fork, 10 to 15 minutes, depending on the size of the paupiettes.

Transfer the cooked fish to a warmed serving platter and keep warm. Strain half the juices into the saucepan of velouté sauce. Bring to a boil, stirring, then lower the heat and simmer until the desired consistency is reached. Add the tomato paste and cream with salt and pepper to taste. Stir in the cooked baby shrimp with a spoon, not a whisk, or you will have chopped baby shrimp. Spoon the shrimp sauce over the paupiettes and serve. SERVES 4

A traditional mother sauce called velouté can always be made in this manner: the roux is cooked and warm stock is whisked in to make a smooth sauce. It is important to add the flour to the butter and the stock to the roux off the heat. The sauce can be simmered up to 1½ hours, with more stock being added when necessary. When flavorings and/or cream are added toward the end of the cooking, the velouté becomes a "little" (petite) sauce.

When a recipe calls for dry white wine, you can always use a French white Burgundy, Chablis, or California Chardonnay with very little oak. For red wine, you can use a red Burgundy, Côte du Rhône, or California Pinot Noir. At Tante Marie's we use Mâcon-Village (Louis Jadot) and Côte du Rhône (E. Guigal). These wines need not be expensive but should be drinkable. For cooking fish, I recommend a very-high-acid, undrinkable white wine, like an Entre-Deux-Mer. Just as lemon brings out the flavor in fish, so does a wine that's high in acid.

How to Deep-Fry

THE BEST METHOD of deep-frying is to use the same pot every time—a deep black frying pan or a wok is ideal. Fill the pot two-thirds full of vegetable oil and place the pot over moderately high heat with the handle turned away from the front of the stove. There should be no pots of boiling water around the oil, and the hot oil should not be moved until it has cooled. The oil gets very hot and will explode if any water drops into it. When it gets really hot it will ignite without even boiling. In other words, be careful!

To tell whether the oil is hot enough for deep-frying, drop in a small piece of bread. If the oil is at 350 degrees, the bread will jump around and begin to cook. At this point slide six or so pieces of food carefully into the oil. It is better to put the food in all at once and take it out all at once rather than trying to figure out which was the first to go in. With a dry metal strainer-type spoon, lift the food and move it around so that it cooks evenly. If it seems to be cooking quickly, add more pieces to the oil. If the food is not cooking quickly, don't add additional pieces. When deep-frying, your temperature control is the amount of food you put in the oil. You can also regulate the temperature with the stove knob. It takes practice to get great results when deep-frying. To tell whether the food is cooked through, cut into one of the first pieces. The color of the batter doesn't tell you whether the food is cooked through; rather, it indicates how hot the oil is. When you lift the food from the oil, be sure to hold the spoon over the oil so that the excess oil drops back into the pan. Transfer the deep-fried food to paper towels without piling the pieces on top of one another. Remember that deep-fried food needs to be served within 15 minutes of cooking.

Unless the deep-frying oil has been used for cooking fish, it can be stored in the refrigerator and reused three or four times. You can tell that the oil has been used too much and needs to be discarded when it bubbles up and doesn't seem to cook the food. Be sure to put all the food in the oil in one batch, let it cook, take it all out at the same time, drain it on paper towels, and let the oil heat up again before cooking the next batch.

Cold Poached Salmon with Sauce Verte

A whole poached salmon with sauce verte may be old-fashioned, but it is still very appealing, especially as part of a cold buffet for a large number of guests. The skin and bones help to keep the fish from falling apart when it is cooking. The sauce verte is a "petite sauce" in the mayonnaise family of sauces.

1 whole salmon (8 to 12 pounds)
2 cups dry white wine
½ cup white wine vinegar
2 bay leaves
½ onion, sliced
1 celery stalk, coarsely chopped
4 sprigs Italian parsley
2 sprigs thyme

FOR THE SAUCE VERTE
8 spinach leaves
¼ cup watercress leaves
¼ cup Italian parsley leaves
2 tablespoons tarragon leaves
1 large shallot, minced
2 cups mayonnaise, preferably homemade (page 112)
Coarse salt
Freshly ground black pepper

1 English cucumber

To prepare the fish, trim off the fins with kitchen scissors and cut the tail to about 1 inch long. With the scissors, dock the tail two or three times to resemble the larger tail.

Make sure to remove all the blood from inside the backbone of the fish.

To make the poaching liquid (court bouillon), put the wine, vinegar, bay leaves, onion, celery, parsley, and thyme in a pan large enough to hold the whole fish. Add a couple of cups of water and bring to a boil on top of the stove. Reduce the heat and simmer for 5 minutes.

Meanwhile, measure the thickness of the fish (not the length of the fish) upward from the counter to the highest point, usually 2½ to 3 inches. Lower the fish into the poaching liquid, add enough water to cover, reduce the heat so that the liquid is barely moving, and let the salmon cook gently for 8 to 10 minutes an inch. Remove the fish from the liquid, and lay it on a counter or a board. With a small sharp knife slit the skin along the top ridge of the fish, around the collar (where the gills were), and along the tail. While the fish is still warm, remove the skin. Gently turn the fish over onto a serving platter and remove the skin from the other side. Before doing this, cut a decorative edge around the collar and the tail so that the skin doesn't tear unattractively.

To make the sauce, blanch the spinach, watercress, parsley, and tarragon in boiling salted water for one minute. Drain and puree in a food processor. Add the puree with the shallot to the mayonnaise. Add salt and pepper to taste.

To decorate the fish, cut the cucumber on a mandoline or with a knife into very thin slices. Spread a thin layer of the sauce verte over the salmon. Place overlapping rows of cucumber over the sauce from back to front to resemble the scales of the fish. (If the fish is to be kept over 4 hours, or overnight, these cucumber scales need to be coated with aspic.)

To serve the fish, cut into the fish with a sharp knife and remove pieces about 2 inches by 3 inches off the bone with a metal spatula or spoon. Do this along the top of the fish, from the head to the tail. With two spoons, lift the tail and the bones off the underside of the fish up to the head and discard. Now you can serve the bottom side of the fish in the same way. The sauce verte should be served separately.   SERVES 16

Although it is fashionable to serve salmon raw or rare, it is important that it be cooked through, or opaque, for this presentation so that the fish comes easily off the bone. If it is over-cooked, it will fall apart and have a metallic taste.

Salmon in Parchment with Beurre Blanc

Salmon in parchment is an old favorite of the students at Tante Marie's. These little packages of fresh fish and vegetables can be made ahead and cooked at the last minute and are perfect for any number of guests, from two people to thirty. You can serve them right in the packages with or without sauce. Be sure to show everyone how to cut into the package and eat right out of the parchment. Otherwise, they will sit and look at it, waiting for guidance, or unwrap it and toss the paper into the middle of the table!

Coarse salt
2 asparagus spears, cut in 1-inch lengths on the diagonal
2 medium-size carrots, sliced in 2-inch length and trimmed to resemble baby carrots
2 tablespoons butter
2 large shallots, finely chopped
Four 4-ounce pieces salmon fillets, about 1-inch thick
¼ cup dry white wine
Freshly ground white pepper
2 round slices lemon, halved
4 sprigs fresh herbs, such as dill or tarragon
1 zucchini, cut into ¼-inch rounds
8 cherry tomatoes, stemmed
8 medium-size mushrooms, halved

FOR THE BEURRE BLANC
1 shallot, finely chopped
¼ cup white wine
¼ cup white wine vinegar
¾ pound (3 sticks) butter, between
refrigerator and room temperature
1 lemon, trimmed and cut in ½-inch
wedges
4 sprigs parsley

To cook the vegetables, bring a large saucepan of water to a boil over high heat. Add ½ teaspoon salt and drop in the asparagus. Cook until the asparagus is tender when pierced with a fork. With a slotted spoon, remove the asparagus, transfer to a strainer, and run under cold running water to stop the cooking. Drop the carrots into the boiling water and repeat. (The other vegetables and the mushrooms do not need to be pre-cooked.) If you wish to make this dish with fewer vegetables, any combination of three would be fine.

To prepare the fish, lay a large piece of cooking parchment on a counter. Fold the paper in half away from you to make a crease. Open it up again. Near the crease, spread a small amount of the butter. Over that, place one-quarter of the chopped shallots. Lay a piece of salmon over the shallots, drizzle the salmon with white wine, and sprinkle generously with salt and pepper. Cover with half a slice of lemon and lay a sprig of fresh herbs over each piece. Surround each piece of fish with one-quarter of the asparagus, carrots, zucchini, cherry tomatoes, and mushrooms. (Do not put the vegetables on top of the fish.) Fold the paper in half and, using scis-

sors, cut a half circle, starting at the crease and leaving a 2-inch border around the fish and vegetables. Fold over the first corner at a 90-degree angle and press the paper to flatten. Continue folding the edges all the way around, using long, narrow folds at angles of about 20 degrees. At the opposite end, fold the last corner as you did the first, at a 90-degree angle. Be sure the edges are sealed tightly so that there are no air holes. Put the parchment-wrapped fish on a baking sheet and chill until ready to cook. (The parchment packages can be made up to 24 hours ahead.)

Preheat the oven to 450 degrees.

To make the beurre blanc, combine the shallot, white wine, and white wine vinegar in a small stainless steel saucepan over high heat. Bring the mixture to a boil and begin reducing. Meanwhile, cut the butter into about 18 pieces. When all but a tablespoon of liquid has cooked away, take the pan off the heat and whisk in two pieces of the butter. Whisk vigorously off the heat until the mixture appears creamy. Return the pan to low heat and continue whisking in the butter one piece at a time, adding one as the other emulsifies. If the mixture begins to boil around the edge of the pan, take the pan off the heat again and continue whisking. Return to the heat and continue whisking and adding butter until all the butter has been incorporated. (It's best to whisk vigorously without watching the butter because when you watch, you slow down.) Remove from the heat and add salt and pepper to taste, and cover with a pot cover.

When ready to serve, place the baking

sheet with the salmon in the oven and bake until the edges of the parchment are lightly browned, about 10 minutes. Transfer each package to a warmed dinner plate, decorate each plate with a sprig of parsley and a lemon wedge, and serve with beurre blanc in a warmed sauceboat on the side.

SERVES 4

There is no real way to tell whether the fish inside the parchment is cooked except to open the first package.

Cooking food encased in parchment, bread, pastry, or salt (en papillote), *enables the food to cook in its own juices. It is important to seal the edges of the parchment so that air doesn't escape during cooking. Some cooks oil the top of the parchment or blow air into the packages before sealing them so that they rise dramatically in the oven.*

Beurre blanc is an emulsion sauce similar to hollandaise. It goes well with poached fish or shellfish and fish cooked in parchment or pastry. You can hold beurre blanc in a tepid water bath for up to 3 hours. Leftover sauce can be stored in the refrigerator and used as a melted butter sauce for dishes such as steamed artichokes.

Salmon in Pastry with Fresh Sorrel Sauce

Here is a magnificent presentation of our favorite salmon that can be made ahead—a piece of salmon encased in puff pastry with a beautiful sauce of fresh green sorrel! Unfortunately, by the time the pastry is cooked the fish is always slightly overcooked, but it looks so great no one will notice. Sorrel is a lemon-flavored grass that is delicious with fish, whether in a sauce or served as a soup. A good substitute for sorrel is young spinach with a squeeze of lemon added toward the end of cooking. You can serve beurre blanc instead of sorrel sauce. Don't worry if your fish doesn't look as decorative as you'd like when it goes into the oven; it will look great when it comes out!

2 leeks, trimmed, white parts only, cut in
   half lengthwise, washed, and thinly sliced
4 tablespoons (½ stick) butter
Coarse salt
1½ pounds puff pastry made with butter
   (see page 385)
Freshly ground black pepper
Four 3-ounce salmon fillets, 1 inch thick
1 egg
2 tablespoons heavy cream

FOR THE SORREL SAUCE
1 tablespoon butter
2 shallots, finely chopped
1 cup finely chopped fresh sorrel leaves
3 cups fish stock
1 tablespoon arrowroot
½ cup heavy cream

To prepare the leeks, put them in a frying pan with the butter and a sprinkling of salt over moderately high heat and cook, stirring from time to time, until they are very soft, about 20 minutes. Transfer to a plate to cool.

If you don't have a fish cutter the size of a fish, about 5 inches long and 3 inches high, make a cardboard template of a simple fish with those measurements.

To prepare the fish, roll out the puff pastry on a lightly floured surface to ⅛ inch thick. (It's easier to roll half the pastry at a time.) Using the fish cutter or template, cut out eight fish shapes. Place four of the pastry shapes on a parchment-lined baking sheet and spoon one-quarter of the leeks in the middle of each. Season the fish with salt and pepper and place a piece of fish on each leek-covered cutout. (You may have to trim some of the fish to fit on the cutouts with a ½-inch rim of dough around each piece of fish.) Brush the rim of dough with water. Cover the fish with the remaining four pastry cutouts. Seal the edges around each fish by pressing with a fork. Lightly beat the egg in a bowl with the cream and a pinch of salt and brush this egg mixture over the top of each fish. With the fork, make small holes to indicate where the gills of the fish would be. With the back of a knife, make lines in the tail. You can also make fins, scales, and eyes with scraps of dough. (It is important to cut out the scraps rather than re-roll them, and if you do make cutouts of dough, be sure they go on the fish and not on the pan. Brush the cutouts with the egg glaze as well.) Chill the fish in the refrigerator while you make the sauce. (At this point, the fish in pastry can be made up to a day ahead or frozen for a few weeks.)

Preheat the oven to 400 degrees.

To make the sorrel sauce, cook the butter and shallots in a medium-size saucepan over medium-high heat. Cook, stirring, until the shallots are soft. Add a cup of the fish stock and simmer until reduced by half. Add another cup of stock and simmer again until reduced by half. Repeat with the remaining stock. Combine a cup of the sauce with the sorrel in a food processor and blend until smooth. Add the sorrel mixture back into the remaining sauce. Continue cooking until the sauce lightly coats the back of a metal spoon, whisk in a mixture of arrowroot and cream, and return to a boil. Add salt and pepper to taste. (The sauce will keep for up to a week in the refrigerator.)

When ready to serve, remove the fish from the refrigerator or freezer, brush once again with egg glaze, and bake for 25 to 35 minutes. Serve on individual dinner plates with sorrel sauce in a sauceboat on the side.

SERVES 4

Don't even think of cooking leeks al dente. Because they are so fibrous, they need to be fully cooked.

Unless you're using a "cheater" dough of cream cheese or sour cream, pastry always needs to be brushed with egg glaze (dorure) before it goes into the oven. Some cooks brush it twice—once when it is assembled and once before it goes into the oven.

The more butterfat there is in an egg glaze,

the darker the pastry will look when it bakes. Egg yolk mixed with cream gives the darkest glaze. Whole egg mixed with cream doesn't come out quite as dark. Some cooks prefer whole egg mixed with milk or even water. It's up to the cook.

This sorrel sauce is an example of a fish reduction sauce. Usually there are three steps to such a sauce: adding the wine and reducing; adding the stock in stages and reducing after each addition; and finishing with cream or butter. In this case, the sorrel replaces the acid of the wine. Reduction sauces would be too salty if made with canned stock or bottled clam juice. This sauce should coat a spoon and taste balanced. It goes well on any poached or baked fish.

Grilled Salmon and Thai Salsa with Basmati Rice

*I*magine a beautiful plate of grilled salmon with a fresh sauce made with mint, ginger, and peanuts. This is a recipe given to me by an old friend. Is it really Thai? Probably not. In fact, this recipe should really be called grilled salmon with mock Thai salsa. Authentic or not, it is a delicious way to present fresh salmon.

¾ cup rice vinegar
½ cup soy sauce
½ cup light corn syrup
½ cup lime juice
2 cups peanut oil
⅓ cup grated fresh ginger
3 garlic cloves, minced
¾ cup coarsely chopped cilantro
1 cup coarsely chopped scallions, equal parts
   white and green
½ cup coarsely chopped mint leaves
3 red jalapeños, chopped
2 cups coarsely chopped peanuts
Eight 4-ounce pieces of fillet of salmon
1 tablespoon vegetable oil
Freshly ground black pepper

Prepare a charcoal fire 45 minutes before serving.

To make the sauce, combine the vinegar, soy sauce, corn syrup, lime juice, and peanut oil in a large bowl. In another bowl, combine the ginger, garlic, cilantro, scallions, mint, jalapeños, and peanuts.

To cook the fish, rub each piece on both sides generously with oil and season with salt and pepper. Grill the fish over the fire until it is resilient to the touch. (It is best to turn the fish only once.) Place each piece of fish on a warmed dinner plate. Mix together the two bowls of sauce ingredients, and spoon generously over the fish. Serve with the rice.

SERVES 8

BASMATI RICE

2 cups basmati rice
Coarse salt
4 tablespoons (½ stick) butter

To make the rice, wash the rice under cold running water to remove excess starch and any debris and until the water is less milky. Put 3½ cups water in a large saucepan and bring to a boil. Add a teaspoon of salt, the rice, and a tablespoon of the butter. Return the rice to a boil, reduce the heat to a bare simmer, and cover tightly. Continue to cook for 5 to 7 minutes. Remove from the heat and let steam, covered, for another 10 minutes. Stir in the remaining butter with a fork. Cover until ready to serve.   SERVES 8

The best way to cut a side (fillet) of salmon into portions is to lay it on a board with the tail (smaller) end on the right. With a thin, long knife cut pieces about 3 inches square with the knife held flat, cutting at an angle toward the tail. This way, the pieces will lie flat and be of equal size and therefore cook evenly.

Here are instructions on how to fillet a whole

salmon. (You'll end up with two sides.) Lay the salmon on a board with the head to the right (if you are right-handed) and the back of the fish close to you. You can see a line in the skin, which is where the backbone is. Off the backbone, bones come straight up to the dorsal fin and others go down toward the belly. With a long, thin knife make a cut with one motion of your knife along the gill cover at an angle to the right. This way you will get the most flesh from the salmon. Cut straight down close to the tail as well. With your fingers, feel along either side of the dorsal fin to see where the bones are on the top of the fish. With the knife cut through the skin of the fish, and with long strokes cut the flesh from off the tops of the bones. (Don't saw away at fish or meat as if it were bread or wood. You want smooth flesh, not jagged.) Using the flexible blade of the knife and your fingers, feel where the bones are. Always remove the fish from the tops of the bones, not the other way around.

When you have cut all along the top of the fish from the gills to the tail and up to the backbone, lift the side of salmon and cut through the little bones on the top of the backbone. Then, using your knife or fingers to guide you, cut down the other side, removing the flesh from the bones. When you reach the belly of the salmon, don't worry about getting all the flesh off perfectly—just blast on through to cut it off the bones. When you have one whole side off, lay the skin side on the board. With the knife, trim any fatty stuff, including the thick belly edge. With needle-nose pliers (or regular pliers), remove any pinbones still in the fillet. To do this, feel for the bones down the center and pull each one in the direction it grew.

To remove the flesh from the skin, grab the tail end in your left hand (you may need to dip your hand in salt for a good grip) and make a cut down to the skin with the knife. Turn the knife away from you and run the blade of the knife parallel to the fish, sliding the blade away from you and pulling the skin taut with your left hand. (Remember, slide rather than saw.) If the knife cuts the skin instead of running parallel to it, turn the fish and do the same thing in the opposite direction. With practice, you will have a smooth, thick fillet of salmon. Do exactly the same thing on the opposite side, keeping in mind that you should always take the flesh off the bones and the flesh off the skin, not the other way around.

With smaller fish you can simply cut into the head on one side of the fish, turn the knife, and run it across the backbone to the tail. There is rarely a call for filleting flatfish, but in that case, the fillets come off in four pieces, two from each side.

The best way to grate ginger is to run it up and down on a ceramic or metal ginger grater with or without peeling it first.

Sautéed Swordfish with Pickled Tomatoes and Couscous

Every once in a while someone shows us a recipe that is just magic—so good that everyone loves it! Here it is—Mary Sue Milliken and Susan Feniger's recipe for pickled tomatoes. Mary Sue and Susan are the very wonderful, energetic, and talented cooks from Border Grill in Los Angeles. Since there is no sauce for this dish, it is imperative to serve lots of juicy tomatoes with it to act as sauce. This is a great summertime dish.

3 pounds red, ripe Italian plum tomatoes, cored and cut in ½-inch wedges
2 bunches scallions, equal parts white and green, sliced at an angle in 2-inch lengths
1 large jalapeño; or 4 serrano chiles, finely chopped
3 tablespoons cumin seeds
1½ tablespoons crushed black pepper
1½ tablespoons mustard seeds (preferably black)
⅔ cup grated ginger
10 garlic cloves, minced
1 tablespoon ground turmeric
1 tablespoon paprika
1¼ cups vegetable oil
1½ cups rice vinegar
¾ cup dark brown sugar
4 tablespoons (½ stick) butter
½ cup flour
¾ cup cornmeal

Eight 4-ounce pieces swordfish, preferably
Pacific, about 1-inch thick
¼ cup vegetable oil

To make the pickled tomatoes, combine the tomatoes, scallions, and chiles in a large glass or ceramic bowl. In a separate bowl, combine the cumin, pepper, mustard seeds, ginger, garlic, turmeric, and paprika. Heat a cup of the vegetable oil in a medium-size frying or sauté pan over medium-high heat. When it begins to smoke, add the spice mixture and let it cook for 2 to 3 minutes. Pour the oil with the spices over the tomato mixture. Cook the vinegar, brown sugar, and salt in another pan over medium-high heat. When it comes to a boil, pour it over the tomato mixture.

To cook the fish, mix the flour and cornmeal in a shallow dish with salt and pepper. Dip both sides of each piece of fish in the mixture. Put enough butter in a large frying or sauté pan over medium-high heat to coat. When the butter and oil are very hot, carefully place the fish pieces in the pan so that they are not touching. It is important that you do not crowd the pan or push the fish around. Cook the fish until it is golden on the bottom, 3 to 4 minutes. Turn over with a metal spatula and cook on the other side until golden. The fish is cooked through when it is firm when pressed with your finger. Remove when it is cooked and repeat with remaining pieces of fish.

To serve, spoon the couscous into the centers of warmed dinner plates. Lay a piece of cooked fish at an angle across an edge of the couscous and spoon plenty of tomatoes with

their juices around the fish and over an edge of the couscous. SERVES 8

COUSCOUS

1½ cups couscous
Coarse salt
4 tablespoons (½ stick) butter

Put 2¼ cups water with a teaspoon of salt and ½ stick of the butter in a medium-size saucepan over high heat. Put the couscous into a glass baking dish. When the liquid boils, pour it over the couscous and stir well. Cover with foil and let stand about 10 minutes. Remove the foil. Fluff the couscous with your fingers or a fork and replace the foil to keep it warm. SERVES 8

Jalapeños are small green or red chiles with shoulders. Serranos are generally smaller and have no shoulders.

Heating spices in oil before adding to a dish makes their flavor more intense.

Do not try to keep these tomatoes for more than 3 days in the refrigerator because they are likely to ferment and if left longer are likely to explode.

Paella

This recipe was taught to us by Marimar Torres, who used to sell wine for her family winery in Spain. Now she makes great wines herself in California under her own name. I recommend serving Torres wine from either place with this traditional paella. This recipe exactly fits in a regular-size wok. It's a great party dish!

16 clams, scrubbed
¾ teaspoon saffron threads
6 garlic cloves
½ cup olive oil
One 3-pound chicken, cut into 8 pieces
Coarse salt
Freshly ground black pepper
1 pound pork chops, boned and cut into
    ½-inch dice
½ pound smoked ham, cut into ½-inch
    dice, preferably Smithfield
1½ pounds squid, cleaned and cut into
    ½-inch rings (optional)
16 large shrimp, in the shell
1 large onion, finely chopped
2 pounds red, ripe tomatoes, peeled, seeded,
    and chopped
3 cups short-grain rice, preferably Arborio
1 cup cooked fresh or frozen peas (1 pound
    in shells)
1 large red bell pepper, seeded, roasted
    (page 25) and cut into ½-inch lengths
1 large lemon, cut in 8 wedges

To cook the clams, put them in a small saucepan with an inch of cold water. Cover the pan and bring it to a boil on top of the stove. After 4 minutes, stir or shake the pan. Most of the clams will open. Discard those that don't. Transfer the clams to a bowl (in their shells) and cover with plastic wrap to prevent them from drying out. Pour all but the last tablespoon of the clam liquid into a measuring cup, then pour this liquid into a larger saucepan with enough water to measure 6 cups altogether. Bring to a boil over high heat. Add the saffron and turn off the heat.

To precook the other ingredients, cook the garlic in a wok or large sauté pan in 2 tablespoons of the oil over moderately high heat, until it is golden. Remove the garlic from the pan and discard. Season the chicken with salt and pepper and sauté the pieces on all sides in the oil, adding more oil as necessary to keep the pan lightly coated, until browned. Transfer the pieces to a plate and continue with the remaining chicken. Fry the pieces of pork and ham in the oil, being careful that the oil doesn't burn, and transfer to a plate. Fry the squid for only a half a minute, transferring them to a plate as they cook. Brown the shrimp in the remaining oil. By now you should have about half a cup of golden oil that is well flavored from the chicken, pork, and seafood. Add the onion to the oil and cook, stirring, until it is soft, about 5 minutes. Add the tomatoes and keep stirring. When the mixture resembles cooked tomato sauce stir in the rice, pork, ham, and squid. Bury the chicken in the rice. (You can prepare this dish ahead up to this point.)

When ready to serve, bring the pan of saffron water to a boil. Stir this into the rice mixture with salt and pepper to taste. Bring the rice mixture to a boil, reduce the heat, and simmer gently for 25 minutes. Stir the paella from time to time so that the rice cooks evenly. When the rice tastes cooked through with no uncooked starch in the center, stir in the shrimp, clams, and peas. Let the paella sit to absorb the flavors for 5 minutes while you garnish the top with the red peppers and lemon wedges.

SERVES 8

To clean the squid, put your finger inside its body and pull out as much of the innards and cartilage as possible, including the head and the tentacles. What doesn't come out the first time you can squeeze out at the tail end. Rinse the body. Some people remove the gray outer filament and some leave it on. Cut the body into rings. Using a small, sharp knife, cut into the

head as close to the eyes as possible. Holding the tentacles in one hand, give a small squeeze and remove the hard beak. Discard all but the body and the tentacles.

To cook fresh peas, drop them into boiling salted water and cook until they are tender when tasted. Strain and refresh under cold running water. The peas do not need to be cooked if frozen; simply leave them at room temperature to thaw.

Feel free to adapt this recipe to suit your desires. For instance, you can make an all-seafood paella or you can make a paella with only sausage and chicken. The recipe never has to be exact.

CHICKEN, DUCK, AND RABBIT

Chicken

Who was it that first used the expression "a chicken in every pot"? Was it King Henry IV of France or President Herbert Hoover? It doesn't really matter! The truth is that for so very long chicken was not accessible or affordable to everyone. Nowadays this good source of relatively inexpensive protein is readily available. Of course, it is much better if the chickens come from farms where they are allowed to range freely, eating grains and seeds, and are grown without added hormones and other chemicals. In my opinion, it is worth the extra dollars to buy these chickens rather than the mass-produced ones. Free-range, organic, and hormone-free are descriptions to look for.

Unlike fish, which is harvested mostly from the wild, most chicken is grown to be slaughtered and therefore is young and tender when sold. If we lived on a farm, chickens would lay eggs for us, and when they got too old to lay, we'd cook them up slowly in a stew. Coq au vin and fricassee of chicken are dishes originally meant for old farm birds. In today's markets, it's hard to find old chickens.

HOW TO BUY CHICKEN

When you are looking at a display of chickens, there is really no way to tell how fresh a chicken is. It's best to buy a chicken not wrapped in plastic and that looks firm, not sitting in liquid. The liquid indicates that the chicken may have been frozen and thawed.

If a chicken has been frozen, the bones of the thigh are dark instead of white. However, you know this only after you've cooked the chicken. A chicken that has been frozen and thawed is acceptable for cooking, and it's better than a fresh chicken that has been sitting in the case for too long. Yellow chickens are not necessarily better than white chickens—they are just a different color.

The very smallest chicken is sold as poussin (or Rock Cornish game hens), usually 1 to 1½ pounds. Chickens that weigh 3 to 4 pounds are called fryers. Roasters usually weigh more than 4 pounds and stewing hens weigh 5 pounds or more.

Roasting a large chicken stuffed with bread stuffing and then carving it at the dinner table belongs to another era. Nowadays it is more common to roast a 4-pound chicken and cut it up before serving. Buying whole chickens is more economical than buying chicken in parts or already boned. You could easily buy several chickens and bone out the breasts for one recipe, make a sauté of the legs for another, and transform the wings into hors d'oeuvres. All the bones and innards (except the liver) can go into the stock pot. You can even store the wings and livers in the freezer. When you have enough of each, make a dish of chicken wings or chicken liver mousse.

How to Cook Chicken

What makes chicken remarkable is that it is easy to cook by any method because it is already tender and has a protective skin that keeps it moist while cooking. It is a common French belief that chicken is best when roasted whole. That way, no juices are lost in the cooking.

However, the French do an equally good job of cooking chicken that is cut up, as in the classic chicken sauté. Like fish, chicken is fully cooked when it is opaque all the way through or when the juices run clear when the thick part of the thigh is pierced. Cooked chicken can keep for a week in the refrigerator.

When cooking chicken, roasting is the best method! All you have to do is put salt and pepper on it, throw it in a hot oven, and toss cooked potatoes in the resulting pan juices. It's even better when the fuel for the oven is hardwood, as in some restaurants, or if the chicken can be turned on a spit as it roasts. Often, you read that a roasting chicken should be trussed. This is to prevent the legs and wings from spreading in the heat of the oven. But I think untrussed chickens roast more evenly. Besides, when you cut it up, no one will see that the legs and wings have spread.

A chicken sauté is a method of cooking unique to chicken. You can even buy pans that are the perfect size: namely, 10-inch sauté pans. The chicken pieces are well browned, and then they cook in their own juices or with a little wine or stock. The dish is finished with cream or butter. Sauté of Chicken with Red Wine Vinegar (page 189) is a real chicken sauté.

Boiled chicken is delicious, especially when it is boiled in a flavorful liquid, and served in a sauce made from that liquid, as in Chicken Pot Pie with Artichokes and Shiitakes (page 192). You can make chicken stock with whole chicken and use the cooked chicken in the pot pie. There's no good reason why you would want to poach or steam chicken.

When chicken is grilled, broiled, or baked, care must be taken that the chicken doesn't dry out. Chicken Olney (page 196) is a terrific baked chicken dish.

In modern cooking, braising and stewing for long amounts of time are not common cooking methods for chicken. Since young chicken does not need long, slow cooking as do tougher cuts of meat, chicken sautés have come to replace braises; and the cooking time for stews has been dramatically shortened, as in Chicken in Red Wine with Onions and Mushrooms (page 194).

You can take chicken off the bone and pan-fry or stir-fry it in a small amount of fat. You can leave it on the bone with or without skin and deep-fry it. Fortunes have been made from the business of fried chicken, an American favorite. Try stir-frying chicken with a ginger-lime sauce (page 201); or deep-frying chicken, as in Chicken Kiev with Melon Seed Pasta Pilaf (page 200).

All over the world, methods of cooking encased chicken have been invented, from cooking in clay in China, to cooking in bread in Italy, to cooking in salt in France. The encased method ensures that no juices are lost, because the chicken cooks in its own juices. Smoking chicken gives chicken added flavor, and it can be added to many dishes such as salads, soups, pastas, and risottos.

How to Sauce Chicken

For most fish dishes, the cook needs to make a sauce. For most chicken dishes, especially when the chicken is cooked on the bone with its skin, the sauce is an integral part of the dish. Of the five families of sauces, the hundreds of little sauces, and the many miscellaneous sauces, most go with boned chicken breasts. That is why chicken is so versatile; it goes with everything. When wondering what sauce to make for chicken, think about capturing the juices of the chicken rather than making a separate sauce.

The Big Problem

Really there is no big problem with cooking chicken; just leave the skin on it, and don't cook it too long. Problems occur when people take the skin off before cooking and try to bake or grill the meat. It just becomes too dry without the skin.

How to Cook Chicken Without a Recipe

To cook a whole chicken, salt and pepper it inside and out, put it in a roasting pan, and stick it in a hot oven for 1 hour. All you have to remember is that a 4-pound chicken cooks in a 475-degree oven for 1 hour. Take it out and let rest for 10 minutes. Put the pan of juices on top of the stove, toss in some fresh and wild mushrooms, and cook until half wilted. Season with salt and pepper and transfer the mushrooms to a warmed serving platter. Cut the chicken into four pieces and place these on top. Instead of mushrooms, you can cook Romaine lettuce cut in 1-inch lengths with slivered garlic in the pan juices. To roast a chicken without a recipe, all you have to do is decide what you like with chicken. The most important thing is to use the juices.

To cook boned chicken breasts, dip the chicken breasts in flour seasoned with salt and pepper. Lay them in a pan with hot butter and oil and cook on one side until golden. Turn with tongs and cook on the other side until golden and firm to the touch. Remove the chicken breasts from the pan and immediately add dry white wine, rinsed capers, and a little chicken stock. This will dissolve the caramelized chicken juices on the bottom of the pan and make pan juices to pour over the chicken—Voilà! Chicken piccata! If you prefer, you can deglaze the pan with Madeira and add heavy cream to make a Madeira sauce. The idea is to cook the chicken breast in a hot pan, feel it with your fingers to see when it is firm and then to remove it from the pan, deglaze the pan with whatever you like, and finish the sauce with a little cream. Capturing the flavors from the bottom of the pan by dissolving them in cold liquid, wine, stock, or water is the most important thing to do when cooking thin pieces of fish, chicken, or meat.

Other Birds and Rabbit

For many years there have been four kinds of domestic poultry: chicken, duck, turkey, and goose. All the rest were considered game and it has long been illegal to sell wild game birds in this country. Chicken and turkey are made up of white meat and are relatively tender whereas domestic duck and goose are made up of dark meat and need special care with cooking because the meat is naturally tough.

There are more and more of what are traditionally classified as game birds being raised for cooking and eating. These include pheasant, quail, and squab. Domestic pheasant is white meat without a lot of taste and can be tough. Quail is white meat and tender and delicate. Squab is a rich dark meat and must

not be overcooked. Order quail and squab whenever you see them on restaurant menus because restaurants have access to quality birds.

A wide variety of game birds are hunted in this country. If someone brings you one of these, the thing to remember is to cook it quickly at high heat to keep it from overcooking. Because there is so little fat on a wild bird, cooks often wrap them in a protective layer of pork fat or bacon. This is called barding.

DUCK

Although you can buy many varieties of ducks in Europe, there is only one variety available in this country—the Peking variety, often called Long Island, even though it may come from Indiana or Wisconsin. The same variety is called Petaluma in California. All domestic duck has lots of fat under the skin and almost no fat throughout the meat. That is why elaborate cooking methods have been developed to try to make the meat tender and moist while the fat is cooked from under the skin. A good solution is to cook the breasts and the legs in different ways, as described in Magret of Duck in Cassis Sauce (page 205) and Braised Duck Legs with Lentils (page 208).

RABBIT

Rabbits are often included in the poultry chapter of cookbooks because they are cooked by methods more similar to those

Marinating and Brining

MARINATING IS USEFUL when cooking anything that is naturally tough. The reasons to marinate are to flavor, to tenderize, to preserve, and to cook (in the case of fish). There are uncooked marinades and cooked marinades. A cooked marinade will flavor and tenderize the food more quickly. There is no great trick to making a marinade. Start with a bottle of red wine, a few tablespoons of red wine vinegar, some sliced shallots, a couple of bay leaves, a few sprigs of thyme, several black peppercorns, and olive oil. Heat the marinade and let it cool if you are cooking the food the same day; otherwise, add the food and chill it overnight, turning the bird or meat a few times. The question always comes up in the cooking school whether you should marinate at room temperature or in the refrigerator. The answer is that it depends on the room temperature. You can safely leave food out in an acidic marinade overnight in 65-degree weather, but it is not a good idea in 90-degree weather.

Marinating should not be confused with brining. After the food is marinated, you can boil up the marinade and use it in the sauce. Brining means to soak food in a salt solution. You can never make a sauce from brine. Other terms for brining are curing, corning, and salting. Brining is done by cooks, especially with modern pork and beef, to make the meat juicy when it is cooked. It is also done to preserve foods before smoking. Dry brines are sometimes called rubs. To make a simple rub, mix together a few tablespoons of black pepper, a teaspoon of cloves, and a stick of cinnamon in a grinder used only for spices, and mix with a cup of coarse salt. This rub would go on a roast just before cooking. You can make a simple liquid brine by mixing ½ cup coarse salt with a gallon of cold water; or you can make a more elaborate brine by adding such ingredients as cinnamon, bay leaf, pepper, or soy sauce. This should be done from four to forty-eight hours before cooking.

FOIE GRAS

HERE IS THE STORY of force-fed duck: Farmers in Alsace and the southwest of France used to fatten their geese at the end of the autumn by bringing them into the barn for about three weeks and overfeeding them. The farmer would sit on a stool three or four times a day with the goose between his legs and put a funnel down its throat through which a grain mixture was forced. When the goose was slaughtered, it had an enlarged liver called foie gras (fat liver). This practice has now been extended to the Muscovy duck and the Moulard, a cross between a Muscovy and Peking duck. Raising ducks (easier than raising geese) has become big business, and there are now good producers of foie gras in New York State and California, such as Hudson Valley Foie Gras and Sonoma Foie Gras.

The problem of what to do with the rest of the geese (or ducks) has resulted in a secondary business of selling the breasts—which are much thicker and meatier than those of other domestic ducks—the legs, and even the fat and the carcasses. If you have access to magrets of force-fed duck, cook them like steak in the recipe for breasts with cassis (page 205)—fantastic! You can cook the legs as in the Braised Duck Legs with Lentils (page 208) recipe or preserve them as in Duck Confit (page 381). If you can get a whole foie gras, serve it hot to waiting guests and then make a terrine with the remainder.

To prepare hot foie gras, cut it in ¼-inch slices with a thin, sharp knife. Put the slices in a hot pan without any butter or oil and cook them quickly. Add a sprinkling of coarse salt and freshly ground black pepper and serve on fine-grained toast with Sauternes or Late Harvest Riesling, depending on what you can afford. You may need practice cooking the first few pieces; the foie gras should be lightly browned and lightly crusty on the outside and slightly pink on the inside.

To make the terrine, carefully remove any veins from the remaining liver. Lay it in a glass baking pan, sprinkle sparingly with Cognac or Armangnac and salt and pepper on both sides, and chill overnight. The next day, place the marinated liver in a ceramic terrine, put the terrine in a larger pan of warm water, and bake it covered in a 300-degree oven until a metal skewer inserted in the middle of the liver is warm to the touch, about 35 minutes. Cool the terrine with a light weight on top so that the cooked liver presses together slightly. Terrine of foie gras should be served in ¼-inch slices (never spread) on fine-grained toast.

used for poultry than for meat. Rabbit is loved by cooks because it adapts well to different flavors. Rabbit Dijonnaise (page 209) is a quick dish; and the woodland-style rabbit (page 210) takes time, but diners will appreciate rabbit off the bone.

Roast Chicken with Beans, Bacon, and Spinach

What cooking teachers have to do is eat at the trendy new restaurants. Here is my interpretation of a fabulous roast chicken dish created by Julia McClaskey, who is the chef-owner of Julia in San Francisco. Shell beans are legumes that are harvested fresh before they are allowed to dry. You can buy shell beans of many different varieties at local farmers' markets or substitute canned beans that have been drained and rinsed—the best are made by Progresso. Either way, this is a relatively easy one-course meal.

> *4 slices thick bacon*
> *One 4-pound chicken*
> *Coarse salt*
> *Freshly ground black pepper*
> *1 large onion, coarsely chopped*
> *1 large carrot, coarsely chopped*
> *1 bunch fresh spinach, stemmed*
> *2 cups cooked cranberry or cannellini beans*
> *2 medium-size tomatoes, peeled, seeded, and chopped*
> *2 tablespoons finely chopped fresh Italian parsley*
> *1 tablespoon finely chopped summer savory*

To cook the chicken, lay the bacon on the bottom of a roasting pan, sprinkle the chicken inside and out generously with salt and pepper, and place the chicken on top of the bacon. Surround the chicken with the carrot and onion and bake in a 475-degree oven until the chicken is well browned, the juices run clear when pierced to the bone with a knife in the thick part of the thigh, and the skin has begun to shrink from the ends of the legs, about 1 hour. Toward the end of the cooking you can baste the chicken once or twice with the cooking juices. Transfer the chicken and bacon to a board and let cool. Discard the vegetables.

To cook the spinach, bring a large pan of water to a boil. Add ½ teaspoon of salt and toss in the spinach. When the spinach is half wilted, remove it with tongs and place four mounds of it on paper towels in a baking pan.

Let the chicken juices cool in the pan for 5 minutes. Pour off all but 3 tablespoons of the fat that rises to the top. Add the onion to the cooking juices and place the pan on top of the stove over moderately high heat. Cook, stirring from time to time, until the onion is soft, about 5 minutes. Add the tomatoes, herbs, and beans and simmer for another 5 minutes, stirring, until the beans are warmed through. Add salt and pepper to taste.

To finish the dish, place the pan of spinach in a 300-degree oven to warm. Cut the bacon into ½-inch pieces and add it to the beans. Cut the chicken into four pieces. Spoon the beans onto four warmed dinner plates, place a mound of spinach next to the beans, and lay a piece of chicken over the spinach and beans. SERVES 4

To cook fresh shell beans, remove the beans from their pods and put them in a pot with half an onion and two sprigs thyme. Cover them generously with cold water and simmer on top of the stove just until they are tender, 8 to 12 minutes. Let them cool in their cooking liquid and then proceed with the recipe.

To cut up a chicken after it is cooked, put the chicken breast side down on a cutting board with the tail toward you. With the back of a knife, draw an imaginary line on either side of the backbone, from the tail to the end of the neck. Use poultry shears or kitchen scissors to cut out the backbone along this line. Cut straight through the breastbone centered as best you can. You should now have two halves of a chicken. Lay the halves bone side down on the board. With your fingers lift one leg, cutting the skin and separating it from the breast. Cut straight down through the thinnest part between the leg, thigh, and breast, trying to keep as much skin covering each piece as possible.

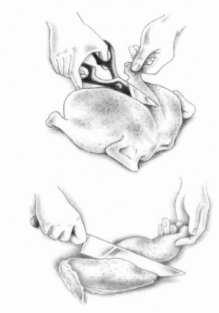

Roast Chicken with New Potatoes and Olives

The trick to making good roast chicken is to have a really hot oven and cook it beyond the recommended cooking time. It tastes so good when it is almost falling off the bone. Here the juices of the chicken are absorbed by the warm potatoes and the flavors are enhanced by the olives.

One 4-pound chicken
Coarse salt
Freshly ground black pepper
2 pounds small new potatoes, such as Yukon Gold or Yellow Finn
1 bunch scallions, equal amounts of white and green parts, chopped
¾ cup chicken stock
⅔ cup fresh Italian parsley leaves, coarsely chopped
⅓ cup minced fresh thyme
½ cup pitted Niçoise olives

To cook the chicken, season it inside and out with salt and pepper. Place the chicken in a roasting pan in a 475-degree oven and roast for approximately 1 hour. You can baste the chicken a few times in the last 15 minutes of cooking.

To cook the potatoes, put them in a saucepan with plenty of cold water and a tablespoon of salt over medium-high heat and bring to a boil. Boil until just tender when pierced with a fork, about 20 minutes. Drain immediately in a colander and shake to evaporate the excess moisture. When the potatoes are cool enough to handle, slice them into ½-inch rounds.

When the chicken is done, remove the pan from the oven and transfer the chicken to a board. When the juices in the pan have cooled, pour off all but 2 tablespoons of the fat, being sure to save the chicken juices. Put the roasting pan over medium-high heat and stir in the scallions. Cook for a minute before adding the chicken stock. Boil up, scraping the sediment. Stir in the potatoes and let cook through without stirring, about 3 minutes. Stir in the parsley and olives, with salt and pepper to taste. Transfer the potato mixture to a serving dish, cut up the chicken into 4 or 8 pieces to go on top of the potatoes, and serve family style. SERVES 4

Remove the innards from the chicken and the blobs of excess fat before cooking. You can rub the chicken with soft butter for added flavor before sprinkling with salt and pepper. You can also fill the cavity with half an onion, a lemon, and sprigs of fresh rosemary or thyme. The important thing is that the chicken roast relatively undisturbed in a hot oven until it is brown and crispy on the outside.

To baste a roast, remove the pan quickly from the oven and close the door. With a bulb baster or a large spoon, squirt or spoon juices all over the roast and especially on the parts of the roast that need to brown. If more liquid is needed, pour it around, not over, the roast. Return the pan to the oven as quickly as possible.

Roast Chicken with Spring Vegetables and Butter Sauce

*T*hank goodness butter is making a come-back! Don't be alarmed by the amount of butter in this dish. As with beurre blanc for fish, you are not going to eat it all. It makes food taste so good, especially the sauce for this chicken. I first ate this dish at a neighborhood restaurant called Pane e Vino; it always has great food.

One 4-pound chicken
Coarse salt
Freshly ground black pepper
1 pound small carrots, peeled and cut into 1½ by ½-inch pieces, trimmed to look like baby carrots
1 pound small white turnips, cut into 1½ by ½-inch wedges
1 pound small green beans, trimmed
½ cup dry white wine
¾ pound (3 sticks) butter, between refrigerator and room temperature, cut into 16 pieces

To cook the chicken, sprinkle it generously inside and out with salt and pepper, place it in a roasting pan in a 475-degree oven, and let it roast until it is well browned, about 1 hour. You can baste the chicken once or twice toward the end of the cooking time by removing the pan from the oven, closing the door to the oven, filling a bulb baster with the juices from the bottom of the pan, and squirting the juices on parts of the chicken that need to brown before returning it quickly to the oven.

To cook the vegetables, bring a large pot of water to a boil. Drop the carrots into the water with ½ teaspoon salt and boil until they are tender when pierced with a fork. Remove them with a slotted spoon to a strainer and run them under cold water until chilled. Do the same with the turnips and then the green beans.

When the chicken is nicely browned, the juices in the thick part of the thigh run clear when pierced with a knife, and the skin has started to shrink from the legs; remove the chicken from the pan and let it rest for 10 minutes. Let the chicken juices cool as well.

To make the sauce, pour off any fat that rises to the top of the chicken juices. Place the roasting pan over high heat and pour in the wine, scraping the brown bits on the bottom of the pan. This is called deglazing. Boil vigorously for 2 to 3 minutes. Strain the juices into a small saucepan and heat over moderately high heat. When the chicken juices are reduced to 3 tablespoons, remove the saucepan from the heat and whisk in two pieces of the butter. When the mixture appears creamy, return it to a low heat and start whisking in one piece of butter at a time. As one disappears, add the next. It is best not to watch the mixture while you're whisking or you will slow down. If the mixture bubbles around the edges of the pan, remove the pan from the heat and let the heat of the pan cook the sauce. When all the butter has been incorporated, remove the saucepan from the heat and add salt and pepper to taste. Cover with a pot lid.

When ready to serve, reheat the vegetables briefly by putting them in a wide frying pan with a tablespoon of butter and shaking them over a high flame for a couple of minutes. Cut the chicken into 4 or 8 pieces and place them on a warmed serving platter surrounded by the vegetables. Spoon some of the sauce over each piece of chicken and serve the remaining sauce separately in a warmed sauceboat.   SERVES 4

This is really a beurre blanc type of sauce made with chicken juices. It will keep warm for up to an hour. Some cooks store it in a Thermos for up to 4 hours.

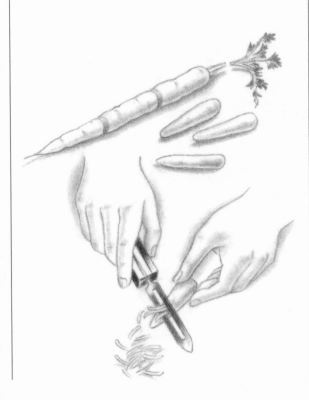

Sauté of Chicken with Shallots

ere is a simple and delicious classic chicken sauté. Serve it with roasted potatoes and buttered green beans and have a good time.

> *One 3½-pound chicken, cut into 8 pieces*
> *Coarse salt*
> *Freshly ground black pepper*
> *4 tablespoons (½ stick) butter*
> *2 tablespoons oil*
> *16 whole shallots, peeled*
> *1 bay leaf*
> *1 cup chicken stock*
> *2 tablespoons minced fresh Italian parsley*

To cook the chicken, sprinkle the pieces generously with salt and pepper. Heat enough of the butter and oil to make a ¼-inch layer in a 10-inch sauté pan. Place the pan over moderately high heat. When the bubbles have subsided, place some of the chicken pieces skin side down with about 1 inch space between them. When the chicken has browned nicely, turn over each piece with tongs and brown on all sides. Do not push the chicken around when browning and do not crowd the pan. Remove each piece of chicken as it browns and put it on a plate. Continue with the rest of the chicken, making sure there is always a layer of butter or oil on the bottom of the pan, even when there is only one piece of chicken left. When all the chicken has browned, pour off all but 2 tablespoons fat from the pan and immediately stir in the shallots. Cook the shallots over moderate heat, stirring, until they are lightly browned. Add the bay leaf and half the chicken stock and bring to a boil, stirring. Return the chicken to the pan with its juices, reduce the heat to a bare simmer, cover, and let cook until the chicken is opaque when cut into with a knife, about 20 minutes.

When the chicken is done, place it on a warmed serving platter and surround it with the shallots. Keep warm. Let the sauté pan cool for 5 minutes and spoon off any fat that rises to the top. Place the pan over moderately high heat and add the remaining chicken stock, scraping up any sediment from the bottom of the pan with a flat wooden spatula. Bring to a boil and simmer for 3 to 4 minutes. Add salt and pepper to taste, spoon the sauce over the chicken, and sprinkle with parsley.   SERVES 4

To cut up a raw chicken, first remove the bag of innards inside the chicken and the blob of fat. Turn the chicken onto its breast with the tail toward you. With a pair of kitchen scissors, cut out the backbone from the tail to the neck on each side. All the innards in the bag except the liver and the backbone can be saved for making chicken stock. At this point, run a sharp knife down the breastbone and cartilage covering the breastbone to slit the filament. With your thumbs on either side of the breastbone and your fingers underneath the breastbone, flip the breastbone up through the cut filament, breaking it on either side. Run your fingers down the cartilage to loosen and remove the breastbone and cartilage. If this seems too complicated, simply try your best to cut down the center of the chicken, dividing it in half. To cut it into quarters, feel for the thinnest part that joins the breast to the thigh. Lay the half chicken on a board, lift a leg, and cut the skin with a sharp knife, then cut straight down between the breast and thigh. Do the same with the other half. To disjoint the leg from the thigh, use the knife to cut down to the joint and wiggle to see exactly where you can slide the knife between the leg and the thigh. To cut the breast and wing quarter in half, cut the breast with your scissors so that it is an equal-sided triangle. This will give the wing piece a bit of breast meat. It looks better if you cut off and discard the last joint of the wing. You should now have eight pieces.

After cutting raw chicken on a wooden or plastic board or counter, always clean the board, knife, and scissors with soap, bleach, and hot water.

To sauté food means to cook it in such a hot pan that it almost jumps around. In a sauté of chicken pieces, the chicken is first browned and then cooked, covered, in a straight-sided pan. It is a dish unique to chicken.

Sauté of Chicken with Red Wine Vinegar
(*Poulet au Vinaigre*)

Just as lemon goes with fish, vinegar goes with chicken! This poulet au vinaigre is a perennial favorite. You can also make this recipe using only legs and thighs. Serve it with garlic potatoes or a potato gratin.

One 3½-pound chicken, cut into 8 pieces
Coarse salt
Freshly ground black pepper
4 tablespoons butter plus 1 tablespoon for finishing the sauce
4 tablespoons olive oil
2 shallots, finely chopped
½ cup red wine vinegar
3 garlic cloves, finely minced
2 medium-size red tomatoes, peeled, seeded, and chopped
1 tablespoon tomato paste
1 tablespoon finely chopped fresh Italian parsley

To cook the chicken, sprinkle it generously with salt and pepper. Add enough of the butter and oil to make a ¼-inch layer on the bottom of a 10-inch sauté pan over medium-high heat. When the bubbles have subsided, place the chicken pieces skin side down with about 1 inch space between them. When the chicken is dark, turn over each piece with tongs and brown on all sides. Do not push the chicken around when browning and do not crowd the pan. Remove each piece of chicken as it browns and put it on a plate. Continue with the rest of the chicken, making sure there is always a layer of butter or oil on the bottom of the pan even when there is only one piece of chicken left. When all the chicken has browned, pour off all but 2 tablespoons fat from the pan and immediately stir in the shallots. Cook them over moderate heat, stirring, until they are soft. Add half the vinegar with ¼ cup water. Bring to a boil, stirring. Return the chicken to the pan with any juices, reduce the heat to a bare simmer, cover, and let cook until the chicken is opaque when cut with a knife, about 20 minutes.

To finish the dish, transfer the chicken to a warmed serving platter. Stir the garlic into the chicken juices and cook, stirring, over moderate heat for a minute. Stir in the remaining vinegar, the tomatoes, and tomato paste. Bring the mixture to a boil, scraping up any browned bits from the bottom of the pan. Reduce the heat to medium and cook for about 5 minutes, or until the sauce has thickened. Turn off the heat from under the pan, dot the top of the mixture with a tablespoon of butter, and swirl to thicken and enrich the sauce. Add salt and pepper to taste. Spoon the sauce over the chicken and sprinkle with parsley. SERVES 4

COOKING WITH WINE AND SPIRITS

UNDERSTANDING DIFFERENT KINDS of alcoholic beverages and how they are used in cooking will help in understanding how to cook.

Wine is basically fermented grape juice. Although it is possible to crush grapes and let them sit and ferment from the natural yeasts on their skins, grape growing and wine making have become very calculated and scientific. Although there are thousands of kinds of grapes from which wine can be made, those that produce the greatest wines are Chardonnay, Sauvignon Blanc, and Riesling of the white varieties; and Cabernet Sauvignon, Merlot, Pinot Noir, Syrah, and Nebbiolo of the red. Many famous wines are made from blends of different grapes; for instance, Bordeaux and Château Neuf-du-Pape.

In California, wines are likely to be named after the grape, whereas in France they are likely to be named after the region where they are grown. Cabernet Sauvignons from California are called Bordeaux in France, and Pinot Noirs from California are called Burgundys in France. Chardonnay is the grape used for white Burgundys.

What a cook wants from wine is the flavor without the alcohol because alcohol gives food a harsh taste. Generally, wine contains 11 to 14 percent alcohol, which means it does not usually ignite when added to a dish but must be cooked for a few minutes so that the alcohol evaporates.

For general cooking purposes, a ten-dollar bottle of wine is fine. Save your expensive wines for drinking. After a bottle of wine has been opened, it will stay fresh for a day or so in the refrigerator. After that, however, it will not be drinkable but can still be used in cooking.

Fortified wines are wines usually from hot climates, made with the addition of alcohol or brandy midway through the fermentation process. These include sherry, port, Madeira, and Marsala. Fortified wines are favored by some cooks because the flavor is stronger and the alcohol ranges from 19 to 22 percent, which means that you can flame foods with them. (Flaming is a fast way of burning off the alcohol but really doesn't enhance a dish.) Another advantage is that you can cook with them, recork the bottle, and keep them for a long time after opening. When cooking with fortified wines, always buy those that are imported and those that are dry rather than sweet.

Vermouth can be used like a fortified wine in cooking. It is actually wine that has been flavored with herbs, spices, and fruits. It is a fine substitute when you have no open white wine; just use a little less because of its intensity.

Brandy is wine that has been distilled, boiled, and its alcohol recaptured. It takes ten bottles of wine to make one bottle of brandy. Its rich brown color comes from aging in wood. It is very high in flavor and in alcohol—40 percent. Whereas wine has to be added at the beginning of cooking, a touch of brandy can be added at the end for extra flavor. Brandy is best for flaming foods such as crêpes Suzettes. In order for brandy to ignite, it needs to be warm. It is a good idea to warm brandy in a ladle held over a flame before igniting it. That way you have control when you pour it over something like cherries jubilee.

Cognac is brandy made in the Cognac area of France. Armangnac is brandy from the southwest of France. Calvados, brandy made from apples, comes from Normandy. When a recipe calls for any of these, regular brandy is an acceptable substitute.

A spirit distilled from the skins, stems, and pips of grapes after they are crushed and the juice is drawn off is called marc in France and grappa in Italy. This is called for occasionally in a recipe, but you can substitute brandy.

Of the distilled spirits—scotch, rye, bourbon, gin, vodka, and tequila—only rum is of interest to the cook. It is used frequently in baking for added flavor. Distilled spirits are distilled from such things as grains, corn, potato, cactus, and molasses.

In northern Europe, where it is too cold to grow grapes, a distilled spirit called eau de vie is made from fruit. Although quality eau de vies are not well known in this country, they can be really delicious and fun to cook with. Kirsch, made from cherries, is the most universally used eau de vie and can be used with any fruit recipe, savory or sweet.

Although there are many liqueurs that can be served after dinner, they are generally too sweet for cooking. The best liqueur for cooking is Grand Marnier. When cooking with other liqueurs such as Kahlúa, Frangelico, and framboise, I recommend adding a little brandy to the liqueurs to sharpen the flavor.

Here's what I recommend having in stock:

1 bottle red table wine
1 bottle white table wine
1 bottle cheap white wine for cooking fish
1 bottle vermouth (Noilly Pratt)
1 bottle Madeira (Sercial)
1 bottle brandy (Korbell is fine)
1 bottle rum (Meyers's dark rum)
1 bottle kirsch (imported)
1 bottle Grand Marnier

Chicken Pot Pie with Artichokes and Shiitakes

*C*hicken pot pie is true comfort food. Boiled chicken in a chicken velouté with mushrooms will make everyone feel comforted. Of course, you can make this dish with any vegetables that go well with chicken, such as cooked carrots, broccoli, kernels of corn, and zucchini. Even such things as hard-cooked eggs and bits of ham or prosciutto work well. With a green salad and a glass of Chardonnay, you have a perfect Sunday night supper!

2 cups flour
Salt
12 tablespoons (1½ sticks) cold butter,
*   cut in 1-inch pieces, plus 2 tablespoons*
½ cup sour cream
One 3¾-pound chicken
1 large onion, cut in 1-inch pieces
1 large carrot, cut in 1-inch pieces
1 stalk celery, cut in 1-inch pieces
4 cups (1 quart) chicken stock
Bouquet garni composed of 4 sprigs parsley,
*   2 sprigs thyme, and 1 bay leaf*
2 fresh artichoke bottoms, trimmed
*   (see page 58)*
1 medium-size lemon
½ pound small shiitakes, stems removed,
*   cut into ½-inch lengths*

FOR THE VELOUTÉ SAUCE
4 tablespoons (½ stick) butter
4 tablespoons flour
½ cup heavy cream
2 tablespoons minced fresh Italian parsley

Coarse salt
Freshly ground white pepper

FOR THE EGG GLAZE
1 egg
1 tablespoon heavy cream

To make the pastry dough for the crust, combine the flour, ½ teaspoon salt, the 12 tablespoons butter, and sour cream in a food processor. Process until the dough comes together in a ball. Wrap the ball of dough in waxed paper and chill for 20 minutes.

To cook the chicken, put the onion, carrot, and celery in a large pot over moderately high heat with the chicken stock. When the liquid comes to a boil, skim and discard the scum. Add the bouquet garni, reduce the heat to a simmer and let cook, stirring from time to time, until the chicken is opaque when cut to the bone with a knife, about 25 minutes. Remove the chicken from the stock. When cool enough to handle, remove the skin and bones. Cut the chicken into pieces about an inch square and put them in a bowl. Season with salt and pepper. Strain the stock into a medium saucepan and discard the vegetables. Bring the stock to a boil and reduce it until you have just 2 cups. Set aside.

To cook the artichokes, bring a medium-size saucepan of water to a boil over high heat. Cut the lemon in half and rub one half on the trimmed artichoke bottoms to prevent them from turning brown. Squeeze the other half into the saucepan of boiling water. Add the artichoke bottoms to the boiling water and cook for 15 minutes or until tender when pierced with a fork. Remove the artichokes from the water and drain upside down on paper towels. When cool enough to handle, remove the center choke, cut the artichokes into ½-inch slices, and add to the bowl of chicken.

To prepare the mushrooms, heat the 2 tablespoons butter in a medium-size frying pan over medium heat. Toss in the mushroom caps and cook until they are half wilted. Remove the mushrooms from the pan and add to the chicken/artichoke mixture. Season with salt and pepper.

To make the sauce, put the butter in a medium-size saucepan over moderately high heat. Remove the pan from the heat and sprinkle in the flour. Beat it down with a wooden spoon. Return the pan to the heat and cook until the roux appears greasy. Remove the pan from the heat again and whisk in the 2 cups warm stock. Return the pan to high heat and continue whisking until the sauce comes to a boil, about 2 minutes. It should thicken considerably at this point. Reduce the heat and let the sauce simmer for 5 minutes. Stir in the ½ cup cream and parsley with salt and pepper to taste. Let simmer another 2 minutes. Carefully fold the sauce into the chicken mixture. Transfer the mixture to a 9-inch-wide by 1-inch-deep pie plate or baking dish and chill.

Preheat the oven to 375 degrees.

To roll out the dough, put it on a lightly floured board and roll it into a circle about ⅛ inch thick and at least an inch wider than the diameter of the pie plate. Mix the egg with the 1 tablespoon cream to make a glaze and brush the edge of the plate with a little of it. Set the circle of dough over the chicken mix-

ture in the pie plate, pressing the edge to the rim of the dish. Double the dough on the edge, fold back, and cut off the excess dough. With your fingers, the end of a kitchen knife, or a fork, make a decorative edge in the pastry around the rim of the dish. Cut four 1-inch-long slashes in a spoke fashion in the top of the pastry. Brush the top of the pastry with the egg glaze. Without balling up the excess dough, make decorative cutouts and place them on top of the pie. Brush these with the egg glaze. If the dough seems to be soft at this point, place the entire dish in the freezer for 10 minutes before baking. (If you do this, brush the top of the pie with egg glaze before putting in the oven.) Bake the pot pie in the upper rack of the preheated oven until the crust is golden, about 35 minutes. Let rest for about 10 minutes before serving. SERVES 6

Chicken in Red Wine with Onions and Mushrooms
(Coq au Vin Rouge)

Two of my favorite restaurants are Bistro Jeanty in the Napa Valley and Jeanty at Jack's in San Francisco. Both are the creations of Phillipe Jeanty. They are warm and friendly and serve real bistro food. (A French bistro used to be a neighborhood café where people could spend the evening eating home-cooked meals, sipping red wine, and smoking Gauloise cigarettes over a game of checkers.) Good, hearty bistro food is always served at Bistro Jeanty. Serve with parsleyed new potatoes (page 185) and, of course, good Napa Valley wine!

2 large onions, sliced

3 shallots, sliced

8 garlic cloves, crushed

Bouquet garni composed of 3 sprigs parsley, 5 sprigs thyme, and 1 bay leaf

1½ bottles hearty red wine, such as Côte du Rhône

Two 3¾-pound chickens, cut into 8 pieces each

Coarse salt

Freshly ground black pepper

4 tablespoons (½ stick) butter

4 tablespoons olive oil

2 tablespoons flour

½ cup brandy

2 cups chicken stock

1½ tablespoons (unsweetened) cocoa powder

½ pound small white onions, peeled

6 slices thick-cut bacon, cut in ½-inch lengths

1 pound small button mushrooms, brushed and trimmed so the stem is flush with the cap

To marinate the chicken, combine the onions, shallots, garlic, bouquet garni, and wine with the chicken pieces in a large stainless steel bowl. Mix well, cover with plastic wrap, and chill for 24 to 48 hours, turning occasionally in the marinade.

To brown the chicken pieces, take them out of the marinade and pat them dry with paper towels. Sprinkle the chicken generously with salt and pepper on both sides. Strain the marinade into a bowl and reserve. Heat enough of the butter and oil to make a ¼-inch layer in a large sauté pan. When the bubbles have subsided, place the chicken pieces skin side down in the bottom of the pan about an inch apart. Do not crowd the pan and do not push the chicken around. As the pieces brown, turn them over with tongs and brown the other side, taking care that the bottom of the pan does not burn. Add more butter and oil as needed to keep the pan from burning. Transfer the cooked chicken to a medium-size heavy casserole, and continue browning the remaining chicken for about 3 minutes on each side, keeping a layer of butter and oil on the bottom of the pan. When all the chicken has been browned, quickly pour off all but 2 tablespoons of the fat. Off the heat, stir the flour into the pan. Cook this roux, stirring, until it is brown, about 2 minutes. Add the brandy and stand back in case it ignites. Strain the marinade and stir to dissolve any brown bits on the bottom of the pan. Pour this sauce around the chicken. Add the chicken stock and bring to a boil. Turn down the heat and let the sauce simmer gently, covered, until the chicken is completely cooked, about 40 minutes.

To finish the sauce, remove the chicken pieces from the casserole. Strain the cooking juices into a bowl and let cool for 5 minutes. With a spoon, skim off and discard any fat that comes to the surface. Return the sauce to the casserole. Place the cocoa in a small bowl and whisk in about ½ cup of the sauce. Stir the cocoa mixture into the red wine sauce. Bring the red wine sauce to a boil, stirring, and continue cooking until the liquid is reduced to about 4 cups. Return the chicken to the casserole.

To boil the onions, put them in a saucepan covered with cold water. Bring to a boil and simmer until the onions are tender, about 8 minutes.

Cook the bacon in a medium-size sauté pan over moderately high heat until it is crisp and brown, about 5 minutes. Stir in the onions and mushrooms and cook, stirring or shaking, until the onions and mushrooms are lightly browned. Remove the bacon, onions, and mushrooms from the pan with a slotted spoon and add them to the casserole with the chicken. (The dish can be made ahead up to this point.)

When ready to serve, reheat the chicken over moderately low heat, stirring from time to time, until it is heated through, about 10 minutes. Add salt and pepper to taste. Serve with parsleyed new potatoes or buttered noodles. SERVES 8

Whenever a recipe instructs you to reduce a liquid, stir the liquid with a flat wooden scraper as it boils to speed up the process.

Brown chicken well before cooking it in liquid because the chicken always whitens during cooking and looks unappealing.

An integral part of many French dishes is small white onions and button mushrooms. They should be about the same size, about an inch across. Pearl onions are too small.

Chicken Olney
(with Zucchini and Ricotta)

*S*ometime in the '70s, I was fortunate enough to see Richard Olney demonstrate this recipe at the old Williams-Sonoma store on Sutter Street in San Francisco. Richard was an inspiration to many of the Bay Area's chefs and cooking teachers. Here, a frittata-type mixture is stuffed under the skin of a flattened chicken, which goes into the oven looking quite green. When it comes out, the chicken is browned, puffed, and glorious, so moist it really doesn't need a sauce. Serve it with garlic potatoes in the winter or a fresh tomato salad in the summer. I'm sure it will become a favorite of yours!

1 large onion, finely chopped
Coarse salt
4 tablespoons (½ stick) butter
1 pound zucchini, grated
3 tablespoons ricotta
1 egg, beaten
1 tablespoon mixed chopped fresh herbs, such as thyme, savory, parsley, and/or chives
3 tablespoons freshly grated Parmesan
Freshly ground black pepper
One 3½-pound chicken
2 tablespoons olive oil

To make the filling, cook the onion with a sprinkling of salt and 2 tablespoons of the butter in a medium-size frying pan over moderately high heat. Cook, stirring from time to time, until the onion is soft, about 5 minutes.

Transfer the onion to a large bowl to cool. Add the remaining 2 tablespoons butter to the pan with the zucchini. Cook, stirring, until all the liquid from the zucchini has evaporated, about 10 minutes. Add the zucchini to the onion and let the mixture cool, stirring from time to time. When it's cool, stir in the ricotta, egg, herbs, and Parmesan with ½ teaspoon salt and ¼ teaspoon pepper.

To prepare the chicken, turn the chicken over onto its breastbone. With poultry shears or kitchen scissors, cut out the backbone of the chicken from each side of the tail to each side of the neck. (It can be added to stock or discarded.) Turn the chicken over, breast side up, and arrange the legs flat on either side, against the ribs. With the palm of your hand, hit the chicken firmly in the middle to break the bones on either side of the breastbone. The flattened chicken should be about the size of a Frisbee.

To make a pocket under the skin, start by putting your fingers between the wings and loosen the skin from the breast and then the thighs and legs. Carefully stuff small handfuls of the filling mixture under the skin starting with the legs, then the thighs, and then the breasts. When all the stuffing is under the skin, use your hands to arrange the legs and thighs, making a clear dent between them and the breasts on either side. This will allow you to see where to carve after the chicken is cooked. You can make a small slit in the skin and poke each leg through the slit to prevent the legs from spreading in the cooking. Alternatively, you can position the legs against the sides of the roasting pan. Either way, it is important to tuck the wing tips underneath the body so they don't spread while in the oven. Rub the outside of the chicken with the olive oil and sprinkle with salt and pepper. (The chicken can be prepared ahead up to this point.)

Preheat the oven to 450 degrees. Place the chicken in the roasting pan on the top rack of the oven and bake for 10 minutes. Reduce the temperature to 375 degrees, and continue roasting. After 30 minutes, baste the chicken at 10-minute intervals with the juices from the bottom of the pan: remove the pan from the oven, close the oven door and, using a bulb baster held straight up and down, squirt the cooking juices over the chicken, especially where the color is light. If the top of the chicken becomes too dark before the time is up, cover it loosely with foil. When the chicken is browned and puffy and the skin has receded slightly from the tips of the legs, about 50 minutes, remove the chicken and transfer it to a warmed serving platter and show everyone how beautiful it is. With a carving knife and fork, cut the legs off before cutting the breast in half.   SERVES 4

The stuffing mixture needs to cool before the ricotta is added because the ricotta will liquefy if hot and the filling won't be as easy to handle.

❧

It is a good idea never to taste mixtures that contain uncooked eggs or raw pork because of the chance of contamination.

❧

You can make this dish with chopped mushrooms instead of shredded zucchini. Cook the mushrooms with the onion in the butter until the liquid is cooked away. Let the mixture cool and add ½ cup bread crumbs with the egg, ricotta, and Parmesan.

Each time you open the oven, the temperature drops about 50 degrees. That is why you want to baste or check for doneness only occasionally.

Crispy Chicken Breasts and Wild Mushrooms with Mashed Potatoes

Everyone loves mashed potatoes, especially with chicken in a sauce of wild mushrooms. It is a common practice to extend lean pieces of meat like chicken and veal by coating them in flour, egg, and bread crumbs. The French term for this is à l'Anglaise.

1 pound yellow-fleshed potatoes, such as Yellow Finn or Yukon Gold
Coarse salt
¼ cup heavy cream
Freshly ground white pepper
½ pound shiitake or other wild mushrooms, trimmed and sliced
4 tablespoons (½ stick) butter
2 tablespoons olive oil
2 shallots, finely chopped
2 tablespoons brandy
3 tablespoons minced fresh herbs, such as parsley, thyme, chives, and/or savory
½ cup heavy cream
1 cup rich chicken stock (reduced from 2 cups)
4 boned chicken breasts
Flour for dredging
2 eggs
1 cup dry bread crumbs
½ cup dry white wine

To cook the potatoes, place them with ½ teaspoon salt in a large saucepan and cover generously with cold water. Bring to a boil over high heat. Reduce the heat and let them boil until they are tender when pierced with a fork. Drain them in a colander and shake them well to allow any excess liquid to evaporate. Peel them, and put them through a potato ricer into a saucepan. Stir in the cream with salt and pepper to taste.

To cook the mushrooms, remove the stems and finely slice them. Slice the mushroom caps into ¼-inch lengths. Heat a tablespoon each of the butter and oil in a medium-size frying or sauté pan over moderately high heat. Add the shallots and cook, stirring, for 2 to 3 minutes until the shallots are soft. Toss in the mushrooms all at once and continue cooking, stirring until the mushrooms are half wilted. Add the brandy and cook for a minute, and add the herbs and cook for another minute. Add the cream and the rich chicken stock and cook for another minute. Add salt and pepper to taste.

To prepare the chicken, place each breast skin side (shiny side) down on a board, cover with waxed paper, and pound with the flat side of a meat pounder to an even thickness.

Prepare three plates for dredging: one of flour seasoned with salt and pepper, one of beaten eggs, and one of bread crumbs. Dip the chicken breasts first in flour, then egg, and then bread crumbs. Heat the remaining butter and oil in a medium-size frying or sauté pan over moderately high heat. When the bubbles have subsided, place a few chicken breasts in the pan. Do not push them around and do not crowd the pan. Cook them gently until they are golden on one side and then cook on the other side. Press the chicken breasts with a spatula fairly often to prevent them from shrinking or put a weight or a cover directly on them as they cook. The chicken breasts are cooked through when they are firm to the touch. Transfer the cooked chicken to a warmed plate and repeat with the remaining chicken breasts. Pour off any fat in the pan, deglaze with the white wine, boil up, and strain the juices into the mushrooms.

To serve, place large spoonfuls of mashed potatoes in the middle of four warmed plates, arrange a chicken breast on each, angled up toward the middle, and spoon the wild mushrooms over the top. SERVES 4

To bone chicken breast halves (boning is to take the meat off the bones), place the chicken breast skin side down on a board, with the thick white bone away from you and the ribs closer to you. With a small, sharp knife and using the thick white bone as a handle, glide the knife along the bones, working toward the ribs. It is important that the knife always stay close to the bone. When the entire breast is removed, run your fingers under the skin to take that off as well.

In French, a boned chicken breast is called a suprême de volaille. *Sometimes the piece closest to the breastbone separates from the rest of the breast. This is called the tenderloin in English and the* blanc de volaille *in French. You can press it back into the breast before cooking to keep it whole.*

If the chicken stock is not rich, reduce it in a small saucepan until it is half the volume.

This recipe would be even better if you added a teaspoon of truffle oil to the mashed potatoes and a few drops to the mushrooms.

Chicken Kiev
with Melon Seed Pasta Pilaf

Even though these little crispy packages of chicken filled with herb butter are common, they are delicious and fun to eat! When cooked right, melted herb butter will ooze from each package as the diner cuts into it. These bundles can be made a day or two ahead and kept in the refrigerator, or frozen for up to nine months. All you have to do is heat up some oil, deep-fry the Chicken Kiev, and you will have dinner in minutes. Serve with rice pilaf or Melon Seed Pasta Pilaf (recipe follows) and a green vegetable or green salad!

½ pound (2 sticks) softened butter
2 tablespoons minced fresh Italian parsley
1 teaspoon minced fresh tarragon
1 garlic clove, minced
Coarse salt
Freshly ground black pepper
12 boneless, skinless chicken breast halves
  (about ½ pound each)
¾ cup flour
3 eggs, well beaten
3 cups fine bread crumbs
Vegetable oil for deep-frying

To prepare the herb butter, place the butter in a bowl and beat with a wooden spoon to soften. Add the parsley, tarragon, and garlic along with salt and pepper to taste. Mix well and form into a block about 4 inches square. Put the herb butter in the freezer for about 30 minutes.

To prepare the chicken, remove all the fat from each chicken breast. Put each one skin (shiny) side down on a board, cover with a piece of waxed paper, and pound with the flat side of a meat pounder to make them an even thickness.

To prepare the coating, prepare three bowls: one of flour well seasoned with salt and pepper; one of the beaten eggs; and one of bread crumbs.

To assemble the bundles, cut the butter into 12 1½ by ½-inch pieces. Put each finger of butter down the middle of a chicken breast, folding over and pinching the chicken meat to get it to stick together. Without rolling the chicken breasts over, coat each side first in the flour, dip them in the egg, and then coat with the bread crumbs. Lay the chicken breasts on a plate with the seam side up. Chill until ready to deep-fry. Care must be taken to close the seam of the chicken and seal it with the flour, egg, and bread crumbs or the Chicken Kiev will open up in the hot fat and release the butter.

When ready to serve, heat at least 4 inches of oil in a wok or deep iron pan to 350 degrees or until a piece of bread dropped into the oil starts to bounce around and cook. Carefully slide three or four of the chicken bundles seam side down into the oil. This is to ensure that the edges seal rather than open up in the oil. If the oil is very hot, the chicken will brown quickly, and the only real way to tell whether they have cooked long enough is to cut into the first one. The chicken meat should be opaque. Remove them as they cook and drain on paper towels. Keep them warm while you cook the remaining chicken breasts. It is always best to add pieces to the oil all at once and take them out all at once. Allow the oil to heat up for a minute or two before adding the next batch. Serve within 15 minutes of deep-frying.

SERVES 12

MELON SEED PASTA PILAF

4 tablespoons (½ stick) butter
1 small onion, finely chopped
Coarse salt
1 garlic clove, minced
6 cups chicken stock
2 pounds melon seed pasta or orzo

To make the pilaf, cook the butter and onion with ½ teaspoon salt in a large saucepan over moderately high heat. Cook, stirring, until the onion is soft, about 5 minutes. Add the garlic, and cook, stirring, for another minute. Add the chicken stock with 6 cups water and bring to a boil. Stir in the pasta and continue stirring until it boils again. Simmer uncovered until the pasta is al dente, about 6 minutes. Drain and keep warm until ready to serve.

SERVES 12

Stir-Fried Chicken and Ginger-Peanut Sauce with Mixed Grain Pilaf

This is a recipe I learned many years ago from Michel Stroot, who for years has been the chef at the Golden Door Spa in southern California. He makes deliciously healthful food! Serve with Mixed Grain Pilaf (recipe follows).

4 chicken breast halves, boned and cut into
*   2 by ½-inch pieces*
Coarse salt
Freshly ground black pepper
¼ cup fresh lime juice
1 tablespoon toasted sesame oil
1 tablespoon soy sauce
1 piece ginger, about 1 inch square, grated
1 garlic clove
1½ tablespoons rice vinegar
1½ tablespoons red wine vinegar
½ tablespoon honey
2 tablespoons (unhomogenized) peanut
*   butter*
Hot chili oil (or Tabasco sauce)
⅔ cup peanut oil
1 tablespoon minced fresh cilantro
4 tablespoons vegetable oil
12 shiitake mushrooms, stemmed and sliced
*   into ½-inch lengths*
6 scallions, cut on the diagonal into 2-inch
*   lengths*

Lightly season the chicken with salt and pepper.

To make the sauce, combine the lime juice, sesame oil, soy sauce, ginger, garlic, rice vinegar, red wine vinegar, honey, peanut butter, and a few drops of chili oil in an electric blender or food processor. Blend until smooth. Once blended, slowly add the peanut oil with the motor running. Stir in the cilantro with a spoon.

To stir-fry the mushrooms, scallions, and chicken, put a tablespoon of the vegetable oil in a large nonstick skillet. When the oil is hot, toss in the mushrooms all at once, season with salt and pepper, and cook over medium high heat until the mushrooms are half wilted. Remove them from the pan, add another tablespoon of vegetable oil, and toss in the scallions. Cook over medium-high heat, stirring constantly, until the scallions are half wilted. Remove from the pan and add the remaining 2 tablespoons of vegetable oil. When the oil is hot, toss in the chicken pieces and continue cooking over high heat, stirring or shaking the pan, until the chicken pieces are golden on all sides and just opaque all the way through. Return the mushrooms and scallions to the pan and pour in enough of the ginger-lime sauce to flavor nicely. (Save the leftover sauce for another day.)

SERVES 6

To bone chicken breasts, see page 199.

When buying chicken, remember that they have only one breast, according to a butcher. When the whole breast is split, there are two halves. This recipe calls for two whole breasts, or four halves.

MIXED GRAIN PILAF

*W*hole grains are fascinating. They can be cooked as a breakfast cereal or a side dish like this pilaf, or ground into flour for baking bread. This side dish can be made with any combination of whole (unpolished) grains. Pilaf can be made ahead and kept covered for 30 minutes to 1 hour before serving.

1 large onion, finely chopped
2 tablespoons olive oil
Coarse salt
1 celery stalk, finely chopped
2 garlic cloves, finely minced
1 teaspoon ancho chile powder
1 teaspoon freshly ground cumin
Cayenne pepper
½ cup short-grain brown rice
½ cup wheat berries
¼ cup wild rice
2¼ cups chicken stock
½ red bell pepper, cut into ¼-inch dice
2 tablespoons minced fresh cilantro

Cook the onion and celery in the oil and salt in a medium-size saucepan over moderately high heat. Cook, stirring from time to time, until the onion is soft, about 5 minutes. Stir in the garlic and cook for another minute. Stir in the chile powder, cumin, and a few grains of cayenne, and cook, stirring constantly, for 2 minutes more. Stir in the brown rice, wheat berries, and wild rice, making sure the grains are coated with the onion mixture. Stir in the stock and bring the mixture to a boil, stirring constantly. Lower the heat to a simmer, cover, and cook until the grains have absorbed all the liquid, about 45 minutes.

When the grains are cooked through, fluff the mixture gently with a fork and stir in the bell pepper and cilantro.　　SERVES 6

All whole (unpolished) grains cook in the same amount of time, about 45 minutes. Polished grains such as white rice cook in 25 minutes. Because of the variation in cooking times, it is best not to combine them.

Whenever you can buy whole spices such as cumin seeds and grind them yourself, do so; the flavor will be much better than using already ground spices.

Chicken Sauté and Preserved Lemons and Olives with Spicy Rice

How can you make chicken more exciting? Rub it with exotic spices the day before cooking it, sauté it with onions and tomatoes, and finish the dish with preserved lemons and olives. This is a great recipe that my fellow Tante Marie teachers and I learned when we were studying with Lydie Marshall at her medieval château in Nyons, a market town in northern Provence. Good cooks keep a big glass jar of preserved lemons in their refrigerator— they're great for adding to salads, vegetables, chicken, and lamb dishes. Serve with Spicy Rice Pilaf (recipe follows).

> One 3¾-pound chicken, cut into
>   8 pieces
> ½ cup olive oil
> 1 teaspoon paprika
> 1 teaspoon turmeric
> ⅛ teaspoon powdered saffron
> Coarse salt
> Freshly ground black pepper
> 4 small onions, halved and thinly sliced
> 6 garlic cloves, minced
> 4 medium-size tomatoes, peeled, seeded,
>   and chopped
> ½-inch piece ginger, peeled and finely
>   chopped
> Juice of 2 fresh lemons
> 1 preserved lemon (see page 390), soaked in
>   cold water for 30 to 60 minutes
> 20 green olives, pitted

To marinate the chicken, place the chicken pieces in a bowl and rub them with 2 tablespoons of the olive oil. Rub the chicken again with a mixture of paprika, turmeric, saffron, ½ teaspoon salt, and ¼ teaspoon pepper. Cover the bowl and refrigerate overnight.

To cook the chicken, heat ¼ inch of olive oil in a medium-size sauté pan over moderately high heat. When the oil is hot but not smoking, place a few pieces of the chicken skin side down in the pan. Do not crowd the pan and do not move the chicken pieces around. When each piece is chestnut brown, turn it with tongs and brown the other side. Transfer the cooked chicken to a plate and continue browning the remaining pieces. Add more oil if needed to keep the bottom of the pan coated. When all the chicken is cooked, pour off all but 2 tablespoons of the fat, add the onions, and cook for 5 to 10 minutes, stirring, until the onions are soft. Add the garlic and cook for a minute more. Stir in the tomatoes and ginger and cook for 5 more minutes, stirring from time to time. Return the chicken pieces and the juices from the plate to the pan. Sprinkle the lemon juice over the chicken and cook, covered, for 20 minutes.

Meanwhile, remove the preserved lemon from the liquid and taste a small piece of the pulp. If it is particularly salty, cut out and discard the soft pulp. Cut the remaining lemon in ¼-inch dice. Test the chicken by cutting into it near the thighbone to see if it is cooked through. Stir in the preserved lemon and olives and cook for a minute. Add salt and pepper to taste. SERVES 4

Traditionally in French cooking, you remove the last joint of the wing—the wing tip—to indicate that it is a domestic fowl rather than a wild one.

Saffron is very expensive because it is the little stamens that have to be handpicked from crocuses. It is better to buy the threads than the powder because they have more flavor.

This recipe could just as easily be made with 8 pieces of dark meat chicken (legs and thighs). It can be cooked 2 to 3 days in advance, refrigerated, and reheated on the stove just before serving.

There is no substitute for preserved lemons, which are completely different from fresh ones. It is really worth the effort to make a jar yourself and keep them in the refrigerator. They can also be purchased in specialty food stores.

SPICY RICE PILAF

1 onion, finely chopped
4 tablespoons (½ stick) butter
Coarse salt
1 garlic clove, minced
1½ cups long-grain white rice
½ teaspoon good-quality curry powder
¼ cup yellow mustard seeds
2¾ cups chicken stock

Cook the onion in the butter with ½ teaspoon salt in a medium-size saucepan over moderately high heat. Cook, stirring from time to time, until the onion is soft, about 5 minutes. Stir in the garlic and cook another minute. Stir in the rice, curry powder, and mustard seeds and cook, stirring constantly, for another minute. Mix in the stock. Bring the mixture to a boil, cover, and reduce the heat to the lowest possible simmer. Cook until all the liquid has been absorbed by the rice, about 25 minutes. Do not stir the rice with a spoon, as it will break up and become mushy. When ready to serve, fluff the rice with a fork. (The rice can be held for up to 30 minutes in the covered pot.)

SERVES 6

In a pilaf, each grain of rice has been coated with butter or oil before being cooked in liquid so that the cooked rice doesn't stick together.

Magret of Duck in Cassis Sauce

This recipe shows us how to make dark duck stock, which is the base for this reduction sauce flavored with cassis. It's important to understand how to get all the flavor from the browned duck bones to make a sauce. Although the term magret *originally meant the boned breast of a force-fed duck, it has come to mean any boned breast of duck. For this recipe Long Island or Petaluma ducks are fine. Muscovy or Moulard are better. It would be best to serve this elegant dish with a potato gratin or puree of root vegetables and a fine Cabernet Sauvignon.*

2 whole ducks
¼ cup cassis liqueur
Coarse salt
Freshly ground black pepper
2 tablespoons olive oil
4 tablespoons butter plus 2 tablespoons for finishing the sauce
1 medium-size onion, coarsely chopped
1 medium-size carrot, coarsely chopped
1 celery stalk, coarsely chopped
½ cup red wine
¼ cup red wine vinegar
4 cups chicken stock
Bouquet garni composed of 2 sprigs parsley, 1 sprig thyme, and 1 bay leaf

To prepare the ducks, remove the legs and thighs of the duck and save for the following recipe or another purpose. With a boning knife, remove the two breast halves (magrets) from each carcass. Remove the skin from each breast by carefully cutting the filament that holds it to the meat. Save the skin to make cracklings if desired, or discard. Trim any fat from the magrets and sprinkle with a few drops of cassis and salt and pepper.

To make the stock, chop the duck bones with a cleaver into 3- or 4-inch pieces. Place the bones in one layer in a 10-inch sauté pan with the olive oil. Brown the bones on all sides over moderately high heat until they are very dark and chestnut brown, being careful not to burn the bottom of the pan. Mix in the onion, carrot, and celery and brown the mixture. Add a cup of the chicken stock and, using a wooden spatula, scrape up any browned bits on the bottom of the pan. Bring the mixture to a boil and simmer until it has thickened slightly. Add the bouquet garni and another cup of the chicken stock, or enough stock just to cover the mixture, and bring to a boil. Boil for 10 to 15 minutes or until the liquid has reduced to just a few tablespoons and is, again, slightly thickened. Add another cup of stock and boil in the same fashion, reducing the stock to a light syrup. Repeat with the fourth cup of stock. When there is about ½ cup liquid in the pan, strain the contents of the pan through a fine strainer into a medium-size saucepan. Pour ½ cup chicken stock or water into the sauté pan to dissolve any remaining sauce and pour this over the bones in the strainer. Press the bones with the bottom of a ladle to release all the juices. Discard the bones. You should have about 1 cup of dark duck stock.

When ready to serve, heat enough butter and oil in the bottom of the 10-inch sauté pan to coat the bottom. When the bubbles have subsided, lay two or three of the magrets in the hot pan. Do not crowd the pan and do not push the duck breasts around. You can press them with the back of a metal spatula or use a weight to keep the duck breasts from curling. When the bottoms of the breasts are nicely browned, turn them over and continue cooking on the other side, pressing gently. When the magrets are slightly resilient when pressed with your finger, remove them from the pan and let rest on a board for 5 minutes while you make the sauce.

To make the sauce, immediately deglaze the pan with red wine and vinegar, scraping up the browned bits on the bottom of the pan with a flat wooden spatula. Add the reduced duck stock and continue cooking until the mixture coats the back of a metal spoon. Add the cassis and let the mixture boil for 3 minutes. Add salt and pepper to taste. Turn off the heat, dot the top of the sauce with 1 tablespoon butter, and swirl to emulsify.

To serve, slice the duck breasts at an angle against the grain of the meat with a thin carving knife. Arrange the slices on warmed dinner plates and spoon 2 tablespoons sauce around each magret.   SERVES 4

To cut up a whole duck, remove the legs and thighs in one piece from each side. To do this, cut into the fatty circle around the top of the leg and glide the knife through the space between the leg and the carcass, keeping the knife close to the carcass. When you reach the joint, fold the leg back to reveal the joint and slide the knife through. Try to get as much meat on either side of the joint as possible with the leg piece. With the knife, remove each breast from each side of the carcass, sliding the meat off the bone from the top of the breastbone, cutting away from yourself down toward the wings.

A delicious way to use duck skin is to cut the skin into large dice, combine it with ½ cup water in a saucepan, and place the pan over moderate heat. The water will help the fat render. Let the duck skin and fat cook gently until all the fat has been rendered from under the skin and the little pieces of skin are crisp. Remove the pieces with a slotted spoon and put them on paper towels. They can be kept in a glass jar in the refrigerator and added to salads or eaten as a snack; just don't forget to salt and rewarm them before serving.

This method of cooking chicken stock over browned bones of other poultry with mirepoix and bouquet garni is a terrific method for making a dark poultry stock in relatively little time. It can be stored in the refrigerator for up to 5 days and frozen for up to 9 months. The stock should be a neutral flavor so that the final dish can be flavored in any way.

To make a good reduction sauce, there are always three steps: deglaze the pan with cold liquid, add the reduced stock and flavoring, and finish with cream or butter. In this recipe, you could deglaze the pan with port and finish the sauce with heavy cream.

To make this recipe with the larger magrets of force-fed ducks, preheat an oven to 450 degrees. Pan-fry the magrets on both sides until brown, then put the entire pan in the oven until the breasts are slightly resilient to the touch. Then proceed with the recipe. (This is a technique very common in restaurant cooking. It is used for fish, poultry, and meat.)

When a recipe calls for straining a sauce through a fine sieve, the best is a conical sieve called a chinois. It really has no other purpose. Use a colander for stock and a round sieve for demi-glace, and a tamis, or drum sieve, for soups because the chinois removes all the texture. The chinois is not recommended for stock, demi-glace, or soups.

Braised Duck Legs with Lentils

*This dish of fully cooked duck legs with fla-
vorful green lentils is quite rustic. Make it
ahead, reheat it, and serve it with a hearty red
wine.*

*8 legs and thighs, cut into 16 pieces
    (or 2 whole ducks cut into 16 pieces)
1 bottle red wine
4 garlic cloves, smashed
2 shallots, thinly sliced
4 sprigs thyme
2 bay leaves
Coarse salt
Freshly ground black pepper
2 tablespoons olive oil
1 onion, finely chopped
1 large carrot, finely chopped
1 celery stalk, finely chopped
6 cups chicken stock
¾ pound (1½ cups) French green lentils
1 tablespoon tomato paste
½ pound thick-cut bacon, cut into 1-inch
    pieces
3 tablespoons minced fresh Italian parsley*

To marinate the duck, place the duck pieces
in a large stainless steel bowl and stir in the
wine, garlic, shallots, thyme, bay leaves, 2
teaspoons salt, and 1 teaspoon pepper. Cover
and chill for 4 hours or overnight, turning
occasionally.

To cook the lentils, put the olive oil in the
bottom of a 3-quart casserole with the onion,
carrot, and celery over moderately high heat,
stirring from time to time. Cook until the
vegetables are soft, about 5 minutes. Stir in
the chicken stock, lentils, and tomato paste,
and bring to a boil. Reduce to a simmer and
cook until the lentils are half cooked, about
15 minutes.

To brown the duck, brown the bacon in
another 3-quart casserole until crisp. Remove
the bacon from the pan and drain on paper
towels. Pour off all but a tablespoon of the
bacon fat. Remove the duck pieces from the
marinade and pat dry with paper towels. Season with salt and pepper. Brown the duck
pieces, skin side down, in the bacon fat,
adding more fat as needed. Turn the ducks in
the pan in order to get a dark brown color on
all sides. Remove the browned pieces of duck
to a plate and repeat until all the duck is
browned, being careful not to burn the bottom of the pan.

In the meantime, strain the duck marinade into a small saucepan. Bring the marinade to a boil over moderately high heat and
cook until it is reduced to a cup.

To assemble the dish, stir the bacon into
the lentils and bury the browned duck pieces
in the lentils. Cover with the reduced marinade and bring to a simmer on top of the
stove.

At this point you can cover and continue
cooking the braised duck legs and lentils over
low heat on top of the stove (or cover the
casserole and place it deep in a 325-degree
oven) until the duck is almost falling off the
bones, about 1½ hours. Add salt and pepper
to taste, and serve sprinkled with parsley. If
made ahead, skim off and discard any fat that
has accumulated on the top of the dish before
reheating and serving. SERVES 8

Rabbit Dijonnaise

*C*are must be taken when making a rabbit *sauté that the meat doesn't get dry. That is why this rabbit with a sauce of cream and mustard is so good—the cream and mustard keep the rabbit moist, and the taste is great!*

One 3-pound rabbit, cut into 6 pieces
Coarse salt
Freshly ground black pepper
2 tablespoons butter plus 2 tablespoons for
  the beurre manié
1 tablespoon olive oil
3 tablespoons minced shallots
½ cup dry white wine
1 cup chicken stock
Bouquet garni composed of 4 sprigs parsley,
  2 sprigs thyme, and a bay leaf
3 tablespoons flour
2 tablespoons Dijon-style mustard
⅓ cup heavy cream

To prepare the rabbit, season the rabbit pieces generously with salt and pepper. Heat enough butter and oil in a heavy skillet or sauté pan to lightly coat the bottom. Place over medium-high heat. When hot, place pieces of rabbit in the pan to brown. Brown the pieces on all sides and remove from the pan, being careful that the bottom of the pan does not burn. Continue with all the pieces. Add the shallots and cook, stirring, for 2 minutes more. Pour in the wine and stock and add the bouquet garni. Return the rabbit to the pan with any juices and simmer gently, covered, for about 10 minutes, or until the rabbit is cooked through, or opaque when cut down to the bone. Remove the bouquet garni, and transfer the rabbit to a warmed serving platter.

To finish the sauce, strain the cooking juices into a saucepan over medium-high heat and reduce by half. Into the juices whisk enough beurre manié to give the juices the consistency of a sauce. (Beurre manié is made by mixing together equal parts of butter and flour to form a paste with the consistency of cookie dough.) Stir in the mustard mixed with the cream and add salt and pepper to taste.   SERVES 4

To cut up a rabbit, cut along the outline of a hind leg from the back toward the stomach and break back the leg to reveal the joint. Disjoint as best you can. To remove the forelegs, start boning some of the meat from on top of the ribs, cutting toward the front of the rabbit. When you reach the legs, do the same as with the hind legs. Cut the rabbit where the ribs meet the saddle. (The rib piece is cooked only for flavor; it is not to be served.) If the rabbit is large, tie a string around the loin and the loose belly flap in two places. Cut the loin in half between the two strings. If the rabbit is small, simply tie with the flaps to make one round piece.

Mustard will separate when heated too long, which is why it is always best to add it to a dish toward the end of the cooking time.

Rabbit Stew Woodland Style with Baked Cheese Polenta

This is an all-time favorite recipe of Tante Marie's students. It was developed by Richard Sax, a well-loved cooking teacher and cookbook writer from New York. Since most of the rabbits available in the United States are young and tender, this method of cooking produces the flavors and style of wild rabbits, which are usually older and need long cooking. It is a joy to eat rabbit off the bone with a thick slice of cheese polenta (recipe follows).

Two 3-pound rabbits, cut into
    6 pieces each
12 juniper berries
2½ cups dry white wine
⅓ cup lemon juice
⅓ cup olive oil plus 4 tablespoons for rabbit
    and 2 for mushrooms
¼ cup brandy
3 garlic cloves, crushed
4 sprigs fresh Italian parsley
3 sprigs fresh thyme
Coarsely ground black pepper
2½ ounces dried porcini (cèpes) mushrooms
2 large onions, finely chopped
1 large carrot, finely chopped
1 celery stalk, finely chopped
½ cup finely diced red bell pepper
Coarse salt
5 garlic cloves, finely minced
½ teaspoon minced fresh thyme
⅓ cup brandy
1⅔ cups dry white wine
2 cups canned Italian plum tomatoes,
    coarsely chopped
5 cups chicken stock
1 bay leaf
1 strip orange zest, 1 by 4 inches
¼ teaspoon red pepper flakes
2 tablespoons olive oil
½ pound small white mushrooms, stems
    trimmed flush with cap
¼ cup minced fresh Italian parsley

To marinate the rabbits, place the rabbit pieces in a large bowl with the juniper berries, white wine, lemon juice, olive oil, brandy, garlic, parsley, thyme, and several grindings of black pepper. Cover and chill for at least 4 hours or overnight, turning the rabbit from time to time.

To reconstitute the dried mushrooms, place them in a glass measuring cup and barely cover with hot water. Let sit for 20 minutes. Remove the mushrooms from their liquor, squeeze out the excess liquid, and finely chop them. Pour off all but the last tablespoon of the liquid to avoid getting grit in the final dish and set aside.

To cook the rabbit, heat enough olive oil in the bottom of a 10-inch sauté pan to lightly coat the bottom and put the pan over medium-high heat. Remove the rabbit from the marinade and pat dry with paper towels. Season with salt and pepper. Brown the rabbit pieces on all sides. Do not crowd the sauté pan and do not push the rabbit pieces around; you want them to stick to the bottom of the pan. Transfer the pieces to an ovenproof casserole. Pour off all but a tablespoon of fat from the sauté pan. Immediately stir in the onions, carrot, celery, and bell pepper with a sprinkling of salt and pepper. Cook, stirring from time to time, until the vegetables are soft and lightly browned, about 8 minutes. Add the minced garlic and thyme and cook, stirring, for 2 more minutes. Add the brandy and wine and bring the mixture to a boil, scraping the bottom of the pan with a wooden spatula to loosen any browned bits. When the liquid has reduced by half, add the tomatoes and cook, stirring, until thickened, about 10 minutes. Pour the mixture over the rabbit in the casserole and add the stock, bay leaf, orange zest, and red pepper flakes. Stir in the reserved mushroom liquor. Bring to a boil, stirring, reduce the heat to a simmer, and cook, partially covered, until the meat is tender, about an hour.

To cook the fresh mushrooms, put 2 tablespoons olive oil in a small frying pan over moderately high heat. When the oil is hot, toss in the button mushrooms and cook, stirring or tossing, until they are half wilted. Add the reconstituted and the fresh mushrooms to the rabbit stew and simmer until the rabbit meat is completely tender and falling off the bones, another 20 to 30 minutes.

To finish the dish, remove the rabbit pieces from the stew. When the meat is cool enough to handle, pull it off in 1-inch pieces and discard the bones. If the sauce seems thin, reduce it over moderately high heat until the desired consistency is reached. If the sauce seems thick, stir in enough water to reach the desired consistency and simmer it for another 10 minutes to meld the flavors. Return the rabbit meat to the stew along with the parsley and salt and pepper to taste. SERVES 6 TO 8

Purchase rabbits that look fresh and moist with no dry spots. There should be no liquid in the display pan.

CHEESE POLENTA

7 tablespoons butter
5 cups milk
4 teaspoons salt
3 cups polenta-type cornmeal
1½ cups grated Parmesan
1 cup grated Gruyère

Generously butter a 9 by 12-inch glass baking dish.

Bring 3 cups of the milk, 5 cups water, and salt to a boil over high heat. Pour the remaining 2 cups milk in a bowl and whisk in the cornmeal. Gradually whisk this mixture into the pan of boiling liquid, whisking vigorously to prevent lumps. Return to a boil, stirring with a wooden spoon, and cook over low heat until thick and smooth, 5 to 8 minutes. Stir in 4 tablespoons of the butter. Pour about one-third of the polenta mixture into the prepared dish. Sprinkle with one-third of each of the grated cheeses. Repeat the layering, ending with a cheese layer. Dot the surface with the remaining butter. Lay a sheet of waxed paper on the surface of the polenta and let cool at least 15 minutes. Uncover and bake in a 425-degree oven until golden brown, about 30 minutes. SERVES 8

Cassoulet of White Beans, Sausage, and Duck Confit

Cassoulet is a dish cooked in the winter in southwest France. It is a winter dish because it is very hearty and uses preserved meats such as sausages and duck confit, cooked with white beans called flageolet. Since cassoulet is a traditional peasant dish, there is no need to buy fancy imported ingredients. Serve it with a green salad, plenty of red table wine, and a simple dessert such as poached oranges.

2 pounds small white beans such as Great Northern, soaked overnight in plenty of cold water

½ pound salt pork or thick-cut bacon, blanched

2 halved onions and 1 chopped onion

1 smashed garlic clove and 1 minced clove

Bouquet garni composed of 4 sprigs parsley, 3 sprigs thyme, and 2 bay leaves

2 quarts chicken stock

1 pound pork sausages, homemade (page 382) or store-bought

4 tablespoons rendered duck fat or olive oil

1 cup dry white wine

1½ pounds red tomatoes, peeled, seeded, and chopped, or one 28-ounce can of tomatoes

Coarse salt

Freshly ground black pepper

1 whole confit of duck, cut in 8 pieces, or 8 whole legs, halved, on the bone

1½ cups toasted bread crumbs

To prepare the beans, drain and put them in an 8-quart casserole with the bacon, the halved onions, the smashed garlic, bouquet garni, and chicken stock. Bring to a boil over moderately high heat. Reduce the heat and simmer over low heat, uncovered, for about an hour. Remove the bacon and cut it into 1-inch pieces. Strain the beans, reserving both the beans and the cooking liquid and discarding the onions and bouquet garni. Set the beans aside in a bowl.

To cook the sausages, prick each one in two places with a fork and put them in the bottom of a 10-inch sauté pan with ¼ inch water. Cook over medium heat, turning from time to time, until the water has evaporated and the sausages are browned on all sides, about 15 minutes. Remove them and cut at an angle into 1-inch pieces. Add 2 tablespoons of the duck fat to the pan with the chopped onion and cook, stirring from time to time, until the onion is soft, about 5 minutes. Add the minced garlic and continue to cook and stir for another minute. Add the white wine and cook for another minute. Stir in the tomatoes and continue cooking for another 5 minutes, stirring from time to time. Season well with salt and pepper and remove from the heat.

To assemble the cassoulet, layer one-third of the beans on the bottom of the casserole and add half the bacon or salt pork, sausages, and duck confit (on the bone). Cover this layer with half the tomato mixture. Repeat with another third of the beans and the remaining bacon, sausages, and duck confit. Cover this with the rest of the tomatoes and then the beans. Add salt and pepper to taste to the bean-cooking liquid. Pour in enough of the bean liquid to come up just to the top of the beans. Cover the entire cassoulet with bread crumbs, dot with the remaining 2 tablespoons duck fat, and bake in a 350-degree oven for an hour and 15 minutes, or until the bread crumbs have formed a crust. You can break through the crust with the back of a spoon three or four times during the cooking to allow the juices to help form a crust.   SERVES 12

To make Duck Confit, see page 381. If you do not have homemade confit, substitute fresh duck. To do this, season the duck well with coarse salt and cut up the duck into 8 pieces, removing any excess fat. Brown the duck in the pan after cooking the sausages, skin side down, over moderately high heat, and proceed with the recipe. The duck is fully cooked when it is falling off the bones.

If you live in or near a metropolitan area, you can buy a roast duck in a Chinese market, cut

it into 8 pieces, and substitute that for the confit of duck.

Often recipes for cassoulet call for a lamb and/or pork stew to be layered with the beans. It seems to me that using many different kinds of meat doesn't improve the dish.

This dish is usually made in an earthenware casserole-type dish called a cassoulet. If using such a dish, more liquid will be needed because the cassoulet is porous.

To toast bread crumbs, simply put them on a baking sheet in a 350-degree oven for about 15 minutes, tossing with a spoon from time to time.

To blanch the salt pork or bacon, simply drop it in a pan of boiling water, turn off the heat, and let sit for 5 minutes.

PORK, VEAL, LAMB, AND BEEF

I T WAS THE FAMOUS food philosopher of the nineteenth century who called himself Brillat-Savarin who said, "One can become a cook, but one is born a roaster of meat." It's a great saying even if it isn't altogether true. The truth is that experience is the best teacher in cooking. If you cook something over and over you will get a feel for it, so much that it even becomes second nature. It could be something as simple as Classic Caesar Salad or as complex as Herbed Rack of Lamb with Béarnaise Sauce. What I think Brillat-Savarin really meant was that there is something so appealing to human beings about the smell and the taste of roasted meats—or grilled meats for that matter. It's irresistible.

HOW TO BUY MEAT

Here is what to look for:

Pork	light gray or pink color with creamy fat
Veal	pale pink to light red color
Lamb	pale red color with brittle fat
Beef	well marbled

Meat should look freshly cut, not dried out or dark. Try not to buy meat in a plastic package. Meat is tough if there is no fat amid the fiber. Tender meat has little lines of fat running through it. Remember, tough cuts need long, slow cooking, and tender cuts need short, hot cooking.

Some restaurants and butchers still age large cuts of beef, which means they keep it in a cool place for up to three weeks. This is done to improve the taste and the texture of the meat. Aging is done less and less now because the meat shrinks as it ages, which means the butcher can't get as much money for it.

The growing, processing, and distribution of meat are pretty much standardized and controlled. Local butchers used to buy whole carcasses. Now the carcasses are already broken down and sold in subprime cuts to supermarkets. The old butchers have been replaced by meat cutters. It's best to buy meat directly from a farmer who treats his animals in a humane way. You can find such meat sometimes at local farmers' markets, or you can look for meats distributed by a company with high standards like Niman Ranch. The only way to know what you are buying is to ask questions, make demands, and get to know a meat salesperson you can trust. Generally, the price you pay indicates the quality. I recommend buying the best meat you can buy and cooking it as simply as possible, preferably on the bone.

After the animal is slaughtered and the carcass is examined, it is graded. Most meat that we buy is graded as good. On rare occasions we can buy the highest grade, called prime. Prime is a deceptive expression because often a standing rib roast of beef is called prime rib, which may not be graded as prime at all. Most of the prime meat in this country is sold to restaurants.

It's hard for the consumer to learn the different cuts of meat, especially of beef. Not only is the same cut of meat called by different names in New York, Chicago, and San Francisco, but it could be called by different names by two different meat handlers in the same city. Terms such as culotte steak, market steak, and châteaubriand all mean different cuts to different handlers. Not only that, but a side of beef can be broken down by the meat cutter according to the American, French, or English system, each giving entirely different cuts. That is why it is so important to get to know the person selling you the meat and learning what's what over time.

How to Cook Meat

Tender cuts of red meat—lamb and beef—should be cooked briefly using dry heat methods: roasting, broiling, or grilling. They should be cooked to medium-rare or 135 degrees on an instant-read thermometer. Tougher cuts of meat can be put in a marinade to be tenderized before roasting or grilling or can be braised or stewed, which tenderizes them at the same time as it brings out the flavor. See page 181 for more on marinating.

Because pork and veal are white meats they need to be fully cooked, which means 150 degrees on an instant-read thermometer. Tender cuts can be cooked in dry heat—roasting, broiling, or grilling. Tender cuts of all meats will toughen with long, slow cooking. That is why stewing and braising are reserved for tougher cuts of meat. In braising and stewing the meat is cooked with wine, stock, aromatic vegetables, and a bouquet garni to enhance the flavor. Browning the meat before cooking gives it added flavor.

Over the last twenty years, the perception of the producers of pork, beef, and even chicken has been that the consumer wants less fat. The truth is that meat with less fat can be rubbery and tough when cooked. Good cooks are now brining pork, beef, and even chicken so that it will be more juicy when cooked. Brining means to submerge the meat for several hours in a salt solution before cooking. See page 223 for more on brines.

The recipes to follow in the meat chapters are examples of the various ways to cook primary meats; namely, pork, veal, lamb, and beef. In the Herbed Rack of Lamb with Béarnaise Sauce (page 234), the lamb is roasted; in the Grilled Skirt Steak with Roasted Potatoes and Salsa Verde (page 242), the steak is grilled over a charcoal fire. These are both dry-heat suitable for tender cuts of meat.

In the Medallions of Pork with Apple Chutney Sauce (page 223) and the Veal Chops with Morels (page 226), the meat is sautéed in a small amount of fat. I don't see any good reason for deep-frying meat. And, instead of boiling meat, which is done the world over, I prefer to braise or stew it by browning it in fat and then simmering it in liquid, as in Lamb Shanks Braised with White Beans (page 241) and Beef (stewed) in Red Wine with Onions and Mushrooms (page 248). The difference between braising and stewing is that usually braising is done in a small amount of liquid, and stewing requires considerably more liquid.

Both braising and stewing can be done with or without browning. When the meat is browned before cooking in the liquid, it has a rich flavor because the sugar in the meat juices is caramelizing. When it is not browned beforehand, the flavor is more delicate. Meats used to be encased in pastry to make it fancy; this is not necessary nowadays. Encasing is a better method for cooking fish, as no juices are lost in the cooking. The most popular meat to cure is pork. Bacon, ham, prosciutto, and pancetta are kinds of cured pork that are then smoked or air dried. Air-dried cured beef is called bresaola; this is delicious served like prosciutto as part of an antipasto plate.

You can try to tell when meat is cooked by feeling it, by cutting into it, and by taking its temperature. None of these may be accurate. The final way to tell is when the meat begins to shrink. When the steak, chop, or roast looks smaller, get it off the heat or out of the oven.

HOW TO SAUCE MEAT

When presented with a piece of fish, chicken, or meat, a good cook has to decide how to cook it and then sauce it. Sauces are a necessity with fish and less so with chicken. With meat the cook can go all out with making luscious sauces. With braises and stews the meat makes its own sauce with the help of wine, stock, aromatic vegetables, and herbs. With roasting and grilling, if the meat is excellent quality, the cook only has to add salt and pepper and roast or grill it on the bone.

There are some points good cooks must keep in mind when saucing less-than-perfect-quality meat and certain tender cuts of meat. The most important thing is to capture the juices from the bottom of the pan. If there is a lot of juice, the pan needs to be cooled for five minutes so that the fat rises to the top. The fat should then be spooned off, which is called degreasing the pan. Return the pan to high heat and add cold liquid in the form of water, wine, or stock to dissolve the caramelized meat juices on the bottom of the pan. This is called deglazing. Be sure to deglaze the pan before it burns!

You can add fortified wine and cream to the pan juices to make a good sauce. But to make a splendid sauce, a good cook goes on to add the basic brown mother sauce called demi-glace (sometimes called espagnole) with a flavoring, as in this chapter's Fillet of Beef Braised with Mushrooms (page 246). A good cook might make a modern reduction sauce by adding essence (stock reduced over pieces of browned meat), as in Medallions of Lamb with Spring Vegetables (page 232). In either case, the demi-glace and the essence are simply the base for the sauce; they still need to be flavored and finished with a little butter or cream.

The Big Problem

The big problem when cooking meat is determining the right method of cooking for each cut. It helps to remember that the most tender part of any animal is the middle of the back—the loin. The more you cook tender cuts of meat, the tougher they will become. The tough cuts of meat are those farther away from the loin. The longer you cook these, the more tender they become. In other words, when the cut of meat is from the back or the hindquarter of the animal it is probably tender—cook it quickly to medium-rare. If it is from the shoulder or the shank, it is tough—braise or stew it until it is well done.

How to Cook Meat Without a Recipe

To cook a steak without a recipe, heat a heavy pan with a thin layer of butter and oil. Season the steak with a little salt and a lot of pepper and place the steak in the hot pan.

Don't move it around. Let it cook until it can be lifted easily, turn it with tongs, and cook it on the other side until it is firm but slightly resilient when pressed with your finger. Take it out of the pan and let it rest for five minutes. Pour off any fat in the pan and immediately add a splash of brandy. Let it boil up and pour in some cream. Taste the sauce and pour it over the steak—voilà!—pepper steak or steak au poivre! You could do the same with a pork chop, throwing some sautéed sliced apples in with the cream; or with a lamb chop, throwing in some garlic and rosemary with white wine instead of brandy and swirling in a teaspoon of butter instead of the cream.

To pan-fry steaks or chops, remember that the meat will feel gushy when it is raw, slightly resilient when it is medium rare, and firm to the touch when it is well done. Tender cuts of lamb and beef will always taste better if cooked medium rare. Pork and veal should always be cooked to well done because they are white meat.

Roasting meat is simple. All you have to do is put salt and pepper on it, put it in a roasting pan in a hot oven, and cook it until it reaches the right temperature. After removing it from the oven, let it rest for a while, pour off any accumulated fat, and deglaze the pan with water to make simple pan juices. The important thing is that the meat is of the highest quality.

PRESERVING

Preserving was far more important to our ancestors than it is to us. In homes without refrigerators or freezers, it was imperative to preserve food in a time of plenty to sustain life in a time of scarcity. Techniques were developed to preserve food at the end of the summer so it could be eaten throughout the winter.

It's hard to imagine what it must have been like not to have had plenty of fresh or frozen vegetables all year round. Now we seldom think of canning or preserving fresh vegetables, except tomatoes. There is no reason to can other fresh vegetables when you can freeze them. To the modern cook, however, some kinds of preserved foods still hold appeal, such as hams, sausages, cheese, smoked fish, and caviar. What follows is a brief lesson on types of preserved foods.

FREEZING

Freezing is a great way to store excess fish, chicken, meat, and vegetables. The food needs to be wrapped tightly and frozen as quickly as possible, except for vegetables, which should be put on a baking sheet, not touching one another, until frozen. They can then be put in plastic bags for storing in the freezer.

There is a perception that fresh food is better than frozen, which is true for the most part. However, sometimes food such as salmon, roast beef, and turkey, when handled properly, frozen quickly, and thawed slowly, can be of better quality than the same food that has been kept in the grocer's showcase for a long time. Commercial companies can freeze food much better than we can in our home freezers. Buy fresh when you really know it's fresh, but otherwise don't worry about buying frozen. When thawing frozen foods (except for vegetables), always thaw them slowly by putting them in the refrigerator.

At Tante Marie's, we keep butter, bread, bread crumbs, chicken bones, walnuts, hazelnuts, and almonds in the freezer; and perhaps the occasional bag of frozen peas or raspberries.

PRESERVING IN SUGAR

Preserving in some form of sugar is an age-old process. Some common examples are whole fruit; preserves (chunky fruit); jam (less chunky fruit); conserves (one or more fruits with added dried fruit and nuts); chutney (fruit with additional ingredients such as vinegar and mustard seeds); marmalade (citrus fruit preserved in sugar); and jelly (clear syrup of fruit preserved in sugar). More unusual items preserved in sugar include apple and other butters, curds such as lemon curd, and cheese such as guava cheese.

To preserve fruit in sugar, the fruit should be closer to underripe than to over-ripe because the amount of pectin in underripe fruit is higher. Generally, in order for the jam or jelly to set up you need ¾ pound (or ¾ cup) of sugar for every pound (or cup) of fruit. The fruit should have some pectin in it and also some acid. You know the jam is set when it reaches 220 degrees on a candy thermometer, and it needs to be put into clean jars when hot, with new lids secured tightly with rings. (Ball or Mason jars are the best.) There is never a need to put fruit preserved in sugar in a water bath to sterilize it, nor do you need to put wax on top.

PRESERVING IN SALT

Foods preserved in salt are usually fish and meat. Salt-preserved fish include anchovies, salt cod, herring, gravlax, smoked salmon, and smoked trout. Caviar is fish roe preserved in salt. Examples of meat preserved in salt include corned beef, pastrami, bresaola, ham, prosciutto, pancetta, bacon, salami, and other kinds of sausages.

To preserve food in salt, you must coat it in a dry brine or submerge it in a wet brine for later drying or smoking. Smoked fish can be cold-smoked, as on page 379, or hot-smoked as in smoked salmon Indian style, or smoked trout or mackerel.

There are two different traditional styles of smoking parts of the hog—the German (or American) style and the Italian (or French) style. In the German style, the back leg or belly of the hog is brined and then hung in a smokehouse to make what I call country ham, such as Black Forest ham, Virginia ham, Kentucky ham, or smoked bacon. For Italian style, the leg or belly is brined and then hung in an airy place to air-dry. Examples of this are prosciutto (the leg) and pancetta (the belly). Bresaola is beef that has been cured in brine and then air-dried. Of course, American ingenuity has produced many products called ham that come from other parts of the hog and are not made using traditional styles.

At Tante Marie's we smoke salmon and chicken. Although we have made our own prosciutto, pancetta, and salt cod, I recommend buying it. Fresh sausages are fun to make (see page 382). Although sausages can be hung to preserve them, they really taste better if stored in the freezer.

PRESERVING IN FAT

Before refrigeration, hogs were raised as much for their fat as their meat. Cooks could store such things as pâtés and sausage patties in barrels of lard to be kept over the winter. The fat prevented any air from getting to the meat and spoiling it.

Confit of duck or goose is still a method of preserving cut-up poultry by salting it and then cooking and storing it in its own fat. See page 381 for how to make your own confit.

PRESERVING IN VINEGAR OR ALCOHOL

Pickles are the most common item preserved in vinegar. When making pickles or relish, it is important to put the mixture into clean jars and submerge the jars in water. The water is brought to a boil and simmered for twenty minutes to seal the jars so that they can be kept indefinitely.

CHEESEMAKING

Making yogurt and fresh or aged cheese is an age-old method of preserving milk. To make yogurt, milk is heated to 90 degrees to kill the unfavorable enzymes, and then a culture (usually some of the last batch of yogurt) is added. The mixture is put in clean glass jars in a warm place overnight (such as a gas oven with only the pilot light for heat). The yogurt is chilled before eating.

To make cheese, cow's, sheep's, or goat's milk is heated to kill any unfavorable enzymes; then a coagulant is added, such as vinegar, lemon, or rennet. Soon the milk breaks down into thick, clotted curd and thin, watery whey. The curd is either salted and served as fresh cheese—called pot cheese, farmer cheese, or cottage cheese—or treated in different ways in different regions to become aged cheese such as Cheddar, Brie, Roquefort, and Gorgonzola.

The best-tasting aged cheeses are made with unpasteurized milk by traditional artisanal methods. They are hard to make at home and not worth the effort. These farmhouse cheeses are so important to culture and cuisine that government regulation would really be a shame. Lesser-quality cheeses are factory made. They are often very smooth and uniform in color. Even lesser-quality cheeses are hydrogenated, including what is commonly called Swiss cheese in the United States, or "American" cheese.

Pork Tenderloins with Onion Compote

*G*erald Hirigoyen, the chef-owner of Fringale and Piperade in San Francisco, is a chef from the Basque region who cooks delicious food for modern California tastes. Here is another of his great recipes! The onion compote can be made for a roast loin of pork instead of a couple of tenderloins. In this case, extend the cooking time to an hour. This dish would go well with any winter vegetables. Thank you, Gerald!

1 large onion, thinly sliced
3 tablespoons olive oil
Coarse salt
¼ cup good-quality balsamic vinegar
¼ cup sherry vinegar
Freshly ground black pepper
1 small green apple, peeled, cored, and cut into ¼-inch dice
3 prunes, pitted and thinly sliced
2 pork tenderloins, about ¾ pound each
½ cup chicken stock
2 tablespoons minced parsley

To make the onion compote, heat the onion with the olive oil and ½ teaspoon salt in a 10-inch sauté pan over moderately high heat, stirring from time to time. Cook the onion until it is golden, about 10 minutes. Add the balsamic vinegar, sherry vinegar, 1 cup water, and a sprinkling of salt and pepper. Continue cooking the onion until all the liquid has evaporated and the onion is completely soft, about 20 minutes. Stir in the apple and prunes and continue cooking another 10 minutes. Preheat the oven to 425 degrees.

To roast the pork tenderloins, remove any silverskin and fat from each tenderloin, and trim the ends. Rub the tenderloins with olive oil and season with salt and pepper. Place the tenderloins in a lightly oiled roasting pan and roast for 10 minutes. Turn over and roast for another 10 minutes. The pork is cooked when firm when pressed with a finger or light pink when cut with a knife. When the tenderloins are done, transfer them to a cutting board and let rest, covered with foil, for 5 minutes before carving. Deglaze the roasting pan with the chicken stock. Boil the juices, scraping up the brown bits on the bottom of the pan. Add the juices to the onion compote with salt and pepper to taste.

To serve, rewarm the compote over low heat. With a thin, sharp knife, slice ¾-inch-thick slices of the roasted pork tenderloins. Put three on each of four warmed dinner plates. Cover with the onion compote, sprinkle with minced parsley, and serve.

SERVES 4

The pork loin is the large muscle that runs down the outside of the backbone. The tenderloin is the small muscle that runs down the inside of the backbone. According to French butchering methods, the meat on top of the backbone from the shoulder to the hip, if taken off the bone, is called the boneless pork loin center and often comes to the meat seller in one piece. According to American butchering meth-

ods, the meat cutter cuts right through the bone to make chops that look like porterhouse and T-bone steaks. To one side of the bone is a large muscle from the loin. The smaller muscle on the other side of the bone is part of the tenderloin.

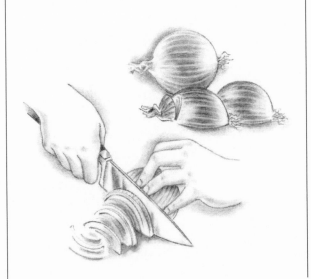

Medallions of Pork with Apple Chutney Sauce

*B*rining pork chops makes them juicier. Boning them and making a sauce from the bones makes them more elegant. Adding apple chutney makes them spicier.

The result is a terrific main course for an autumn dinner to be served with Butternut Squash and Hashed Brussels Sprouts (pages 255 and 256).

Coarse salt
4 loin pork chops, about 1 inch thick
Freshly ground black pepper
3 tablespoons olive oil
3½ cups good-quality chicken stock
2 tablespoons butter
¼ cup Spicy Apple Chutney, store-bought or homemade (page 388)
Watercress leaves for garnish

To make the brine, combine ½ cup salt with 2 quarts cold water in a plastic container large enough to hold the pork chops. Stir well. Submerge the pork chops in the brine and chill for 4 to 48 hours. Remove the chops from brine, pat dry with paper towels, and discard the brine.

To remove the bones from the pork chops, place them on a board and, holding a small, sharp knife straight up and down, cut the meat off the bone, following the bone with the knife. Trim most of the fat from the medallions. (They should be somewhat round.) Any meat cut from the ends of the chops should be saved for the sauce. Season the medallions with salt and pepper and set aside.

To make the essence (the base for the sauce), heat 2 tablespoons of the oil in a 10-inch frying or sauté pan over medium heat. Carefully place the bones and/or cubed meat at ½-inch intervals around the pan. Brown the meat on all sides and allow the juices on the bottom of the pan to caramelize. The meat, bones, and bottom of the pan should be dark brown. Pour on the stock, one ladleful at a time, reducing after each addition. After four additions of stock the essence should be dark and thick and coat the back of a metal spoon. Strain the contents of the pan through a conical strainer into a measuring cup. Rinse out the pan with ½ cup water and pour that over the meat and bones in the sieve to retrieve any extra meat juices. You should have about a cup of essence.

Twenty minutes before serving, heat the remaining tablespoon of olive oil with a tablespoon of the butter in the same 10-inch sauté pan over moderately high heat. When the bubbles subside, place the medallions of pork in the pan, leaving an inch between them. When each medallion is nicely browned, turn it with tongs and cook the other side, 2 to 3 minutes each side. The pork chops are done when they are barely firm to the touch. Put the medallions on a plate and keep warm while you make the sauce. Immediately pour off any excess fat and pour in the remaining ½ cup chicken stock, deglazing the pan. Bring to a boil. Remove any fat from the top of the reserved stock and pour that into the pan. Bring to a

boil, reduce the heat to a simmer, and cook, stirring, until the sauce lightly coats the back of a metal spoon. Stir in the apple chutney with salt and pepper to taste. Return the sauce to a boil, turn off the heat, and dot the sauce with the remaining tablespoon of butter, swirling to incorporate. Serve the medallions with their sauce on warm plates garnished with sprigs of watercress.

SERVES 4

If the pork medallions are not cooked through after browning on both sides for 2 to 3 minutes, deglaze the cooking pan with the remaining stock and return the medallions to the pan. Let them simmer gently for 2 to 3 minutes, covered, until they are firm to the touch.

Browning the meaty bones and bits of meat as described is called making an essence. This is the base for a reduction sauce in modern cooking. It must not be confused with the sauce itself. There are always three parts to making a reduction sauce: deglazing the cooking pan with cold liquid; adding the sauce base and flavoring; finishing with cream or butter.

Roast Pork
with Dried Apricots and Prunes

We have been cooking this recipe for years and years at Tante Marie's. It's still delicious, especially served with Spinach with Walnuts (page 259) and Celery Root with Lemon (page 259). A great winter dinner!

12 pitted prunes and 12 dried apricots
¾ cup full-bodied white wine
One 4-pound pork loin roast, off the bone
Coarse salt
Freshly ground black pepper
4 tablespoons (½ stick) butter
2 tablespoons olive oil
1 cup veal or chicken stock
Bouquet garni composed of 3 sprigs parsley,
    2 sprigs thyme, and 1 bay leaf
¾ cup heavy cream
2 tablespoons red currant jelly
1 teaspoon lemon juice
1 teaspoon grated orange zest
1 teaspoon cornstarch

To marinate the prunes and apricots, put them in a stainless steel bowl with the wine and let them marinate at room temperature for 2 to 4 hours.

To prepare the pork, make a ½-inch hole through the center of the roast from one end to the other with a long, thin knife. Using the handle of a wooden spoon, push half the apricots and prunes into the opening. Tie the pork loin with kitchen twine at 1-inch intervals to help it keep its shape when cooking. Season the roast with salt and pepper.

Put enough butter and oil in the bottom of an oval casserole (preferably Le Creuset) to make a ¼-inch layer and heat over medium-high heat. When the bubbles subside, brown the roast on all sides and on the ends, being careful not to burn the fat in the bottom of the pan. Remove the roast, pour off any excess fat, pour in the stock, and bring the mixture to a boil, stirring constantly. Return the roast to the pan with the bouquet garni, cover the pan, and put it deep in a 375-degree oven for about an hour, or until the internal temperature of the roast reaches 150 degrees. To take the temperature, remove the pan from the oven, closing the oven door, and insert an instant-read thermometer about two-thirds of the way into the middle of the roast.

When the meat has reached the correct temperature, transfer it to a board to rest for 10 minutes while you make the sauce. Discard the bouquet garni. Let the pan cool for 5 minutes and spoon off the fat that rises to the top. Place the pan of juices over high heat and reduce the liquid in the pan by one-third. Stir in the cream and the jelly and cook until the jelly dissolves. Stir in the lemon juice, the orange zest, and the remaining dried fruit with salt and pepper to taste. To thicken the sauce, mix the cornstarch with a tablespoon of cold water in a small bowl. Whisk a spoonful of this into the pork sauce and let it boil. Keep adding the slurry of cornstarch and water until the desired consistency has been attained. The sauce should lightly coat the back of a spoon.

To serve, carve the meat with a thin, sharp knife into ¼-inch slices and place them overlapping on a warmed serving platter. Surround the meat with some of the sauce and the dried fruit, and serve the rest of the sauce separately in a warmed sauce boat.

SERVES 6

Cornstarch, arrowroot, and potato flour always need to be dissolved in cold liquid before being added as a thickener to a sauce. They give the food a slightly gelatinous quality.

All white meat, including pork and veal, is unappealing unless fully cooked. However, it is no longer necessary to cook pork or sausages to 170 degrees for health reasons. The parasite that causes trichinosis in humans is killed at 138 degrees.

When a recipe calls for a roasting pan, you should use a pan that is heavy, can go in the oven, and that can be heated on top of the stove. This is because often after something has been roasted in the oven, the pan needs to be deglazed over high heat. You can be assured that a glass baking dish will break if you try to deglaze in it. Roasting pans have low sides so the meat is exposed to direct heat.

Veal Chops with Morels

*I*n classical French cooking a term used for very rich dishes is financière. *Here is a dish to cook when you feel as rich as a financier. Big, juicy veal chops cooked with morels and cream will at least make you feel happy even if you have spent all your money!*

> 3 ounces fresh morels
> Vinegar
> 6 veal chops, about 1-inch thick
> 3 tablespoons olive oil
> 1 quart good-quality veal stock
> Coarse salt
> Freshly ground black pepper
> 1 tablespoon butter
> 3 tablespoons Madeira
> ½ cup heavy cream

To clean the morels, put them in a bowl and cover with cold water. Add a dash of vinegar and let sit for 5 minutes. Remove the morels and discard the liquid. Trim the little rings from the ends of each morel and slice the morels into ¼-inch lengths.

To make strong veal stock, put the veal stock in a saucepan and reduce until you have about a cup.

To prepare the veal, trim the chops of excess fat and score the edges at 1-inch intervals to prevent the chops from curling when heated.

To cook the veal chops, season them on both sides with salt and pepper. Heat the remaining oil and the butter in a 10-inch sauté pan over moderately high heat. When the bubbles subside, arrange three of the chops in the pan. Do not crowd the pan and do not push them around. Turn the chops with tongs when they are golden on the bottom, about 2 minutes, and cook on the other side. Remove the browned chops and continue with the remaining chops. Always have a layer of oil or butter on the bottom of the pan even when there is only one chop left. Otherwise, the pan will burn and you will lose those wonderful caramelized meat juices. When all the chops have been browned, pour off any excess fat, immediately deglaze the pan with the Madeira, and cook over high heat to evaporate the alcohol. Stir in the reduced veal stock and return the veal chops to the pan. Reduce the heat to low, cover the pan, and let the veal chops cook gently until they are just firm to the touch and slightly pink on the inside, about 15 minutes.

To make the sauce, transfer the cooked veal chops to a warmed serving platter and keep warm. Reduce the pan juices until they are slightly thickened. Add the cream and continue cooking until the sauce lightly coats the back of a metal spoon. Stir in the morels and continue to cook another 2 minutes. Add salt and pepper to taste. Spoon the sauce over the chops and serve.   SERVES 6

If fresh morels are unavailable, you can substitute an ounce of dried morels. To reconstitute the dried morels, place them in a glass measuring cup and barely cover with hot water. Let sit 20 minutes. Remove the mushrooms, squeeze out the excess liquid, and slice them into ¼-

inch slices. The morel liquor can be added with the Madeira and the sliced mushrooms added with the cream.

For this recipe, it is important to make veal stock yourself or buy good-quality stock. Canned stock, if reduced, would make the sauce too salty.

Veal Ragoût with Olives and Homemade Spaetzle

If you follow this recipe exactly, you will know how to make a stew. The whole idea is to create a layer of brown stuff on the bottom of the pan, often called sediment, really caramelized meat juices, which you capture with the addition of onions, wine, and tomatoes. The browned pieces of meat are then cooked in a flavorful liquid. The juices from the meat go into the cooking liquid and the cooking liquid goes into the meat, creating an interchange of flavors. The meat tenderizes in the long, slow cooking while the sauce thickens with the juices of the meat. Not only are stews delicious, they are better if made ahead and reheated. You can make this stew with 10 pounds of pork stewing meat instead of veal. It's just as delicious.

*5 pounds breast of veal, cut in
    2 by 1-inch pieces*
*5 pounds veal shoulder, cut in
    1-inch-square cubes*
4 tablespoons (½ stick) butter
4 tablespoons olive oil
3 onions, finely chopped
2 garlic cloves, minced
½ cup flour
4 cups dry white wine
*2 pounds red, ripe tomatoes, peeled,
    seeded, and chopped*
2 to 3 cups veal or chicken stock
*Bouquet garni composed of 4 sprigs parsley,
    3 sprigs thyme, and 1 bay leaf*

24 Picholine olives, pitted
24 Niçoise olives, pitted
Coarse salt
Freshly ground pepper

To brown the meat, heat a large sauté pan over moderately high heat with a ¼-inch layer of butter and oil. Season the meat with salt and pepper. When the bubbles subside, arrange the meat in the pan at ½-inch intervals. Using tongs, turn the meat to brown it on all sides. As it browns, transfer it to a 3-quart enamel casserole. Continue with the rest of the meat, keeping a layer of oil and butter on the bottom of the pan and taking care not to burn the pan. If there is a spot on the pan that looks as though it may burn, move pieces of meat to that spot.

When all the meat has been browned, pour off all but 2 tablespoons of the fat in the pan and stir in the onions with ½ teaspoon salt. Cook, stirring with a wooden spoon or spatula, until the onions are soft, about 5 minutes. Add the garlic and cook for a minute more. Sprinkle in the flour and press into the onions with the back of the spoon. Cook until the flour becomes brown in color. Pour in the wine and bring to a boil, stirring. After a minute, add the tomatoes and bring the mixture to a boil. Pour this mixture over the meat in the casserole. Pour in enough veal stock to barely come up to the top of the meat. Bring to a boil, stirring, on top of the stove. Add the bouquet garni, then cover the casserole, and cook it in a 350-degree oven until the meat is tender when tasted, about 1½ hours. Stir in the olives and continue cooking the casserole in the oven for another 30 minutes. (This dish can be made ahead up to this point and chilled for up to 5 days.)

When ready to serve, remove and discard any fat that has risen to the top of the stew. Discard the bouquet garni. Reheat the stew over moderate heat on top of the stove, stirring to make sure it doesn't stick. (If you would like a more elegant presentation, you can go through and remove the small rib bones.) Add salt and pepper to taste.

SERVES 12

If breast of veal is hard to find, substitute 5 pounds of additional veal stew meat (shoulder). If the butcher has a breast, ask him or her to divide it lengthwise on the saw so that you have short rather than long ribs. You can separate the ribs yourself. Using veal breast on the bone will give the stew much more natural thickener.

Even though tough cuts of meat cooked in this manner make their own sauce, the dish still needs thickener. Some cooks dredge the pieces of meat in seasoned flour before browning them. Others sprinkle flour over the browned meat and roast the meat in the oven to cook the flour before adding liquid. I find that adding the flour at the end to make a roux and cooking the roux on top of the stove gives you more control over the thickness and the flour is less likely to burn.

If the meat is perfectly cooked and there is too much liquid in the stew, remove the meat with a slotted spoon and boil down the sauce until the desired consistency is reached. To do this, be sure to move a wooden spatula back and forth to hasten the evaporation of the excess liquid. You must taste the sauce for saltiness constantly during the reduction. You can reduce the amount of excess liquid but salt doesn't reduce—it only intensifies. If the sauce becomes salty enough and the sauce still has too much liquid, you can add a beurre manié or a slurry of cornstarch or arrowroot dissolved in cold liquid.

There is no point in halving a recipe for a stew or a ragoût because it's practically the same amount of work. Just freeze the uneaten stew for another dinner or two.

SPAETZLE

> *3½ cups flour*
> *Coarse salt*
> *2 eggs*
> *¼ pound (1 stick) butter, melted*
> *Freshly ground black pepper*

To make the dough, put the flour on a board or a counter. Make a well in the center of the flour large enough to hold the eggs. Sprinkle salt on the flour. Crack the eggs into the center of the well and add a cup of water. With a fork, break the yolks of the eggs and mix well. Mix the eggs with the water and then bring in the flour. When all the ingredients are combined, you should have a smooth dough.

To cook the spaetzle, bring a large pan of water to a boil and add a teaspoon of salt.

Divide the dough into three or four pieces. Press each piece onto the bottom of a cake pan to a thickness of ¼ inch. With a wet knife, cut ¼-inch slivers of the dough and slide them off the cake pan into the boiling water. Return the water to a boil and cook the spaetzle until they rise to the surface and are tender, about 6 minutes. Remove with a slotted spoon and toss them in a warmed serving dish with the melted butter. Continue with the rest of the dough. Season the spaetzle with salt and pepper and serve immediately. SERVES 6

It is fashionable to add fresh herbs to the spaetzle dough and make these irregular noodles in tiny shapes.

Osso Buco
with Risotto Milanese

*Y*ou *never forget the first time you ate osso buco—a traditional Italian dish of braised veal shanks. Because the meat is from the shank, the long, slow cooking makes the resulting sauce gelatinous and rich. Connoisseurs eat the marrow from the center of the bones with marrow spoons.*

1 large onion, finely chopped
1 large carrot, finely chopped
1 celery stalk, finely chopped
4 tablespoons (½ stick) butter
Coarse salt
1 garlic clove, minced
2 strips lemon zest, 2 by ½ inch
7 pounds veal shank, split into 2-inch-high
*   rounds*
¾ cup flour
½ cup olive oil
Freshly ground black pepper
1 cup dry white wine
6 red, ripe tomatoes, peeled, seeded,
*   and chopped*
3 cups veal stock
Bouquet garni composed of 4 sprigs parsley,
*   2 sprigs thyme, and 1 bay leaf*

FOR THE GREMOLATA
*   (OPTIONAL)*
1 garlic clove, minced
1 teaspoon grated lemon zest
1 teaspoon minced fresh Italian parsley

To cook the mirepoix, put the onion, carrot, and celery with the butter and ½ teaspoon salt in a heavy casserole just large enough to hold all the veal shanks in one layer. Cook over moderately high heat, stirring from time to time, until the vegetables are soft, about 7 minutes. Stir in the garlic and cook another minute. Add the lemon strips and remove from the heat.

To brown the meat, tie each piece of veal shank around the middle with string using a surgeon's knot. (It's just like a square knot with another loop; put right over left, then right over left a second time, then left over right.) Dip each piece of veal shank carefully in a plate of flour seasoned with salt and pepper. Make sure a light coating of flour covers each piece just before it is to be browned. Heat a large sauté pan with a ¼-inch layer of butter and oil over moderately high heat. When the bubbles subside, arrange some of the veal shanks in the hot pan at ½-inch intervals. Cook the veal until golden on all sides, turning with tongs. As the pieces brown, stand them on top of the cooked mirepoix in the casserole. As soon as all the pieces have been removed from the sauté pan, pour in the wine to deglaze the pan. Bring the wine to a boil to evaporate the alcohol. Stir in the tomatoes and continue stirring until the sauce thickens. Pour the tomato sauce over the veal shanks and pour the stock over as well. Add the bouquet garni. Bring the contents of the casserole to a simmer on top of the stove, stirring here and there to keep it from sticking. When the mixture comes to a simmer, cover and put the casserole deep in a 325-degree oven and cook until the veal is almost falling off the bones, about 2½ hours. (This dish can be made ahead to this point and chilled for up to a week.)

To serve, reheat the casserole of veal in a 325-degree oven for 40 minutes if not already heated. Transfer the osso buco to a warmed serving platter. Cut each string with scissors and remove. If the sauce is not thick enough, place the casserole over medium-high heat and simmer, stirring with a wooden spatula, until the desired consistency is reached. Add salt and pepper to taste. Spoon the sauce over the meat. If the osso buco does not have enough flavor for you, make a gremolata by mixing the garlic, zest, and parsley and sprinkle it on the osso buco before serving.   SERVES 6

Veal shanks are the lower part of the hind legs and forelegs of calves. In small calves the shanks are usually split in two crosswise, giving a cross-section of the meat and bone with the marrow. More pieces can be cut from larger shanks. They should be 2 to 3 inches thick. The reason they are tied with string is to keep the fully cooked meat from falling off the bone.

RISOTTO MILANESE

1 small onion, finely chopped
7 tablespoons butter
Coarse salt
1½ cups Arborio rice
3½ cups veal or chicken stock, heated
⅓ teaspoon saffron threads
¼ cup freshly grated Parmesan

Put the onion, 4 tablespoons of the butter, and ½ teaspoon salt in a medium-size heavy saucepan over moderately high heat, stirring from time to time. When the onion is soft, about 5 minutes, stir in the rice, making sure the rice is coated with the onion mixture. Stir in 1½ cups of the stock and stir slowly so that the rice absorbs the liquid. When most of the liquid is absorbed, add another ladleful of stock and continue stirring. After about 15 minutes, add the saffron to the hot stock. After 20 minutes, start tasting the rice to determine whether the centers of the grains are swollen and there is no uncooked starch when tasted. Immediately stir in the remaining butter and the Parmesan. Cover the pan and let it rest for 5 minutes to absorb the flavors. It is always better to slightly undercook the rice than to let it overcook. Serve with osso buco. SERVES 6

Medallions of Lamb with Spring Vegetables

With a little preparation and last-minute cooking, you can have an elegant lamb presentation reminiscent of the era of nouvelle cuisine.

2 racks of lamb, 1½ pounds each, 8 chops each
Coarse salt
Freshly ground black pepper
3 tablespoons olive oil
3 cups veal or chicken stock
4 medium-size carrots, cut into château shapes
3 medium-size turnips, cut into château shapes
½ pound small green beans (preferably haricots verts), trimmed on both ends and cut on the diagonal into 1½-inch lengths if long
8 tablespoons butter
½ cup white wine
⅓ cup heavy cream

To prepare the lamb, remove the entire piece of meat from the ribs. To do this, hold the ribs in one hand and with a small, sharp knife start at the top of the ribs, gliding the knife away from you and following the contours of the bones. When the whole piece of meat has been removed, trim the fat and silverskin from it. To remove the silverskin, slip the knife under it and pull. It will pull easily in one direction and tear the meat in the other. Trim the ends of the tenderloin so that the width of the meat is even. Cut out any bits of meat from the fat. (These bits will be used to make the essence.) With a long, thin knife, cut the loin into medallions about 1 inch thick. Season these with salt and pepper. Set aside.

To make the essence or base for the reduction sauce, heat 2 tablespoons of the oil in a 10-inch sauté pan over moderately high heat. Carefully place the meat bits at ½-inch intervals around the pan. Do not crowd the pan. Turn the meat with tongs to brown on all sides. The meat should be dark brown but not burned. Pour off and discard any fat from the pan. Immediately pour in a cup of the stock over the bones, deglazing the sediment on the bottom of the pan. Let the stock reduce over the meat until it thickens and stir another cup of the stock. Continue to reduce the sauce again until it is thick. Stir in a third cup of the stock and reduce again. When the sauce lightly coats the back of a metal spoon, strain it through a conical sieve into a glass measuring cup. Pour the meat and bones into the sieve as well. Pour ½ cup cold water into the sauté pan to get out any drops of sauce, and pour this over the meat in the sieve. You should have about a cup of liquid. (This essence can keep for a week in the refrigerator or six months in the freezer.)

To precook the vegetables, bring a large saucepan of water to a boil. Add a teaspoon of salt. Drop in the carrots and cook them until they are tender when pierced with a fork, about 7 minutes. Remove the carrots with a slotted spoon, put them in a sieve or colander, and run under cold water to stop the cooking. Do the same with the turnips.

At this point you may need to add more water to the pan. Bring the water back to a boil and drop in the green beans. Cook the beans until they are tender when pierced with a fork, about 6 minutes. Pour out the beans and the water into a sieve. Run cold water over the beans. (Any vegetables can be prepared this way and stored in plastic bags in the refrigerator for up to 3 days.)

When ready to serve, put a ¼-inch layer of oil and butter in a 10-inch sauté pan over medium-high heat. When the bubbles subside, arrange some of the medallions at ½-inch intervals in the bottom of the pan. Let them cook undisturbed until well browned, 2 minutes each side. Turn them over with tongs and brown on the other side. Be careful that the bottom of the pan doesn't burn. The meat is medium-rare when it is somewhat resilient to the touch. Transfer the cooked medallions to a plate and continue with the rest, keeping a layer of oil or butter on the bottom of the pan even when there is only one medallion cooking. As soon as they are all cooked, pour off any fat and quickly pour in the wine to deglaze the bottom of the pan. Use a flat wooden spatula to scrape up the sediment. Let the mixture boil for a minute or two. At this point, strain the sauce into a small saucepan if the mixture is not smooth. Bring the mixture to a boil, add the essence of lamb, and reduce again until the sauce coats the back of a metal spoon. Add the cream and boil again. Add salt and pepper to taste.

To reheat the vegetables, heat them with butter in a wide frying pan while stirring or shaking. To serve, spoon 2 to 3 tablespoons of the sauce on warm dinner plates. Carefully arrange three of the lamb medallions on the lower side of the plate, and place little bundles of carrots, turnips, and green beans on the upper side of the plate.

SERVES 4

Some cooks prefer to reheat blanched vegetables by dropping them again into boiling water and serving them in butter. It's the chef's choice.

To turn vegetables or make them into château shapes is a technique used in the past. The idea was to shape vegetables such as potatoes, carrots, and turnips by carving them with a small knife so that they had seven sides and were about the size of large olives. That way they would cook evenly when blanched and roll around a pan easily when reheated in butter. Since this medallion of lamb recipe with spring vegetables is old-fashioned, it would be attractive to make a few turned vegetables for each plate.

I prefer to make this dish with local lamb rather than lamb imported from New Zealand. Although New Zealand lamb tastes fine, the racks are very small.

Herbed Rack of Lamb with Béarnaise Sauce

Go ahead and splurge—buy a rack of the best lamb you can find and roast it just for a dinner for two. When it's cooked medium-rare, you need no sauce, but if you want to go all out you will really impress your dinner partner by making Béarnaise Sauce (recipe follows). A great way to serve the Béarnaise is in a hollowed out and warmed tomato half. When the diner finishes the lamb, he or she can eat the tomato!

1 rack of lamb, 1½ pounds, 8 chops,
  prepared for roasting
Coarse salt
Freshly ground black pepper
½ tablespoon finely minced fresh tarragon
½ tablespoon finely minced fresh chives
½ tablespoon plus 1 tablespoon finely
  minced fresh Italian parsley
1 shallot, finely minced
½ cup fine fresh bread crumbs
2 garlic cloves, finely minced

Preheat the oven to 450 degrees.

To prepare the lamb, trim any excess fat from the rack and make a crisscross pattern with a knife in the fat that covers the meat; the lines should be about an inch apart. Season it with salt and pepper.

In a small bowl combine the tarragon, chives, the ½ tablespoon parsley, and the shallot. Rub this mixture all over the lamb, pressing gently. Put the rack on a small roasting pan in the oven and cook until the internal temperature of the lamb reaches 110 degrees, about 25 to 30 minutes. (The rack of lamb can be made ahead to this point and held for up to 2 hours at room temperature.)

While the lamb is cooking, combine the bread crumbs, the 1 tablespoon parsley, and the garlic. Press this mixture over both sides of the rack of lamb.

When ready to serve, return the pan to the oven and cook for 10 minutes more for rare lamb. Transfer the rack to a cutting board to rest for 10 minutes. Deglaze the pan with ½ cup cold water, boil, and strain into the Béarnaise sauce, if making. To carve, stand the rack up with a carving fork held up and down and glide a thin, sharp knife along one edge of the chops, using the bone as a guide.

SERVES 2

Whenever you carve, always use a thin, sharp knife and glide it through the meat, letting the knife cut the meat. Do not press hard and do not saw like bread or wood.

The garlic mixture is added only in the last 10 minutes of cooking because garlic is likely to burn, and when it does, it tastes horrible.

TOMATOES FILLED WITH BÉARNAISE SAUCE

6 small red tomatoes
Coarse salt
¼ cup tarragon or white wine vinegar
¼ cup dry white wine
2 shallots, finely chopped
1 sprig fresh or ¼ teaspoon dried tarragon
  plus 1 tablespoon minced fresh tarragon
  or parsley
Freshly ground white pepper
3 egg yolks
12 tablespoons (1½ sticks) softened butter
Lemon juice

To prepare the tomatoes, cut the tops from them, leaving an opening almost as wide as the tomatoes. With a grapefruit spoon or a kitchen spoon, remove the seeds and the pulp from each tomato. Sprinkle the inside of each tomato with salt and drain upside down on a rack to release excess moisture.

To make the tarragon flavoring for the sauce, combine the vinegar, wine, shallots, and tarragon sprig with a sprinkling of salt and pepper in a small stainless steel or ceramic saucepan. Bring this mixture to a boil over moderately high heat and let boil until about 2 tablespoons liquid remain. Let cool.

To make the béarnaise sauce, put the egg yolks in the top of a double boiler or in a small bowl that will fit on top of a pan of simmering water. Off the heat, beat the yolks with a wire whisk until thick and lemon colored. Strain in the tarragon flavoring and beat well. Place the bowl over the simmering water, whisking vigorously so that every part of the bottom of the bowl is touched by the whisk. Start adding the butter by the tablespoon, and as each piece of butter disappears, add another piece. The idea is that the heat and the whisking create a medium in which the egg yolks will absorb the butter to form a smooth, warm emulsion. The bowl should never get so hot that the mixture begins to bubble around the edges or that you can't hold your finger on the bottom of the bowl. The sauce should be made quickly over slightly increasing heat; adding the butter slowly won't help the emulsion. When all the butter has been added, remove the bowl from the simmering water and add the lemon juice and salt and pepper to taste. Add the fresh tarragon or parsley and cover with a metal top to keep warm.

When ready to serve, invert the tomatoes onto a baking pan and place them in a 350-degree oven for 10 minutes to reheat. Strain some of the lamb juices into the béarnaise sauce. Fill the tomatoes with the warm béarnaise and serve with the roasted rack of lamb.

Since the lamb recipe serves 2 and the tomatoes serve 6, you need to decide if you want to make béarnaise for 2 and have a lot left over or to increase the recipe for the lamb to serve 6.

Boned Leg of Lamb with Orange-Herb Stuffing

This old-fashioned recipe for butterflying a leg of lamb, stuffing it with an orange-herb stuffing, and coating it with flour, eggs, and bread crumbs is still good. It is a great way to take an ordinary leg of lamb and make it very appealing for a dinner. Since lamb doesn't reheat very well, it is best to make the roast ahead, put it in the oven when the guests arrive, and spend a few minutes finishing the sauce while your guests are at the table.

1 small onion, finely chopped
Coarse salt
4 tablespoons (½ stick) butter
1½ cups fine bread crumbs
4 tablespoons mixed fresh herbs, such as Italian parsley, chives, and/or thyme
Zest and juice of 1 orange
Freshly ground black pepper
1 leg of lamb, butterflied, about 7 pounds
¾ cup flour
2 eggs, beaten
2 tablespoons butter, melted
1 medium-size onion, sliced
1 tablespoon flour
1 cup chicken stock
1 tablespoon red currant jelly

To make the stuffing, heat the onion with ½ teaspoon salt and 2 tablespoons of the butter in a medium-size frying or sauté pan over moderately high heat. Cook the onion, stirring from time to time, until it is soft, about 5 minutes. Mix in ½ cup of the bread crumbs, herbs, and orange zest and juice with salt and pepper to taste and remove from heat.

To stuff the lamb, first roll the lamb with both hands to resemble a football to see how the final roast should look. Trim any excess fat, leaving the thin membrane covering the leg, which is called the fell. Open it up and season the meat with salt and pepper. Lay the orange-herb stuffing down the middle of the length of the leg. Roll the lamb again into a football shape. Tie the roast in three or four places along the width of the roast. (You want to make the roast long so that it will be easier to carve later.) Tie another string around the roast lengthwise. Try to tie the roast in as few places as possible, because when you take the strings off later, the crust will come off, too.

To coat the lamb, make three plates: one of flour seasoned with salt and pepper, one of beaten eggs, and the remaining bread crumbs. With the seam side down and using your hands, cover the roast with seasoned flour, then with egg, and then with the bread crumbs. Without rolling the roast over, place the lamb in a roasting pan without a rack, seam side down, pour over the melted butter, and put it deep in a 350-degree oven. The lamb is cooked to medium-rare when an instant thermometer inserted in the thick part of the meat registers 120 degrees, about an hour.

To make the sauce, transfer the roast to a warmed serving platter to rest for 10 minutes. Carefully remove all the strings. Add the sliced onion to the roasting pan and cook over moderately high heat, scraping up any brown bits on the bottom of the pan. Sprin-

kle the onion with the tablespoon of flour and press in with a wooden spoon. Cook, stirring, until the flour begins to color. Stir in the stock and the jelly. Bring to a boil and cook until the mixture thickens. Add orange juice and salt and pepper to taste. Strain the sauce into a warmed sauceboat.

To serve, put the lamb on a serving platter and carve enough ½-inch slices for each person and leave the rest of the roast whole. Lay the slices overlapping, spoon a little of the sauce down the middle of the slices, and serve the rest separately. Serve with glazed onions, carrots, and buttered green beans. Arrange these vegetables in mounds around the roast.

SERVES 8

To butterfly a leg of lamb, lay the leg on a board with the rounded side down. First, remove the "aitch" bone, part of the hip. To do this, use a small, sharp knife to slide the meat away from the bone. Always cut away from yourself and use your fingers to feel where the contours of the bone are. It is easy to start boning up the leg bone rather than disjointing it by feeling for the round shiny end of the bone embedded in the aitch bone. Be sure to cut around the bone, keeping the knife close to the bone. After the aitch bone is removed, use the knife to slide the meat off from around the lower part of the leg. Now there is only one bone left. With your knife held straight up and down, cut into the meat, making a cut along the top of the remaining leg bone and cutting down to the bone. Without cutting toward yourself, run the knife around the bone in both directions without cutting down to the board. You should be able to remove all the leg and thigh bones. Now the butterflied leg of lamb has a flat side and a rounded side. With the knife held parallel to the board, cut through the thick round part to open it up like a book and lay it flat. Remove the thick piece of fat about the size of a large marble; otherwise it will give the final dish a muttony taste.

According to butchers, lambs have only two legs, which are the back legs. The front legs are cut to make lamb shanks and shoulder of lamb (lamb stew meat).

Boning a leg of lamb means to take the bones entirely out of the roast without cutting the meat. Butterflying means cutting the meat in such a way that it will lie flat. There is no such word as "deboning"—it's like using the word "un-thawing."

Instead of an orange-herb stuffing, you can make a tapenade stuffing. In this case, do not put red currant jam or orange juice in the final sauce. To make tapenade, mix together 4 ounces pitted black olives, ½ tablespoon rinsed capers, 4 anchovy fillets, and 1 garlic clove in a food processor. Pour olive oil on top of the roast instead of butter.

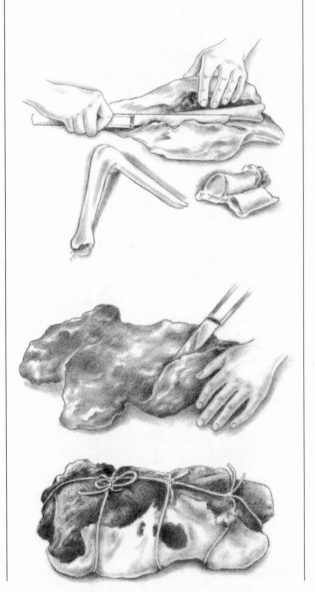

Spring Lamb Stew
(Navarin Printanier)

Here is a gorgeous presentation. The three colorful vegetables give this lamb stew the appearance of spring. You could make this stew with lamb, veal, pork, or a combination of all three.

4 tablespoons butter plus 6 tablespoons for the vegetables
2 tablespoons olive oil
2 pounds lamb riblets
2 pounds lamb shoulder, cut in 1½-inch pieces
1 large onion, finely chopped
Coarse salt
3 garlic cloves, minced
3 tablespoons flour
1 cup dry white wine
3 red, ripe tomatoes, peeled, seeded, and chopped, or 14 ounces canned tomatoes, coarsely chopped
3 cups chicken or veal stock
Bouquet garni composed of 3 sprigs parsley, 2 sprigs thyme, and 1 bay leaf
Freshly ground black pepper
8 medium-size carrots, cut into château shapes
6 medium-size turnips, cut into château shapes
1 pound small green beans trimmed on both ends and cut on the diagonal into 1½-inch lengths if long

To brown the meat, heat a large sauté pan with a layer of butter and oil over medium-high heat. When the bubbles subside, arrange the meat in the pan at ½-inch intervals. Using tongs, turn the meat to brown it on all sides before transferring to a 3-quart enamel casserole. Continue with the rest of the meat, keeping a layer of oil and butter on the bottom of the pan and taking care not to burn the pan. If there is a spot on the pan that looks as though it may burn, move pieces of meat onto that spot.

When all the meat has been browned, pour off all but 2 tablespoons of the fat in the pan and stir in the onion with ½ teaspoon salt. Cook, stirring with a wooden spoon or spatula, until the onion is soft, about 5 minutes. Add the garlic and cook for a minute more. Sprinkle in the flour and press into the onion with the back of the spoon. Cook this until the flour becomes brown in color. Pour in the wine and bring to a boil, stirring. After a minute, add the tomatoes and bring the mixture to a boil. Pour this mixture over the meat in the casserole. Pour in enough stock to barely come up to the top of the meat. Bring to a boil, stirring, on top of the stove. Add the bouquet garni, cover the casserole, and cook in a 350-degree oven until the meat is tender when tasted, about 1½ hours. (This dish can be made ahead up to this point and chilled for up to 5 days.)

To precook the vegetables, bring a large saucepan of water to a boil and add a teaspoon of salt. Drop in the carrots and cook them until they are tender when pierced with a fork, about 7 minutes. Remove with a slotted spoon, put them in a sieve or colander, and run under cold water to stop the cooking. Do the same with the turnips. At this point you may need to add more water to the pan. Bring the water back to a boil and drop in the green beans. Cook the beans until they are tender when pierced with a fork, about 6 minutes. Pour out the beans and the water into a sieve. Run cold water over the beans.

When ready to serve, remove and discard any fat that has risen to the top of the stew. Reheat the stew over medium heat on top of the stove, stirring to make sure it doesn't stick. Discard the bouquet garni. Add salt and pepper to taste. Reheat each vegetable in a separate saucepan in butter. Mound the stew in the middle of a warmed serving platter. Surround it with little piles of vegetables, alternating carrots, turnips, and green beans.

SERVES 8

When you are cooking in a heavy enameled iron pan such as Le Creuset brand, it doesn't matter too much whether you cook at a low simmer on top of the stove or in the middle of the oven. Either way, you should check the pan every once in a while to make sure the cooking is slow and even. When stew boils too vigorously, the meat becomes like tough little bullets. The same thing will happen when you cook a tender cut of lamb, such as a leg.

For a Moroccan variation on this classical French stew, add 1 teaspoon ground cumin and ½ teaspoon ground ginger to the stew with the tomatoes instead of the bouquet garni. Instead of carrots, onions, and green beans, cook a cup of peeled fava beans and 4 trimmed artichokes separately, each in a cup of the lamb cooking

liquid taken out of the stew after the meat is cooked. Return the cooked vegetables to the stew with a preserved lemon, rinsed and coarsely chopped, and 10 black olives. Simmer for 10 minutes for the flavors to meld. Add salt, pepper, and lemon juice to taste.

Lamb Shanks Braised with White Beans

The French love lamb shanks braised with white beans, and so will you! Sometimes you need to special-order lamb shanks from the butcher. They are in great demand among passionate cooks because they become juicy and delicious in long, slow braising.

1 pound small dried white beans, such as Great Northern
4 tablespoons (½ stick) butter
2 tablespoons olive oil
6 lamb shanks
Coarse salt
Freshly ground black pepper
2 onions, coarsely chopped (about 2 cups)
4 medium-size carrots, coarsely chopped (about 2 cups)
2 garlic cloves, minced
½ cup flour
2 cups dry white wine
6 tomatoes, peeled, seeded, and chopped, or one 28-ounce can Italian plum tomatoes, coarsely chopped
5 cups chicken or veal stock
Bouquet garni composed of 4 sprigs parsley, 2 sprigs thyme, and 1 bay leaf
2 tablespoons minced fresh Italian parsley

To prepare the beans, put them in a baking pan and sort through them, looking at each one, searching for pebbles. Soak the beans overnight in plenty of cold water. The next day drain them, discarding the water. (For the quick-soak method, see page 23.)

Season the lamb shanks on all sides with salt and pepper. Heat enough butter and oil in a 2-quart enamel casserole to make a ¼-inch layer on the bottom. Place the pan over moderately high heat. When the oil and butter are hot, arrange two or three of the shanks in the pan and brown them on all sides. When they are browned, transfer them to a plate and continue with the rest of the lamb shanks, adding oil as necessary to keep the bottom of the pan covered. When all the shanks have been browned, pour off all but a tablespoon of the fat in the pan and immediately stir in the onions and carrots with ½ teaspoon salt. Cook until the vegetables are soft and lightly colored, about 8 minutes. Stir in the garlic and cook, stirring, for another minute. Sprinkle the flour over the vegetables, and press it in with the back of a wooden spoon. Cook this roux until the flour is nicely browned. Pour in the wine and bring the mixture to a boil. Add the tomatoes and bring to a boil, stirring. Cook until the tomato mixture thickens slightly. Add the beans to this mixture, as well as the lamb shanks with any accumulated juices on the plate. Stir in the stock and the bouquet garni. Reduce the heat to a feeble bubble, cover, and simmer gently on top of the stove or place it deep in 350-degree oven, until the lamb is practically falling off the bones, about 1½ hours. If the beans are still somewhat hard, transfer the lamb shanks to a plate and continue cooking the beans until they are tender when tasted. Add salt and pepper to taste. Return the lamb shanks to the beans. (The dish can be prepared ahead up to this point and chilled overnight.)

To serve, reheat gently over medium-high heat, stirring. Serve on warmed dinner plates and sprinkle with parsley. Serve with a full-bodied Burgundy and crusty country bread.

SERVES 6

Canned white beans in this recipe won't work; what makes this dish so good is that the beans cook with the lamb juices.

Grilled Skirt Steak with Roasted Potatoes and Salsa Verde

*M*any people are trying to eat more vegetables and fruit and less meat. Here is a terrific way to serve less meat, and the dish is so delicious no one will even notice. Slices of grilled steak are piled on a bed of lightly dressed greens and roasted potatoes and topped with a salsa verde, to complement the beef.*

*2 skirt steaks or 1 full flank steak
    (1½ to 2 pounds)
Half a lemon, plus the zest and juice of
    2 lemons
6 tablespoons olive oil, plus some for
    potatoes
Coarse salt
Freshly ground black pepper
1 large shallot, chopped
4 tablespoons fresh Italian parsley, chopped
2 tablespoons capers, rinsed
2 anchovy fillets (optional)
2 tablespoons sherry vinegar
½ cup olive oil
2 pounds baby new potatoes
2 bunches arugula or watercress, coarse
    stems removed
1 tablespoon red wine vinegar
3 tablespoons extra-virgin olive oil*

To prepare the steak, rub both sides of the steak with the cut side of the lemon half and 2 tablespoons of the olive oil, and season with salt and pepper. Let stand at room temperature for 30 minutes.

To make the salsa verde, put the shallot, parsley, capers, anchovies, and vinegar in a food processor. Pulse until the mixture is finely chopped. Add the ½ cup olive oil to make a moist sauce; process again only until mixed but not liquefied. Add salt and pepper to taste.

To roast the potatoes, place them in a roasting pan, rub all over with plenty of olive oil, and season well with salt and pepper. Roast the potatoes in a 400-degree oven, tossing from time to time, until they are tender when pierced with a fork, about 35 minutes.

Prepare a charcoal fire about an hour before serving (see box on page 244). Grill the steak until it is firm but resilient when pressed with your finger, about 3 minutes on each side. Transfer the steak to a wooden board and let rest for 10 minutes.

To prepare the salad, place the greens in a large bowl. In the bowl of a spoon held over the greens, dissolve ½ teaspoon salt in the red wine vinegar. Spoon this onto the greens with the extra-virgin olive oil and a grinding of pepper. Toss well. Mound the greens in the center of a warmed, oval serving platter. Mound the warm potatoes on either side of the platter. With a long, thin knife held at an angle, slice ¼-inch-wide slices of meat and overlap them on top of the greens. Pour any juices over the meat. Spoon salsa verde diagonally across the meat from one side to the other. Serve immediately.

SERVES 4

Even though the recipe calls for skirt or flank steak, you could use a 1-inch-thick sirloin, New York, or ribeye. In this case the edges of the steak need to be scored. Scoring a piece of meat means to cut right through the fat and silverskin into the meat itself at 1-inch intervals around the edge of any steak or chop to prevent it from curling when it cooks.

Charcoal is wood that has been baked at a high temperature without igniting. This happens in nature when a forest fire burns all the oxygen at the top of the trees, and the wood underneath is simply heated at a high temperature.

HOW TO CHARCOAL-GRILL

To GRILL FOODS over a charcoal fire, follow these steps. Start the fire with newspaper and kindling, an electric starter, or a chimney starter. The charcoal should be piled with space between the pieces to create a draft. When the charcoal is flaming, remove the electric starter. Continue to move the charcoal on top of the flaming coals with tongs. When all the charcoal has burned to the point that the coals are white, the charcoal fire is ready. At this point, place a clean grill about 4 inches from the fire and let it heat for 3 minutes. (Either the food you are cooking or the grill should be lightly oiled.) You can tell when the fire is hot enough to cook fish, chicken, or meat when you hold your hand 4 inches from the grill and it gets too hot before 4 seconds are up. If you can count to 4, the fire is not hot enough. Place the food on the grill so that there is air circulation between the pieces of food. Let the food cook until it no longer sticks to the grill. With a wide metal spatula, quickly turn it and cook it on the other side. Do not cover the food if it is less than 2 inches thick. The cover creates an oven effect that bakes the food rather than grills it.

The best fuel for a charcoal grill is hardwood or mesquite charcoal. If this is not available, charcoal briquets can be used. Never use charcoal starter, lighter fluid, or self-starting charcoal. Not only is this a pollutant of the environment, it gives food an unpleasant taste.

Pan-Fried Fillet of Beef with Red Wine Sauce and Truffle Butter

Although the fillet (or tenderloin) of beef is the most tender cut of meat, it really benefits from a good sauce. Here you can go all out to make two sauces, a red wine reduction sauce made with an essence of beef and a compound butter with truffles or minced herbs. This is an elegant and delicious presentation. Serve it with Mashed Potato Gratin with Truffle Oil (page 272) and a green vegetable such as spinach. Bon appétit!

1 whole tenderloin of beef, untrimmed, about 6 pounds
Coarse salt
Freshly ground black pepper
2 tablespoons olive oil
1½ quarts good-quality veal stock
¼ pound (1 stick) butter, softened, plus 2 tablespoons
1 black truffle, minced, or 2 tablespoons minced fresh herbs, such as parsley, chives, thyme, tarragon, or chervil
3 tablespoons flour
2 cups good-quality red wine
2 tablespoons brandy

To prepare the meat, remove all the fat and silverskin from the beef. Along one side of the whole tenderloin is a 1-inch piece that almost pulls off. This is called the chain. Remove this and trim off most of the fat. When removing the silverskin, be careful not to trim off the thick sirloin end, which is part of the cut of meat. With butchers' string, tie the roast at 1½-inch intervals, including the thick end piece. With a thin knife, cut the meat into 12 fillet steaks, each wrapped with a string to help the meat keep its shape when it cooks. Season both sides of each fillet with salt and pepper.

To make the essence of beef, cut the tenderloin trimmings into 1-inch squares. Heat a 10- or 12-inch heavy skillet or sauté pan with enough oil to lightly coat the bottom. Carefully place the squares of meat around the bottom of the pan, making sure to have at least ¼ inch between the pieces of meat. Brown the meat well on all sides, turning with tongs, and being careful not to burn the sediment on the bottom of the pan. When all the meat has been browned, add a cup of the stock and reduce over medium-high heat, stirring from time to time. Repeat, adding cupfuls of the stock and reducing until the essence is thick enough to coat the back of a metal spoon. Strain the essence through a fine sieve (or chinois) into a glass measuring cup. To capture any remaining drops of essence, add ½ cup water to the skillet or sauté pan, swirling to dissolve any brown bits, and pour this over the pieces of meat in the sieve. Chill and remove any fat that accumulates on the top.

To make the compound butter, beat the ¼ pound butter in a bowl with a wooden spoon until light. Add the chopped truffle (or the minced herbs) with salt and pepper to taste.

To make the beurre manié, mix together the remaining 2 tablespoons butter and the flour until you have the consistency of cookie dough.

When ready to serve, pan-fry the fillets over high heat until the meat feels resilient to the touch and is medium-rare. Remove the meat from the pan and keep warm. Pour off any excess fat from the pan and without hesitation deglaze with the red wine. Let the mixture boil up, stirring to evaporate the alcohol. Stir in the brandy and continue to reduce. Pour in the essence and boil again. Continue to reduce this mixture until it is thick enough to lightly coat a metal spoon. Taste. With the mixture boiling, whisk in enough beurre manié to make a sauce consistency. Add salt and pepper to taste.

To serve, put a ladle of red wine sauce on a warmed plate, lay a cooked fillet in the middle of the sauce, and top with a teaspoon of compound butter. SERVES 12

An essence can be made of duck, pork, veal, lamb, or beef. It is simply intensified caramelized meat juices that can be used as a sauce base. To make a sauce from an essence, it is imperative that the pan in which the meat was cooked be deglazed with wine, fortified wine, or brandy, then reduced. The essence is incorporated, and again the mixture is reduced. When the desired consistency and taste have been achieved, the sauce is finished with butter or cream. Of course, any finished sauce must have a flavoring component.

In this recipe, the essence is the base of the reduction sauce. It cannot be made with canned stock.

Fillet of Beef Braised with Mushrooms

The whole fillet or tenderloin is the very tender muscle that runs down the inside of the backbone of the steer. Here it is browned on all sides, then braised in an old-fashioned French brown sauce called demi-glace. The sauce is finished with sautéed mushrooms. It is a wonderful way to present this elegant cut of beef. Serve it with Tomatoes Filled with Creamed Spinach (page 262) and the best wine you can find!

FOR THE DEMI-GLACE SAUCE
4 tablespoons (½ stick) plus 3 tablespoons butter
½ small onion, finely chopped
1 medium-size carrot, finely chopped
1 small celery stalk, finely chopped
Coarse salt
2 tablespoons flour
1½ to 3 cups veal or beef stock, heated
1 red, ripe tomato, seeded and coarsely chopped
2 fresh white mushrooms, coarsely chopped, plus ½ pound sliced
Bouquet garni composed of 4 sprigs parsley, 2 sprigs thyme, and 1 bay leaf

3½ pounds tenderloin of beef, trimmed
Freshly ground black pepper
2 tablespoons olive oil
3 tablespoons butter
2 cups red wine

To make the demi-glace, combine the ½ stick butter, onion, carrot, and celery with ½ teaspoon salt in a small saucepan over moderately high heat. Cook, stirring, until the vegetables are soft, about 5 minutes. Take the pan off the heat and sprinkle in the flour, pressing it into the vegetables with the back of a wooden spoon. Return the pan to the stove and cook, stirring with the wooden spoon, until the flour turns a nutty brown. Off the heat, whisk in 2 cups of the stock. Return the pan to the heat and whisk until the mixture comes to a simmer. Stir in the tomato, chopped mushrooms, and bouquet garni. Turn down the heat and continue simmering the sauce for at least 30 minutes, preferably for 1½ hours, adding more stock as necessary and skimming off and discarding any scum that accumulates on the surface. Strain. (This basic brown sauce can be made with canned stock and can be chilled for up to 5 days or frozen for up to 6 months.)

To cook the beef, tie the meat securely at 1½-inch intervals with kitchen string. The meat must be tied so that it will hold its shape while cooking. Season the roast on all sides with salt and pepper. Heat a large enamel pan with the oil and 2 tablespoons of the butter. When the bubbles subside, brown the tenderloin on all sides, including the ends, being careful not to burn the fat on the bottom of the pan. When the meat is browned, remove it to a board, pour off any excess fat in the pan, and immediately pour in the wine to deglaze the pan. Add the prepared demi-glace. Bring to a boil over moderately high heat and return the roast to the pan. Cover the pan and place it in a 350-degree oven, or continue cooking it on top of the stove over a very low flame, until the meat reaches the temperature of 120 degrees on an instant-read thermometer, about 35 minutes. When the meat is done, remove it from the pan, remove the strings, and let it rest on a platter for 10 minutes while you finish the sauce. Let the sauce cool in the pan for 5 minutes. Skim off and discard any fat that rises to the surface. Check the sauce for consistency—it should coat the back of a metal spoon. If it is too thin, reduce it over medium heat while stirring. If it is too thick, add some stock or water and simmer for another 10 minutes.

To cook the sliced mushrooms, heat the remaining tablespoon of butter in a small frying pan over moderately high heat. Toss in the mushrooms all at once so that they absorb the butter evenly. Season with salt and pepper. Cook the mushrooms until they are half wilted and add them to the sauce. Add salt and pepper to taste.

To serve, carve 1-inch-thick slices of the tenderloin, enough for one per person, and leave the rest of the roast whole. Overlap the slices on the platter and spoon some of the sauce with the mushrooms down the middle of the meat. Serve the remaining sauce separately in a warm sauceboat.   SERVES 8

The way to take the temperature of something cooking in the oven is to quickly open the oven, remove the pan, place it on top of the stove, and close the oven door. Stick an instant-read thermometer two-thirds of the way into the meat and let it warm up for a few seconds before reading it. Sometimes thermometers are wrong, so always check the juices that run out of the hole made by the thermometer. Return the pan to the oven. Every time you open the oven, you reduce its temperature by 50 degrees. The more you open it, the longer it will take things to cook.

A variation on this recipe is tenderloin tips in Bordelaise sauce. To make this, cut the trimmings of the tenderloin into long, thin pieces, 2 inches long and ¼ inch thick. Season well with salt and pepper. Heat a pan with oil and butter, stir-fry the meat over high heat until barely cooked, and remove the meat from the pan. Stir in 1 shallot, minced, and cook for a minute. Stir in 6 mushrooms, thinly sliced, and cook until half wilted. Remove the mixture from the pan. Add a cup of dry red wine and bring to a boil. Add a cup of demi-glace and bring to a boil. Add salt and pepper to taste. Stir the beef and mushrooms back into the sauce, sprinkle with minced parsley, and serve with buttered noodles.

Beef in Red Wine with Onions and Mushrooms
(Boeuf Bourguignon)

Beef Bourguignon is an old favorite that remains popular even today. This recipe is relatively quick and easy to prepare. Serve this stew with parsleyed new potatoes, followed by a green salad.

4 tablespoons (½ stick) butter plus
    2 tablespoons
2 tablespoons olive oil
4 pounds beef chuck, cut into 1-inch
    cubes
¼ cup flour
3 cups red Burgundy (Pinot Noir)
1 tablespoon tomato paste
Bouquet garni composed of 4 sprigs parsley,
    3 sprigs thyme, and 2 bay leaves
1 pound small white onions, peeled
1 pound small white mushrooms, stems
    trimmed flush with caps
Coarse salt
Freshly ground black pepper

To brown the meat, heat a layer of butter and oil in a large sauté pan over medium-high heat. When the bubbles subside, arrange the meat in the pan at ½-inch intervals. Using tongs, turn the meat to brown it on all sides before transferring to a 3-quart enamel casserole. Repeat with the rest of the meat, keeping a layer of oil and butter on the bottom of the pan and taking care not to burn the pan. If there is a spot on the pan that looks as if it may burn, move pieces of meat onto that spot.

When all the meat has been browned, pour off all but 2 tablespoons of the fat in the pan and, off the heat, sprinkle in the flour and press it into the fat with the back of a wooden spoon. Return the pan to the heat and cook this roux until the flour becomes dark brown in color. Pour in the wine and bring to a boil, whisking to prevent lumps. After a minute, add the tomato paste and bring the mixture to a boil. Pour this mixture over the meat in the casserole. Bring to a boil, stirring, on top of the stove and add the bouquet garni. Cover the casserole and place it in a 350-degree oven until the meat is tender when tasted, about 1½ hours. Discard the bouquet garni.

To prepare the onions, put them in a pan covered generously with cold water, bring to a boil, and simmer until the onions are tender, about 8 minutes. Drain the onions and add them to the stew.

To prepare the mushrooms, heat the butter in a medium-size frying pan over moderately high heat. Toss in the mushrooms all at once. Season with salt and pepper and continue tossing them until they are lightly browned. Add them to the stew.

When the casserole is removed from the oven, check the consistency of the sauce. If the sauce is too thin, remove the meat and vegetables with a slotted spoon and place the casserole over high heat. Cook, stirring with a flat wooden spatula, until the sauce is reduced to the desired consistency. Return the meat and vegetables to the pan. Add salt and pepper to taste.   SERVES 8

Braised Short Ribs with Horseradish Mashed Potatoes

*W*hether you call it stew, ragoût, or daube, it's all the same method of cooking— tough meat is cooked long and slow so that it essentially makes its own sauce. In this dish, the meat is cooked until it's almost falling off the bones and is served with mashed potatoes with a hint of horseradish.

6 cups dry red wine
3 garlic cloves, minced
1½ bay leaves
2 tablespoons minced fresh thyme
2 strips orange zest
1 tablespoon whole black peppercorns
4 pounds beef short ribs
2 tablespoons olive oil
2 tablespoons butter
1 medium-size onion, finely chopped
1 medium-size carrot, finely chopped
2 tablespoons flour
3½ cups veal or beef stock
Coarse salt
Freshly ground black pepper

To prepare the marinade, combine the wine, garlic, bay leaves, thyme, orange zest, and peppercorns in a large stainless steel or enamel pan. Bring to a boil and simmer over medium heat for 10 minutes. Remove the pan from the heat and cool completely. When cool, add the short ribs. Let marinate for 4 hours at room temperature or overnight in the refrigerator.

When ready to cook, remove the meat

from the marinade and pat it dry with paper towels. Strain the marinade into a saucepan and reduce it over moderately high heat until it is reduced by one-quarter.

To brown the meat, heat a large sauté pan with enough oil and butter to make a ¼-inch layer on the bottom. Place the pan over moderately high heat. When the bubbles subside, arrange the meat in the pan at ½-inch intervals. Using tongs, turn the meat to brown it all over before transferring to a 3-quart enamel casserole. Repeat with the rest of the meat, keeping a layer of oil and butter on the bottom of the pan and taking care not to burn the pan.

When all the meat has been browned, pour off all but 2 tablespoons of the fat in the pan and stir in the onion and carrot. Cook, stirring with a wooden spoon or spatula, until the vegetables are soft, about 5 minutes. Sprinkle in the flour and press it into the vegetables with the back of the spoon. Cook until the flour becomes brown in color. Pour in the reduced marinade and bring to a boil, stirring. Pour this mixture over the meat. Add enough stock to barely come up to the top of the meat. Bring to a boil, stirring, on top of the stove. Cover the casserole and place it in a 350-degree oven until the meat is tender, about 3 hours. (This dish can be made ahead up to this point and chilled for up to 5 days.)

To finish the daube, allow it to rest for 10 minutes and spoon off any fat that accumulates on the top. If reheating, stir gently over moderate heat until the stew begins to simmer. At this point you need to determine if you have the right amount of liquid for the stew. If there is too much liquid, remove the meat to a plate and reduce the liquid over high heat, stirring with a flat wooden spatula until the desired consistency is reached. Remove the bones and gristle from the ribs if desired. Return the meat to the stew. Add salt and pepper to taste. Serve with horseradish mashed potatoes (recipe follows).

SERVES 6

HORSERADISH MASHED POTATOES

*2½ pounds yellow-fleshed potatoes,
    halved if large*
Coarse salt
½ cup olive oil
¼ pound (1 stick) softened butter
*2 tablespoons grated fresh horseradish
    or prepared horseradish to taste*
Freshly ground black pepper

Put the potatoes with ½ teaspoon salt in a large saucepan, generously cover with cold water, and place over moderately high heat. Allow the potatoes to boil, uncovered, until they are tender when pierced with a fork, about 30 minutes. Drain in a colander and shake vigorously to allow any excess liquid to evaporate. Peel the potatoes. While the potatoes are still warm, press them through a potato ricer back into the saucepan. With a wooden spoon, beat in the olive oil, butter, horseradish, and salt and pepper to taste. Be sure to taste the potatoes as you add the horseradish so as to judge the amount to add.

SERVES 6

If you find fresh horseradish, take it home and remove the yellowish-brown skin. Either grate it on the medium-size holes of a box grater or grate it into a food processor. Put it in a glass jar and cover with white wine vinegar. Storing it like this will prevent it from discoloring. It will keep for a year and can be used to flavor beef dishes.

California Choucroute Garnie

Traditional Alsatian choucroute garnie is a variety of preserved pork products, such as salt pork, pork sausage, smoked pork chops, or smoked ham, served on sauerkraut that has been cooked a long time and is served with boiled new potatoes and mustard. This California version presents smoked pork chops and fresh cooked cabbage for a lighter effect. Try it—you'll like it!

*4 pork sausages (homemade, see page 382;
    or store-bought)*
2 tablespoons olive oil
2 large onions, coarsely chopped
2 large carrots, coarsely chopped
2 celery stalks, coarsely chopped
Coarse salt
2 garlic cloves, minced
1 green apple, peeled and coarsely chopped
*½ head cabbage, preferably Savoy, cored
    and cut in ½-inch-wide strips*
2 cups dry white wine
⅓ cup white wine vinegar
*2 pounds new red or white potatoes, peeled;
    halved or quartered if large*
2 smoked pork chops
1 slice smoked ham, cut in half
Coarse salt
Freshly ground black pepper

To cook the sausages, prick them several times, lay them in a large enamel casserole with ¼ inch water, and place the pan over medium-high heat. Cook, turning from time to time, until the water has evaporated and the sausages are browned on all sides, about 15 minutes. Remove the sausages, pour off any excess fat in the pan, and add the olive oil, onions, carrots, and celery to the pan with ½ teaspoon salt and cook, stirring, until soft, about 5 minutes. Stir in the garlic and cook another minute. Add the apple, cabbage, wine, and vinegar and continue cooking until the mixture begins to simmer. Cover and cook gently for 15 minutes.

To cook the potatoes, put them with ½ teaspoon salt in a pot, cover generously with cold water, and put over high heat. Boil the potatoes until they are tender when pierced with a fork, about 25 minutes. Immediately drain them in a colander, shaking off any excess moisture.

To assemble the choucroute, bury the sausages in the cabbage and place the smoked pork chops and the ham on top of the cabbage. Place the casserole in a 375-degree oven and bake, uncovered, until the chops are lightly colored, about 20 minutes. Add salt and pepper to taste.

To serve, arrange the cabbage in the middle of a serving platter and cover the cabbage with the sausages, pork, and ham. Arrange the potatoes at the ends of the platter or in a separate bowl. Serve prepared mustard on the side. SERVES 4 TO 6

If smoked pork chops are not available, substitute regular pork chops that have been soaked in a brine solution for an hour and then browned. (The brine solution ratio should be ½ cup coarse salt to 2 quarts cold water.)

VEGETABLES

VEGETABLES are the little miracles of the food world! A seed or a bulb is planted in dirt and in time, with the help of water and sunshine, it becomes a beautiful, colorful plant that gives us pleasure and nutrients. If you have the opportunity to pick vegetables fresh from your garden—fantastic! The next best thing is to buy vegetables from local farmers at your nearest farmers' market—terrific! The next best thing is to encourage your local market to carry only the best local, seasonal vegetables.

Vegetables can be divided into categories of green vegetables—vegetables that grow above the ground—such as green beans and broccoli; and root vegetables— vegetables that grow below the ground— such as parsnips, carrots, and rutabagas. The third category is green leafy vegetables, often used in salads. You can also classify vegetables according to season. Spring is the season of asparagus, peas, and artichokes. Summer brings us tomatoes, corn, eggplants, and peppers. Autumn is the season of squash, such as pumpkins and butternut squash, while winter is the season of leeks, celery root, and fennel.

How to Cook Vegetables

Vegetables can be cooked using all methods—steaming, boiling, roasting/baking, grilling/broiling, sautéeing, deep-frying, braising, and stewing. Three special vegetable presentations are vegetable purees, timbales, and gratins. A puree is a smooth mixture usually made with added butter or cream that will hold its shape when spooned onto a plate. A timbale is a chopped or grated mixture baked in a mold with eggs and cream and then unmolded on the plate. A gratin is usually cooked vegetables covered with a béchamel sauce baked in a flat dish in the oven.

A common way to cook green vegetables is to blanch them—that is, to drop them into plenty of boiling salted water until they are tender when pierced with a fork, then drain them and hold them under cold running water or plunge them into an ice bath to stop the cooking. This is what the frozen food companies do before freezing vegetables. The vegetables can then be reheated by being dropped briefly into boiling water or warmed briefly in butter.

The best way to cook beets is to trim the tops, leaving an inch of stems, wrap each uncut beet in foil, and bake them for 1 to 2 hours in a 350-degree oven. They can then be peeled and made into a variety of dishes.

The best way to cook winter squash is to cut it in half, remove the seeds and fiber, place them cut side down on an oiled baking sheet, and bake them in a 350-degree oven until very soft. The squash is spooned out of the skin and made into dishes such as soup or filling for mezzaluna.

For delicious corn on the cob, cut off the silk and loose leaves, place the unhusked corn in a 325-degree oven, and bake for 10 minutes. The only problem with cooking corn this way is that you need to remove the husks with oven mitts while the corn is hot, but it's worth the effort.

The best way to cook new potatoes is to coat them with olive oil, sprinkle them wih coarse salt and freshly ground pepper, and roast them at 400 degrees until they are tender when pierced by a fork.

The Big Problem

It's hard to figure out what to do with unfamiliar vegetables. When you find a vegetable you have never seen before, try blanching it in boiling water and serving it with butter. Alternatively, try roasting it in a 400-degree oven until tender when pierced with a fork.

How to Cook Vegetables Without a Recipe

You can make a wonderful side dish or first course with vegetables by gathering a colorful assortment, washing them, and cutting them into uniform sizes—about 2 inches long by ¼ inch wide. Heat some olive oil in a frying pan, add the harder vegetables first, and cook, stirring constantly for 2 to 3 minutes. Add the softer vegetables and cook another 2 to 3 minutes, then add the very soft vegetables and cook for another minute. The best way to flavor a vegetable mélange like this is with a sprinkling of coarse salt and a tablespoon of extra-virgin olive oil. You could also chop together some garlic, parsley, and grated lemon zest and sprinkle this mixture over the warm vegetables. This is called a gremolata.

Butternut Squash with Pecans

Butternut squash is so good—and good for you!

3 tablespoons butter
2½ pounds butternut or other winter
    squash, peeled, seeded, and cut into
    ½-inch dice
Coarse salt
Freshly ground black pepper
½ cup coarsely chopped fresh
    pecans
3 tablespoons minced fresh Italian
    parsley

Heat the butter in a 10-inch frying or sauté pan over moderately high heat. Toss in the squash all at once and pour in ½ inch water and ½ teaspoon salt. Cover and cook over moderate heat, stirring from time to time, until the squash is tender when pierced with a fork, about 15 minutes. Stir in the pecans with salt and pepper to taste. Transfer to a warmed serving bowl, sprinkle with parsley, and serve. SERVES 6

Whenever you cut off the skin of any winter squash, place the squash on a board or a counter and cut it with the knife always turned away from you. Because the skin is hard, it is easy to cut yourself.

Of the many kinds of winter squashes, the best-tasting are butternut, Kabocha, Preservation, and Sugar Pumpkin. The squash with the least taste is Acorn.

Since pecans are so perishable, buy them fresh when you need them, preferably in bulk.

Hashed Brussels Sprouts with Brown Butter and Capers

Even Brussels sprouts haters love them when they are cooked this way!

2 pounds fresh Brussels sprouts
6 tablespoons butter
2 tablespoons capers, rinsed and drained
Coarse salt
Freshly ground black pepper

Remove the rough outer leaves of the Brussels sprouts and trim the stem of each sprout. Drop them through the slicer attachment of a food processor to shred them. Heat the butter in a 10-inch frying or sauté pan over moderately high heat. When the butter turns brown, toss in the shredded Brussels sprouts along with the capers. Cook until the sprouts soften, about 7 minutes. Add salt and pepper to taste.　　　SERVES 8

Julienne of Autumn Vegetables

This is a colorful display to accompany chicken or meat.

4 tablespoons (½ stick) butter
1 pound white turnips, peeled and cut into 2 by ¼-inch julienne
1 pound rutabagas or parsnips, peeled and cut into 2 by ¼-inch julienne
Coarse salt
1 pound snow peas, cut into ¼-inch-wide strips
1 red bell pepper, cut into ¼-inch-wide strips
Freshly ground black pepper

Combine the butter with the turnips and rutabagas with ½ cup water and ½ teaspoon salt in a 10-inch frying or sauté pan over moderately high heat. Cook, stirring constantly, until the vegetables begin to soften, about 10 minutes. Stir in the snow peas and bell pepper and continue to cook another 2 minutes. Add salt and pepper to taste.　　　SERVES 8

Roasted Winter Vegetables

hese vegetables look absolutely fabulous when arranged carefully on a plate. They should look as if they just came from the garden.

¼ cup olive oil
6 small new potatoes (about ½ pound),
　cut in half
6 small thin leeks (about ½ pound),
　equal parts white and green, trimmed
6 whole shallots (about ½ pound), unpeeled
　and cut in half
6 small parsnips (about ½ pound),
　trimmed and cut in half or quarters
　lengthwise
Coarse salt
Freshly ground pepper
¼ cup good-quality balsamic vinegar

Pour the olive oil on the bottom of a heavy roasting pan. Arrange the vegetables cut side up in the dish and add enough water to come ½ inch up the sides of the dish. Season the vegetables generously with salt and pepper. Then roast the vegetables in the oven at 425 degrees until they are tender when pierced with a fork, about 20 minutes. Add the balsamic vinegar to the dish and return to the oven for 5 minutes. Serve warm or at room temperature. It is best not to toss the vegetables together when they are cooking so that you can arrange them attractively on dinner plates. SERVES 6

Grilled Winter Endive and Radicchio

These grilled bitter vegetables would be delicious served with grilled fish.

3 Belgian endives, trimmed and split in half lengthwise (make sure each piece is attached to the core)
2 medium-size heads radicchio, cut vertically into 4 wedges (make sure each piece is attached to the core)
½ cup extra-virgin olive oil
Coarse salt
Freshly ground black pepper
½ cup freshly grated Parmesan

Toss the vegetables with half the olive oil and a sprinkling of salt and pepper.

Prepare a charcoal fire or preheat the broiler.

To grill the vegetables, place them on the rack over the fire or on a broiler pan under the broiler. Grill or broil until the endives are a deep golden brown and the radicchio is lightly browned on both sides, about 5 minutes on each side. Place the vegetables on a warmed serving platter and sprinkle with the remaining olive oil and the Parmesan.

SERVES 6

Buttered Green Beans

Simple cooking is often the best, especially when it is to accompany flavorful food.

1 pound small green beans, trimmed on both ends
Coarse salt
4 tablespoons (½ stick) butter
Freshly ground black pepper

Heat a saucepan of water over moderately high heat. When the water comes to a boil, add a teaspoon of salt and drop in the green beans. Let the beans boil vigorously until they are tender when pierced with a fork, about 6 minutes. Drain the beans and run cold water over them to stop the cooking.

When ready to serve, heat the beans with the butter in a 10-inch frying or sauté pan over moderate heat. Cook, shaking the pan or stirring often, until the beans are warmed through. Season with salt and pepper and serve.

SERVES 4

If you are blanching a large amount of beans, it is better to stop the cooking by submerging the beans briefly in ice water. Professional cooks often reheat vegetables by plunging them into boiling water for a few seconds.

Celery Root with Lemon

*C*elery root and spinach are both vegetables suitable for serving in the winter with hearty meats.

3 pounds celery root
4 tablespoons butter
2 tablespoons lemon juice
Coarse salt
Freshly ground black pepper
2 tablespoons minced fresh Italian parsley

Peel the celery root and cut it into very thin strips (julienne) just before cooking. Melt the butter in a skillet and toss in the celery root. Cook, stirring, for 2 to 3 minutes. Cover and let cook over medium heat for 5 to 8 minutes until tender when tasted. Stir in the lemon juice with salt and pepper to taste and sprinkle with the parsley.   SERVES 8

Spinach with Walnuts

4 pounds fresh spinach
Coarse salt
4 tablespoons butter
½ cup walnuts, coarsely chopped and lightly toasted
Freshly ground black pepper

To cook the spinach, bring a pot of water to a boil over high heat. Drop in a tablespoon of salt with the spinach and cook until the spinach is half wilted. Remove the spinach and drain.

Put the butter in 10-inch skillet or sauté pan. Add the cooked fresh spinach and heat through. Toss in the walnuts with salt and pepper to taste.   SERVES 8

Peas Cooked with Lettuce and Onions

This very French vegetable dish is suitable to serve with rich food such as duck.

1 head butter lettuce, core removed and
    leaves shredded
3 pounds fresh peas, shelled, or 1 pound
    frozen little peas
12 pearl onions, peeled
4 tablespoons (½ stick) butter
Sugar
4 sprigs fresh Italian parsley
Coarse salt
Freshly ground black pepper

To assemble this dish, place the lettuce on the bottom of a 10-inch sauté pan and place the peas on top of the lettuce. Scatter the onions over the top and dot with the butter. Sprinkle with a pinch of sugar, lay parsley across, and season with salt and pepper. Cover the pan and place it over moderately high heat. Cook, shaking the pan occasionally, for about 10 minutes if the peas are fresh and 5 minutes if the peas are frozen. Remove the parsley sprigs before serving. Serve the mixture directly from the pan.   SERVES 6

Vegetables Printanier

These spring vegetables will enliven any dish.

1 pound baby carrots, trimmed and scraped,
    or large carrots, trimmed to look like
    baby carrots
Coarse salt
8 small white turnips, halved or quartered
    if large
1½ pounds fresh peas, shelled, or 1 pound
    frozen peas
4 tablespoons (½ stick) butter
⅓ cup chicken stock
2 tablespoons minced fresh Italian parsley
Freshly ground black pepper

To blanch the vegetables, heat a large pot of water over high heat. When the water boils, add ½ teaspoon salt and drop in the carrots. When the carrots are tender when pierced with a fork, remove them with a slotted spoon to a strainer, and run cold water over them to stop the cooking. When the water comes to a boil again, drop in the turnips. Let the turnips boil until they are tender when pierced with a fork, about 10 minutes. Remove them with a slotted spoon to a strainer and run cold water over them. Drop the peas into the water and let them cook until they are tender, about 5 minutes for fresh peas and 2 minutes for frozen. Strain the peas into a strainer and run cold water over them.

To give the carrots and turnips a slight glaze, combine them with the butter and chicken stock in a 10-inch frying or sauté pan over moderately high heat. Toss or stir them until they are lightly browned. Add the peas and cook for a minute more, just heated through. Add salt and pepper to taste. Put the vegetables in a serving dish and sprinkle with the parsley.　Serves 8

If you like the look of a little of the stem of the carrots and turnips attached, by all means cut them this way. They definitely look appealing with the stems on even if the stems are not good to eat. If baby turnips are not available, cut large turnips into château shapes (see page 234). Do not peel vegetables before turning them; it is twice as much work.

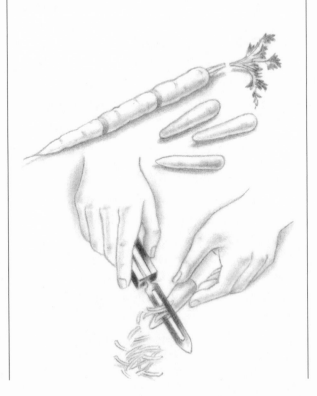

Glazed Onions

When you cook root vegetables with just a little sugar, you can give them a nice caramel color. They are traditional with roasted meats.

> *½ pound small white onions*
> *1 teaspoon sugar*
> *1 tablespoon butter*
> *Coarse salt*
> *Freshly ground pepper*

To peel the onions, bring a large saucepan of water to a boil. Cut off the onion roots and make a cross in the root end. Drop the onions into the water and let cook for 2 minutes. Drain the onions and when cool enough to handle, gently slip off the outer skin by pinching the end opposite the roots.

To glaze the onions, return them to the cleaned-out saucepan with the sugar, butter, and salt and pepper to taste. Cook over moderately high heat, shaking from time to time, for about 8 minutes. Stir or shake the pan for another 2 minutes so that the onions are tender and caramelized on all sides.

Serves 4

Glazed Carrots

1 pound carrots, trimmed, peeled, and cut
    into 1½ by ½-inch sticks
1 teaspoon sugar
1 tablespoon butter
Coarse salt
Freshly ground pepper

Combine the carrots with ½ cup water, the
sugar, and butter in a 10-inch frying or sauté
pan over moderately high heat. Simmer the
carrots, stirring from time to time, until the
carrots are tender and the water has evaporated. Toward the end of the cooking, shake
or stir the carrots so that they caramelize all
over. Add salt and pepper to taste.

SERVES 4

Tomatoes Filled
with Creamed Spinach

This old-fashioned recipe still looks appealing and tastes delicious!

12 medium-size red tomatoes
Coarse salt
4 pounds fresh spinach, stems removed,
    leaves washed and left damp
6 tablespoons butter
4 tablespoons flour
1½ cups milk, heated
1 cup heavy cream
Freshly ground black pepper

To prepare the tomatoes, cut off the top
quarter of each tomato. With a grapefruit
knife or a small metal spoon, remove the
seeds and the pulp from the inside of each
tomato, leaving a shell about ½ inch thick.
Sprinkle the inside of each tomato with salt
and invert the tomatoes on a rack set over a
baking sheet for an hour to release excess
moisture.

To cook the spinach, put the damp
spinach leaves in a 10-inch sauté pan over
moderately high heat. Cover the pan and let
cook for 3 minutes, until the leaves begin to
wilt. Remove the lid and start lifting the
wilted spinach on the bottom of the pan
over the uncooked spinach. Continue
doing this for another 3 or 4 minutes, until
all the spinach is completely wilted. Drain
the spinach and press it between two plates to
remove the cooking liquid. Finely chop the
spinach.

To make the béchamel sauce, melt 4 tablespoons of the butter in a small saucepan over moderate heat. Off the heat, beat in the flour with a wooden spoon. Return to the heat and cook this roux, stirring constantly, until it appears greasy. Off the heat, whisk in the milk. Return the pan to the heat and whisk constantly until the sauce has thickened and is smooth. Whisk in the cream and continue to cook another 5 minutes. Add salt and pepper to taste. (Cover this sauce with a piece of waxed paper or plastic wrap.)

To flavor the spinach, combine it with the remaining tablespoons of the butter in a saucepan over moderate heat. Cook briefly and stir in the béchamel sauce. Return the sauce to a simmer, stirring constantly. (The spinach can be made ahead to this point. It needs to be covered with a piece of waxed paper right on top of the sauce to prevent a crust from forming.)

To serve, invert the tomatoes onto a lightly buttered baking dish, reheat the spinach mixture, and spoon it into each tomato. Place the filled tomatoes in a 375-degree oven for 5 minutes.   SERVES 12

Celery Root and Potato Puree

A puree is an elegant way to serve vegetables. In a French restaurant, purees may be made with vegetable trimmings.

1¼ pounds celery root, peeled and cut into
    1-inch dice
6 garlic cloves, unpeeled
Coarse salt
¾ pound yellow-fleshed potatoes, such as
    Yukon Gold or Yellow Finn, peeled and
    cut into 1-inch dice
4 tablespoons (½ stick) butter
½ cup milk

Combine the celery root with the garlic cloves in a large saucepan with plenty of water and ½ teaspoon salt over moderately high heat. Boil the celery root for 15 minutes, then add the potato pieces. Cook until the vegetables are tender, about 25 minutes total. Drain them well in a colander, shaking vigorously to allow excess moisture to evaporate. Press the cooked vegetables through a potato ricer or a food mill into the cleaned-out pot. The puree should have a consistency such that it holds a definite shape in the spoon. If the mixture is too runny, heat the puree over moderate heat, stirring constantly to evaporate any excess moisture. When the desired consistency is reached, stir in the butter and the milk. Add salt and pepper to taste.

SERVES 6

Celery root is a cousin to celery, cultivated for its bulbous root. Celery root starts to discolor as soon as it is cut, which is why it is a good idea to store it in a bowl of cold water with a squeeze of lemon if you're not cooking it immediately.

Carrot and Rutabaga Puree

1 pound new potatoes, peeled
Coarse salt
6 tablespoons butter
1 cup heavy cream
½ pound carrots, peeled and cut in
    1-inch dice
½ pound rutabagas, peeled and cut in
    1-inch dice
Freshly ground black pepper

To cook the potatoes, put them in a large saucepan with ½ teaspoon salt and plenty of cold water over moderately high heat. Boil the potatoes until they are tender when pierced with a fork. Drain in a colander, shaking the colander to allow any excess liquid to evaporate. Press the potatoes through a potato ricer or a food mill into the cleaned-out pan. Add half the butter and half the cream.

To cook the carrots and rutabagas, put them into a large saucepan of boiling water with ½ teaspoon salt. Boil until they are tender when pierced with a fork. Drain and put the vegetables in a sauté pan with the remaining cream. Shake the pan back and forth over low heat until the cream has reduced and coats the vegetables. Puree the creamed vegetables in a food mill or a food processor. Mix the vegetable puree with the mashed potatoes. The puree should have a consistency such that it holds a definite shape in the spoon. If the mixture is too runny, heat it over moderate heat, stirring constantly to allow any excess moisture to evaporate.

When the desired consistency is reached, stir in the remaining butter and the cream. Add salt and pepper to taste.

Carrots always taste better when bought in bunches with their greens still attached.

What is called a rutabaga in California is sometimes called a yellow turnip in other parts of the country.

Spinach Timbale

These unmolded vegetable custards are an elegant way to present spinach or other cooked vegetables.

> 1 pound fresh spinach
> Coarse salt
> Freshly ground black pepper
> 3 tablespoons butter
> 2 teaspoons flour
> ¾ cup milk
> ½ cup heavy cream
> 3 eggs

To prepare the spinach, remove the stems by pinching them off at the leaf and wash them in plenty of water. Put the wet spinach with a sprinkling of salt in a 10-inch sauté pan over moderately high heat. Cover and let steam for a minute or two. Remove the cover and start turning the wilted spinach over the uncooked spinach, adding more spinach as the size of the pan allows. When all the spinach is cooked, put it on a plate and press with another plate over a sink to drain the excess moisture. Chop the spinach coarsely and season it with salt and pepper.

To make the sauce, melt the butter in a small saucepan and let it cook until it is quite brown and literally smoking. Mix in the cooked spinach with a fork. Off the heat, sprinkle in the flour and beat it in with a wooden spoon. Return the pan to the heat and cook the flour for 2 to 3 minutes. Off the heat, stir in the milk and cream. Return the pan to the heat and bring the mixture to a boil, stirring constantly. Off the heat, stir in the eggs one at a time, beating well after each addition. Fill six to eight buttered ramekins or custard cups with the spinach mixture and place them in a larger pan of warm water in a 375-degree oven until the custard is set, 25 to 30 minutes. To serve, run a knife around the very top of the custard and unmold the timbales onto warm plates.

SERVES 6 TO 8

When a recipe calls for cooking something in a larger pan of water, a bain-marie, it is done to provide the dish with even heat.

Root Vegetable Gratin

In modern cooking, there is not much call for béchamel; however, this dish stands out with the addition of this traditional sauce.

¼ pound (1 stick) butter
½ pound carrots, peeled and cut into
*   ¼-inch rounds*
½ pound rutabagas, peeled and cut about
*   the same size as the carrots*
½ pound parsnips, cut about the same size
*   as the carrots*
4 tablespoons flour
4 cups milk, heated
Coarse salt
Freshly ground black pepper
4 tablespoons freshly grated Parmesan
½ cup fine bread crumbs

To prepare the vegetables, melt half the butter in a 10-inch frying or sauté pan over moderate heat. Toss the carrots, rutabagas, and parsnips into the pan, making sure they are all coated with the butter. Add ½ cup water with ½ teaspoon salt. Cover and cook until the vegetables are tender when pierced with a fork.

To make the béchamel sauce, melt the remaining butter in a small saucepan over moderately high heat. Off the heat, stir in the flour and beat it down with a wooden spoon. Return the roux to the heat and cook, stirring, until it appears greasy. Off the heat, whisk in the warm milk. Return the sauce to the heat and continue whisking until it comes to a boil. Let simmer 5 minutes. Add salt and pepper to taste.

To assemble the dish, when the vegetables are cooked, add them to the béchamel and stir in the Parmesan. Pour them into a buttered 2-quart gratin dish. Sprinkle with the bread crumbs and bake in a 375-degree oven until the top is golden brown, about 20 minutes. (This dish can be made ahead and reheated.) SERVES 8

Ratatouille Niçoise

Ratatouille is a famous vegetable stew from the South of France composed of eggplant, zucchini, tomatoes, onions, and peppers. It really should be cooked until the vegetables blend together.

¾ cup olive oil
1 large onion, halved and sliced
2 red or yellow bell peppers, cored, seeded, and cut in ½-inch strips
Coarse salt
2 garlic cloves, minced
4 medium-size zucchini (about 1 pound), cut in ½-inch rounds
1 medium-size eggplant (1 to 1½ pounds), cut in 1-inch cubes
6 medium-size tomatoes (about 1½ pounds), peeled, seeded, and chopped
2 tablespoons minced fresh Italian parsley
Freshly ground black pepper

To prepare the vegetables, heat ¼ cup of the olive oil with the onion, peppers, and ½ teaspoon salt in a 10-inch sauté pan over moderately high heat. Cook, stirring from time to time, until the onions and peppers are soft, about 5 minutes. Add the garlic and cook, stirring, for a minute more. Transfer the onion mixture to a plate.

Add a thin layer of oil to the pan. When it is hot, add the zucchini in one layer and lightly brown on both sides, turning with tongs. Transfer the browned zucchini to a plate and continue with the rest of the zucchini and then the eggplant. Be careful not to add too much olive oil because the eggplant will absorb as much as you use.

When all the zucchini and eggplant have been browned, layer the vegetables back in the pan, starting with half the onions and peppers, then half the zucchini and eggplant, and then half the tomatoes sprinkled with parsley. Season each layer with salt and pepper. Repeat with the remaining vegetables. Cover the pan and let the vegetables stew over moderate heat for 35 minutes to meld all the flavors. (This dish can be made ahead and stored in the refrigerator for up to 3 days.) Serve warm or at room temperature.

SERVES 6

Cooks used to salt the eggplant slices and let them rest to give off bitter juice. There is no need to do this, since today's eggplants lack the bitterness.

This recipe will taste better if cooked with fresh tomatoes in the summertime.

California Succotash

This is a recipe I developed years ago to go with turkey and mashed potatoes for a Thanksgiving dinner.

1 pound pearl onions, trimmed and peeled
4 medium-size zucchini, cut in ½-inch dice, each with some of the green skin
Kernels from 4 ears yellow corn
2 cups heavy cream
1 red bell pepper, cut in ½-inch dice
Coarse salt
Freshly ground black pepper

Put the onions in a saucepan and cover generously with cold water. Bring to a boil, reduce the heat, and simmer for 5 minutes. Drain.

To make the succotash, heat the cream in a 10-inch frying or sauté pan over moderately high heat. Simmer gently until the cream is reduced by half, about 5 minutes. Stir in the onions and red pepper and simmer gently 3 minutes. Add the zucchini and corn and cook another 2 minutes. Season with salt and pepper and serve.

SERVES 8

Vegetable Charlotte

This recipe is a lot of work but it's worth it for a spectacular Thanksgiving presentation of all the vegetables everyone likes in one dish. The final dish is a colorful display of vegetables held together by mashed potatoes. It is designed to be eaten with turkey gravy.

Coarse salt
1 pound green beans, at least 3 inches long, both ends trimmed
2 to 3 large carrots, cut in strips the same size as the beans
2 yellow squash cut in ¼-inch-thick rounds
2 zucchini, cut in ¼-inch-thick rounds
½ cup Brussels sprouts, halved
½ medium-size cauliflower, cut into ½-inch florets
¼ cup shelled fresh peas
3 pounds yellow-fleshed potatoes, such as Yellow Finn or Yukon Gold
¼ pound (1 stick) butter, plus some for the mold
½ cup heavy cream
Freshly ground pepper

To blanch each kind of vegetable, bring a large saucepan of water to a boil over high heat. Add ½ teaspoon salt and drop in one kind of vegetable at a time. When cooked, remove and cook the next. Cook the vegetables until they are tender when pierced with a fork. Remove the vegetables with a slotted spoon, put them in a strainer, and run them under cold water. As you finish cooking each vegetable, put it separately on a tray.

To cook the potatoes, cut them in half if large and put them with ½ teaspoon salt in another large saucepan with plenty of cold water. Bring to a boil over high heat and cook until the potatoes are tender when pierced with a fork. Drain and shake the potatoes in a colander to allow the excess liquid to evaporate. Peel the potatoes. Press the potatoes through a potato ricer or a food mill into the cleaned-out pan. Stir in half the butter, the cream, and salt and pepper to taste.

To assemble, generously butter the inside of a 2-quart soufflé dish or charlotte mold. Arrange a row of peas around the inside edge of the bottom of the dish. Inside that, make a circle of overlapping slices of yellow squash, then a circle of overlapping slices of zucchini. The bottom of the dish should be covered with peas, squash, and zucchini. To continue up the sides of the dish, stand the green beans and carrots, alternating them around the inside of the dish. (You may have to press some of the mashed potatoes against them to make them stand up.) When the border is finished, spread half the mashed potatoes in the bottom of the dish. Place a circle of Brussels sprouts around the edge of the mashed potatoes and fill the center with the cauliflower florets. Cover these vegetables with the remaining mashed potatoes. On the top, place overlapping layers of yellow squash and zucchini. Dot the top of the squash with the remaining butter. Trim the ends of the carrots and beans with scissors so they are even with the top of the dish. (This dish can be prepared up to 3 days ahead and stored in the refrigerator.)

When ready to serve, place the dish holding the vegetable mold in a 350-degree oven to heat through, about 30 minutes. To serve, put a warmed round serving platter on top of the dish and without hesitation, invert the dish onto the platter. Be sure to lift the dish straight up and off the mold.

SERVES 6

Garlic Potatoes

*T*his recipe for potatoes cooked with whole, unpeeled garlic cloves has been a favorite of Tante Marie's students ever since it was taught to us by Judith Olney. The secret is to cook the potatoes and garlic in plenty of olive oil so the garlic doesn't burn. Serve this dish with roasted chicken or a chicken sauté.

¾ cup olive oil
12 medium-size new potatoes
(about 1 pound), halved if necessary
to keep them uniform in size
24 garlic cloves, unpeeled
6 bay leaves
4 sprigs thyme
4 sprigs rosemary
Coarse salt
Freshly ground black pepper

Cover the bottom of a glass baking dish with the oil. Toss in the potatoes and garlic, making sure both are coated with the oil. Toss in the bay leaves and sprigs of herbs and season generously with salt and pepper.

Bake this dish in a 425-degree oven until the potatoes are tender when pierced with a fork, about 35 minutes. Open the oven and stir the potatoes twice during the cooking time. (When serving, be sure to show the guests how to squeeze the softened garlic and mash it into the potatoes.)

SERVES 6

Choose firm and fresh-looking new (thin-skinned) potatoes. Any long thin-skinned potatoes can be called fingerlings. The yellow-fleshed ones are Yellow Finn and Yukon Gold, and there are many varieties of white and pink potatoes. I find the purple potatoes have the least flavor.

Potato Gratin

This recipe is a Christmas tradition with my friends the Connells in Toronto.

3 pounds baking potatoes, peeled, halved, and thinly sliced
1 quart milk
Bouquet garni composed of 4 sprigs parsley, 2 sprigs thyme, and 1 bay leaf
2 tablespoons butter
Coarse salt
2 cups grated Gruyère
1 cup heavy cream
Freshly ground black pepper

Put the potatoes in a large saucepan with the milk, bouquet garni, a tablespoon of the butter, and a sprinkling of salt over moderately high heat. When the milk begins to bubble, reduce the heat to a simmer and cook the potatoes until they are barely tender. Drain the potatoes, discarding the cooking liquid and the bouquet garni. Season the potatoes with salt and pepper.

Rub a 9 by 13-inch ceramic or glass baking dish with the remaining tablespoon of butter. Mix the cheese and cream together in a small bowl. Spread half the potatoes in the baking dish, cover with half the cheese and cream mixture, and season with salt and pepper. Spread the remaining potatoes and the remaining cheese and cream over the mixture. Season again with salt and pepper. Bake the gratin in a 375-degree oven until it is bubbly and lightly browned, 50 to 60 minutes.

SERVES 8

Inexperienced cooks like to mix everything with a whisk. Really, a whisk is best for keeping flour from lumping in a sauce or for whipping up a sauce or heavy cream. It doesn't need to be used for all mixing; for instance, for stirring cheese into spinach.

Mashed Potato Gratin with Truffle Oil

This luxurious recipe for mashed potatoes with Fontina and white truffle oil very suitably was taught to me by my friend Jerry DiVecchio, who loves luxury!

> 4½ pounds baking potatoes, peeled and
>   cut in quarters
> ¾ cup milk
> ¾ cup heavy cream
> 8 ounces imported Fontina, grated on large
>   holes of box grater
> 3 tablespoons white truffle oil
> Coarse salt
> Freshly ground white pepper

To cook the potatoes, put them with ½ teaspoon of salt in a large saucepan and cover generously with cold water. Bring to a boil over high heat and cook until the potatoes are tender when pierced with a fork, about 35 minutes. Drain the potatoes in a colander, shaking them vigorously to evaporate any excess water. Force the cooked potatoes through a ricer back into the cleaned-out pot. Stir in the milk, cream, half the Fontina, and half the truffle oil. Beat the mixture with a wooden spoon until it is smooth. Spoon the potatoes into a 3-quart baking dish and top with the remaining Fontina. (This dish can be prepared up to 3 days ahead at this point and stored in the refrigerator.)

To serve, put the potato dish on the top

rack and broil just until the cheese is lightly browned, about 5 minutes. Drizzle with the remaining truffle oil and serve.

SERVES 8

Since there are many bad imitations of truffle oil, it is important to check the ingredients to make sure the oil was infused with real truffles.

Squash, Pepper, and Hominy Stew

I*t's the combination of spices that makes this dish so appealing to the taste, and the colors of the vegetables that make it so appealing to the eyes. Serve this autumn vegetable stew as a first course before grilled chicken or a hearty pasta.*

3 tablespoons olive oil
1 large onion, finely chopped
Coarse salt
Freshly ground black pepper
6 garlic cloves, finely minced
¾ pound butternut, Kabocha, or Preservation squash, peeled, seeded, and cut into ½-inch cubes
1 teaspoon dried Greek oregano, crumbled
½ green bell pepper, cut into ½-inch dice
½ red bell pepper, cut into ½-inch dice
2 tablespoons ancho chile powder
½ teaspoon freshly ground cumin
1 tablespoon flour
1 cup dry white wine
2 cups chicken or vegetable stock
6 red, ripe tomatoes, peeled, seeded, and chopped, or one 28-ounce can tomatoes, coarsely chopped
½ pound green Swiss chard, stemmed and cut in 1-inch lengths
One 29-ounce can hominy, drained and rinsed
¾ cup sour cream or whole-milk yogurt
¼ cup chopped fresh cilantro or green onions for garnish

Put the oil, onion, and ½ teaspoon salt in a 10-inch frying or sauté pan over moderately high heat. Cook, stirring from time to time, until the onion is soft, about 5 minutes. Add the garlic and cook for another minute. Stir in the flour and cook for another minute. Stir in the squash, oregano, green pepper, red bell pepper, chile powder, cumin, and flour, and cook the mixture for 2 minutes more, stirring constantly. Season with salt and pepper. Stir in the wine, stock, and tomatoes, bring to a boil, stirring, and lower the heat to simmer the stew until the liquid begins to thicken and the vegetables are tender, about 35 minutes.

To cook the Swiss chard, bring another pot of water to a boil. Add a sprinkling of salt and the chard and cook until the chard is tender, about 3 minutes. Drain the chard in a colander and run cold water over it to stop the cooking. Using a ladle, press out the excess moisture from the chard and chop it coarsely.

Stir the chard and the hominy into the stew and cook until all the vegetables are tender, about 15 more minutes. If the stew is very liquid at this point, transfer the vegetables to a plate and reduce the liquid, stirring it constantly with a flat wooden spatula until the liquid thickens. Add the vegetables back into the pan to reheat. Add salt and pepper to taste. Serve in warmed bowls with a dollop of sour cream on each serving and a sprinkling of fresh cilantro.   SERVES 6

If the stems of the Swiss chard are large and coarse, grab the stem in one hand and the leaves in the other and pull. The stem should pull right out. Some cooks save the stems for another purpose; some of us put them in the compost.

Although it is generally better to cook with fresh herbs rather than dried, in this case the dried Greek oregano adds a special dimension to this dish.

Curried Eggplant and Chickpeas

This delicious curry could be served as a side dish with grilled chicken or fish or made into a vegetarian entreé served with brown rice pilaf.

½ cup olive oil
1½ teaspoons cumin seeds
½ teaspoon fennel seeds
½ teaspoon black peppercorns, cracked
2 medium-size onions, thinly sliced (about 2 cups)
12 garlic cloves, sliced
2 teaspoons dry mustard
1 teaspoon red pepper flakes
1 teaspoon turmeric
Coarse salt
1 small eggplant, about ¾ pound, cut into ½ by 2-inch pieces (about 3 cups)
3 pounds tomatoes, quartered lengthwise, or 28 ounces canned tomatoes, coarsely chopped
One 14-ounce can chickpeas, drained and rinsed
Freshly ground black pepper
2 tablespoons minced fresh cilantro

To toast the spices, heat the oil in a 10-inch sauté pan over moderately high heat. When the oil is hot, add the cumin seeds and cook until dark brown, about 15 seconds. Add the fennel seeds and peppercorns and cook another 5 seconds.

To make the stew, add the onions and cook, stirring from time to time, until the onions are soft, about 5 minutes. Add the garlic and cook another minute. Stir in the dry mustard, red pepper flakes, turmeric, a teaspoon of salt, the eggplant, and ½ cup water. Cook, stirring gently, about 10 more minutes, until the eggplant is soft. Stir in the tomatoes and cook 5 more minutes, stirring, until the tomatoes are soft. Gently stir in the chickpeas. Cover and simmer over low heat for 10 minutes, until the liquid thickens and flavors have blended. Add salt and pepper to taste. Serve sprinkled with cilantro.

SERVES 6

Seven Vegetables with Spiced Couscous

Couscous is a traditional Moroccan dish in which the little grains of pasta are steamed over a flavorful stew, which gives the couscous its flavor. This is a modern adaptation—a big platter of colorful vegetables on top of cooked couscous—for a vegetarian main course!

3 tablespoons olive oil
1 large onion, finely chopped
Coarse salt
1 garlic clove, minced
½ teaspoon ground turmeric
½ teaspoon ground cumin
Cayenne pepper
6 medium-size ripe tomatoes, peeled, seeded, and chopped, or one 28-ounce can of tomatoes, coarsely choppped
1 pound parsnips, peeled and cut into 1-inch dice
1 pound rutabagas, peeled and cut into 1-inch dice
1 pound carrots, peeled and cut into 1-inch dice
1 pound yams or sweet potatoes, peeled and cut into 1-inch dice
Freshly ground black pepper
Juice of 2 lemons
2 tablespoons minced fresh cilantro
10 cardamom pods
2 whole allspice berries
1 cinnamon stick
1 whole clove
½ teaspoon cumin seeds
½ teaspoon black peppercorns, crushed
¼ pound (1 stick) butter
3 cups couscous

To cook the vegetables, put the oil and the onion with ½ teaspoon salt in a large sauté pan over moderately high heat. Cook, stirring from time to time, until the onion is soft, about 5 minutes. Stir in the garlic, turmeric, cumin, and a pinch of cayenne and cook for a minute more. Stir in the tomatoes and continue cooking for 3 minutes more. Season the parsnips, rutabagas, carrots, and sweet potatoes with salt and pepper, and stir them into the tomato mixture. Continue to simmer the vegetables until they are tender when pierced with a fork, about 30 minutes. If the mixture seems dry, add water. Stir in the lemon juice, cilantro, and salt and pepper to taste.

To make a flavorful liquid for the couscous, combine the cardamom, allspice, cinnamon, clove, cumin seeds, peppercorns, and 5 cups of water in a large pot over high heat. When the water comes to a boil, reduce the heat and let simmer for 10 minutes.

Spread the couscous in a glass baking dish. Reheat the liquid if necessary, add the butter and 1½ teaspoons salt, and strain the liquid into the couscous. Stir the couscous once with a fork, cover the dish with foil, and let sit for 10 minutes. Before serving, break up any lumps with a fork.

To serve, spoon the couscous on a warmed serving platter and cover with the vegetable mixture.   SERVES 8

Couscous is like polenta—it really doesn't taste good by itself. Rather, couscous and polenta are both used as vehicles for flavorful foods.

To give an even more exotic taste to this dish, stir into the vegetables 2 tablespoons of diced preserved lemons at the end instead of the lemon juice.

Black-eyed Pea Stew Served in a Pumpkin

This is a really fun dish to serve around Halloween. It is also healthful and delicious!

1 cup black-eyed peas, sorted and soaked overnight in plenty of cold water
1 onion, quartered
1 dried red chile pepper
1 large sugar pumpkin shaped like a tureen
3 tablespoons olive oil
1 large onion, chopped
Coarse salt
5 garlic cloves, minced
½ teaspoon freshly ground cumin
1 teaspoon ancho chile powder
½ jalapeño without seeds and ribs, minced
1 red bell pepper without seeds and ribs, cut in 1-inch dice
1 cup dry white wine
6 medium-size red, ripe tomatoes, peeled, seeded, and chopped, or one 28-ounce can tomatoes, coarsely chopped
2 cups butternut or other winter squash, peeled and cut in ½-inch dice (½ pound)
2 medium-size zucchini, trimmed and cut into ½-inch rounds (½ pound)
2 ears fresh corn, cut in 1-inch rounds
Freshly ground pepper
1 pint sour cream
3 tablespoons coarsely chopped cilantro

To cook the black-eyed peas, drain them well, discarding the soaking liquid, and put them in a medium-size saucepan with the onion and dried chile. Add enough cold water to cover and bring to a boil. Reduce the heat to medium-low and simmer until the peas are tender, about 30 minutes. Drain well, discarding the onion and pepper.

To prepare the pumpkin, with a large knife slice off the top 4 to 5 inches down from the stem. Remove the seeds and fiber from the top and cavity of the pumpkin with a large metal spoon. Put the pumpkin in a round pie plate or baking dish and bake in a 350-degree oven for about 45 minutes. The pumpkin should be just tender but still hold its shape.

To prepare the vegetables, put the olive oil with the onion and ½ teaspoon salt in an enamel casserole over moderately high heat. Cook, stirring from time to time, until the onion is soft, about 5 minutes. Stir in the garlic with the cumin and chile powder and cook for another minute. Stir in the jalapeño and bell pepper and cook for another minute. Add the wine and tomatoes with 4 cups water. Bring the mixture to a boil, stirring constantly, and simmer for 10 minutes. Add the winter squash and cook for another 20 minutes. Add the cooked black-eyed peas, the zucchini, and corn and simmer for another 5 minutes. Add salt and pepper to taste.

To serve, reheat the pumpkin in a 350-degree oven for 15 minutes, fill it with the warmed stew, and present it at the table. Serve with dollops of sour cream and chopped cilantro. SERVES 8

When a recipe calls for sorting dried beans, it means to look at every one (preferably on a baking sheet) to make sure it isn't a stone.

For the quick-soak method for cooking beans, see page 23.

Good cooks like to use ancho chile powder because it is much purer than regular chile powder, which contains ingredients like dried garlic. If you can't find ancho chile powder, use red pepper flakes, only considerably less.

Black Bean Chili

For over twenty years, black bean chili has been served at Greens Restaurant in San Francisco. The food at Greens is so good you don't even notice it's vegetarian!

2 cups black turtle beans, sorted and soaked
   overnight in cold water
1 onion, quartered, plus 3 large onions,
   chopped
1 bay leaf
4 teaspoons cumin seeds
4 teaspoons dried Greek oregano
4 teaspoons paprika
½ teaspoon cayenne pepper
3 tablespoons vegetable oil
Coarse salt
5 garlic cloves, minced
2 teaspoons ancho chile powder
6 red, ripe tomatoes, chopped, with their
   juices
2 teaspoons chopped chipotle chile (if using
   a dried chile, soak in warm water until
   soft before chopping; if using canned
   chipotle, drain before using)
1 tablespoon rice vinegar
Freshly ground black pepper
4 tablespoons chopped fresh cilantro,
   plus 2 tablespoons cilantro leaves
2 fresh poblano or Anaheim chiles
1 cup sour cream
1 cup grated Monterey Jack
2 tablespoons cilantro leaves

To cook the beans, drain them, discarding the soaking liquid. Put them in a large enamel casserole or saucepan with 6 cups fresh water, the quartered onion, and the bay leaf over moderately high heat. Bring to a boil, reduce the heat, and simmer until the beans are half cooked, about 30 minutes.

To toast the spices, heat the cumin seeds in a small, dry saucepan over moderately high heat. Cook, shaking, for about a minute. Add the oregano and cook for a minute more, shaking the pan often. Remove the pan from the heat and add the paprika and cayenne. Let the spices cool. Grind the spices and herbs together in a coffee grinder reserved for spices.

To prepare the base for the chili, put the oil, the chopped onions, and ½ teaspoon salt in a large saucepan over moderately high heat. Cook, stirring from time to time, until the onions are soft, about 5 minutes. Stir in the garlic, ground spices, and the ancho chile powder. Continue to cook, stirring, for another 5 minutes. Stir in the tomatoes with their juice and half the chipotle chile and cook for another 15 minutes. Add this tomato mixture to the black beans with enough water so that the beans are covered by an inch. Bring this mixture to a boil again and simmer until the beans are tender, about an hour. Stir in the vinegar with salt and pepper to taste and add more chipotle to taste. Stir in the chopped cilantro.

To prepare the garnish, put the poblano chiles over a gas flame or under the broiler in an oven and roast, turning occasionally, until charred on all sides. Put the charred pepper in a bowl and cover tightly with plastic wrap. After 5 minutes, remove the pepper and peel off all the charred skin. Remove the stem, seeds, and veins and shred the pepper. (The chili can be prepared several hours ahead up to this point and stored in the refrigerator.)

To serve, reheat the chili, stirring, over moderate heat. Ladle into warmed bowls. Serve with a dollop of sour cream and a sprinkling of shredded poblano chile, grated Monterey Jack, and cilantro leaves.

SERVES 8

Grilled Vegetable Brochettes and Tofu with Brown Rice Pilaf

Here is another recipe I have adapted from Greens Restaurant. It is absolutely the best way to serve tofu!

1 pound firm tofu, cut into 1-inch cubes
½ ounce dried porcini (cèpe) mushrooms
2 teaspoons dried Greek oregano, toasted in a dry pan until fragrant
2 garlic cloves, thinly sliced
½ cup olive oil
½ cup sherry vinegar
½ cup red wine
½ cup tamari sauce
2 tablespoons red wine vinegar
1 garlic clove, finely minced
1 tablespoon Dijon-style mustard
1 tablespoon minced fresh herbs, such as Italian parsley, thyme, and marjoram
¾ cup olive oil
Coarse salt
Freshly ground black pepper
8 cherry tomatoes, stemmed
4 zucchini, cut into ½-inch rounds
4 Asian eggplants, cut into ½-inch rounds
16 medium-size fresh mushrooms, stems trimmed flush with the caps

To remove the excess liquid from the tofu, place the cubes in a single layer in a glass baking dish. Cover them with a smaller baking dish to weight them down and let sit for 30 minutes.

To make the marinade, put the porcini in a small saucepan with enough water to just cover. Place the pan over low heat and simmer for 15 minutes or until the mushrooms are soft. Add the toasted oregano to the mushroom liquor with the garlic, olive oil, sherry vinegar, red wine, and tamari sauce. Bring this mixture to a boil and simmer gently for 5 minutes. Drain the liquid from the tofu and strain the marinade over it through a strainer lined with a damp paper towel. Discard the solids from the marinade. Let the tofu marinate in the refrigerator for 1 to 5 days, turning occasionally.

Four hours before serving, prepare the marinade for the vegetables by combining the vinegar, garlic, mustard, herbs, and olive oil with salt and pepper to taste. Toss in the tomatoes, zucchini, eggplants, and mushrooms. Soak 8 wooden skewers in warm water.

Prepare a charcoal fire.

To assemble, remove the tofu from the marinade and alternate the vegetables and tofu on the 8 skewers, finishing each skewer with a mushroom. Grill the skewers over the fire for 3 to 4 minutes on each side. Slide the tofu and vegetables from the skewers and serve over brown rice pilaf.

SERVES 8

BROWN RICE PILAF

6 tablespoons butter
1 large onion, finely chopped
Coarse salt
1 garlic clove, minced
2 cups short-grain brown rice
4 cups vegetable stock

Heat the butter and onion with ½ teaspoon salt in a medium-size saucepan over moderately high heat. Cook, stirring from time to time, until the onion is soft, about 5 minutes. Add the garlic and cook, stirring, for another minute. Stir in the rice and coat well with the onion mixture. Stir in the stock and bring to a boil. Reduce the heat to a low simmer, cover, and let cook undisturbed until all the liquid has cooked away and the grains of rice are tender, about 45 minutes. The rice can hold, covered, for up to an hour before serving. When serving, be sure to fluff the rice with a fork rather than stir it with a spoon so that it will not break up.   SERVES 8

Tofu is soybean curd, which comes in many textures that range from silky to firm. It is very versatile.

PLANNED LEFTOVERS

As a broad generalization, I have observed that people who don't like to eat do an extraordinarily bad job of cooking. They make things worse for themselves by not thinking ahead. What they do is go to the store each day to shop for dinner. People who love to eat good food and love cooking are always thinking about how to make less work for themselves in the kitchen. For instance, when cooking vegetables, pasta, risotto, or polenta, they might make extra to use in a later meal. Here are some ideas for planned leftovers:

POLENTA

Whenever you make creamy polenta for dinner, make double the amount, spread the rest in a well-buttered baking pan, and store it, covered with plastic wrap, in the refrigerator. It can be cut into 3-inch squares, which can be grilled or sautéed and served another day with a sauce of red peppers and sausages, for example (page 139). Or you can cut the cold polenta into 2 by ½-inch "fingers" that can be coated in fine bread crumbs, deep-fried, and served with a fresh tomato sauce (see page 73). Another idea is to cut the cold polenta into 1-inch squares, make a hole in them with a melon baller, reheat them in the oven, and fill them with a stew or Black Bean Chili (page 279).

RISOTTO

Leftover risotto, no matter what the flavor, can be filled with fresh mozzarella cheese and deep-fried for a hot hors d'oeuvre. To do this, cut ¼-inch squares of cheese, make a plate of fine bread crumbs, and heat a large pan of vegetable oil to 350 degrees. For each cup of leftover risotto, stir in a beaten egg. Coat one hand with a little cold water; in the hollow of that hand put the cold risotto, and fill it with cheese. Put more risotto around the cheese, roll the risotto ball in fine bread crumbs, and repeat with the remaining risotto. These balls can be stored in the refrigerator for a few hours or overnight. When ready to cook, deep-fry them in the oil and serve in a basket lined with a napkin (see page 165 for how to deep-fry).

PASTA

Leftover pasta can also be made into a hot hors d'oeuvre or a breakfast or luncheon dish called frittata. For every 2 cups of cooked pasta you will need 3 eggs, ⅓ cup Parmesan, 2 tablespoons parsley, and salt and pepper. Mix the ingredients while melting 4 tablespoons butter in a 12-inch frying pan. When the butter is hot, spread the frittata mixture over the bottom of the pan. Cook for 3 to 4 minutes over moderate heat without disturbing. Start tilting the pan and lifting the edges of the frittata so that some of the uncooked egg goes underneath. When the bottom of the frittata has turned a nice golden color, invert it onto a round plate and slide the frittata back into the pan to cook it on the other side until it too is golden. To serve, transfer to a warmed plate and cut into wedges or squares.

VEGETABLES

Leftover cooked vegetables can be served as an hors d'oeuvre with a flavored dip such as aïoli or in salade Niçoise with tuna, or made into a frittata as described above.

FISH

Leftover uncooked fresh fish can be made into seviche. To do this, cut the fish into ½-inch pieces (without skin), and let it marinate covered in lime juice or equal parts of lime and lemon juice for 4 to 24 hours. Add ingredients such as chopped tomatoes, cubed avocado, fresh kernels of corn, and cilantro to make an hors d'oeuvre to be served on tortilla chips.

Leftover cooked fish can be put in a glass or ceramic plate and covered with lots of sliced white onions, julienned red peppers, a little minced garlic, minced jalapeños, and plenty of white wine vinegar and white wine to make escabeche. This will keep for up to 3 days and can be served as a first course.

SALMON

Leftover uncooked salmon can be cured to make gravlax (page 18) or cured before smoking in a cold smoker (see page 379). Remember, gravlax should always be served with a sauce, such as sour cream mixed with sweet mustard. Smoked salmon should be served with lemon and freshly ground black pepper.

SMOKED SALMON

A great way to use the odd bits of smoked salmon—the pieces that won't slice easily—is to weigh them and mix them in a food processor with butter, a little lemon juice, and a little pepper. The ratio of salmon to butter is 3 to 2. This should be put in a small crock or a ramekin and served on a plate surrounded by small squares of brown bread or crackers as an hors d'oeuvre.

CHICKEN

If you save your chicken wings in the freezer, you can thaw them and make them into what look like miniature drumsticks. To do this, separate the two parts of each wing. With a small, sharp knife, cut the skin on the thinnest part of the larger end of the wing. With your fingers, pull the skin and flesh down to the thicker end of the wing. Dip the wing first in Dijon-style mustard, then in bread crumbs seasoned with salt and pepper and mixed with minced fresh herbs. Place the wings on a baking sheet. Making the smaller part of the wing into a little drumstick takes another step because there are two bones. Sever the bones from each other at both ends, and with your fingers, start working the skin and flesh up toward the larger end while pulling out the smaller bone. The resulting little drumstick should look like the others. When the wings are prepared, you can store them in the refrigerator for up to 4 hours or overnight. To cook them, place the baking pan in a 375-degree oven and bake until they are golden brown and firm to the touch, about 20 minutes. Serve them as a hot hors d'oeuvre.

CHICKEN LIVERS

Leftover chicken livers can be poached and mixed with soft butter to make a chicken liver mousse. The chicken livers must first be poached in chicken stock with a few slices of onion and a sprinkling of salt. The ratio is 1 pound chicken livers to 1 cup chicken stock. Poach them gently in the liquid until they are barely pink on the inside. Remove, strain, and let cool. When they are cool, blend them in the food processor with ¾ pound (3 sticks) butter, 2 tablespoons brandy, ½ teaspoon quatre épices, and salt to taste. Press this mixture into a small bowl and serve on a larger plate, surrounded by squares of thin white bread toasted and cut into quarters. This chicken liver mousse will turn a very unattractive color fairly quickly when exposed to the air. This is why it is imperative to cover the top of the mousse with a thin layer of finely minced parsley. Quatre épices is made by grinding together equal amounts of black peppercorns, white peppercorns, allspice, cinnamon, and coriander. It is a spice mixture used in pâtés in France.

SMOKED CHICKEN

Cut thin slices of baguette, toast them on both sides, and cover them with thin slices of smoked chicken (or turkey). Dot with Spicy Apple Chutney (see page 388) or Spicy Cranberry Chutney (see page 388). These can be served as an hors d'oeuvre.

PORK, VEAL, LAMB, AND BEEF

Most meats do not reheat very well, especially pork and lamb. Pork would be great made into toasts as described above. For lamb, remember these two things: tapenade and aïoli. (For tapenade, see page 238; for aïoli, see page 34.) You can make great sandwiches with cold meat and tapenade, aïoli, and arugula (or watercress) on crusty country bread. Leftover beef can be made into a beef salad. Slice the beef thinly and arrange it with slivers of red onions and French potato salad (see page 67). Spoon a mustardy vinaigrette or salsa verde over the top (see page 243).

DESSERTS

ESSERT HAS BEEN CALLED "a delicious dish that holds the guest to the table with a final tempting of his sensuality." It's true that all too often you think you can't eat anymore just when a luscious dessert is served that you can't resist. A good dessert should be the perfect finish to a meal. It can be followed by a cup of coffee if you wish, but coffee should never be served before or with dessert; it dulls one's sense of taste.

Just as a good sauce should have a balance of salt, sweet, acid, and bitter, a good dessert should have a balance of sweet and acid. If a dessert is too sweet, it lies flat in your mouth. This is why I always like to add a few grains of salt to most desserts; it sharpens the sweetness. Lemon juice or some form of alcohol such as vanilla extract, kirsch, or brandy can do the same. A good dessert should not be bigger than your fist; the trend of serving huge desserts is very unappealing. It is hard to pair dessert wines with desserts because all too often the dessert is too sweet for the wine. I prefer to offer dessert wine instead of dessert. A nice dessert wine with a bis-cotti is a good finish to a meal. Biscotti are twice-baked Italian cookies meant to be dipped in a liquid, not eaten alone. They can be dipped in red wine, coffee, or a sweet dessert wine such as vin santo.

Just as food made with care and served hot needs no decorating, neither does a dessert. Garnishes such as mint leaves, lemon slices, and raspberries have no place on a lot of desserts. It is fine to show what kind of dessert it is with lemon slices or raspberries, if it's a lemon or raspberry dessert. Otherwise, let the dessert stand on its own. Sieving confectioners' sugar over a dessert is a fine way to hide a slightly burned dessert; however, sprinkling confectioners' sugar or cocoa on everything is pretty silly. Food doesn't taste better with these embellishments.

KINDS OF DESSERTS

Fresh fruit is always a welcome dessert. A simple frozen dessert can be made at home by freezing fruit juice or flavored beverages in ice cube trays and chopping the frozen ice in a food processor. This is called granita, as in Strawberry Granita (page 290). A more refined fruit juice or fruit puree frozen dessert with a fine texture is made with sugar syrup and is called sorbet, as in Plum Sorbet in Tulipes (page 294).

Custards can be stirred, as in Gratin of Fresh Berries (page 296); or baked, as in Meyer Lemon Crème Brûlée (page 298). Ice cream can be simply good-quality flavored and sweetened heavy cream that is frozen and aerated at the same time, as in Lemon Verbena Ice Cream (page 295). Or ice cream can be made with a base of stirred custard—crème anglaise—which is flavored, frozen, and aerated, as in Caramel Ice Cream (page 307). Gelato is dense Italian ice cream, which can have intense flavor because it has less air than traditional sorbet or ice cream.

A dessert soufflé can be an ethereal finish to a meal, especially the Grand Marnier Soufflé in this chapter (page 304). A soufflé is amazing. Beaten egg whites are folded into a cooked base, usually milk, flour, and sugar with added egg yolks and flavoring. It is put in a slippery-sided dish in a hot oven, where it rises dramatically. The cooked flour is the stabilizer—it prevents the soufflé from falling too much. The egg yolks are the glue—they prevent it from falling over the sides of the dish when it rises. The beaten egg whites act as the leavener—it's what makes the soufflé rise.

A soufflé by definition has extra egg whites to help it rise in the oven; a mousse often has extra egg yolks for richness. When the base of the mousse is viscous like chocolate, there is no need to stabilize it. However, if it is made with cream, as in Blueberries in Lemon Mousse (page 292) it will begin to break down in 3 to 4 hours. When gelatin is incorporated, a mousse mixture can be kept chilled up to 5 days. When a mousse is stabilized with a little gelatin and formed to look as if it rose in the oven, it is called a cold soufflé, as in Cold Lemon Soufflé (page 310). When it is stabilized with gelatin, chilled, and unmolded, it is called a Bavarian cream, as in Hazelnut Praline Bavarian Cream (page 311). In the old days, mousse mixtures with or without gelatin were formed in a mold lined with ladyfingers so that they could easily be unmolded. Now the same effect comes from lining the mold with plastic wrap and attaching the ladyfingers later with whipped cream. These are called charlottes.

A kind of French dessert not often made in this country is a parfait. It consists of sugar syrup cooked to the soft-ball stage and poured on beaten eggs, essentially cooking the eggs. After this mixture is beaten and cooled, whipped cream is folded in. This must not be confused with ice cream layered with sauce—it's a completely different dessert.

KINDS OF DESSERT SAUCES

Although you can make many different kinds of sauces, the classic dessert sauces in French cooking are crème anglaise, a cold pourable custard sauce; sabayon, a warm egg yolk, sugar, and fortified wine sauce, which is sometimes served as a dessert by itself; caramel sauce, sugar cooked until it turns an amber color with added cream and butter; chocolate sauce, chocolate melted with cream; and fruit puree, a sauce of pureed fruit, sometimes with the addition of brandy or liqueur to enhance the flavor.

PLANNING DESSERTS

If the main course is light, you can go all out with a rich chocolate dessert such as Chocolate Pudding Cake (page 315). However, a chocolate dessert is totally inappropriate after fish—Blueberries in Lemon Mousse (page 292) would be a better choice. A spicy main course should be followed by a custard-like dessert to smooth the taste buds, Gratin of Fresh Berries (page 296), for example. Something as rich as paella, cassoulet, or choucroute garni would be best followed by fresh fruit, such as Oranges with Strawberry Sauce (page 293).

Dessert wine with biscotti makes for a fine dessert, as does a selection of cheeses with breads or crackers. You can serve a tisane of fresh herbs after dinner or a pot of decaffeinated coffee. Please don't ask your guests what they would like, just serve what you want to.

The Big Problem

The big problem with desserts is finding the time to make them. If you prefer cooking to baking, plan a very simple dessert. If you prefer baking to cooking, plan a simple main course. There just isn't enough time for the home cook to do it all.

How to Make Dessert Without a Recipe

Ask what fruits are in season. Can you serve them with yogurt, ice cream, or pound cake? Would they go with honey or maple syrup? Would walnuts, almonds, or pecans improve their flavor? A favorite dessert of mine is fresh seasonal fruit such as peaches, blueberries, or strawberries in large wineglasses or glass bowls with a generous amount of whole milk yogurt (such as Brown Cow, Stonyfield Farm, or Nancy's) spooned over and honey or maple syrup drizzled on top. You can thicken thin yogurt like Pavel's by spooning it into a plastic sieve over a bowl and letting it drip in the refrigerator for a couple of hours.

Yogurt is cultured milk. It is healthful and delicious and needs no artificial thickeners. Neither low-fat nor nonfat yogurt should be substituted—they are essentially pudding mixtures with lots of additives.

Strawberry Granita

Granita is a frozen dessert with the texture of ice crystals. It is very easy to make, thanks to the food processor. This one really brings out the flavor of the fresh strawberries when they are in season!

2 pints fresh strawberries, stems removed
    and berries wiped with a damp towel
½ cup sugar
2 teaspoons good-quality balsamic vinegar

To macerate the strawberries, put them in a bowl with the sugar and vinegar and let rest for 20 minutes.

To make the granita, put the strawberry mixture in a food processor and process until smooth. Pour the mixture into ice cube trays and cover with plastic wrap. Freeze until hard. Just before serving, place the cubes in the bowl of a food processor with the blade and process until you have finely chopped strawberry ice. Serve in wineglasses.

SERVES 8

You can make a granita by freezing any good-quality fruit juice in ice cubes and processing as described. You can even try coffee or tea granitas. This mixture can also be frozen in an ice cream machine.

Strawberry Fool

What the English call a fool is a dessert composed of a fresh fruit puree folded into whipped cream. It will keep for up to four hours. Make this dessert in the spring when strawberries are at their best. It can also be made with a puree of other fresh seasonal fruits, peaches, gooseberries, or blackberries, for example. It's easy and fun!

2 pints fresh strawberries, stems removed
    and berries wiped with a damp towel
2 teaspoons lemon juice
½ cup sugar
1½ cups heavy cream

To macerate the strawberries, place them in a bowl with the lemon juice and sugar and let sit for 20 minutes.

To make the fool, puree the strawberry mixture until smooth in a food processor fitted with the blade. In a separate large bowl, whisk the cream until it holds soft peaks. Fold the strawberries into the cream. Carefully ladle the mixture into wineglasses and chill until ready to serve.

SERVES 6

You can take the stems out of fresh strawberries with a strawberry huller or a kitchen knife inserted in the berry. It is a bad habit to simply cut off the stem end of the strawberry with a sharp knife because not only is it wasteful, it distorts the look of the berry—the stem end should be rounded, not flat.

To whip cream by hand, put the cream in a large metal bowl. With a sauce whisk (with straight sides) use a circular motion to beat the cream. It is perfectly all right to whip cream in an electric mixer. It's best to whip it to soft peaks in the machine, then switch to a sauce whisk to reach the desired consistency. Balloon whisks (large and rounded) should be used only for egg whites. When you use a balloon whisk for cream, it easily overwhips it, turning it to butter. If this happens, whisk in a considerable amount of additional cream.

When you are whipping cream by hand or by machine, it will gradually get thicker. It is called partially whipped cream when you can see a line in the cream when you draw the whisk through it. Partially whipped cream is used for gelatin desserts. It has reached the right consistency to serve with fruit or other desserts when you can hold some of the cream on the end of the whisk in a soft peak. It is piping consistency when the peak on the end of the whisk is firm. If the cream has reached the desired consistency, stir in flavorings such as sugar and vanilla with a spoon, not the whisk.

To "fold" an ingredient is to mix it into another ingredient or combination of ingredients so that the maximum amount of air is kept in the mixture. To do this, use a large rubber spatula to cut down the middle of the two mixtures, lift the ingredient on the bottom up and over the top of the other without pressing, and then turn the bowl. If you keep turning the bowl, you will eventually fold the entire mixture. It is folded when there are no longer streaks of one mixture showing.

Green Apple Sorbet with Calvados

This is a wonderfully refreshing dessert to have after a heavy meal. It is best made at the end of summer and early fall, when apples are in season.

2½ pounds Granny Smith or other green
    apples
¼ cup lemon juice
1 cup plus 2 tablespoons sugar
Calvados

Peel and core the apples, then cut them into 1-inch chunks. Place the cut apples in a bowl with the lemon juice and toss. Combine the sugar with 1⅓ cups water in a medium-size saucepan over moderately high heat. Bring to a boil, stirring from time to time. Add the apples and cook for 1½ minutes more. Remove from the heat. Transfer the apples and the cooking liquid to a blender and puree until completely smooth, scraping down the sides of the blender. Chill the mixture. Transfer the mixture to an ice cream machine and freeze.

Serve with a shot of Calvados that the guest can pour over the sorbet.

SERVES 8

Blueberries in Lemon Mousse

Here is a light, refreshing dessert for a summer's evening!

2 pints fresh blueberries, raspberries, or blackberries, picked through
4 eggs, separated
½ cup sugar
⅓ cup lemon juice
1 tablespoon grated lemon zest
1 cup heavy cream
Salt
Mint leaves for garnish

To make the mousse, heat the egg yolks, sugar, and lemon juice and zest in a bowl over a saucepan of gently simmering water. Whisk constantly until the mixture thickens, about 4 minutes. Remove from the heat and let cool to room temperature, stirring from time to time. Put the cream in a large bowl and beat with a sauce whisk until it forms soft peaks. Fold three-quarters of the cream into the lemon mixture, reserving one-quarter for decorating the dessert. Put the egg whites in a clean copper bowl with a few grains of salt. Whisk with a balloon whisk, lifting the egg whites out of the bowl, until the whites hold stiff peaks. Fold this mixture into the lemon-cream mixture. Fold in the berries. Spoon the mixture into the 6 wineglasses. Whip the remaining cream with a sauce whisk until it is stiff enough to pipe. Spoon or pipe the remaining cream on top of each glass of mousse. Decorate with additional berries and mint leaves. (This dessert will hold in the refrigerator for up to 4 hours.)

SERVES 6

This recipe does not work well with strawberries because most strawberries are so large, they have to be sliced, and the sliced strawberries will make the mousse weep; in other words, they will give the recipe a watery texture.

When buying eggs, look for ones that are grown locally, naturally, hormone-free, even organically. Keep them in their original container in the refrigerator. Leftover egg whites will keep refrigerated for weeks. Leftover yolks can be poached and sieved onto salads.

Oranges with Strawberry Sauce

This colorful light dessert will be welcome after almost any meal!

4 large oranges
3 tablespoons Grand Marnier
2 cups ripe fresh strawberries, stemmed,
  plus 6 whole berries for garnish
2 tablespoons red currant jelly, melted
1 teaspoon lemon juice
6 fresh mint leaves for garnish

To prepare the zest, remove the zest from the oranges with a vegetable peeler in long strips from top to bottom, being careful to take only the orange part of the skin and avoiding the white pith. Put a small pot of water on to boil. Layer the strips of orange zest on top of each other and with a sharp knife, cut tiny slivers of the orange zest crosswise. Drop the zest into the boiling water, turn off the heat, and let sit for 5 minutes. Drain off the liquid. (This is to remove the bitter taste of the zest.) Combine the orange zest in a bowl with a tablespoon of the Grand Marnier.

To make the strawberry sauce, puree the strawberries in a food processor until smooth. Strain through a fine strainer to remove the seeds. Mix the strawberry puree in a bowl with the remaining 2 tablespoons Grand Marnier, the red currant jelly, and the lemon juice.

To section the oranges, cut off both ends of the orange down to the flesh. Stand the orange on end and cut off the remaining rind in 1-inch-wide pieces, cutting from top to bottom. Remove any remaining pith with a small, sharp knife. With the orange in one hand and the small knife in the other, cut along the membrane on each side of the section. The remaining sections can be removed by cutting along the top membrane toward the center of the orange and turning the knife to come out the other side.

To serve, spoon the strawberry sauce onto the middle of six dessert plates. Arrange the orange sections in a pinwheel design on top of the sauce and place a whole strawberry and a mint leaf in the center. Scatter the zest over the oranges. SERVES 6

When a recipe calls for grated zest of oranges or lemons, you can grate the orange on a grater or use a zester, but do not use a vegetable peeler as described here. This is a technique for julienne zest of orange, not grated zest.

Plum Sorbet in Tulipes

I*t's lots of fun to make your own ice cream and sorbets. You can invest as little as sixty dollars in a small electric ice cream maker with a container of coolant that has to be chilled in the freezer, or you can spend upward of five hundred dollars for one that has a chilling unit built in.*

1 cup sugar
1 pound fresh plums, nectarines, skinned
   peaches, or apricots, pitted and cut into
   1-inch chunks
Salt
Port or brandy to taste
8 tulipes (recipe follows)

To make the sugar syrup, combine the sugar with a cup of water in a small saucepan over low heat. Swirl the pan from time to time to dissolve the sugar. Turn up the heat and let simmer gently for 5 minutes. Chill.

To prepare the fruit, put it in pieces in the food processor fitted with the blade and process until smooth. Mix the pureed fruit with the cooled sugar syrup and add a few grains of salt. Taste and add up to a tablespoon of alcohol if the flavor needs enhancing. Freeze in an ice cream maker until firm.

MAKES 1 QUART

Sorbet should be made with a sugar syrup of 1 part sugar to 1 part water. If making a fruit sorbet with juice, use the ratio of 1 part fruit juice to 1 part sugar syrup. If using fruit puree, *the ratio should be ⅔ fruit puree to ⅓ sugar syrup.*

Alcohol is essentially an antifreeze; that is why you never want to use more than 2 tablespoons to a quart of ice cream or sorbet.

TULIPES

4 tablespoons (½ stick) butter, softened
½ cup sugar
2 egg whites
¼ teaspoon vanilla extract
½ cup flour

Preheat the oven to 350 degrees and line two cookie sheets with parchment. Make a template to use as a guide for the cookies by taking a thin piece of cardboard and cutting out a round about 6 inches in diameter.

To make the dough, put the butter in a bowl and beat it with a wooden spoon until it is light. Switch to an electric mixer and beat in the sugar. Continue beating until the mixture is light and fluffy. Beat in the egg whites and the vanilla and stir in the flour. Put the template on the parchment, place a heaping tablespoon of the dough in the center, and spread it thinly with a metal spatula. Remove the cardboard and use it to form the remaining cookies. Bake the cookies until lightly browned around the edges, about 6 minutes. Remove from the oven and slide a spatula underneath to lift the cookies off the paper. Lay each cookie, flat side up, on an overturned little spice jar to form a flower-shaped container. Let cool a minute or two. If the cookies harden, return them to the oven for a couple of minutes. Tulipes should be as thin as possible.   MAKES 8 COOKIES

Butter is made from cream that has been churned until it is thick. Recipes can call for melted butter, softened butter, cold butter, and sometimes even for clarified or brown butter. Clarified butter is pure fat with the milk solids removed; brown butter has more taste than melted butter.

Butter can be measured in tablespoons, cups, ounces, or pounds. It is important not to get them confused. Remember, one stick of butter equals 8 tablespoons, which equals ½ cup, which equals 4 ounces, which equals ¼ pound. Please unwrap the butter before cutting into it.

Compote of Fresh Berries with Lemon Verbena Ice Cream

This is a simple dessert that tastes great. If you don't have a lemon verbena bush growing in your backyard, you can substitute fresh mint.

> 1 pint fresh strawberries
> ½ pint fresh raspberries
> ½ pint fresh blackberries
> 1 cup sugar
> 6 leaves fresh lemon verbena or
>   fresh mint

To prepare the fruit, pick over the berries, removing any dirt or green stems. Put the berries in a bowl.

To prepare the syrup, combine the sugar with 2 cups water in a medium-size saucepan. Dissolve over low heat, stirring slowly until the liquid is clear. Add the lemon verbena leaves and remove from the heat. Let cool.

To assemble, add the fruit to the syrup and chill for 30 minutes before serving. Serve in large red-wine glasses.   SERVES 6

Often recipes call for sugar syrup, which is nothing more than sugar dissolved in water. It can be light, medium, or heavy, depending on the need. Light syrup is 1 part sugar to 2 parts water, medium is 1 sugar to 1. Heavy syrup is made with a ratio of 2 parts sugar to 1 part water.

FRESH LEMON VERBENA ICE CREAM

2 cups good-quality heavy cream
⅔ cup sugar
1 cup fresh lemon verbena leaves or
  ¾ cup fresh mint leaves
1 cup whole milk

Combine the cream, sugar, and verbena leaves in a large saucepan over moderate heat. When bubbles begin to form around the edges of the pan, remove from the heat, cover, and let steep for an hour. Strain and discard the verbena leaves. Add the milk. Chill. When the mixture is cold, put it in an ice cream machine and freeze until firm.

MAKES 1 QUART

Lemon verbena has a very special taste. The best is to buy a lemon bush and plant it. That way you can make pots of lemon verbena tisane all summer long. To do this, be sure to keep trimming the bush to keep it from flowering. The plant needs to be pruned in the winter and probably brought inside in snow country.

Gratin of Fresh Berries

This is a delightful summer dessert—fresh red berries barely covered in custard and lightly browned. The idea is to give the illusion of a crème brûlée with fruit.

1 pint fresh wild strawberries or raspberries
  (2 cups)
4 cups heavy cream (1 quart)
8 egg yolks
½ cup sugar plus additional for top
1½ teaspoons vanilla extract
Salt

To prepare the fruit, pick through it to remove any grit or green stems. Spread the berries over the bottoms of eight 5-inch gratin dishes.

To make the custard, heat the cream in a saucepan over moderate heat until bubbles appear around the edge of the pan. Combine the egg yolks with the ½ cup sugar in a bowl and whisk until light and lemon-colored. Slowly mix the warmed cream into the yolk mixture. Remove it from the heat and stir in the vanilla with a few grains of salt. Pour this mixture through a strainer over the fruit. Bake in the oven at 325 degrees for 35 to 40 minutes. Cool.

When ready to serve, sift over the remaining 4 tablespoons sugar. Brown the sugar with a blowtorch to make a crust and serve.

SERVES 8

All custards (eggs cooked with sugar and milk or cream) need to cool to room temperature before being refrigerated. They do not hold up well going from the oven to the refrigerator.

Summer Pudding

Whenever you have the good fortune to find fresh red currants in the farmers' market, this is the dessert to make. This wonderful comforting dessert of summer, a tradition in England, can be made with cranberries if you can't find red currants; both have lots of pectin, which helps set this pudding.

¾ cup fresh raspberries
¾ cup fresh red currants or coarsely chopped cranberries
¾ cup fresh blackberries
¾ cup sugar plus additional for sweetening the cream
8 slices white bread, crusts removed
¾ cup heavy cream, whipped

To prepare the fruit, remove any stems and dirt from the berries and put them in a pan with the sugar. Bring to a boil over medium-high heat, cover, and cook gently until the currants or cranberries are tender, 5 to 10 minutes. Drain the fruit, reserving the juices.

To assemble, line the bottom and sides of a 1-quart glass bread pan with the bread. Spoon the cooked fruit mixture into the lined pan, packing it well. Pour in about ½ cup of the reserved juices. Place the remaining bread on top of the fruit. Weight the pudding and chill overnight. The next day, unmold onto a plate and serve in slices with lightly sweetened whipped cream.

SERVES 6 TO 8

There are many kinds of berries sold as blackberries. They have names such as boysenberry, loganberry, and olallieberry.

Sauce whisks have straight sides so they can get in every corner of a saucepan. Balloon whisks are large and rounded for lifting egg whites to get air into them. When you whip cream with a balloon whisk, the cream will whip quickly but it will also overwhip quickly as well. This is why I recommend whisking whipping cream with a sauce whisk, or with an electric mixer and finishing with a sauce whisk.

The way to have cranberries in the summer to make this dessert is to freeze them in the fall when they come on the market.

Meyer Lemon Crème Brûlée

*M*eyer lemons are becoming more available because they are so sweet and uniquely flavored. This is simply a variation on that perennial favorite, crème brûlée. It's fine to make this recipe with limes; just add a little more sugar.

Grated zest of 4 Meyer lemons (or 6 limes)
1 quart heavy cream
8 egg yolks
4 tablespoons plus ¾ cup sugar
Salt

To make the custard, heat the zest with the cream in a medium-size saucepan over moderate heat. Combine the yolks with the 4 tablespoons of sugar in a large bowl. Whisk until light and lemon colored. Strain the scalded cream into the yolk mixture. Add a few grains of salt. Pour the mixture into eight 3- or 4-inch ramekins or ceramic gratin dishes. Place the molds in a larger pan, put the pan on the middle shelf in the oven, and fill the dish with enough warm water to come halfway up the sides of the molds. Cover the molds with one piece of foil and bake the custards in a 350-degree oven until barely set, about 35 minutes. Cool at room temperature. Chill.

To brown the tops of the crème brûlée, put the remaining ¾ cup sugar in a fine sieve. Shake the sugar over the crème brûlée, making an even layer about ¼ inch thick. Using a blowtorch, brown the sugar lightly to create a crust. Leave at room temperature to cool. Do not refrigerate again, or the sugar on top will liquefy.   SERVES 12

Using a blowtorch is fun; just be sure to light it facing away from you. It is best not to move the blowtorch around to brown things—keep it in one place until the desired color is reached.

Whenever a recipe calls for sieving an ingredient on top, always put the ingredient in the sieve over the counter, not over the food. Otherwise you will have a mass of sugar or whatever where it fell through the sieve.

Peaches
with Champagne Sabayon

*T*o eat a peach when it is perfectly ripe is sublime. But sometimes you can't get perfect peaches. That's when you can enhance them by serving them with a dollop of Champagne sabayon. Sabayon (in French) or zabaglione (in Italian) is often a whipped egg, sugar, and alcohol dessert served warm. It can be made up to three hours ahead by folding in heavy cream whipped to about the same consistency as the warm dessert sauce. It's delicious served with other fruits or winter desserts such as gingerbread or chocolate pudding cake.

6 large yellow peaches
4 egg yolks
⅓ cup sugar
¾ cups Champagne (or still white wine)
1 cup heavy cream
2 tablespoons kirsch

To peel the peaches, drop them into boiling water for 60 seconds. Lift out with a slotted spoon and remove the peels with a paring knife. Cut the peaches into ½-inch-wide wedges and put into eight wineglasses.

To make the sabayon, put the eggs with the sugar in the top of a double boiler or a bowl that fits over a saucepan. Off the heat, whisk the egg mixture vigorously with a sauce whisk until thick. Still off the heat, whisk in the Champagne. Place the pan over the boiling water, without letting it touch the water, and whisk vigorously until the mixture is very thick. Remove it from the heat.

Place the heavy cream in a metal bowl and whisk with a sauce whisk until you can see a line when the whisk is drawn through the cream. From time to time, slowly stir the sabayon mixture as it cools. With a rubber spatula, fold the partially whipped cream into the cooled sabayon with the kirsch.

Spoon the cool sabayon over the peaches in the glasses. SERVES 8

To make this as a warm dessert for two, whip together 2 egg yolks and 3 tablespoons sugar with ¼ cup dry Marsala or sherry and a strip of lemon. Whip vigorously and serve in glasses while still warm.

Rhubarb-Strawberry Compote with Lattice

This recipe of Janet Rikala, a beloved pastry chef, is perfect for modern tastes. It is composed of a bowl of stewed fruits of summer served with a dollop of slightly sweetened whipped cream (crème Chantilly) and covered by a sugar cookie that resembles a lattice.

FOR THE DOUGH
2½ cups flour
⅛ teaspoon salt
⅓ cup sugar
½ pound (2 sticks) butter, cut into
 1-inch pieces
1 egg yolk
1 teaspoon vanilla extract

FOR THE COMPOTE
1 pound fresh strawberries, stemmed and
 halved
1 vanilla bean, split lengthwise
1 cup sugar
1 pound rhubarb, cut in 1-inch pieces
2 teaspoons cornstarch dissolved in
 1 tablespoon water
½ teaspoon grated orange zest
¼ teaspoon ground cinnamon

½ cup heavy cream

To make the short crust (pâte sablé), combine the flour, salt, sugar, and butter in the bowl of a food processor with the blade. Process until the mixture resembles coarse bread crumbs. Mix the egg yolk with the vanilla and 2 teaspoons cold water. With the machine running, pour the egg mixture through the feed tube and process until the dough comes together into a ball. Wrap the dough in waxed paper, press into a disc, and chill for 10 minutes before using.

To cook the fruit, heat the strawberries, vanilla bean, and ½ cup of the sugar in a medium-size saucepan over medium heat. Cook, stirring from time to time, until the berries are soft, about 20 minutes. Mash with a potato masher. Stir in the rhubarb, cornstarch, orange zest, cinnamon, and the remaining ½ cup sugar. Cook, stirring from time to time, until the rhubarb is soft, about 10 minutes more. (This compote can be made several hours or a day ahead and stored in the refrigerator.)

Preheat the oven to 350 degrees and line two baking sheets with parchment paper.

To make the lattice, roll out the dough on a lightly floured board or counter. Lightly flour the dough and the rolling pin. Roll the dough down and forward. Turn the dough a quarter turn and roll away from you. Continue rolling and turning until the dough is a

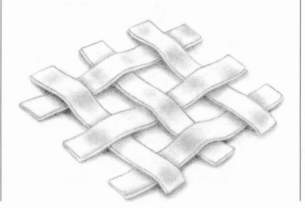

rectangle about ⅛ inch thick. With a pastry wheel or pastry cutter, cut the dough in 24 strips, ½ inch wide and 6 inches long. Place three of these strips ½ inch apart on one of the parchment-lined baking sheets. To make the lattice, fold the two outside strips halfway back and lay one more strip across the remaining strip. Lay the two back, then one over from the opposite direction, and place another strip, across this. Repeat this step and you'll have six strips woven together to look like a lattice. Press the strips slightly so that they stick together. Sprinkle the lattice with sugar and bake until lightly browned around the edges, 15 to 20 minutes. (They can be stored in a tin for up to 2 weeks.)

When ready to serve, lightly whip the cream with a whisk, adding a sprinkling of sugar. Ladle the compote into four wide soup bowls. Place one-fourth of the cream off center in each bowl and lay a cookie across the cream at an angle. SERVES 4

Strawberries taste best when small and deep red in color. They should be wiped with a damp cloth instead of washed because they are likely to absorb water, which dilutes their taste.

Rhubarb grown outdoors has dark red stems while hothouse rhubarb has pinkish stems. Either way, rhubarb is always sold without its leaves, which are poisonous.

Although vanilla beans are expensive, they can really improve the taste of some desserts, especially this one. A vanilla bean is the pod from a

parasitic plant that grows on other plants in the tropics. To slightly ferment them, they are picked ripe, dipped in hot water for a few seconds, and allowed to dry. If you cut one open, you can see hundreds of tiny seeds. I recommend using vanilla bean in vanilla ice cream so that the taste will shine and vanilla extract in something like peach ice cream, where vanilla is just an accent flavoring.

A kind of pastry dough that can be made in the food processor is short pastry (pâte sablée or pâte à foncer). Because it has more butter and sugar, it can be pressed out, rolled out, and handled much more than sweet pastry (pâte sucrée). It is a brittle pastry rather than an elastic one.

Lemon Curd Soufflé

Lemon curd is a kind of preserve popular in England. It can be used as a filling for cakes or tarts. Here it's the base of a scrumptious dessert soufflé.

4 tablespoons (½ stick) butter
½ cup sugar
4 egg yolks
⅓ cup lemon juice
2 tablespoons freshly grated lemon zest
5 egg whites
Salt

To make the lemon curd, combine the butter, ¼ cup of the sugar, egg yolk, lemon juice and zest in a bowl set over a pan of gently simmering water. Whisk the mixture constantly until it thickens, 15 to 20 minutes.

To prepare the mold, generously butter a 1-quart soufflé dish or six ½-cup ramekins and sprinkle the inside with sugar, shaking out the excess. Preheat the oven to 400 degrees.

When ready to serve, if the lemon curd has cooled completely gently rewarm it over a pan of simmering water just until it is warm to the touch. Combine the egg whites with a few grains of salt in a clean copper bowl and beat with a balloon whisk until the egg whites are stiff and shiny and you can turn the bowl over your head without the egg whites falling out. Whisk in the remaining ¼ cup sugar, a tablespoon at a time, beating well after each addition. With a rubber spatula, fold one-third of the meringue mixture into the soufflé base then fold the soufflé base back into the remaining meringue. (It is acceptable to have some white streaks showing.) Pour the soufflé mixture into the prepared mold and smooth the top with the rubber spatula. With your thumb an inch into the mixture and your forefinger hooked on the edge of the mold, turn the mold with your other hand to make a dent all the way around the soufflé so that a cap will form when it bakes. Turn the oven down to 375 degrees and place the soufflé on the bottom shelf for 25 to 30 minutes. (Do not open the oven for 15 minutes.) The soufflé is done when it has risen and is lightly browned and is firm yet soft when shaken slightly. To serve, bring the soufflé to the table and cut into it with two spoons. Serve on warm plates.

SERVES 6

The only thing that causes a soufflé to fall is heat. When the soufflé mixture gets too hot (from staying in the oven too long), the eggs curdle and the soufflé falls. A soufflé always begins to fall when it is taken from the oven. That's why it must be served right away.

All soufflés can be made up to an hour ahead if the egg whites are folded into a warm soufflé base, put in the prepared dish, and the whole thing covered with a bowl, because the heat of the mixture slightly poaches the egg whites.

Dried Apricot Soufflé

*D*ried apricots really do have more flavor than fresh. Here, they're highlighted in this airy soufflé.

½ pound dried apricots (bright orange and moist-packed)
1⅓ cups sugar plus more for the ramekins
4 tablespoons brandy
5 egg whites
Salt

To make the apricot puree, combine the apricots with a cup of water in a saucepan over moderately high heat. Let simmer until they are completely soft, about 10 minutes. Puree the apricots in the food processor.

To prepare the molds, generously butter the sides and bottoms of eight 3- to 4-inch ramekins. Add a handful of sugar to one, run it all around, and pour it into the next ramekin. When all the ramekins have been sugared, place them on a baking sheet.

To make the soufflé base, put the cup of sugar in a small saucepan with enough water to make a paste. Heat over low heat and swirl the pan to dissolve the sugar. When all the sugar has dissolved, increase the heat to high and let it boil without stirring until the sugar reaches the hard-ball stage, 260 degrees on a candy thermometer. Stir in the apricot puree with 2 tablespoons of the brandy.

Preheat the oven to 400 degrees.

To make the soufflés, combine the egg whites with a few grains of salt in a clean copper bowl and beat with a balloon whisk until they are stiff and you can turn the bowl over your head without their falling out. Fold one-quarter of the egg whites into the apricot mixture and then fold the apricot mixture back into the larger amount of egg whites. Turn down the oven to 375 degrees. Spoon the soufflé mixtures into the prepared ramekins, making swirls on top, and bake on the bottom shelf. The soufflés are done when puffed and lightly browned, 12 to 15 minutes. Serve immediately.   SERVES 8

If a soufflé doesn't rise, it is probably because the egg whites were overbeaten until they are no longer smooth but chunky; or the egg whites were folded too thoroughly into the soufflé base. That is why I recommend always using a copper bowl with a balloon whisk to beat the whites. It is hard to overbeat the egg whites in copper, and you can even beat them ahead and keep them smooth by stirring them slowly. When folding, it is important to remember that it's acceptable to have streaks of egg whites showing when you fill the molds.

Grand Marnier Soufflé

What could be better than a boozy, eggy, airy dessert after a rich meal? Nothing! That is why everyone loves Grand Marnier soufflé. This one is special because tiny bits of Grand Marnier–soaked candied orange peel are dispersed throughout the soufflé.

⅔ cup candied orange peel, cut in small dice, homemade (page 389) or a good-quality store-bought
¼ cup Grand Marnier
3 tablespoons flour
¾ cup milk
½ cup sugar
4 egg yolks
2 tablespoons softened butter
5 egg whites
Salt
2 teaspoons vanilla

If using homemade orange peel, cut the peel into tiny dice and measure ¼ cup of the syrup. If using store-bought candied orange peel, soak the peel in the Grand Marnier for an hour.

To make the soufflé base, whisk the flour with some of the milk in a medium-size saucepan off the heat. Blend in the rest of the milk with ¼ cup of the sugar. Stir over moderately high heat until the mixture thickens and comes to a boil. Let it boil for 5 minutes to cook the flour. Remove the pan from the heat and whisk in the egg yolks, one at a time, beating well after each. Stir in the butter. (If making ahead, put a piece of plastic wrap right down on top of the soufflé base so that it does not form a crust.)

Preheat the oven to 400 degrees. Generously coat a 6-cup soufflé dish or eight ½-cup ramekins with butter and sugar.

Twenty minutes before serving, put the egg whites into a clean copper bowl with a few grains of salt. Beat them with a balloon whisk until they are stiff and you can turn the bowl over your head without their falling out. Beat in the remaining ¼ cup sugar. Drain the orange peel if necessary, reserving the Grand Marnier. With a sauce whisk, stir the Grand Marnier and the vanilla into the soufflé base. Fold one-quarter of the meringue into the soufflé base. Then fold the soufflé base back into the rest of the meringue. Pour half this mixture gently into the prepared soufflé dish or eight ½-cup ramekins on a baking sheet. Scatter with the candied orange peel. Cover with the remaining soufflé mixture. Smooth the top with the rubber spatula. For the large soufflé, hook your finger on the edge of the soufflé dish and your thumb about an inch into the top of the soufflé and an inch from the edge. Turn the bowl to bring the soufflé full circle. This is to make a cap when the soufflé bakes.

Turn the oven down to 375 degrees. Put the soufflé (or soufflés) on the bottom shelf. The large soufflé will cook in 25 to 30 minutes and the small soufflés will cook in 12 to 15 minutes. (If the soufflés get too brown in the oven, quickly sift a little confectioners' sugar over them before serving.) Serve immediately.   SERVES 6 TO 8

Remember, there are three things that always have to be done before you start beating your egg whites for a soufflé—you need to make a soufflé base, you need a prepared dish, and you need a hot oven.

There are three different kinds of dessert soufflés, depending on the texture; namely, liqueur, chocolate, or fruit puree. Liqueur soufflés are the most stable, chocolate soufflés are fairly stable, and fruit purees are the most fragile. Soufflés fall in the oven when it gets so hot that the eggs curdle. That is why it is important to take them out of the oven when they are ready— puffy and lightly browned.

This is a very traditional recipe for a liqueur soufflé. You can make it into an amaretto soufflé by substituting ground amaretto cookies for candied orange peel and an amaretto liqueur for Grand Marnier. You can also experiment with other liqueurs. The reason Grand Marnier works so well is that it isn't too sweet. When substituting other liqueurs, add a couple tablespoons of brandy to cut the sweetness.

SERVING CHEESE

SERVING CHEESE AT THE END of the meal can be fun and interesting! I would serve at least three cheeses of differing textures and tastes. Cheeses should always be served at room temperature, which means taking them out of the refrigerator an hour or so before eating them. I suggest passing them around the table on a large platter, each cheese with its own knife for cutting. Soft white cheeses can be served with walnut bread, and others with slices of sweet baguettes or mildly flavored crackers. Some cheeses, particularly Stilton, go well with walnuts. Some cheeses can be matched with dried fruits or fruit compote; however, I don't recommend serving grapes or sliced apples with cheese. It is much better to pair cheeses with fine wines or ports.

Although cheeses can be classified according to their region of origin or according to the kind of animal that produced the milk from which the cheese derives, the most common way of categorizing cheeses is by their texture. Examples of fresh cheeses are cottage cheese, cream cheese, and mozzarella. The soft-ripened cheeses include Brie and Camembert. The triple creams include St. André and Explorateur. The blue cheeses include Stilton and Gorgonzola. The semisoft cheeses include Bel Paese and Port Salut. The semihard cheeses include the various kinds of Cheddar, Gruyère, and Emmenthal. And the hard, grating cheeses include Parmesan. Some cheeses, notably Gouda, can be sold semisoft, semihard, or aged.

Caramel Ice Cream

This ice cream is simply delicious!

½ cup plus ¾ cup sugar
2 cups milk
6 egg yolks
1 cup heavy cream
Salt

To make the caramel, put the ½ cup sugar in a small saucepan with enough water to make a paste over low heat. Swirl the pan from time to time until the sugar has dissolved. Turn up the heat and boil the syrup without stirring until the mixture turns a light amber color. Place the saucepan in a larger pan of warm water to stop the cooking.

To make the ice cream, scald the milk. Combine the egg yolks in a large bowl with the ¾ cup sugar. Whisk the yolks and sugar together until the mixture is light and lemon colored. Whisk a ladleful of the warm milk into the yolk and sugar mixture to temper the eggs. Return the yolk mixture to the saucepan and start stirring it slowly over gentle heat with a wooden spoon. Keep the bowl and whisk handy. The sauce will begin to thicken when the bubbles subside and a little steam rises. Pay close attention; the mixture should coat the back of the spoon and should not boil. If it gets to the boiling point by mistake, pour the mixture into the bowl and whisk vigorously. Otherwise, quickly pour the mixture into the bowl and stir in the cream with a few grains of salt. Stir in the

caramel. Freeze in an ice cream machine. Serve the same day it is made.

SERVES 6

It is easy to make caramel if you add water to help the sugar to start to melt. To do this, put granulated sugar in a heavy pot with enough water to make a paste. Stir the mixture with a spoon. Stop stirring and let it melt over gentle heat without letting it boil until the resulting syrup is clear, swirling the pan from time to time. When all the sugar crystals have melted, increase the heat to high and let the mixture boil vigorously over high heat until it begins to turn yellow. If you stir it or cook it over too low a heat, the sugar will crystallize before it caramelizes. If this begins to happen, cover it quickly and let it continue to cook. If this trick doesn't work, you need to start over.

You can adapt this recipe to make vanilla ice cream. Instead of making caramel, simply steep the milk with a split vanilla bean for 10 to 15 minutes before proceeding.

The technique described here is exactly how crème anglaise (custard sauce) should always be made. Remember that eggs thicken at 180 degrees and liquid boils at 212 degrees. This means that the mixture should not come close to boiling.

Caramel has been used for color and flavoring for years in French cooking. In a way, it serves the same purpose as brandy or fortified wines in cooking in that it has a strong taste and an acid element. Therefore, it is not a good idea to try to use both alcohol and caramel.

Cappuccino Brûlée

Imagine a coffee cup filled with a creamy, rich custard, covered with meringue, that looks like cappuccino! It's great fun to make because you have to use a blowtorch to brown the edges of the meringue. This is my adaptation of a recipe from Roland Passot, of La Folie in San Francisco, who loves to make food for people.

> 1 quart heavy cream
> 1 tablespoon instant (not freeze-dried)
>   espresso powder
> 8 egg yolks
> 1 cup sugar plus 1½ cups for the meringue
> 6 egg whites
> Salt

To make the custard, heat the cream with the espresso powder in a saucepan until bubbles form around the edges. (This is called scalding.) Let steep for 5 minutes. Put the egg yolks in a bowl, whisk in 1 cup of the sugar, and continue whisking until the mixture is a light lemon color. Stir in the warm cream. Strain the mixture into 12 small, ovenproof coffee or demitasse cups. Place the cups in a baking pan and fill the pan with warm tap water to come halfway up its sides. Cover all the coffee cups with one piece of foil and bake in a 325-degree oven until the custard is set but still soft, about an hour. Carefully remove the pan from the oven and remove the cups from the water to let cool at room temperature.

To prepare the meringue, combine the egg whites in a bowl of an electric mixer with a few grains of salt. Using the whip, beat the egg whites slowly at first and then more quickly until they are quite stiff. With the mixer running, add the remaining 1½ cups sugar, a tablespoon at a time, beating well after each addition. The meringue should be firm and glossy. Put a generous spoonful of the meringue on top of each custard, using a spoon to spread it to the edges of the coffee cup, making swirls on the top. Lightly brown the meringue with a blowtorch. Serve the cappuccino brûlées in their cups on saucers.

MAKES 12

To make a good meringue, the egg whites should be so stiff before the sugar is added that you can turn the bowl of egg whites over your head and they won't fall out. When all the sugar has been added, you can tell whether the resulting meringue is stiff enough by putting an egg right on top; it won't sink in. When making meringue, a foam of egg whites essentially suspends the granules of sugar. Don't add the egg whites too soon or too quickly, or the sugar will liquefy and make the meringue mixture runny.

Whenever a recipe calls for egg yolks and sugar to be mixed together, do not throw the sugar onto the eggs and leave it because the sugar will start to cook the eggs. You will notice how quickly egg yolks and sugar liquefy; this is because sugar is closer to a liquid than it is to other dry ingredients.

When using a blowtorch, always hold the nozzle away from you when you light it. Adjust the flame and run it gently over the meringue. There is no real trick to it. You can buy a fancy little blowtorch at cookware shops or use one from the hardware store. If the idea doesn't appeal to you, sift a little unsweetened cocoa powder on top to give the illusion of brûlée.

A custard made with milk and baked in a mold lined with caramel is called crème caramel. A custard made with cream and baked in a little pot or cup is called pot de crème. This dessert is really a pot de crème with meringue on top. A rich custard with a burned sugar crust on top is called crème brûlée.

Cold Lemon Soufflé

A cold soufflé is a kind of gelatin dessert formed in a soufflé dish and decorated to look like a soufflé that has risen. It never goes into the oven. Cooks add gelatin to a basic mousse mixture so that it can be made ahead. This is my all-time favorite dessert. It is a perfect finish to an elegant dinner!

1 tablespoon (1 package) granular gelatin
3 cups heavy cream
5 eggs, separated
1½ cups sugar
Juice and grated zest of 4 lemons
    (about 1 cup juice and ¼ cup zest)
5 egg whites
Salt
Pistachios, finely chopped
Lemon slice
Mint leaf

Rinse a 1-quart soufflé dish in cold water, shaking out any excess water. Using a sheet of parchment or waxed paper long enough to wrap around the dish, fold it in thirds lengthwise. Wrap it around the outside of the dish to form a collar at least 2 inches above the rim. Tie the collar tightly around the top of the dish with string.

Melt the gelatin with ⅓ cup water in a small saucepan over low heat. Whip the cream in a large bowl set over a bigger bowl of ice only until you can draw the whisk through the cream, and see the line. (This is called partially whipped cream.) Remove the bowl of cream from the ice and set the bowl of ice aside.

To make the mousse, heat the egg yolks, sugar, and lemon juice and zest in a bowl over a pot of simmering water. Whisk constantly until mixture is thick, about 10 minutes. Remove from the heat and let cool, stirring, for a couple of minutes. Transfer one-third of the partially whipped cream to another bowl and reserve for garnish. Fold the thick lemon mousse into the remaining cream and stir in the melted gelatin. Place this mixture over the bowl of ice. Test with a rubber spatula to determine when the gelatin is beginning to set. (You can tell that it's almost set when the edge of the pan looks frosted.) With a balloon whisk, beat the egg whites in a copper bowl with a few grains of salt until they are firm. When the gelatin is beginning to set, fold in the stiffly beaten egg whites and pour the mixture into the prepared soufflé dish, smoothing the top. Chill for at least 4 hours.

To finish the dessert, cut the string holding the collar and, running a kitchen knife around the collar, discard the collar. Whip the remaining cream with a sauce whisk until soft peaks form. Spread this over the top of the cold soufflé with a metal spatula. With the soufflé dish in one hand, use the other hand to press chopped pistachios around the top of the cold soufflé where the paper was removed. Whip the remaining cream a few more times. Fill a pastry bag fitted with a ½-inch star tube filled with the cream and pipe rosettes around the edge of the cold soufflé. Ignore the impulse to make one more rosette in the middle; it will ruin the design. Cut the slice of lemon from the center to the rind with a knife and holding the slice in both hands, twist each end away from the other, making a decoration for the center of the soufflé. Put a mint leaf under this. Always serve this dessert with spoons, not cut in wedges like a cake.   SERVES 8

When working with gelatin, always get out a bowl of ice, no matter what the instructions are in the recipe. There is no other way to tell when the gelatin is beginning to set. You must fold in the lighter ingredients at exactly the setting point to suspend the gelatin throughout the dessert. If you fold too soon, you will have a thin layer of yellow jelly on the bottom of the soufflé dish. If you wait too long, you will have little blobs of yellow jelly suspended throughout the mixture.

Cooks who train with European teachers always use sheet gelatin while the rest of us use granular gelatin. Sheet gelatin needs to be soaked in cold water before being melted and added to the mixture to be set. Five sheets of gelatin will set 4 cups of liquid, as will a tablespoon of granular gelatin. You can estimate how many cups of liquid there are by counting the cups of cream and sugar and guessing at the cups of egg yolks. Remember, sugar is considered liquid because it liquefies when mixed with eggs.

Hazelnut Praline Bavarian Cream
(Bavarois)

A Bavarian cream (bavarois) is a classic French dessert with a flavored base of crème anglaise, lightened with whipped cream and beaten egg whites and stabilized with gelatin. It is always served unmolded. Although this praline-flavored Bavarian cream is a lot of work, it is truly memorable.

1 cup hazelnuts
2 cups sugar
1½ tablespoons granular gelatin
½ teaspoon instant espresso
6 egg yolks
1 cup milk, warmed
1½ cups heavy cream
6 egg whites
1 tablespoon vanilla extract

To toast the nuts, place them on a baking sheet in a 375-degree oven for 5 to 7 minutes. Rub the hazelnuts in a towel or over the bottom of a metal colander to remove the skins. (Don't worry if you don't get all the brown skins off.) Return the nuts to the oven until they are a golden brown, about 6 minutes. Place the toasted nuts on a lightly oiled baking sheet.

To make the praline, combine a cup of the sugar with enough water to make a paste in a heavy pan over low heat. Stir to mix. Swirl the pan gently until the sugar is dissolved.

Increase the heat to high and boil, without stirring, until the mixture turns a deep, dark (not golden) color. Pour the mixture over the toasted nuts and set aside to cool. When cool, crack the praline and grind the mixture in a food processor until it becomes a fine powder.

Sprinkle the gelatin and the instant espresso over ½ cup water in a small saucepan. Prepare a large bowl of ice and rinse a 2-quart decorative mold (or eight 1-cup molds) with water.

To make the Bavarian cream, combine the egg yolks and the remaining cup of sugar in a large bowl and whisk until thick and lemony in color. Slowly add the warmed milk to the egg yolks and return this mixture to the saucepan over moderate heat. Keep the whisk and bowl handy. Cook, stirring constantly, until the mixture thickens and coats the back of a spoon, being careful not to let it boil. Pour the warm mixture into the bowl. Melt the gelatin-coffee mixture over low heat and stir it into the custard sauce (crème anglaise). In a separate bowl, partially whip the cream with the vanilla just until you can draw a line through it. Fold one-third of the cream into the egg yolk mixture and place the bowl with this mixture in the large bowl of ice. Feel with a rubber spatula to test when the gelatin begins to set up. Remove the bowl from the ice and stir in the praline powder. Meanwhile, beat the egg whites with a few grains of salt in a copper bowl with a balloon whisk until stiff but not dry. When the gelatin begins to set, fold in the stiffly beaten egg whites. Pour this mixture into the prepared molds. Refrigerate the Bavarian cream until set, at least 4 hours. (It can be kept in the refrigerator for up to 5 days.)

To unmold the Bavarian (or Bavarians), bring a large pan of water to just below the boiling point on top of the stove. Holding the molds with towels, dip them in the water for 10 seconds. Loosen a corner of the Bavarian with a small knife and invert it onto a serving platter or individual dessert plates. Do not keep putting the molds back into the hot water. If the Bavarian does not unmold, the chances are there is a vacuum holding it in and dipping it repeatedly in the hot water will simply melt it. The best solution is first to try loosening it with a knife to break the seal and then to wrap a hot towel around it. Whip the remaining heavy cream until it holds soft peaks. Put it in a pastry bag fitted with a ¼-inch star tube and decorate the tops of the Bavarians.

SERVES 8

To pipe decorations on any dessert, drop a pastry tip into the bottom of a pastry bag. Fold 2 or 3 inches of the top of the bag back over one of your hands to make a collar. With your little finger or elbow against the bowl, reach into the bowl with a rubber spatula in the other hand and lift out a spoonful of whipped cream. Spoon the cream deep into the bag, cleaning off the spatula by pressing it against the hand under the collar. Do not fill the bag above the edge of the collar; you can always refill it. To pipe, close the top of the bag over the cream and press all the cream down to the tip end. Pipe the first blob of cream back into the bowl to get out any air bubbles. Hold the top of the bag twisted in one hand and guide it with the other. The bottom hand should have its thumb down. Do not squeeze with this hand, only with the top hand. Look at where you are piping from, in front of your hands, not behind.

To make a rosette, hold the bag straight up and down about ½ inch from the dessert. Squeeze from the top, stop squeezing, then do a little down/up motion with the bag. It's a good idea to practice rosettes on waxed paper before trying them on finished desserts. Remember, don't squeeze in the middle and always look over the bag, not behind it.

Caramel and praline have two distinctly different tastes and colors (praline has a much stronger taste). In caramel, the cooking of the sugar is stopped when it's a light brown, the color of a maple butcher block. In praline, the cooking is stopped when the sugar is dark brown, the color of mahogany wood.

Espresso–Chocolate Truffle Ice Cream

For years the French have been making irregular little balls of chocolate candy that look like truffles that grow in the ground. This ice cream will have little bits of exquisite chocolate interspersed in a rich coffee ice cream.

> 4 ounces semisweet or bittersweet
>   chocolate
> 2 tablespoons butter
> ⅓ cup sifted powdered sugar
> 3 tablespoons dark rum
> 2 cups heavy cream
> 6 egg yolks
> ¾ cup granulated sugar
> 2 teaspoons instant espresso
> 1 cup milk
> 1 teaspoon vanilla extract
> Salt

To make the chocolate truffles, melt the chocolate and the butter with 2 tablespoons water in a bowl set over a pot of barely simmering water. When the chocolate is melted, remove the bowl from the heat and stir in the powdered sugar and rum. Freeze the mixture until firm.

To make the custard base, scald the cream in a medium-size saucepan over moderately high heat. Combine the egg yolks with the granulated sugar in a bowl and whisk until the mixture is light and lemon colored. Pour half the hot cream slowly into the egg mixture and whisk constantly. Return the mixture to the saucepan and stir with a wooden spoon. Keep the whisk and the bowl nearby. Cook the custard over moderate heat, watching carefully for the moment when the eggs thicken enough to coat the back of the spoon. This will happen when the bubbles subside and the mixture begins to steam. It is important that the mixture does not come to a boil. If it does, pour it immediately back into the bowl and whisk vigorously. Strain the sauce into a bowl and stir in the instant espresso, milk, vanilla, and a few grains of salt. Pour half the mixture into an ice cream machine and freeze until firm.

To finish the ice cream, form ¼-inch chunks of the chocolate truffle mixture with a teaspoon. Transfer the frozen ice cream to a bowl and stir in half the truffles. Repeat with the rest of the ice cream mixture and the remaining truffles.

MAKES 1½ QUARTS

Whether ice cream is made with flavored cream or a custard base, it may have three different textures from a cook's point of view, and the flavorings are added at different times, depending on the texture. When the flavoring has no texture at all, like vanilla or coffee, it can be added at the beginning. When the flavoring has some texture, like puree of strawberry or peaches, the puree needs to be added to the machine halfway through the freezing process. When there is definite texture, like nuts or truffles, the ingredients need to be stirred in after the ice cream is made.

🍂

Just as heat brings out flavor, chilling deadens flavor. So when you taste an ice cream mixture at room temperature, remember that it will *have less taste after it has been frozen. Therefore, make sure there is always plenty of flavor in the ice cream mixture before it goes into the machine.*

Chocolate Pudding Cake

*E*veryone is making warm chocolate pudding cakes these days, but this is the best!

¼ pound (1 stick) butter, plus more for
   buttering the molds
2 teaspoons flour, plus more for dusting the
   molds
6 ounces good-quality bittersweet or
   semisweet chocolate, chopped
2 eggs plus 2 egg yolks
¼ cup sugar
½ cup heavy cream (optional)

To prepare the molds, butter and flour four
3- to 4-inch ramekins, and place them on a
baking pan.

To melt the chocolate, put it with the butter in a bowl over gently simmering water.
The water should not touch the bottom of
the bowl.

To make the puddings, combine the eggs,
yolks, and sugar in a medium-size bowl.
Whisk until the mixture is light and lemon
colored and stir in the melted chocolate. It is
important that the two mixtures be about the
same temperature. Stir in the flour. Spoon
the chocolate mixture into the prepared
molds and place them on a baking sheet.
(They can be prepared up to 4 hours ahead at
this point.)

Preheat the oven to 450 degrees.

When ready to serve, place the puddings
in the oven for 12 minutes. Invert them onto
four warm dessert plates and without hesitation slide a kitchen knife under one corner of
the molds to lift them off. Serve with lightly
sweetened whipped cream on the side, if
desired.   Serves 4

*The best chocolate to use when making this dish
is Valrhona. The next best is Scharffen Berger.
After that comes a whole range of cooking
chocolate made by different companies—Callebaut, Guittard, Lindt, and Ghirardelli.*

*To melt chocolate, cut it into shards with a
knife. Put the shards in a clean, dry metal bowl
over a smaller pan of gently simmering water.
The bowl must not touch the water. You can use
a double boiler, or you can melt the chocolate in
the microwave. It is terribly important that no
moisture drop into the chocolate partway
through the melting process. This may cause the
chocolate to seize, that is, to clump up. This can
happen if small amounts of liquid get into the
chocolate after it has started to melt. A cover
may cause condensation and a wet spoon may
cause it to seize. That is why I advise not to stir
it at all. Just let it melt uncovered and take it
off the heat when melted. Let the chocolate cool
until it is about the temperature of the other
ingredients before you mix it in.*

Raspberry-Chocolate Crème Brûlée

This is probably the most popular dessert at Tante Marie's! It's my version of a dessert I ate years ago at Tra Vigne in the Napa Valley. It looks like classic crème brûlée with a few macerated raspberries and a mint leaf in the middle. When you look closely, however, you realize that it is really a chocolate-coated cookie on top of a rich custard. The dessert can be made in advance, and it's really worth investing in the individual gratin dishes—it doesn't work nearly as well in any other kind of dish.

FOR THE CUSTARD
1 quart heavy cream
1 vanilla bean, split lengthwise
8 egg yolks
½ cup sugar
Salt

FOR THE COOKIE
¼ pound (1 stick) butter
½ cup sugar
2 tablespoons flour
2 tablespoons milk
½ cup ground blanched or unblanched almonds

FOR THE GARNISH
1 pint fresh raspberries
1 teaspoon sugar
2 tablespoons kirsch (or framboise)
4 ounces semisweet chocolate
8 fresh mint leaves

To make the custards, combine the cream and the vanilla bean in a large saucepan over moderately high heat until bubbles form around the edge of the pan. Combine the egg yolks with the sugar in a large bowl and whisk until they are light and lemon colored. Slowly stir in the warm cream with a few grains of salt. Strain the mixture into eight 5-inch shallow gratin dishes. Bake in a 325-degree oven until barely set, about 45 minutes. Remove the custards from the oven and cool at room temperature.

To make the cookies, preheat another oven to 375 degrees. To make the cookies, combine the butter, sugar, flour, milk, and ground almonds in a small sauce-pan with a few grains of salt. Cook over low heat, stirring constantly, until the butter melts, about 5 minutes. Drop the dough by the tablespoonful onto a parchment-lined baking sheet, four cookies to a sheet; they will spread out when they bake. Bake until they are lightly browned around the edges, about 7 minutes. Remove from the oven and slide the paper off onto a rack to cool. Let the cookies sit for about a minute. Remove the parchment paper from the cookies—do not bend the cookies back. Let cool on a rack. Repeat with the remaining dough. (It will take practice to make the cookies the same size as the gratin dishes.)

To macerate the raspberries, mix them lightly in a small bowl with the sugar and the kirsch.

To assemble the dish, melt the chocolate in a bowl set over a pan of simmering water. When the cookies are cool, brush a thin layer of melted chocolate on the flat side of each.

Place each cookie, chocolate side down, on top of each cooled custard. Put a small spoonful of berries in the center of each cookie and garnish with a mint leaf. (The dessert can be assembled up to 4 hours before serving.)   SERVES 8

These cookies can be rolled around a dowel or a clean pencil before they are completely cooled to make rolled almond cookies, with both ends dipped in melted chocolate.

New cooks love to line every pan with parchment. Parchment, called grease-proof paper in England, is really designed for baking when there is butter in the batter, for example, to line pans for cookies and cakes. Parchment should not be used for lining a pan that bread is to be baked on, when making candy, or when baking an angel food cake, which has no butter.

Tiramisù

T iramisù is a modern Italian dessert made by soaking ladyfingers or cake with coffee and layering it with mascarpone cream. I learned this recipe from a woman who made it for the restaurant at Badia a Coltibuono, Lorenza de' Medici's home near Siena. I hung out in the kitchen waiting for her, and then tried to figure out what she was doing. Since I spoke no Italian and she spoke no English, our common language was food! This is the original recipe.

4 egg yolks
½ cup plus 1 tablespoon sugar
1 pound mascarpone
¼ cup light rum
1 tablespoon lemon juice
1 tablespoon vanilla extract
1 cup heavy cream
1 tablespoon confectioners' sugar
4 egg whites
48 soft ladyfingers, about 2 inches in length
2 cups strong coffee
2 teaspoons instant espresso
3 ounces unsweetened chocolate, finely
*   chopped*

To make the mascarpone cream, put the yolks in a bowl and whisk in the ½ cup sugar. Whisk this mixture until it is light and fluffy, about 3 minutes. With a wooden spoon, mix in the mascarpone until the mixture is smooth. Stir in the rum, lemon juice, and vanilla. In a separate bowl, whisk the cream with the confectioners' sugar until it forms very soft peaks. Fold the cream into the egg yolk mixture. In another bowl, whisk the egg whites until stiff but not dry and gently fold them into the yolk mixture.

To assemble, line a 9 by 13-inch baking dish with ladyfingers. Mix the coffee with the instant espresso and the tablespoon of sugar in a flat bowl. Dip the bottoms of the ladyfingers lightly in the coffee mixture and arrange them over the bottom and sides of the dish. Spread half the mascarpone cream over the ladyfingers. Dip the rest of the ladyfingers in the coffee mixture and arrange them in one layer over the cream. Spread the remaining cream on top. Cover the dish with the chopped chocolate. Chill the tiramisù for at least an hour and up to 3 days before serving.   SERVES 10 TO 12

Mascarpone is really a thickened Italian cream even though it is sometimes called cheese. Crème fraîche is a thickened French cream, while Devonshire cream is a thickened English cream.

It is better to make ladyfingers or buy them in a bakery than to buy the dry packaged ones. You could also make this dessert with a plain cake like génoise; pound cake is really too rich.

The best way to chop chocolate for this recipe is to put 1-inch squares of chocolate in a food processor with the blade and chop the chocolate until fine. Unsweetened cocoa on top does not give nearly the same effect; it is too powdery.

LADYFINGERS

This ladyfingers recipe was taught to us by the brilliant chocolatier Alice Medrich. They are not meant to be eaten plain but are used as an ingredient in other recipes.

4 eggs, separated
½ cup plus 4 tablespoons sugar
1½ teaspoons vanilla extract
Salt
1 cup minus 2 tablespoons sifted cake flour
¾ cup confectioners' sugar

Preheat the oven to 325 degrees and line two baking sheets with parchment paper. Have ready a pastry bag fitted with a ½-inch round tip. To keep the ladyfingers equal in length, draw 3-inch-long lines with a pencil on the parchment paper, spaced 3 inches apart. Turn the paper over.

To make the egg yolk mixture, combine the yolks with the 4 tablespoons of sugar and the vanilla in the bowl of an electric mixer. Using the whip, beat the mixture until it becomes pale and thick. (This can be done in a bowl with a whisk if you don't have two bowls and whips for your electric mixer.)

To make the egg white mixture, combine the whites in the bowl of an electric mixer with a few grains of salt. Using the whip, beat the whites slowly at first and then at high speed until soft peaks form. Add a tablespoon at a time of the ½ cup sugar. When the meringue mixture is firm, scoop one-third of the meringue onto the yolk mixture. Over this, sift one-third of the flour. Fold gently until the mixture is nearly incorporated.

Continue with another third of the meringue and another third of the flour. Finally, fold in the last third of the meringue and the last third of the flour. Work quickly and do not overfold. The batter should be delicate and remain as stiff as possible. Scoop the batter into the pastry bag and pipe out strips, 3 inches in length, onto the prepared baking sheets, letting the batter fall onto the pan. Do not press it down. Bake the ladyfingers until they are lightly golden. Cool briefly on the pan on a rack.

MAKES 2 DOZEN LADYFINGERS

If you overfold the two mixtures, they will fall. If you underfold them, they will fall. This isn't a problem if you're using the ladyfingers for tiramisù, since they are soaked in coffee and covered with cream.

Bread Pudding with Dried Apricots and Cherries

This is a great dessert for a cold winter's evening. The strong flavors of the dried fruits and caramel go well with modern California food.

¼ pound dried apricots, quartered
¼ pound dried cherries or dried
*   cranberries*
4 cups sugar
2 cups milk plus 1 to 2 additional cups
3 cups heavy cream
8 egg yolks
1½ pounds white sandwich bread (such as
*   Orowheat, Northridge, Arnold, or*
*   Pepperidge Farm brands)*

To cook the dried fruit, combine the apricots and cherries with a cup of the sugar and 2 cups water in a medium-size saucepan. Bring the mixture to a boil over moderately high heat. When it comes to a boil, turn off the heat and let the fruit sit for 20 minutes until soft. Remove the fruit and reserve the liquid.

To make the custard, heat the milk with 2 cups of the cream in a medium-size saucepan over moderately high heat until bubbles form around the edge of the pan. Put the egg yolks and sugar in a mixing bowl. Whisk until light and lemon colored. Slowly beat the warmed milk and cream into the yolk mixture.

To assemble the pudding, trim the crusts

from the bread and cut the slices in half. Lightly butter a 9 by 13-inch glass or ceramic baking dish. Overlap half the bread slices over the bottom and sides of the dish. Spread all the fruit over the bread. Cover the fruit with another layer of bread, overlapping the slices slightly to create a decorative pattern. Pour the custard mixture over the bread and add perhaps as much as 2 cups more milk, enough to barely cover the bread. Bake the bread pudding in a 350-degree oven until the bread on top is lightly browned and the custard is almost set, about an hour and 15 minutes.

To make the caramel sauce, heat the remaining cup of sugar with ¼ cup water in a medium-size saucepan over low heat. Cook, swirling the pan from time to time, until the sugar dissolves. Do not stir the melting sugar and do not let it boil, or it may crystallize. When the sugar has melted and air bubbles start to form in the mixture, increase the heat to high and cook until the mixture turns light amber in color, about 7 minutes. Remove the pan from the heat and stir in a cup of the reserved fruit-soaking liquid. Return the pan to the heat and continue cooking until the mixture is the consistency of honey, about 10 minutes more. Remove the pan from the heat and stir in the remaining cup of cream. (It may boil up.) Let the sauce sit for 30 minutes.

To serve, spoon a generous amount of the fruit caramel sauce around the bottom of individual dessert plates and spoon a serving of the bread pudding on top. (This dessert can be made ahead and stored in the refrigerator for up to 5 days, well covered with plas- tic wrap.) It is best served warm or at room temperature.   SERVES 8

When adding cream and/or butter to caramelized sugar, be sure the pan is always large enough because the mixture may boil up, especially if the cream is cold.

Dried Fruit Compote with Cardamom Pound Cake

A cardamom-flavored pound cake served *with a spicy compote of dried fruit is a great dessert for the ski cabin—a warm, comforting winter dessert! This compote would also be great served over good-quality whole milk yogurt in pretty glasses.*

8 ounces dried prunes, pitted
4 ounces dried apricots
4 ounces dried figs, stems removed
1 cup dry white wine
3-inch cinnamon stick
¼ cup brandy
1 cup orange juice
¼ cup honey
¼ teaspoon ground allspice
¼ teaspoon ground cinnamon
¼ teaspoon ground ginger
One 2-pound pound cake, store-bought or
    homemade (recipe follows)
¾ cup heavy cream
Sugar for sprinkling
1 teaspoon vanilla

To make the fruit compote, combine the prunes, apricots, and figs in a medium-size saucepan with the wine, cinnamon stick, and 1⅔ cups water. Bring the liquid to a boil, stirring, and simmer until the fruit is tender, about 15 minutes. Transfer the mixture with a slotted spoon to a serving bowl, remove the cinnamon stick, and sprinkle with the brandy. Add the orange juice, lemon juice, honey, allspice, cinnamon, and ginger to the liquid in the saucepan. Cook the mixture over medium-high heat until it is reduced by half. Let the liquid cool, then pour it over the fruit. Let sit for at least an hour before serving. (This mixture can be kept for up to 3 months in a covered container in the refrigerator.)

To serve, put the cream in a bowl and whisk it until it holds soft peaks. Stir in sugar to taste and vanilla.

To serve, place a ¼-inch slice of pound cake in the middle of each plate, put a dollop of whipped cream to one side of the cake, and spoon a generous amount of the dried fruit and the syrup over the top.

SERVES 8

In this recipe the allspice and cinnamon can be ground together but the ginger has to be bought already ground.

If the cream has exactly the texture you want for whipped cream, stir the sugar and vanilla in with a spoon rather than the whisk, because the whisk will continue to work the cream.

CARDAMOM POUND CAKE

*T*he pound cake is a basic cake in French cooking. It is called quatre-quarts, *the four equal parts being butter, sugar, eggs, and flour. This is a recipe from Diane Dexter, who taught at Tante Marie's for years. Whenever a cake has as much fat as this one does, it will keep for a long time.*

*1½ cups all-purpose flour plus extra
    for the pan
1½ cups cake flour
1 teaspoon baking powder
¾ teaspoon salt
¾ pound (3 sticks) butter, softened, plus
    extra for the pan
1½ cups sugar
5 eggs
1 teaspoon vanilla extract
½ teaspoon ground cardamom
2 teaspoons grated lemon zest
⅔ cup buttermilk*

Preheat the oven to 325 degrees. Generously butter the inside of a tube pan and lightly coat it with flour, tapping out any excess. Sift together the flours, baking powder, and salt in a sieve over waxed paper.

To make the cake, put the butter in the bowl of an electric mixer and beat it with a wooden spoon until soft. Transfer the bowl to the mixer and beat at low speed until the butter is light and fluffy. Gradually beat in the sugar and continue beating until the mixture is very fluffy. Beat in the eggs one at a time, beating well after each addition. Beat in the vanilla, cardamom, and lemon zest and remove the bowl from the mixer. With a spoon, mix in the dry ingredients, alternating with the buttermilk. Mix until the batter is smooth and soft. Pour the batter into the prepared pan and bake until the cake is firm to the touch and pulls away from the edge of the pan, about an hour and 15 minutes. Cool the cake in its pan on a rack for 10 minutes before inverting onto the rack.

MAKES 1 CAKE

You can beat butter, sugar, and eggs as much as you want, but flour should not be beaten in when making cookies, squares, and cakes because beating a dough once the flour is added will make it tough. In bread recipes, you want the flour to become elastic. In pastry and cakes, you do not.

Baking soda is an older leavener than baking powder. Whenever it was used in a recipe, a form of acid had to be added as well, such as lemon juice, vinegar, molasses, or sour milk. Baking powder is a newer form of leavener; it already contains acid in the form of cream of tartar.

Gingerbread Napoleon with Poached Pears and Caramel Sauce

This recipe, which consists of poached pears layered with spicy gingerbread and served with caramel sauce, is suitable for an autumn dinner when pears are in season. The best pears to cook with are French butter pears, d'Anjou, Comice, and Bosc.

2 cups sugar
2-inch piece fresh ginger
2 tablespoons lemon juice
6 ripe pears, peeled, halved, and cored
4 tablespoons (½ stick) butter
1 cup heavy cream
*1 gingerbread, store-bought or homemade
   (recipe follows)*

To cook the pears, combine a cup of the sugar with 4 cups water and the ginger and lemon juice. Bring this mixture to a boil, stirring to dissolve the sugar. When the sugar has dissolved, add the pears. Reduce the heat to low and poach the pears until they are tender when pierced with a fork. Remove the pears from the syrup and cool, reserving the liquid.

To make the caramel sauce, combine the remaining cup sugar with ½ cup water in a medium-size saucepan over low heat. Swirl the pan from time to time until the sugar dissolves. Add a cup of the pear-poaching liquid and increase the heat to high. Boil the mixture without stirring until it turns amber in

color. Remove the pan from the heat and add the butter and cream. Be careful; the mixture may bubble up. Stir gently and let sit for 30 minutes.

To assemble, cut 8 rounds from the gingerbread with a 3-inch round cutter. Slice each round horizontally into thirds. Slice the cooled pears lengthwise, about ⅜-inch thick. Place a generous spoonful of the caramel sauce in the middle of a dessert plate. Assemble the napoleon by layering a piece of gingerbread, a few pear slices, another piece of gingerbread, a few more pear slices, and another piece of gingerbread. Drizzle additional caramel sauce over the napoleon. Serve the remaining sauce separately.

S ERVES 8

GINGERBREAD

This is a recipe from the late Rosemary Manell, a great friend and passionate cook!

2½ cups flour
2½ teaspoons ground ginger
1 teaspoon ground cinnamon
½ teaspoon salt
*¼ pound (1 stick) butter, at room
   temperature*
½ cup light brown sugar
1 cup unsulfured molasses
2 teaspoons baking soda
1 egg
*¾ cup candied ginger, cut into ¼-inch dice
   and tossed with 2 teaspoons flour*

Preheat the oven to 375 degrees and butter a 9 by 13-inch baking pan. Sift together the flour, ginger, cinnamon, and salt.

To make the cake, put the butter in the bowl of an electric mixer and beat with a wooden spoon until it is soft. Put the bowl on the mixer with the whip attachment and beat until the butter is fluffy. Gradually add the sugar and continue beating until the mixture is light and fluffy, scraping down the sides of the bowl as needed. Combine the molasses with the baking soda and a cup of boiling water in another small bowl and stir to mix. Pour the molasses mixture into the butter mixture and continue to mix. Beat the egg. Remove the bowl from the mixer and stir in the sifted dry ingredients with a wooden spoon. Stir in the candied ginger. Pour the mixture into the prepared pan and bake in the oven for 15 minutes. Turn the oven temperature down to 350 degrees and continue to bake for another 15 minutes. The cake is done when it is firm to the touch and begins to pull away from the sides of the pan. Cool on a rack in the pan for 30 minutes. Invert the cake onto a rack and let cool.

SERVES 8

Sugar is usually refined from sugarcane. The result is granular and white; the by-product is molasses. Manufacturers add a little molasses back into sugar to make it golden brown, or even more molasses to make it dark brown. Sometimes it is ground very fine and mixed with up to 5 percent cornstarch to make powdered or confectioners' sugar.

Recipes can call for fresh ginger, ground ginger, crystallized (or candied) ginger, and ginger in syrup. They are not really interchangeable.

CAKES AND PASTRIES

WHEN YOU THINK about it, it is really amazing what you can make with butter, sugar, eggs, and flour. With these four ingredients plus various flavorings, you can make so many kinds of pastries and cakes to serve at luncheons, picnics, and dinner parties as well as with afternoon coffee or tea. And they can be displayed magnificently in a dessert buffet or a pastry shop!

There are really two kinds of cooks in this world—savory cooks and pastry cooks. I believe that people who like to cook meat and other savory dishes are a little wild and crazy. Even though they make the same dish over and over, they know it will never come out quite the same. That is why they don't have to measure their ingredients and why they must taste the food to see if it is what they want. Pastry cooks, on the other hand, are more precise. They know exactly what to expect when they mix their ingredients. In fact, they don't even have to taste their food; it will come out the same every time. I like to compare savory cooks to Ferrari drivers, who throw caution to the wind, and pas-

try cooks to Porsche drivers, who admire precision!

In this country we have one word for the people who make pastries and bread: bakers. In France, there are two different professions: the bread baker is called the *boulanger,* and the pastry cook is called the *pâtissier.* One works with yeast and the other doesn't. The reason I don't refer to all cooks and bakers as chefs is that there is really only one chef in a kitchen—the boss!

Kinds of Pastry

Although the classifications of pastry are not as well defined as the kinds of sauces in French cooking, here are the kinds of pastry that an accomplished pastry cook or baker should know:

What I call short crust pastry (pâte sablée or pâte à foncer) is essentially a cookie dough. Because it has added butter and sugar, it can be made in the food processor and pressed into a tart tin. It is quite brittle; the same dough is used in Caramelized Almond Tart (page 336),

Tropical Fruit Tart (page 337), and Caramelized Walnut Tart (page 339).

What I call flaky pastry is made in exactly the same way as sweet pastry (pâte brisée and pâte sucrée). The difference is that one has sugar and the other doesn't. In this method, the cold fat is cut into the dry ingredients and the liquids are added in such a way that the pastry, when baked, is light and flaky. This is best for tarts and covered pies in which there needs to be some strength to the pastry so that it will hold together when served. Good examples of this are Fresh Cherry Open Tarts (page 327), Fresh Apricot Tart (page 329), and Upside-Down Caramelized Apple Tart (page 333).

Choux pastry (pâte à choux) is a kind of French pastry that becomes hollow when baked. Pastry Ring Filled with Praline and Strawberries (page 340) and Pepper-Gruyère Cheese Puffs (page 38) are made with choux pastry. Other examples are éclairs and profiteroles.

The king of the French pastries has always been puff pastry (pâte feuilletée). Although it takes time to make, the results are spectacular. It is a dough in which the butter is rolled between layers of the dough in such a way that when it is baked, it rises dramatically in the oven. Rectangular Tart Filled with Peaches and Blackberries (page 342) and Salmon in Pastry with Fresh Sorrel Sauce (page 169) are made with this kind of pastry.

The kinds of cakes in French cooking are: génoise, in which the leavener is beaten eggs; biscuit, in which egg whites are folded into an egg-yolk-and-sugar mixture; and pound cake *(quatre-quarts)*, which traditionally con-tained equal amounts by weight of eggs, sugar, butter, and flour. Examples of cakes are Almond Génoise with Fresh Fruit and Raspberry Sauce (page 347), Torta Regina with Chocolate and Caramel Sauces (page 348), and Cardamom Pound Cake (page 322).

A layered meringue pastry is called a vacherin. See page 343 for Raspberry Vacherin. A meringue pastry with nuts is called a dacquoise. See page 345 for Hazelnut Dacquoise.

The kinds of French pastry that the traditional bread baker would make are brioches and croissants.

The kinds of fillings a baker might make are crème patissière (page 329), frangipane (page 331), whipped cream (crème Chantilly) (page 300), ganache (page 352), and curd (page 302). Although buttercream (crème au beurre) (page 345) is usually used as an icing, it can be used as a filling.

The Big Problem

Because pastry for tarts, tartlets, and pies is the most commonly used, here are some of the things that can go wrong with this pastry in the oven:

- If it shrinks, it has too much water or was overworked.
- If it's too hard, too much salt was added or not enough water.
- If it's too brittle, too much sugar was added.
- If it leaks, it needed an egg yolk to be added with the liquid.
- If it's tough, it was handled too much.

How to Make Pastries Without a Recipe

It is really impossible to make pastries without a recipe. The ratios of ingredients need to be exact. You can layer génoise with meringue, with mousse, or with whipped cream. You can make wonderful creations, but you need recipes for the basic elements.

Fresh Cherry Open Tarts

*T*hese individual open tarts can be made with any fresh fruit in season, such as peaches, apples, or plums, but the best is cherries!

FOR THE DOUGH
3⅓ cups flour
¼ teaspoon salt
2 tablespoons sugar
½ pound (2 sticks) plus 2 tablespoons cold butter, cut into ½-inch pieces

FOR THE ALMOND FILLING
¾ cup (4 ounces) almonds, blanched or unblanched
2 tablespoons sugar
3 tablespoons butter

FOR THE FRUIT
4 pounds ripe Bing cherries, pitted
⅓ cup kirsch or brandy
1 egg
Salt
Sugar for sprinkling

1 cup heavy cream

To make the dough, combine the flour, salt, and sugar in a bowl and cut in the cold butter with a pastry cutter. When the mixture looks like bread crumbs or oatmeal flakes, stir in 8 to 10 tablespoons cold water with a fork held straight up and down. Bring the mixture together with the fingers of one hand. Put the dough on a board or a counter and knead lightly just until the dough comes together. Wrap it in a piece of waxed paper, press to form a patty, and chill for 20 minutes.

To make the almond filling, combine the almonds, sugar, and butter in a food processor and process until smooth.

Preheat the oven to 375 degrees and line two baking sheets with parchment.

To assemble the tarts, roll out the dough on a lightly floured surface until it is about ⅛ inch thick. To do this, flour the dough, the board, and the rolling pin. Pound the dough a little in all directions to get it started. Lift it and turn it. Roll down and out away from yourself and then turn the dough and repeat. The idea is to have only as much flour as you need to prevent the dough from sticking, and to keep it moving so that it doesn't stick to the board. With a kitchen knife, cut six rough circles about 6 inches in diameter. Put the rounds on the prepared pans, divide the filling among the rounds, and spread lightly with the back of a spoon. Mound one-sixth of the cherries on top of the filling, leaving a 1½-inch rim. Brush the inside rim of each round with water and press the sides up and around the fruit. Sprinkle the cherries with kirsch, leaving a large window of fruit on the inside.

To make the egg glaze, mix the whole egg with a teaspoon of water and a few grains of salt. Brush the surface of the tarts with this egg glaze *(dorure)*, sprinkle the dough and fruit generously with sugar, preferably large crystals, and bake on the upper rack of the oven until the bottoms of the tarts are golden, about 40 minutes. Served with lightly sweetened whipped cream on the side.

SERVES 6

To pit cherries, remove the stem and put each cherry in a cherry (or olive) pitter with the stem side up. When you press the pitter, the pit should be pushed through. If it isn't, eat the cherry yourself.

The moisture content of all-purpose flour varies, depending on where the flour was milled and stored. It is for this reason that most recipes can't tell you exactly how much water to add to a dough to make it come together. After a while, you will be able to determine by feel.

Egg glaze is called dorure *in French. It is whole egg or egg yolk mixed with water, milk, or cream. The more butterfat there is in the egg glaze, the darker the pastry will look when it is baked.*

Fresh Apricot Tart

When you first see these apricot tarts at the beginning of summer in Paris, you can't believe that the tips of the apricots are burned. But then you taste them and you realize that the combination of caramelized fruit and rich, thick pastry cream is so delicious!

FOR THE DOUGH
1⅔ cups flour
⅛ teaspoon salt
1 tablespoon sugar
9 tablespoons cold butter, cut in 1-inch pieces
1 egg yolk

FOR THE PASTRY CREAM
2 cups milk, heated
6 egg yolks
1 cup sugar
4 tablespoons flour
4 tablespoons cornstarch
1 teaspoon vanilla extract

FOR THE FRUIT
24 fresh apricots, halved and pitted
Sugar for dusting

To make the dough, mix the flour, salt, and sugar in a medium-size bowl. Cut in the cold butter with a pastry blender until the mixture resembles oatmeal flakes. Mix the egg yolk with 3 to 5 tablespoons of cold water in a small bowl. Stir this into the flour mixture with a fork held straight up and down. Bring the dough together with the fingers of one hand. Turn the dough onto a counter and, using the heel of your hand, smear parts of the dough across the counter. Mound the dough back together using a pastry scraper. Do this three or four times to bring the dough together with a minimum of handling. Wrap in waxed paper and press into a patty. Chill for 20 minutes.

To make the crème pâtissière, heat the milk in a medium-size saucepan over low heat until bubbles appear around the inside of the pan. Combine the egg yolks in a medium-size bowl with the sugar and mix with a whisk until the mixture is light in texture. Whisk in the flour and cornstarch a tablespoon at a time. Stir in the heated milk and return the mixture to the saucepan. Bring the mixture to a boil over moderately high heat, whisking constantly until thickened. (At the point when the flour begins to expand, whisk vigorously to prevent lumping.) Let simmer for 5 minutes to cook the flour. Remove the pan from the heat and stir in the vanilla. Transfer the pastry cream to a flat bowl, cover directly with plastic wrap, and let cool at room temperature.

Preheat the oven to 375 degrees.

To line the tart shell, roll the dough out on a lightly floured board or counter. Always roll away from yourself and always turn the dough to make sure it will come off the counter. When the dough is about ⅛ inch thick, roll it back onto the rolling pin and lay it carefully over a 9-inch metal tart tin with a removable bottom. Lay the dough around the tart tin without stretching it. With scissors, cut off the excess dough around the shell, leaving a 1-inch border. For an even edge, always turn the tart so that you are handling the edges of the tart at 12 o'clock. With your fingers, double the dough back to reinforce the edges and press the dough firmly into the edges of the pan, giving an edge about ½ inch higher than the rim of the pan. Make a decorative edge by twisting the dough or pinching it with tongs. Chill the dough again for 5 to 10 minutes.

To assemble the tart, spread the pastry cream over the bottom of the pastry. Cover the pastry cream with overlapping halves of apricots in such a way that all the apricots are angled into the pastry cream with the cut side up so very little pastry cream is showing. Sprinkle with a tablespoon of sugar. Bake the tart on the top rack of the oven until the tips of the fruit are literally black and the tart shell has begun to shrink away from the tin, about 45 minutes. (This tart is best eaten the same day it is made.)

SERVES 6 TO 8

What makes pâte brisée (flaky pastry) and pâte sucrée (sweet pastry) light and flaky is that the little bits of cold butter produce steam in the hot oven. That is why it is so very important to be sure that the pastry is always cold and the oven always hot. If the dough gets warm when being worked, chill it. Remember, pastry always bakes best when it is cold.

Pastry cream (crème pâtissière) is a traditional cooked custard filling for filling pastries such as napoleons made with puff pastry, éclairs made with choux pastry, or fresh fruit tarts. It is usually put into a tart shell after the shell is baked and covered with fresh or poached fruit. It will keep for 2 weeks in the refrigerator. Always whisk it before spreading it. Some cooks lighten it by folding in lightly whipped cream.

Fresh Fig and Plum Tart

Who would have thought that these two beautiful purple fruits of summer would go so well together? They certainly do in this pastry shell with an almond filling called frangipane.

FOR THE DOUGH
2½ cups flour
¼ cup sugar
½ pound (2 sticks) butter, cut in 1-inch pieces
⅛ teaspoon salt
1 egg yolk
½ teaspoon vanilla extract

FOR THE FRANGIPANE
¾ cup (4 ounces) almonds, unblanched
2 tablespoons sugar
1 egg
1 teaspoon flour
4 tablespoons (½ stick) butter
2 teaspoons port or brandy plus one teaspoon for the glaze

FOR THE FRUIT
1 pound fresh figs, halved vertically
1 pound fresh plums, halved and pitted

FOR THE GLAZE
½ cup red currant jelly

To make the short crust dough, combine the flour, sugar, butter, and salt in the bowl of a food processor fitted with the blade. Pulse until the mixture resembles coarse bread crumbs. Mix the egg, vanilla, and 2 tea-spoons cold water together and add to the dough. Process until the dough comes together to form a ball. Press the dough into a 10-inch tart pan with a removable bottom. Prick the dough two or three times with a fork and chill.

Preheat the oven to 375 degrees.

To make the frangipane filling, combine the almonds with the sugar in the bowl of a food processor and process until the almonds are finely ground. Add the egg, butter, and 2 teaspoons of the port and process for a minute more. Spread the mixture on the bottom of the cooled tart shell. Arrange the figs and plums cut side up in alternating circles over the filling, covering the filling with as much fruit as possible. Bake on the upper rack of the oven until the tips of the fruit are browned, about 35 minutes. Cool on a rack.

To make the glaze, heat the jelly with the 1 teaspoon port in a small saucepan over moderate heat until melted. Transfer the tart to a round serving platter, and with a pastry brush, lightly coat the fruit with the glaze.

SERVES 8

The best way to remove a tart from a pan with a removable bottom is to put the tart over a cylindrical jar or container and let the ring fall on the counter. It is best to slide the tart onto a flat plate without the round from the pan, but sometimes this is not possible.

Traditional glazes for tarts and other pastries are apricot or red currant jam melted with a little water, fortified wine, or liqueur. The kind of jam used depends on the color of the fruit.

FLOUR

ALTHOUGH FLOUR can be made from any dried grain, vegetable, or tuber such as barley, rye, corn, or potato, the term "flour" usually refers to a substance ground from wheat. The whole grain called wheat berry is made up of the germ, the endosperm, and the bran. When wheat berries are ground, they turn into whole wheat flour. When this is sieved, the germ and the bran are removed, leaving what is commonly called white flour, which is slightly yellow in color. In time the flour will whiten naturally, but often it is artificially bleached white to accelerate the process.

This fine white powder called "flour" is, in fact, the ground endosperm, which is about 67 percent carbohydrate, 9 percent to 14 percent protein, and the rest water. The amount of protein in flour can vary according to what kind of wheat is used. Generally, wheat from the northern United States and Canada is hard wheat, and wheat from the South is soft wheat. Soft wheat has less protein than hard wheat. What the mills do is blend flour from different wheats so that the amount of protein is consistent. This is done so their flour will work the same way every time it is used.

Since the bread baker wants flour with lots of potential for producing gluten, bread flour usually has 14 percent to 18 percent protein. Remember, when exercised, the protein in flour turns to gluten. On the other hand, pastry cooks and bakers don't want their cakes and pastries to be strong and elastic, so cake flour has about 9 percent protein. For the rest of us who don't keep different containers of flour, mills make all-purpose flour with about 12 percent protein.

When flour is refined, it has a long shelf life. When it is made of whole wheat, it should be stored in the refrigerator; the fat from the germ makes it more perishable than white flour.

Upside-Down Caramelized Apple Tart
(*Tarte Tatin*)

FOR THE FRUIT
¼ pound (1 stick) butter
1 cup sugar
2½ pounds green apples, such as Granny
   Smith or pippins, peeled, cored, and
   thickly sliced

FOR THE DOUGH
1⅔ cups flour
⅛ teaspoon salt
9 tablespoons cold butter
1 egg yolk

FOR THE GARNISH
¾ cup heavy cream
Sugar
1 teaspoon vanilla extract
Almond extract (a few drops)
⅓ cup sliced almonds

To caramelize the apples, spread 4 tablespoons of the butter in the bottom of a heavy iron or copper 10-inch pan. Sprinkle with ½ cup of the sugar and press into the apples. Sprinkle the apples with the remaining ½ cup sugar and dot with the remaining 4 tablespoons of butter. Cover the pan and cook it over high heat for 5 minutes. Remove the cover and cook over moderate heat until the sugar begins to turn yellow (caramelizes), about 15 minutes.

To make the pastry, combine the flour and salt in a bowl. Cut in the butter with a pastry cutter until the mixture resembles oatmeal flakes. In a small bowl, mix the egg yolk with 3 to 5 tablespoons water. Pour the egg mixture into the middle of the flour mixture and stir, holding the fork straight up and down. Bring the mixture together with the fingers of one hand. Knead the dough across a board or counter 3 or 4 times to get the dough to come together. Wrap in waxed paper, press into a patty, and chill for 20 minutes.

Preheat the oven to 350 degrees.

When the apples are ready, roll out the dough on a lightly floured board, roll it back onto the rolling pin, and unroll it over the apples. Tuck the corners in all around the edge of the skillet, and quickly put the skillet on the top rack of the oven and bake until lightly browned on top, about 35 minutes.

To whip the cream, place the cream in a bowl and beat it with a whisk until it holds soft peaks. Add sugar to taste, the vanilla, and almond extract.

To serve the tart, invert the tart onto a round serving plate when it is still warm. Do this by putting the plate on top of the pan and turning both the plate and the pan at the same time in a down-up-down motion. If all the apples don't come out, use a metal spatula to patch them into the dessert. If the tart is not caramelized enough, sprinkle it with additional sugar and run it under the broiler for a minute or two. Serve with the sweetened whipped cream on the side.

SERVES 8

There are two ways to get the rolled-out dough into the pan. One is to roll it back onto the rolling pin, holding it with your thumbs to keep it from unrolling, and laying it across the pan. The other way is to fold the dough in half, fold it in half again, and put the point of the dough in the middle of the pan and unfold it. Either way, it is important not to stretch the dough or it will shrink when it bakes in the oven. In the case of this tarte Tatin, it is important to work quickly because the pan holding the apples is hot and will start to melt the pastry. Don't worry how it looks; the pastry will be on the bottom when it is served.

Whenever you are serving a tart or a cake at the table, do not divide it exactly according to how many people are at the table. Cut into the tart and remove the wedges of the tart with a knife and a pie server without touching the tart with your fingers.

Lemon Tarts
(Tartes aux Citrons)

The first time I went to Paris, I got so excited about the windows of the pâtisseries that I overlooked the little yellow tarts down in the corner. These are lemony, buttery tarts that are a specialty of Paris. I like to put candied lemon slices on top to show what they are.

FOR THE DOUGH
3⅓ cups flour
¼ teaspoon salt
2 tablespoons sugar
½ pound (2 sticks) plus 2 tablespoons cold
    butter, cut into small pieces
1 egg yolk

FOR THE TOPPING
1 cup sugar
2 lemons, thinly sliced

FOR THE FILLING
3 egg yolks
3 eggs
1 cup sugar
½ cup lemon juice
1 tablespoon grated lemon zest
1 teaspoon cornstarch
7 tablespoons butter, melted and cooled

To make the dough, combine the flour, salt, and sugar in a medium-size bowl. Cut in the cold butter with a pastry cutter until the mixture resembles oatmeal flakes. In a small bowl, using a fork, mix the egg yolks with 8 to 10 tablespoons cold water. Stir this into the flour mixture with the fork held straight up and down. Bring the mixture together with the fingers of one hand. Put the dough on a board and knead gently to get it to come together roughly; this is called *fraisage.* To do this, use the heel of your hand to spread the mixture across the board or counter. Bring the dough together with a pastry scraper and press it quickly with your hands. (Do not press as if you are making a snowball. You'll warm the dough.) Repeat three or four times until the dough comes together. Wrap it in waxed paper, press it together in a patty, and chill for 20 minutes.

To candy the lemon slices, put the sugar in a small saucepan with 1 cup water. Stir gently while the sugar dissolves and the mixture comes to a boil. With a thin knife cut thin rounds from the lemons, discarding the ends. Slide the lemon rounds into the sugar syrup and poach gently until the rinds are slightly translucent, about 15 minutes. Remove the lemon slices with tongs and put on a plate.

Preheat the oven to 375 degrees.

To line six 4-inch tart tins with removable bottoms, roll out the dough on a lightly floured surface, always moving it around to make sure it will come off the counter. When the dough is ⅛ inch thick, cut rounds with a sharp knife about an inch larger than the tins. Place these gently in the tins, laying them on the bottoms of the tins without stretching the dough. Roll the rolling pin over the edges of the tins to cut off the excess dough. Prick the tarts once or twice with a fork straight up and down and transfer them to a baking pan. Chill for 5 to 10 minutes. Put a piece of parchment or waxed paper in the bottom of each tart, fill these with beans, rice, or pie weights, and bake on the top rack of the oven until the tarts are lightly golden around the edges, about 12 minutes. Remove the paper and the beans, and continue to bake until the bottom of the pastry shell is lightly golden, about 10 minutes more. Press the pastry down if it rises. Remove from the oven and chill immediately.

To make the filling, mix the 3 egg yolks and whole eggs, 1 cup sugar, lemon juice and zest, and cornstarch in a bowl with a wooden spoon. Stir in the melted butter. Pour the mixture into the cooled tart shells, no more than two-thirds full. Lay three lemon slices over each filled tart. Bake in an oven turned down to 325 degrees until the filling is set, about 15 minutes. Let cool on a rack for 10 minutes before unmolding. The best way to unmold tart tins with removable bottoms is over a small bottle such as a spice jar. (These tarts are best eaten the day they are made.)

SERVES 6

The purpose of the technique of baking pastry with a false filling is to get it to hold its shape without the sides falling in and the center puffing up. This is called to bake blind. At the cooking school we keep a large container of dried beans that are used over and over for baking blind.

Because there is so much butter and eggs in this lemon filling, it would be inappropriate to decorate these tarts or serve them with whipped cream.

❦

It is best not to use a whisk to mix the filling because bubbles would form. A wooden spoon is better.

Caramelized Almond Tart

Here is a tart we have been enjoying at Tante Marie's for many years. It was developed by Lindsey Shere, the beloved pastry chef and partner of Chez Panisse in Berkeley. Chez Panisse is a mecca for passionate cooks. For a double delight, serve this tart with Caramel Ice Cream (page 307).

FOR THE DOUGH
1 cup flour
1 tablespoon sugar
¼ pound (1 stick) butter
A few drops vanilla extract
A few drops almond extract
Salt

FOR THE TOPPING
¾ cup heavy cream
¾ cup sugar
A few drops almond extract
1 tablespoon Grand Marnier
1 tablespoon kirsch or amaretto
1 cup sliced almonds

Preheat the oven to 375 degrees.

To make the crust, combine in the food processor the flour, sugar, butter, vanilla and almond extracts, a few grains of salt, and 1 teaspoon cold water. Pulse until the mixture forms a ball. Press the dough into a 9-inch tart pan and chill. Save a teaspoon of the dough for patching. Bake in the oven until lightly browned, 7 to 10 minutes. Let cool on a rack and patch any cracks.

Increase the temperature of the oven to 450 degrees.

To make the filling, in a saucepan mix together the cream, sugar, almond extract, Grand Marnier, and kirsch. Heat this mixture, stirring, until the sugar melts, then stir in the almonds. Pour this nut mixture into the baked shell and put on the top rack in the oven for 15 to 20 minutes. Turn the oven down to 400 degrees and bake for another 15 minutes, turning the shell often so that the sugar mixture caramelizes evenly. When the filling is nicely browned, remove the tart from the oven and let cool on a rack for 5 minutes before removing from the pan.

The best-tasting almonds for cooking are unblanched. Sometimes they need to be blanched for aesthetic purposes, and sometimes a recipe calls for slivered or sliced almonds. Please don't use slivered or sliced almonds anytime a recipe calls for almonds, because they just don't taste as good as whole almonds. However, when sliced almonds are caramelized with cream and sugar, as in this recipe, they taste pretty good.

To remove the skins from the almonds, or blanch them, bring a pot of water to a boil, turn off the heat, and drop in the almonds. Take the almonds out of the water small batches at a time and squeeze the nuts out of the skins. If you drain a large amount all at once, they may start to dry out again and it won't be easy to remove the skins.

Tropical Fruit Tart

The French call them les fruits exotiques; *we call them tropical fruits. Whatever you call them, they look great mounded over almond filling in this open tart.*

FOR THE DOUGH
1¼ cups flour
2 tablespoons sugar
¼ pound (1 stick) cold butter
⅛ teaspoon salt
1 egg yolk
½ teaspoon vanilla

FOR THE FRANGIPANE
¾ cup (4 ounces) almonds, blanched
¼ cup sugar
¼ pound (1 stick) butter, softened
2 eggs
2 tablespoons flour
2 drops almond extract

FOR THE FRUIT
1 mango, peeled and sliced in ¼-inch slices
1 banana, peeled and sliced in ¼-inch slices
2 kiwis, peeled and sliced in ¼-inch slices
½ pint raspberries or strawberries, with stems removed
1 papaya, peeled and sliced in ¼-inch slices

FOR THE GLAZE
½ cup apricot jam

To make the short crust dough, combine the flour, sugar, butter, and salt in the bowl of a food processor fitted with the blade. Pulse until the mixture resembles coarse bread crumbs. Mix the egg with the vanilla and 2 teaspoons cold water, add to the dough with the machine running, and process until the dough comes together to form a ball. Press it into a 10-inch tart pan with a removable bottom. Prick the dough two or three times to prevent it from puffing in the oven. Chill for 20 minutes.

Preheat the oven to 375 degrees.

To make the frangipane filling, put the almonds and sugar in the bowl of a food processor and grind them to a fine powder. Add the butter, eggs, flour, and almond extract and process just until combined. Chill for 20 minutes.

Fill the tart shell with the frangipane filling, and bake on the top rack of the oven until the filling is firm to the touch and the pastry is golden, about 35 minutes. Remove from the oven and let cool on a rack.

To assemble the tart, take the tart out of the pan and transfer it to a round serving plate. Heat the apricot jam in a small saucepan with a tablespoon of cold water over low heat until melted. Paint the top of the almond filling with the apricot jam. Mound the fruit decoratively on the tart and paint the fruit with the glaze. This tart is best served the day it is made.   SERVES 8

This tart can easily be made into miniature tarts. To make these, press a tablespoon of the dough into the edges and up the sides of miniature tart tins (1½ inches in diameter), fill them no more than half full with the frangipane mixture, and bake them until they begin to shrink away from the edge of the pan. Let them cool on a rack and squeeze each tin gently to unmold. Put the miniature tarts on a serving platter. Paint them with apricot glaze and mound one fruit on each, for instance, a cluster of raspberries or a round of kiwi. It is best to have only one type of fruit in each tart. These can be served with tea or as part of a dessert buffet.

You can also make miniature tarts using prebaked shells. To prebake the shells, we press a tablespoon of the short crust dough into a miniature tart tin, then press another tin inside it so that the pastry holds its shape when baked. These bake for 15 minutes with the other tin inside and 5 minutes without. When they are cooled, they can be filled with lemon curd (page 302) or chocolate ganache (see pages 352 and 353). You can also put a teaspoon of raspberry or red currant jam in the bottoms of the prebaked shells and cover with caramelized walnuts (see page 339).

If making a selection of miniature tarts— say, raspberry, kiwi, lemon curd, chocolate ganache, and carmelized walnut—you will need to make additional batches of the short crust dough.

Of course, you don't have to make all five kinds of miniature tarts, but please don't mix the flavors. Lemon curd and chocolate ganache don't need to be covered with raspberries and kiwi.

Caramelized Walnut Tart

*I*f you love nuts, caramel, and almond filling,
you will adore this tart. This winter tart is so
rich, it is best for a celebration.*

FOR THE DOUGH
1¼ cups flour
2 tablespoons sugar
¼ pound (1 stick) cold butter
⅛ teaspoon salt
1 egg yolk
1 teaspoon vanilla extract

FOR THE FILLING
8 ounces almond paste
¼ pound (1 stick) butter
¼ cup sugar
2 eggs
2 tablespoons flour

FOR THE TOPPING
¾ cup sugar
1 tablespoon light corn syrup
4 tablespoons butter
¼ cup heavy cream
2 cups walnut pieces, lightly toasted

To make the short crust dough, combine the
flour, sugar, butter, and salt in the bowl of a
food processor fitted with the blade. Pulse
until the mixture resembles coarse bread
crumbs. Mix the egg yolk with the vanilla
and 2 teaspoons cold water and add to the
dough with the machine running. When the
dough comes together to form a ball, press it
into a 10-inch tart pan with a removable bottom. Prick the dough two or three times to
prevent it from puffing in the oven.

Preheat the oven to 375 degrees.

To make the filling, in a food processor or
with an electric mixer beat the almond paste
until light. Add the butter and sugar and continue beating. Add the eggs one at a time and
beat in the flour. As soon as the flour has been
added, stop the beating. Pour the filling into
the crust and bake on the top shelf of the oven
until the crust begins to come away from the
sides of the pan, about 30 minutes. Let cool on
a rack and unmold onto a round serving platter.

To make the topping, heat the sugar, corn
syrup, and enough water to make a paste in a
medium-size saucepan over low heat. Stir to
mix. Swirl the pan from time to time until
the sugar has dissolved. Increase the heat to
high and let it boil, without stirring, until the
sugar syrup turns a golden caramel color. Off
the heat, add the butter and cream. Be careful
because the mixture may bubble up. Stir in
the toasted walnuts with a wooden spoon.
Continue stirring until the mixture just
begins to lose its shine. Quickly spread the
caramel over the top of the tart. Do not
refrigerate.

SERVES 8

*A caramel coating will weep in the refrigerator.
There is no danger in keeping desserts with lots
of sugar at room temperature.*

*Never try to toast more than 2 cups of nuts at a
time. If you forget them and they burn, you
have wasted too many nuts. Always toast them
in batches.*

Pastry Ring Filled with Praline and Strawberries
(Gâteau Paris-Brest)

A gâteau Paris-Brest is usually a ring of choux pastry filled with praline-flavored buttercream. Here is my adaptation of this famous dessert—I flavor whipped cream with praline and add strawberries. It's light, airy, and delicious!

FOR THE DOUGH
¼ pound (1 stick) butter
⅛ teaspoon salt
1 cup flour
4 eggs
3 tablespoons sliced almonds

FOR THE FILLING
½ cup hazelnuts and/or almonds
1 cup sugar
2 cups heavy cream
1 pint small red strawberries, stems removed
Confectioners' sugar for dusting

Preheat the oven to 400 degrees. Line a baking sheet with parchment and draw the outline of a 10-inch circle on it. Turn the paper over.

To make the choux pastry, melt the butter with the salt and a cup of water in a small heavy saucepan over moderate heat. Do not let the mixture come up to a boil until the butter melts. When the butter has melted, increase the heat and let boil for a minute.

Turn off the heat and dump in the flour all at once. Beat it vigorously against the edges of the pan with a wood spatula or spoon. The more you beat the mixture, the higher it will rise in the oven. Let cool for 10 minutes. Break the eggs into a bowl and mix them with a fork until you can't distinguish yellow from white. Add a small amount of egg to the dough and beat it against the edge of the pan, slowly at first. Continue adding egg and beating until all the egg has been incorporated. At this point the mixture should stick to the edges of the pan and be hard to stir. If this point has not been reached, beat up another egg and start adding it until the desired consistency has been reached. Fill a large pastry bag fitted with a 1-inch plain tube with the dough. Squeeze from the top and starting at 12 o'clock, pipe half the dough in a ring on the paper outline. Pipe another ring on top of the first. Always aim to attach the top ring to the outside of the bottom ring, because it will try to fall toward the inside. When ready to stop pressing the pastry out of the bag, cut it off with a kitchen knife. Sprinkle the top with the almonds. Turn up the oven to 425 degrees and bake until the dough is very dark and puffy, about 50 minutes. Turn off the oven. Remove the pan from the oven and with a serrated knife make four slits around the ring horizontally. Return to the oven for 10 minutes to dry the inside of the ring of choux pastry.

To make the praline, remove the skins from the hazelnuts and/or the almonds and roast them on a baking sheet at 350 degrees until lightly toasted. Transfer to a lightly oiled baking sheet. Heat the sugar in a small heavy saucepan with enough water to make a paste. Stir to mix. Swirl the mixture over low heat without stirring until the sugar dissolves. Turn up the heat and let it boil, without stirring, until the sugar turns a dark chestnut brown. It should be smoking at this point. Quickly pour this over the toasted nuts. When completely cool, crack the praline with a meat pounder and put it in the food processor to grind to a powder.

To whip the cream, put it in a metal bowl and beat with a sauce whisk or an electric beater until it holds firm peaks. Fold in the praline powder.

To assemble, cut the ring of choux paste in half horizontally with a serrated knife. Transfer the top, without turning, to a board and transfer the bottom, without turning, to a serving platter. (If you don't turn either part of the pastry, the top and bottom should line up when reassembled.) With a small spoon, remove and discard any damp dough in the bottom. Spoon the praline-flavored whipped cream into the bottom ring. Arrange the strawberries all around the cream and cover with the top ring. Press the top lightly and sieve over it a light coating of confectioners' sugar. To serve, cut into 2-inch pieces with a serrated knife.   SERVES 8

The technique described here for making choux pastry is how it should be made whether it is to be deep-fried or baked or used for a savory or sweet dish. This is the dough used for éclairs, profiteroles, religieuses, and many other kinds of pastries.

To remove the skins from almonds, drop them into a pan of boiling water, turn off the water, and let them sit for 5 minutes before removing them a few at a time from the water and slipping off the skins.

To remove the skins from hazelnuts, place them on a baking sheet and bake them at 350 degrees for 10 to 15 minutes, then rub in a dish towel. Don't worry if all the brown skins don't come off.

Rectangular Tart Filled with Peaches and Blackberries

Here roasted peaches sit on top of a long tart of puff pastry, a beautiful presentation of some of the fruits of summer.

FOR THE TART SHELL
1 pound puff pastry (store-bought or homemade, page 385)
1 egg yolk
1 tablespoon heavy cream

FOR THE ALMOND FILLING
3 tablespoons soft butter
2 tablespoons sugar
¾ cup almonds, blanched

FOR THE FRUIT
4 ripe peaches
1 pint blackberries
4 tablespoons butter
2 tablespoons sugar

1 cup heavy cream to serve

To prepare the pan, line a baking sheet with a piece of foil. One side of the foil should be against the long side of the baking pan and the other should make an edging about 4 inches away. What you will have is a mold for the tart, about 4 inches wide and 16 inches long. This is to prevent the sides from falling over when the dough bakes. Make another mold on the other side of the pan.

To make the tart shell, roll out the dough on a lightly floured surface into a rectangle about ⅛ inch thick. With a sharp knife, cut it into two pieces 4 by 14 inches. Turn these over onto the foil molds. Brush the edges with water. Cut four strips of the dough ½ by 14 inches and place these along the sides of the rectangles to form a border. Prick the bottom of the shell all over with a fork (this is called docking). In a small bowl mix the egg yolk with the cream. Brush the trim with this egg glaze, being careful it doesn't run down the sides of the dough. Chill for 20 minutes. Preheat the oven to 425 degrees. Bake the dough in the top rack of the oven until the bottom is golden brown. Open the oven three or four times during the baking and press down the dough that rises in the middle to prevent the center from rising. Remove the tart shell from the oven and let cool on a rack.

To make the filling, mix together in a bowl the soft butter with the sugar and the ground almonds.

To cook the fruit, drop each peach into a pan of boiling water for 30 seconds, take it out with a slotted spoon, remove the skin, and cut each peach in half, discarding the pit. Melt the butter in a medium-size frying pan, lay the peach halves in it, sprinkle with sugar, and cook over medium-high heat on top of the stove for about 5 minutes. Turn over to cook on the other side. Toss in the blackberries. Cook, shaking the pan, until the fruit is slightly softened. Allow to cool slightly, then cut the peaches into thick slices.

To assemble, spread the filling over the two baked rectangular shells. Cover the center of the pastry entirely with the peaches and blackberries and their juices. Serve the tart warm with sweetened whipped cream on the side. SERVES 8

As with flaky pastry (pâte brisée) or sweet pastry (pâte sucrée), it is very important to bake puff pastry (pâte feuilletée) when the pastry is cold and the oven is hot. Otherwise, it won't rise properly.

Raspberry Vacherin

*T*his colorful, light layer cake has a perfect balance of texture and taste! The crisp sweetness of the meringue contrasts with the soft texture and the acid of the raspberries as well as the smoothness and blandness of the cream. It's a truly great dessert!*

FOR THE MERINGUE
6 egg whites
Salt
1½ cups sugar

FOR THE FILLING
1 cup heavy cream
½ pint fresh raspberries, picked over
  but not washed
Confectioners' sugar for dusting

Mint leaves for garnish

Preheat the oven to 250 degrees and line two baking sheets with parchment paper. On each sheet, draw 16 circles 3 inches in diameter, using a drinking glass as your guide. Turn the paper over onto the pans.

To make the meringue, combine the egg whites with a few grains of salt in the bowl of an electric mixer. Beat them slowly at first, then at a higher speed, until they are stiff and almost chunky and you can turn the bowl over your head without the whites falling out. Beat in the sugar a tablespoon at a time. Use a smidgen of meringue to glue each piece of parchment to the baking pan. Place a generous tablespoon of meringue in each circle on the paper. With a small metal spatula, spread each round roughly the size of the outline; the edges should be about ½ inch high, not thin. Make swirls on top of rounds. Bake until almost firm, about an hour. Let cool on the paper on a rack. Then peel off the paper from the baked meringues.

To prepare the cream, put it in a large bowl and beat it with a sauce whisk or an electric mixer until it can hold soft peaks.

To assemble, place eight of the less attractive meringue discs on a board and spread a thick layer of cream on each, saving a little for garnish. Divide the raspberries among the eight discs, reserving eight for garnish. (It is important that the raspberries show at the edges of the meringues.) Press the eight remaining discs on top. Sieve a light dusting of confectioners' sugar over the meringues. Place a smidge of cream in the middle of each vacherin, with a mint leaf and a raspberry as garnish. Transfer to individual dessert plates.

SERVES 8

Egg whites without any yolk in them can keep in a plastic container in the refrigerator for 3 to 4 weeks. You can pour them out in blobs that roughly equal one egg white. There are a generous 8 egg whites in a cup.

Meringues always weep a little in the oven, where the sugar syrup comes out. They will weep more if the oven is turned up during baking or if they are made on a humid day.

When a recipe calls for a metal spatula, I mean a straight, thin metal blade about 1 inch wide and 9 inches long. Sometimes pastry cooks use offset metal spatulas. These are different from the square metal piece of equipment angled on a handle called a pancake turner.

Hazelnut Dacquoise

In the 1980s all the famous food people stayed at San Francisco's Stanford Court Hotel. It was a great time! This is a dessert that was always served at the hotel's fine restaurant, Fournou's Ovens. It's still a very special treat.

FOR THE MERINGUE
¾ cup (4 ounces) almonds, blanched
2½ cups sugar
6 egg whites
Salt

FOR THE BUTTERCREAM
2 eggs
1 cup sugar
¾ pound (3 sticks) butter, cut in
    1-inch pieces
2 tablespoons coffee extract
½ cup finely chopped hazelnuts

2 tablespoons confectioners' sugar for dusting

Preheat the oven to 250 degrees. Line two baking sheets with parchment paper and on each sheet of paper trace a 10-inch circle. Turn the paper over onto the pans. Put the almonds and ¾ cup sugar in a blender or food processor and finely grind.

To make the meringues, put the egg whites with a few grains of salt in the bowl of an electric mixer and, with the whisk attachment, beat them until they are stiff and you can turn the bowl over your head without their falling out. With the machine running, add the remaining 1¾ cups sugar, a table-

spoon at a time. Remove the bowl from the electric mixer and with a large rubber spatula loosely fold in the ground almond mixture. (Thorough mixing is not necessary.) Put the meringue mixture in a large pastry bag fitted with a 1-inch round tip. Pipe two solid discs of meringue in a coil, starting on the outside of the outline. It is important to let the meringue fall onto the paper—do not press it down. Bake until the meringues are almost firm, about an hour. Switch the pans on the shelves halfway through the cooking time. Remove the pans from the oven and let cool on racks for about 15 minutes before carefully peeling off the parchment.

To make the buttercream, put the eggs in the bowl of an electric mixer and beat with the whisk attachment for a minute. Heat the sugar with enough water to make a paste in a small saucepan and stir to mix. Cook, swirling from time to time, over low heat until the sugar is dissolved. Turn up the heat and continue to boil, without stirring, until the sugar syrup reaches 242 degrees on a candy thermometer. With the mixer running moderately high, slowly pour the sugar syrup into the eggs. Continue beating the mixture until the bowl is cool to the touch, at least 10 minutes. Add the butter, one piece at a time. As each one is absorbed, add another. When all the butter is incorporated, beat in the coffee extract with a few grains of salt. If the mixture begins to separate, stop adding the coffee extract and keep beating.

To assemble, put the less attractive disc of meringue on a 9-inch round of cardboard. (If the discs of meringue are uneven, you can saw the edges with a serrated knife to make them even.) Spread all the coffee buttercream over the meringue and place the other layer on top. Smooth the buttercream around the outside edge. Lift the cake in one hand and press the chopped hazelnuts around the edge with the other hand. Sieve a light layer of confectioners' sugar over the top. Place the dacquoise on a round serving platter in the refrigerator for 30 minutes before serving.

SERVES 6 TO 8

The best-tasting coffee extract is made by dissolving two tablespoons of instant espresso powder (not freeze-dried) in a tablespoon of hot water.

There are two ways of shaping meringue layer cakes: the more rustic way with a rubber spatula, as in raspberry vacherin, and the more professional way, described in the hazelnut dacquoise. Take care when using a pastry bag that the meringue doesn't lose a lot of air.

When making meringues, what you are doing is beating egg whites until they break down into millions of little bubbles. Adding the sugar slowly or folding it in helps keep the sugar in crystal form so that it doesn't liquefy. You can be sure that the meringue mixture will have too much liquid if you add the sugar before the egg whites are really stiff (too soon), or if you pour in the sugar all at once (too quickly).

Buttercream can be made in three different ways. This is the way I find most reliable. It is terribly important that the temperature of the sugar syrup be exact. If it is too hot, the mixture will crystallize when it is beaten. If it is not hot enough, the mixture will be runny. Buttercream is primarily a frosting or glaze, even though it is often used as a filling.

The reason nuts are ground with sugar is to keep the nuts from turning into nut butter.

Almond Génoise with Fresh Fruit and Raspberry Sauce

This is a wonderfully light almond cake covered with fresh fruit and served with a raspberry sauce. It looks and tastes great!

Generally génoise is not made with almond paste. This is simply a delicious variation.

To make these into individual cakes, cut rounds from the almond génoise with a 3-inch cutter and proceed with the recipe, mounding the fruit as described.

FOR THE CAKE
Butter for preparing the pan
½ cup flour
⅛ teaspoon salt
2 tablespoons almond paste
6 tablespoons sugar
2 whole eggs
1 egg yolk
½ teaspoon vanilla extract
½ teaspoon grated lemon zest
2 tablespoons butter, melted

FOR THE FRUIT
1 kiwi, peeled and sliced
1 banana, sliced
1 mango, sliced
½ pint strawberries or raspberries
¾ cup ground and toasted almonds

FOR THE GLAZE
½ cup apricot preserves

FOR THE SAUCE
10 ounces frozen raspberries

Preheat the oven to 350 degrees. Butter the sides of a 9-inch cake pan, put a round of parchment on the bottom, and butter that as well. Put the flour and salt in a sieve on a piece of waxed paper.

To make the génoise, put the almond paste in the bowl of an electric mixer and beat slowly for 1 to 2 minutes until soft. Add the 6 tablespoons of sugar and continue to beat until the mixture is smooth. Add the eggs and egg yolk and continue to beat until the mixture triples in volume, or until you can write an M in the mixture with the beater. Add the vanilla and lemon zest and beat until just blended. Remove the bowl from the mixer. Sift in the dry ingredients and fold them into the batter, using as few strokes as possible. Mix a large spoonful of the batter into the melted butter and fold that mixture back into the batter with no more than 15 strokes. Pour this cake batter into the prepared pan. Cook on the top rack of the oven until the cake is firm to the touch and pulls away from the sides of the pan, about 35 minutes. Cool on a rack for 10 minutes before inverting onto the rack.

To make the sauce, puree the raspberries in a food processor until smooth. Strain the mixture through a fine sieve to remove the seeds. Add sugar to taste.

To assemble, put the cake top side down on a flat serving plate. Brush what is now the top and sides with the melted preserves. Mound the fresh fruit decoratively over the top of the cake. Press the almonds onto the sides of the cake.

To serve, put a spoonful of sauce on each

of six or eight dessert plates and put a wedge of the cake in the center.

SERVES 6 TO 8

A génoise is a type of French cake with the beaten whole eggs as the only leavener. It is very important that there be a minimum of folding in of the flour and melted butter so that the maximum amount of air remains in the egg yolk foam and will allow the cake to rise. If the génoise is overfolded, there will be a rubbery layer on the bottom where the butter has sunk.

There are two things you always need to do before baking a cake: preheat the oven and prepare the pans.

You can always tell that the cake is done when it pulls away from the sides of the pan and is firm to the touch.

Torta Regina with Chocolate and Caramel Sauces

When Emily Luchetti was the pastry chef at Stars, she taught us how to make this cake flavored with chocolate, hazelnuts, and orange zest. The presentation is clever because it hides the fact that this cake is really easy to make and takes no decorating expertise. Wedges of chocolate-orange cake are overlapped on a plate and served with vanilla bean ice cream, decorated with chocolate and caramel sauces— what could be more delicious?

FOR THE CAKE
Butter for preparing the pan
1½ cups (8 ounces) hazelnuts, skins removed
5½ ounces bittersweet chocolate, chopped
1 teaspoon grated lemon zest
2 teaspoons grated orange zest
6 eggs, separated
½ cup sugar

FOR THE ACCOMPANIMENTS
Ice cream for serving
Chocolate sauce (recipe follows)
Caramel sauce (recipe follows)

Preheat the oven to 350 degrees. Butter the inside of a 9-inch round cake pan, line the bottom of the pan with a round of parchment paper, and butter the paper.

To prepare the flavoring, combine the hazelnuts, chocolate, and lemon and orange

zest in the bowl of a food processor fitted with the blade and process just until it is coarsely chopped.

To make the cake, put the yolks with half the sugar in the bowl of an electric mixer with the whisk attachment. Whisk on high speed until light yellow and doubled in volume, about 3 minutes. Decrease the speed to low, add the nut mixture, and mix to combine. (The batter will be very stiff at this point.)

Put the egg whites in a clean bowl of the electric mixer. With a clean whisk attachment, beat the egg whites at medium speed until frothy, about 2 minutes. Increase the speed to high and whip the whites until soft peaks form. Continue to whip while adding the remaining ¼ cup of sugar, a tablespoonful at a time. Whip until the whites are stiff and shiny, no more. Fold half of the egg whites into the chocolate/egg yolk batter. When the mixtures are almost combined, fold in the remaining whites. Pour the batter into the prepared pan and bake until a skewer or toothpick inserted in the center comes out clean, about 25 minutes. Cool the cake on a rack for 10 minutes before removing it from the pan. This cake can be stored covered with plastic wrap in the refrigerator for up to a week or in the freezer for up to a year.

To serve, cut the cake into 8 wedges. Cut each wedge in half horizontally with a serrated knife. Crisscross the two wedges on individual dessert plates cut sides up, put a scoop of vanilla ice cream on the plate, and drizzle caramel and chocolate sauces over the top. The best way to do this is with plastic squirt bottles filled with the two sauces.

SERVES 8

The texture you want in this cake is rough, with the nuts, chocolate, and orange zest identifiable. Therefore, it is important not to process them too much in the food processor.

The best store-bought vanilla ice cream is Hä n-Dazs. If you want to make your own, use the Caramel Ice Cream recipe (page 307), but leave out the caramel flavoring and add vanilla.

The reason desserts served in restaurants are often served on chocolate or caramel sauce, or even a blob of whipped cream, is to prevent the dessert from sliding around as it is brought to the table.

CHOCOLATE SAUCE

1½ cups heavy cream
10 ounces bittersweet or semisweet chocolate,
chopped

Pour the cream into a heavy saucepan over low heat to warm. Remove the pan from the heat and stir in the chocolate. Cover and let sit for 5 minutes. Stir until smooth.

CARAMEL SAUCE

1 cup sugar
1 cup heavy cream, at room temperature
4 tablespoons (½ stick) butter, at room
temperature

Combine the sugar in a heavy, medium-size saucepan with enough water to make a paste. Stir to mix. Swirl the pan from time to time over low heat until the sugar is dissolved. Increase the heat to high and let the mixture boil until it begins to turn color. At this point watch the mixture very carefully. When the sugar syrup is golden, the color of a maple butcher block, remove the pan from the heat and add the cream and butter. Stir to mix and let the sauce sit for 30 minutes.

Both chocolate and caramel sauces can be kept for weeks in the refrigerator.

Queen of Macadamia Torte

*I*t was Julia Child and friends who brought us the concept of queen of nuts cakes (Reine de Sheba), and it was her partner Simone Beck who took it one step further to make this Queen of Macadamia nut cake. It is a kind of French cake that is so rich you need serve only a small wedge!

FOR THE CAKE
8 ounces bittersweet or semisweet
*   chocolate, chopped*
4 eggs, separated
¼ pound (1 stick) butter, softened, plus
*   some for coating the pan*
5 ounces macadamia nuts, rinsed
*   if salty*
⅓ cup potato starch
½ cup sugar

FOR THE GLAZE
6 tablespoons bittersweet or semisweet
*   chocolate, chopped*
4 tablespoons (½ stick) butter, softened
1 tablespoon corn syrup

Preheat the oven to 375 degrees. Butter the inside of a 9-inch cake pan, line the bottom of the pan with parchment paper, and butter the paper as well.

To make the cake base, combine the 8 ounces chocolate with ⅓ cup water in a stainless steel bowl set over a pot of simmering water, making sure the water does not touch the bottom of the bowl. When the chocolate is melted and smooth, remove the bowl from the heat and stir in the egg yolks, one at a time. Place the bowl back over the pot of water and stir until the mixture thickens slightly, about 3 minutes. Remove the bowl from the heat and stir in the butter until the mixture is smooth.

To prepare the nuts, put them on a baking pan in the oven. Cook for 6 to 8 minutes, shaking the sheet from time to time, until the nuts are lightly browned. Coarsely chop 5 to 6 of the nuts and set them aside for garnish. When the remaining nuts are cooled, place them in a food processor with the potato starch and ¼ cup of the sugar. Process the nut mixture until it is fine and stir it into the chocolate mixture.

Whisk the egg whites with a few grains of salt in a clean copper bowl with a balloon whisk until they can hold soft peaks. Sprinkle the remaining ¼ cup of sugar into the whites a tablespoon at a time and continue beating until the whites are stiff and glossy. Carefully fold the meringue into the chocolate mixture with a wire whisk. Pour the batter into the prepared pan and bake until the cake has puffed slightly and a toothpick inserted into the center comes out with just a slightly wet crumb, about 25 minutes. Allow the cake to cool on a rack for at least 45 minutes before removing it from the pan.

To make the glaze, combine the 6 ounces of chocolate with the ½ stick of butter and the corn syrup in a stainless steel bowl set over a pot of simmering water, making sure the water is not touching the bottom of the bowl. Cook until the mixture is fully melted and smooth. Remove the bowl from the heat and allow the glaze to cool for about a minute. Invert the cake onto a rack set over a baking sheet and remove the parchment paper. Pour the glaze through a sieve over the top of the cake. Run a flat metal spatula across the cake in no more than four different directions to spread the glaze evenly over the top and down the sides of the cake. It is acceptable to patch the sides of the cake with the chocolate that has fallen into the pan. Do not go back over the top or it will become dull. Decorate the rim of the cake with the reserved chopped nuts. (This cake will keep, covered by a bowl, for up to a week at room temperature.) SERVES 8

When you make a cake with lots of ingredients such as brandy, walnuts, and apricots, you can use a lesser-quality chocolate. But when the recipe has fewer ingredients the quality of the chocolate is more noticeable. This cake can easily be made with Callebaut, a reliable Belgian cooking chocolate. The difference between semi-sweet and bittersweet varies with different manufacturers and is so minimal that you can use either.

Using potato starch, rice flour, or cornstarch instead of white flour will give the cake a smaller crumb. All three are more pure forms of starch than all-purpose, cake, or pastry flour.

You know the chocolate has seized when it lumps together and appears greasy. To save it, add a considerable amount of hot water, at least half a cup, from the double boiler and stir until smooth.

I recommend always beating egg whites for soufflés in a copper bowl with a balloon whisk because it's very difficult to overbeat egg whites in a copper bowl. However, when making meringue (egg whites and sugar), it's all right to overbeat the whites a little. An electric mixer does a better job when you start adding sugar, as the mixture becomes very heavy.

Nut Meringue Layered with Praline, Coffee, and Ganache
(Gâteau Marjolaine)

M*any recipes exist for this spectacular dessert, a nut meringue layered with praline, coffee, and ganache made famous at Fernand Point's Restaurant de la Pyramide near Lyon. I think this is one of the best! It's a rectangular cake of meringue-like pastry, layered with the fillings of three colors. The cake is left unfrosted at the ends to show off the distinct layers. This is definitely a cake to make for special occasions!*

FOR THE CAKE
1 cup hazelnuts plus ½ cup for the praline, skinned and toasted (see page 93)
1 cup almonds plus ½ cup for the praline, blanched and toasted (see page 337)
1 cup sugar plus ½ cup for the praline
¼ cup flour
6 egg whites
Salt
2 tablespoons confectioners' sugar

FOR THE GANACHE
1½ cups heavy cream
6 ounces semisweet chocolate, chopped

FOR THE BUTTERCREAM
1 cup sugar
2 eggs
½ pound (2 sticks) butter
3 tablespoons coffee extract

Preheat the oven to 450 degrees. Generously butter an 11 by 18-inch Swiss jelly-roll pan lined with parchment, and butter the paper as well. Put the 1 cup hazelnuts and 1 cup almonds in a food processor with a cup of the sugar and the flour and finely grind.

To make the nut meringue, combine the egg whites with a few grains of salt in the bowl of an electric mixer with the whip attachment and whisk them until they are stiff but not dry. With a large rubber spatula, fold the nut mixture into the egg whites; it is better to leave some of the nut mixture distinguishable than to overmix, as it will be further mixed when spread out. Spread the mixture in the prepared pan. Sift the confectioners' sugar over the top and bake until slightly firm to the touch, about 7 minutes. Invert the meringue immediately onto a fresh sheet of parchment paper and let cool. Cut the cooled meringue widthwise into four equal strips.

To make the chocolate ganache, heat the cream in a small, heavy saucepan over moderately high heat for 2 minutes. Remove the pan from the heat and stir in the chocolate until the mixture is smooth. Chill.

To make the praline, put the remaining hazelnuts and almonds on a lightly oiled baking sheet. Place the ½ cup of the sugar with enough water to make a paste in a small saucepan over low heat. Swirl the pan from time to time until the sugar has dissolved. Increase the heat to high and boil without stirring until the mixture turns a dark brown color and is beginning to smoke. Immediately pour this over the nuts and let cool. When cool, break up the praline into 1-inch pieces and put them in the bowl of a food processor. Blend to a fine powder.

To make the buttercream, combine a cup of the sugar with ½ cup water in a medium-size saucepan. Swirl the pan over low heat until the sugar has dissolved. Turn up the heat and boil, without stirring, until it reaches the soft-ball stage, 238 degrees on a candy thermometer. While the sugar is cooking, put the eggs in the bowl of an electric mixer with the whip attachment and beat briefly. As soon as the sugar reaches the desired temperature, turn on the mixer and pour the syrup in a thin, steady stream into the eggs. Continue beating the mixture until it is thick and the bowl is cool to the touch, about 10 minutes. When the mixture is cool, beat in the butter a tablespoon at a time. The mixture will have a thick frosting consistency when it is made properly. Divide the buttercream evenly into two bowls. Add the coffee extract to one bowl and ½ cup of the praline powder to the other bowl. (The remaining praline powder can be stored in a jar at room temperature for another use.) If the buttercream is too soft to spread, chill it.

To assemble the cake, finely chop the remaining ½ cup of nuts. Place a strip of meringue on a serving platter. Tuck short pieces of waxed paper under the edges of the meringue to cover the plate to keep it clean. Spread the praline buttercream in a thick layer on the first, making sure not to round off the edges. Cover with another strip of meringue, pressing down to square it off. Spread half the chocolate ganache over this layer. Add another strip of meringue on top, pressing to square it off. Spread the coffee buttercream on this layer. Top with the final strip of meringue, once again pressing to square it off. Cover the top and two long sides of the cake with half the remaining chocolate ganache. Put the rest of the ganache in a small pastry bag fitted with a ¼-inch star tube. Pipe a ridge of small shells down both sides of the top of the cake. Press the remaining nuts into the long sides of the cake. With a serrated knife, cut off the ends of the cake to show the layers. Each layer should be at least ½ inch high. Remove the pieces of waxed paper carefully. Chill the cake for at least 30 minutes before serving. Serve by cutting ¾-inch-thick slices and laying them flat on dessert plates. SERVES 8

*To pipe decorations onto any dessert, drop a tip into the bottom of a cloth pastry bag. Fold 2 or 3 inches of the top back over one of your hands to make a collar. Using the little finger of that hand or your arm against the bowl of the mixture, reach into the bowl with a rubber spatula and lift out a spoonful of the mixture. Put this deep into the bag, cleaning off the spatula by pressing it against the hand under the collar. Do not fill the bag above the edge of the collar; you can always refill it. To pipe, close the top of the bag over the mixture, and press all the mixture down to the tip end. Pipe the first blob of mixture back into the bowl to get out any air bub-*bles. *Hold the top of the bag twisted in one hand and guide it with the other. The bottom hand should have its thumb down. Do not squeeze with this hand, only with the top hand. Look at where you are piping from, in front of your hands, not behind.*

To make small shells, hold the bag straight up and down about ½ inch from the dessert. Squeeze from the top, push the bag away from you so the ganache falls on itself, stop squeezing, then pull the bag toward yourself. Repeat a little closer to yourself so that the shells overlap in a line. It is a good idea to practice these on waxed paper before trying it on the finished desserts.

The technique described here is how you always make ganache. Chocolate is so dense that all it needs is some thickened cream to make it into a filling. Ganache is technically a filling for such things as cakes, tarts, and the centers of chocolate candies, even though it is often used as a glaze or frosting.

It is recommended to decorate the Marjolaine with chopped nuts rather than the remaining praline because all the sugar in the praline will make it watery.

BREADS, COOKIES, AND CHOCOLATES

WHAT I HAVE TRIED to do in this book is to organize it according to a menu. You might have an hors d'oeuvre to nibble on before dinner. You would usually have a first course, a main course, and dessert. The first course could be something like vegetables in vinaigrette or soup, salad, pasta, or risotto. The main course might be seafood, poultry, meat, pasta, risotto, or a vegetable stew. Dessert could be fruit, custard, tarts, or cakes. A dinner would be quite memorable were you to offer home-made bread with the first course or the main meal (not before) or a plate of cookies and/or confections after the meal. Breads, cookies, and chocolate are just the little extras you might want to offer your guests.

If you really think about it, there is nothing so special in the sharing of your-self with others as cooking for them. Whether it is as simple as throwing a steak on a grill or as complex as spending hours and days preparing for a celebration, the fact that you are preparing food for your family and friends is what makes you a welcome member of a civilized society.

Don't ever worry about whether your food is good enough or others will like it; it is enough that you care. The giving of your-self through food is so very important. Sharing meals when people sit at a table and have conversation is what separates us from wild animals, which just eat when and where they find food. I hope you enjoy learning to cook through this book and that you have fun cooking everything from hors d'oeuvres to chocolates.

Breads

Bread is alive—it has a soul, and it is dif-ferent from any other food we make or cook (except wine)! It knows whether it is being handled by human hands or machine; it knows whether it is being made with loving care; and it gives great pleasure to the baker who nurtures his or her loaf from beginning to end, to anyone smelling the aroma of bread baking in the oven, and to the diner who may smear warm slices of bread with butter and jam, or layer it with meats and cheeses, or soak up the juices of a stew with it. Is bread the

355

staff of life? I don't know; however, it is certainly one of the great pleasures of life!

What we call bread comes in a variety of forms. There are flatbreads, with no leavener or very little, such as lahvosh, pita, and matzo. There are quick breads leavened by baking soda or baking powder such as banana bread and cranberry bread. When people talk about breads, they are mostly talking about yeast breads. Yeast breads are almost always made with wheat flour (white or whole wheat), salt, water, and yeast.

Sometimes bakers add specialty flours, such as rye, buckwheat, oat, and corn. Generally, with flour made from grains other than wheat, you need to always have a percentage of wheat flour for the yeast to work and the gluten to develop. Yeast essentially eats the flour—it loves refined white flour from wheat.

A fundamental point you need to understand in bread baking is that yeast is essentially a living bacterium; it needs warmth, moisture, and food to grow. The food can be in the form of sugar, but mostly it is flour. Yeast comes in several forms: fresh (or cake) yeast; active dry yeast; instant yeast; rapid-rise yeast; and in natural form from things like grape skins.

What the yeast does in a warm moist environment is eat the endosperm of the wheat (the carbohydrate) and produce bubbles of carbon dioxide. Yeast is very hardy. Once it has been activated and has food, it will grow and grow. Heat kills it. Most of the rising occurs in the oven, just before the yeast dies and the bread begins to bake.

The other important point to understand is that when you mix and then knead the ingredients in yeast bread made with wheat flour, the protein in the flour changes to gluten, which gives the bread its elasticity. A good loaf of bread is exercised until it is very elastic and thus holds its shape and retains the bubbles produced by the yeast. There is not enough protein in specialty flours to give the bread elasticity, which is why breads such as rye contain some wheat flour. It is much easier for yeast to consume the flour if the bran and germ have been removed. That is why it takes longer to make a whole wheat bread that still contains the bran and germ.

It's important to always add the salt to the flour, not directly to the yeast, because too much salt will kill the yeast. The dough will rise nicely in a bowl covered with a dry towel or in a plastic container. (You have to keep it covered to prevent a dry crust from forming on the outside.) A warm place for the bread to rise could be in a gas oven with a pilot light or an electric oven with a pan of hot water underneath. A sunny window does not provide even heat. The longer it takes to make the bread, the better will be the flavor and the texture. That is why I don't like rapid-rise yeast.

To punch down the dough, simply punch your fist into the middle of the dough, bring it into a ball on a counter or table, and begin to shape it—it is not necessary to knead at this point. Bread to be baked in bread pans needs less gluten development, in other words, less kneading. Bread to be baked free-form needs more kneading to make the dough elastic so it will hold its shape while baking in the oven. Bread baked directly on tiles or bricks will have a harder crust. So too will bread baked with moisture in the oven. That is why some home cooks go to elaborate lengths to put moisture in the oven in the first few minutes of baking and why some professional bakers have steam blown into the ovens.

The Big Problem

When beginners start to knead bread they add too much flour at first, making the dough too dry after it is kneaded. The moisture content of flour varies dramatically, depending on what wheat was used and where it has been stored. That is why most recipes don't give an exact measurement for flour and water. What you want to do is knead your bread, trying to add only enough flour to hold the dough together. As you knead it the dough will become dryer, so add only a little flour at a time. The less flour you use, the bigger the holes in the bread will be in the final product. A well-kneaded dough will feel smooth like a baby's bottom.

How to Make Bread Without a Recipe

Because yeast grows and expands, a tablespoon of granular yeast will raise 4 to 5 cups of flour. It will also raise 10 cups of flour. To make two loaves of bread, proof a spoonful of yeast with a pinch of sugar in a cup of hot water until it bubbles. Mix a tablespoon of salt into a bowl of flour. Substituting flour from other grains for part of this flour would be fine as long as you understand that the rising time will be longer. Into the center of the flour add enough warm water with the yeast to make dough. Mix, knead, let rise covered, in a warm place (about 65 degrees is best), punch down, shape, let rise again, and bake. Of course, you can add ingredients such as olive oil or sugar to the first ingredients and knead in ingredients such as raisins and nuts after the first rising. Just start doing it, and you'll see how much fun it is!

If you have to leave during the bread baking, just punch down the dough, shape it into a ball, place in a covered container at room temperature for 10 minutes, then place it in the refrigerator. The next day, remove the dough and let it sit at room temperature for at least 1½ hours before shaping the loaves. You can keep punching down and chilling the dough for a couple of days.

Traditional Scones

Scones are wonderful biscuits that were originally made in England, Ireland, and Scotland. They should be freshly made and served warm with clotted cream, thick cream, or butter with homemade jam, and tea.

3 cups flour
⅓ cup sugar
1½ teaspoons baking powder
¾ teaspoon baking soda
¾ teaspoon salt
12 tablespoons (1½ sticks) butter, cut into
    1-inch pieces and very cold
1½ cups buttermilk
¾ cup currants

FOR THE GLAZE
⅓ cup milk
1 tablespoon sugar

Preheat the oven to 400 degrees. Line a baking sheet with parchment.

To make the dough, sift the flour, sugar, baking powder, baking soda, and salt into a bowl, and drop in the butter. With a pastry cutter, cut the butter into the dry ingredients until the mixture resembles oatmeal flakes. Stir in the buttermilk and the currants using a fork held straight up and down until just blended; do not overmix. Turn the dough out onto a work surface and knead briefly just to bring it all together. Using the heel of one hand, gently press the dough into a round about ¾ inch thick. With a 3-inch fluted cutter, cut rounds of dough and transfer them to the baking pan. If there is excess dough, press it together and cut additional rounds.

To bake the scones, glaze the tops of each scone by brushing with a mixture of the milk and sugar. Bake on the top rack of the oven until the scones are very lightly browned, about 12 minutes. Let cool on a wire rack.

MAKES 12 SCONES

In Great Britain, the fancy tea served with sandwiches and cakes at four o'clock in the afternoon is called afternoon tea or cream tea. High tea is totally different; it is actually a full meal served as an early dinner.

Whipped heavy cream cannot substitute for clotted or thickened cream; if you have a source of thick cream like Devonshire, crème fraîche, or mascarpone to go with your scones, great. If not, butter is fine.

All biscuits, scones, and small cakes will be lighter if the dough is not handled too much.

You can vary this scone recipe by replacing the currants with fresh fruit such as plums or raspberries. Or you can add ½ cup grated Cheddar and a tablespoon of chopped scallions for savory scones.

Cornsticks

Y ou don't need to serve butter with these cornsticks because they have plenty of butter in them! You do, however, need those wonderful little iron pans that give you cornbread in the shape of corncobs. Bradley Ogden of The Lark Creek Inn and One Market fame taught us how to make these many years ago.

1 ear yellow corn
½ cup yellow cornmeal
½ cup flour
2 tablespoons sugar
1¼ teaspoons baking powder
1 teaspoon salt
5 tablespoons butter, melted, plus extra for coating the pans
1 cup minus 2 tablespoons heavy cream
1 egg, separated
Salt

Preheat the oven to 425 degrees. When the oven is hot, place empty cast-iron cornstick molds in the oven to warm. Remove the kernels from the ear of corn.

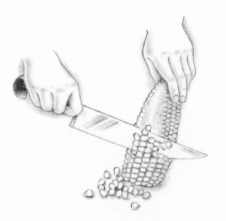

To make the dough, mix the corn kernels with the cornmeal, flour, sugar, baking powder, and salt in a large bowl. In a separate bowl, beat together the butter, cream, and egg yolk. Stir this mixture into the cornmeal mixture and blend well. Beat the egg white with a few grains of salt until stiff but not dry and gently fold it into the other ingredients.

To bake the cornsticks, remove the hot cornstick molds from the oven and coat them lightly with some butter. Spoon or pipe the mixture into the molds (they should be no more than two-thirds full) and return them to the oven. Bake for 15 to 20 minutes, until golden brown on the bottom and slightly pulled away from the sides of the pan. Serve warm.   MAKES 12 CORNSTICKS

Breadsticks

Jim Dodge was the talented pastry chef of the Stanford Court Hotel when he started teaching at Tante Marie's. Here is his recipe for olive oil breadsticks.

> 2 tablespoons dry active yeast
> 5 cups flour
> Sugar
> 1½ tablespoons salt
> ¾ cup olive oil plus some for coating the
>   pans
> Cornmeal for dusting
> Coarse salt

To proof the yeast, warm a measuring cup with tap water, then measure ¾ cup hot (115 to 120 degrees) water and mix in the yeast. (If using instant yeast, add a pinch of sugar.) Let the mixture sit until it bubbles up.

To make the dough, mix the flour and salt in the bowl of an electric mixer with your fingers. When the yeast has proofed, make a well in the center of the flour and pour in a cup of warm water and the olive oil. Pour the yeast mixture into the center and stir with a wooden spoon until roughly mixed. Place the bowl in the mixer with the dough hook and mix the dough on medium-low speed until the dough is elastic and pulls away from the sides of the bowl, about 7 minutes. (You can also knead the dough by hand on a lightly floured surface instead of in a mixer, for approximately 15 minutes.) Either way, shape the dough into a round, roll it over in a lightly oiled bowl, cover with a towel, and put in a warm place to rise until doubled in bulk, about an hour.

Preheat the oven to 400 degrees and spread a light layer of cornmeal on two baking sheets.

To shape the dough, punch it down and roll it out into a log about 16 inches long on a board or counter. With a pastry scraper, cut off 1-inch pieces from the log. Roll each piece between your hands until it is about 16 inches long, and arrange the pieces ½ inch apart on the baking sheets. When all the breadsticks are done, lightly brush them with olive oil and sprinkle with coarse salt. Bake until they are lightly golden on the bottom, 12 to 15 minutes.

MAKES 30 TO 40 BREADSTICKS

You don't really have to let these breadsticks rise a second time because they are thin. Most of the rising happens in the oven. Although they can be baked a day or more ahead, they really are better eaten the day they are baked.

Zamboni

These wonderful little rounds of warm bread with a slight sprinkling of Parmesan and red pepper have nothing to do with the machine that smooths the ice at hockey games. It's just what I called them after eating them one afternoon at the Cheese Board in Berkeley!

2½ tablespoons dry active yeast
Sugar
6 cups flour
1 tablespoon salt
⅓ cup olive oil
2 tablespoons freshly grated Parmesan
Red pepper flakes
Coarse salt

To proof the yeast, warm a glass measuring cup with tap water, then measure ½ cup hot water (115 to 120 degrees) and mix in the yeast with a pinch of sugar. Let sit until bubbles form, about 10 minutes.

To make the dough, mix the flour and salt in a large bowl. Make a well in the center of the flour and pour into it 2 cups warm water. Stir the yeast mixture into the water and then into the flour mixture with a wooden spoon. Mix until the dough comes away from the edges of the bowl, and then turn it out onto a lightly floured work surface and knead until you have a smooth dough. Don't add more flour than is absolutely necessary. Make the dough into a round ball, roll it over in a lightly oiled bowl, cover with a dry towel, and place it in a warm place, free of drafts, to rise until doubled in bulk, about an hour.

To shape, punch the dough down. Put it onto a board or counter and shape it into a log about 2 inches wide. Cut the dough with a pastry scraper into 1-inch pieces. With the flat of your hand, roll a piece on the board to make it smooth and round and then stretch the dough to make smooth spheres, pinching the dough together underneath. Place these on a baking sheet sprinkled with cornmeal. Let rise, covered with a light cloth, for about 30 minutes.

Preheat the oven to 400 degrees.

Before baking, paint each round of dough with additional olive oil and sprinkle some Parmesan, a tiny bit of red pepper flakes, and a few grains of salt on each. Bake in the top third of the oven until golden brown on the bottom, about 20 minutes.

MAKES 8 ROLLS

For baking breads and cakes, convection ovens (or convection settings on a regular oven) work extremely well. The air is circulated, making the cooking temperature more even throughout the oven and allowing you to reduce the baking time by as much as 20 percent. If using the convection setting, make sure to check for doneness about three-quarters through the recommended baking time.

Whole Grain Breakfast Bread

There is much appeal in a loaf of home-made mixed grain bread with a lot of texture. You can either buy whole grains and grind them yourself in a wheat grinder or buy 5 Grain Rolled Cereal by Bob's Red Mill, which can be found at most quality grocery stores. Serve the bread with good butter and home-made jam!

2 tablespoons active dry yeast
Sugar
2 cups unbleached all-purpose flour
2 cups whole wheat flour
1 tablespoon salt
2 tablespoons honey
2 tablespoons dark brown sugar
*½ cup safflower or other vegetable oil plus
   additional for coating the pans*
*2½ cups 5 Grain Rolled Cereal or 2 cups
   7 Grain Hot Cereal plus ½ cup 5 Grain
   Rolled Cereal*

To proof the yeast, warm a measuring cup, then measure 1 cup hot (110 to 115 degrees) water. Stir in the yeast with a pinch of sugar and let rest until it is quite bubbly, about 10 minutes.

In a large bowl mix 2 cups of the all-purpose flour, the 2 cups whole wheat flour, and the salt. Make a well in the center of the flour and pour in a cup of warm water and the honey, brown sugar, and safflower oil. Pour the proofed yeast mixture into the center. Stir the liquids together with a wooden spoon. Bring in the flours and keep stirring until smooth. Cover the bowl and set it in a warm, draft-free place to rise until the dough is bubbly, about an hour. Stir in the cereal and mix until the dough begins to pull away from the sides of the bowl. Cover and let rest for 10 minutes. Dump the dough onto a board or a counter with a cup of the all-purpose flour next to it. Begin kneading by pushing the dough down, turning it, and pushing it down again. (Always toss the flour to be incorporated under the dough; don't sprinkle it on top because it may clump.) Use the cup of flour to keep a light film of flour on the board and your hands. You want to try to keep the dough as moist as possible. Continue kneading until the dough is smooth and elastic, at least 15 minutes. Shape the dough into a ball. Lightly oil a large bowl, put in the ball of dough, and turn it over so that the top of the dough is oiled. Cover the bowl with a dry towel and let it rise again in a warm place for 1 to 2 hours.

Return the dough to the board. Punch the dough once, then bring it into a mass again and cut it into two equal pieces. (It is not necessary to knead the dough again or add additional flour.) Shape the dough into free-form rectangles about 2 inches high. Put them on two lightly oiled baking sheets and cover with a light towel for 30 minutes. Paint the top of each loaf with water, scatter additional rolled cereal over the tops, and bake at 375 degrees until the bread feels firm to the touch, 30 to 45 minutes.

MAKES 4 SMALL LOAVES

If you use 7 Grain Hot Cereal in this bread, it will have a crunchier texture than if you use 5 Grain Rolled Cereal.

Breads made with whole grain always take longer to rise. Sugar helps the yeast to work faster, and oil slows it down. What yeast really likes best is refined white flour, so when baking with whole grain flour and meal, have patience.

When a recipe calls for flour, generally what is meant is refined white flour from wheat, although flour can be made from many different grains, tubers, and vegetables. White flour from wheat can be used to thicken sauces, to make pastry, and to bake bread. Some cooks prefer a more pure starch as in potato, rice, cornstarch, or arrowroot to thicken sauces. Some bakers like to add flour from other grains to bread such as rye, oats, and barley. These specialty flours do not work as well with yeast but provide interesting taste and texture.

Walnut Bread

One of the best things about eating dinner in a restaurant in France is the cheese course served after the main course and before dessert. The soft white cheeses are especially good with slices of walnut bread!

    2 tablespoons active dry yeast
    7 to 8 cups flour
    Sugar
    1 tablespoon salt
    1 cup walnut oil
    2 cups fresh walnuts, coarsely chopped

To proof the yeast, warm a measuring cup with hot tap water, then measure ½ cup hot water (115 to 120 degrees) and mix into it the yeast (add a pinch of sugar if using instant yeast). Let the mixture sit until bubbles form, about 10 minutes.

To make the dough, mix 7 cups of the flour with the salt in a large bowl. Make a well in the center, pour in 2½ cups warm water, and add the yeast mixture with ¼ cup of the walnut oil. Mix with a wooden spoon to incorporate the yeast into the water, then bring in the flour. When the dough begins to come together, put it on a lightly floured work surface and knead it until it is smooth and elastic, about 15 minutes. Put the remaining cup of flour on the board beside the dough. Add flour underneath the dough as needed to prevent it from sticking. The idea is to add as little flour as possible and still have a smooth dough. Make the dough into a round ball. Place a teaspoon of the walnut oil in a deep bowl and turn the dough over to coat the top with oil. Put the dough in the bowl and cover it with a dry towel. Place in a warm area and let rise until doubled in size, about 1½ hours.

To shape the dough, punch it down and mix in the chopped walnuts with another ½ cup of the walnut oil. Knead only to incorporate. Return the dough to the bowl and let it rise again, covered, until doubled in size, about an hour.

Punch down the dough, divide into two portions, and shape each into a large, smooth ball. Place the loaves on a lightly oiled baking pan and let rise one more time, lightly covered with a cloth, for about 45 minutes. Brush the loaves lightly with the remaining walnut oil and bake on the top rack of a 400-degree oven until golden on the bottom and the loaves are firm to the touch, about 35 minutes. MAKES 2 LOAVES

The more oil or butter there is in a loaf of bread, the longer it will keep. It is best to keep bread at room temperature. If the bread is warm, it should be stored in a paper bag. After it has been cut into, or when it is completely cool, the bread can be stored in a paper bag, which can then be placed in a plastic bag. This will maintain the best flavor.

Ginger Spice Cookies

These cookies go well with tea.

¾ cup unsulfured molasses
¼ pound (1 stick) butter
½ cup dark brown sugar
1 egg yolk
2 cups flour
2 teaspoons ground ginger
1 teaspoon ground cinnamon
¼ teaspoon ground cloves
⅛ teaspoon freshly ground black pepper
¼ teaspoon baking soda
¼ teaspoon salt
Granulated sugar for dusting

Preheat the oven to 375 degrees. Line two baking sheets with parchment.

Put the molasses in a saucepan large enough to hold all the ingredients and melt over gentle heat until liquid. Stir in the butter and brown sugar and remove from the heat. Let cool for 5 minutes before stirring in the yolk. Sift in the flour combined with the ginger, cinnamon, cloves, baking soda, and salt. Stir to mix. Chill until firm. With your hands, roll balls of dough ½ inch in diameter, roll in the granulated sugar, and place them 2 inches apart on the pans. Flatten the cookies as thin as possible with a flat meat pounder and bake until crisp, about 10 minutes. Cool on racks and store in a tightly covered tin.

MAKES 48 COOKIES

Cornmeal-Raisin Biscotti

A terrific finish to an Italian meal is twice-cooked biscuits or cookies dipped in vin santo or late-harvest Riesling.

1½ cups golden raisins
1 pound (4 sticks) butter
1½ cups sugar
2 eggs
1½ teaspoons vanilla extract
3½ cups flour
1½ cups cornmeal
1½ teaspoons salt

To prepare the raisins, bring a saucepan of water to a boil. Turn off the heat and drop in the raisins. Let sit for 10 minutes, then drain thoroughly and set aside.

Preheat the oven to 325 degrees.

To make the dough, put the butter in the bowl of an electric mixer and beat with a wooden spoon until it is soft. Put the bowl in the mixer and beat in the sugar until the mixture is light and fluffy. Add the eggs one at a time, beating well after each addition, then the vanilla. Sift in the flour, cornmeal, and salt, and mix until the dough barely holds together. Stir the raisins into the dough. Roll the mixture into two logs, each of which is about 2 inches wide; chill until firm. Bake on the top rack of the oven until the dough is somewhat firm to the touch, about 1 hour. Let cool on a rack for 5 minutes. Cut the logs across into ½-inch-wide slices and lay these cut side down on the baking sheet. Return them to the oven for 5 minutes to dry them out, turn off the oven, and let them continue to dry for another 5 minutes. Cool and store in airtight containers.

MAKES 48 BISCOTTI

Raspberry- or Lemon-Filled Cookies

These cookies are a treat for afternoon tea or as little cookies served after the meal with coffee or fresh herb tisane.

14 tablespoons butter (2 sticks minus
    2 tablespoons), at room temperature
1 cup sugar
1 egg
1 teaspoon vanilla extract
2 cups flour
½ teaspoon salt
¾ cup raspberry preserves or
    1 recipe lemon curd (page 302)

To make the dough, put the butter in the bowl of an electric mixer and beat it with a wooden spoon until soft. Put the bowl in the mixer and beat in the sugar until the mixture is pale and fluffy. Beat in the egg and vanilla. Sift in the flour with the salt. Wrap the dough in waxed paper and chill until firm.

Preheat the oven to 350 degrees. Line two baking sheets with parchment.

On a lightly floured board or counter, roll out the dough to a thickness of about ⅛ inch. With a 1- or 2-inch cookie cutter, cut out rounds and place them on the prepared pan. With a ½-inch round cutter, cut out the centers from half the rounds to make them look like flat doughnuts or rings. Spread ½ teaspoon raspberry preserves in the center of each of the whole rounds, place the rings on top, allowing the raspberry preserves to show in the center, and bake until they are lightly golden around the edges, about 15 minutes. If you want to use the lemon curd, bake the rounds and rings unfilled, as the curd should not go in the oven. When they are cool, spread the curd on the rounds and top with the rings. MAKES 40 COOKIES

To make fresh herb tisane, put several sprigs of fresh lemon verbena and/or fresh mint in a teapot. Cover with boiling water, let steep for 3 to 4 minutes, and serve.

Florentines

These elegant cookies would be a perfect ending to a holiday meal.

½ cup sugar
⅓ cup mixture of half milk and
   half heavy cream
⅓ cup light corn syrup
2 tablespoons butter
¼ cup flour
1 cup sliced, blanched almonds
⅓ cup Candied Orange Peel (page 389),
   cut in ¼-inch dice
1 ounce semisweet chocolate, chopped

Preheat the oven to 375 degrees. Line an 11 by 19-inch baking sheet with parchment.

To make the cookies, combine the sugar, cream, corn syrup, and butter in a medium-size saucepan. Swirl the mixture over low heat until the sugar dissolves. Increase the heat to high and let it boil until it reaches the soft-ball stage, 238 degrees on a candy thermometer. Transfer the mixture to a bowl and stir in the flour. Stir in the almonds and candied peel. Drop the batter in teaspoonfuls 2½ inches apart on the prepared pan and bake until the cookies are lightly browned around the edges, about 10 minutes. Let cool for a minute, and with a metal spatula invert them onto a rack to cool completely.

To finish the cookies, melt the chocolate in a bowl over a pan of gently simmering water. Don't let the bowl touch the water. Paint the bottom of each cookie with a thin layer of chocolate and drag the tines of a fork or a pastry comb through the chocolate to make a design. Let the chocolate cool. Serve the florentines with the chocolate side down. MAKES 24 COOKIES

The reason we don't cook with light cream or half-and-half is that it doesn't taste good. It is a product intended for adding to coffee, not for cooking. It is better to mix equal amounts of milk and heavy cream to make half-and-half.

Raspberry Truffles

These are unusual truffles because they are composed of a chocolate mixture wrapped around a fresh raspberry!

8 ounces bittersweet or semisweet
  chocolate, chopped
6 tablespoons butter
½ cup raspberry jam, melted and
  strained
2 tablespoons framboise
  (or kirsch)
16 fresh raspberries
¼ cup unsweetened cocoa powder

To make the truffle mixture, heat the chocolate with the butter in a bowl over a saucepan of gently simmering water, without allowing the water to touch the bottom of the bowl. Stir the mixture gently until melted and smooth. Let cool for a moment, then stir in the raspberry jam and the framboise. Chill until firm.

To form the truffles, sift the cocoa onto a plate. Scoop out a teaspoon of the truffle mixture, and with your fingertips press it around a fresh raspberry and drop it into the cocoa. Roll the truffle around in the cocoa and lift it with a fork to transfer it to a little candy cup. Repeat with the remaining chocolate mixture and raspberries. Chill. Serve within 24 hours.

MAKES 16 TRUFFLES

If you look at old cookbooks, you will find that thirty years ago cooks were using coffee to make cooking chocolate taste stronger. Now, fortunately, we can buy a variety of good cooking chocolates. For flavored chocolate truffles, Callebaut bittersweet or semisweet is a fine cooking chocolate.

Chocolate Pecan Toffee

The waiters at Insalata's in San Anselmo, the restaurant of my esteemed student Heidi Krahling, all know to bring me a little plate of this toffee after dinner. It's the best!

1½ cups sugar
9 ounces light corn syrup
1 pound butter, cut in 1-inch pieces
2½ cups lightly toasted chopped pecans
12 ounces semisweet or bittersweet chocolate
4 ounces milk chocolate

Heat the sugar with 6 tablespoons water in a large saucepan over low heat. Swirl from time to time to dissolve the sugar. Add the corn syrup and the butter. Increase the heat to bring to a boil, stirring from time to time. When the mixture reaches the hard-crack stage, about 300 degrees on a candy thermometer, after about 20 minutes, quickly stir in a cup of the nuts and pour the mixture onto a Silpat-lined cookie sheet. With a metal spatula, spread the candy as thin as possible. Let cool to room temperature, then remove from the Silpat.

To finish the candy, melt the chocolates in a bowl over a pan of gently simmering water. Spread the chocolate on top of the candy and sprinkle the remaining pecans on top. Let cool.

When the chocolate has set, break it into pieces. Store in an airtight container.

MAKES 2 POUNDS

Always taste a pecan before buying because they go rancid quickly.

Chocolate chips are fine for cookies but no substitute for semisweet chocolate in recipes like these because they contain too many stabilizers.

Silpats are great for caramel and chocolate work. They can be bought at kitchen shops and need to be stored flat.

Melted sugar goes through several stages as it heats and before it caramelizes, each stage of which is important in candy making:

thread	215°
soft ball	238°
hard ball	250°
soft crack	275°
hard crack	305°

CHOCOLATE

CHOCOLATE STANDS BY ITSELF! There is no other ingredient like it in cooking. When it first came to Europe from the New World, it was consumed as a beverage for a hundred years before it was discovered it could be made into a confection. Since then it has been used in all forms of desserts as well as candy.

Chocolate comes from cocoa beans grown on trees in the tropics. The beans are removed from the pods, fermented, and dried on the cocoa plantations. To be made into chocolate, the beans must be roasted to develop aroma and flavor, then crushed, hulled, and ground into a paste called chocolate liquor. Chocolate liquor is about 53 percent cocoa butter—a white waxy fat—and cocoa powder. This liquor used to be made in the country of origin and shipped to manufacturers around the world, who made it into cooking chocolate. Now many producers like to start with their own beans.

To make the chocolate liquor into cooking chocolate, the liquor must be milled and conched to become smooth. Conching can take anywhere from four hours to five days. Afterward, sugar, vanilla, and an emulsifier are added, and sometimes extra cocoa butter. Finally, the chocolate is formed into ten-pound blocks, which are sold to bakers and confection makers.

As a cook, how do you know what cooking chocolate to buy? The best one to buy is bittersweet or semisweet because it has the most pure taste. Each manufacturer makes several kinds of these chocolates, with names like French Vanilla and LeNoir. The absolute best chocolate for cooking is made by Valrhona. Because it is so expensive, save it for special desserts like Chocolate Pudding Cake (page 315). For most cooking, Callebaut is fine. What it comes down to is that choosing a cooking chocolate is a matter of personal taste. Good cooking chocolate is made by Scharffen Berger, Lindt, Guittard, and Ghirardelli; again, it's a matter of taste.

What you should look for in quality cooking chocolate is chocolate that has a nice shine and that breaks like shale when cut, a minimum of graininess in your mouth, and a minimum of emulsifiers.

The difference between bittersweet and semisweet varies from company to company. Milk chocolate has powdered milk added and more sugar than bittersweet or semisweet. White chocolate is made from just the cocoa butter. The only kind of white chocolate to buy is Callebaut.

To melt chocolate, do so slowly over gentle heat. Chocolate will seize if it gets too hot or if liquid is added partway through the melting process. Chocolate is like a cat— sometimes it works for you and sometimes it doesn't. If it gets too hot, you can bring it back by stirring in a considerable amount of hot water. If you do this, be sure to taste it to make sure it doesn't have a burned taste.

For many years Nick Malgieri, the well-known New York pastry chef, has been teaching the students of Tante Marie's how to temper chocolate. It's a great class, but the accomplished home cook never needs to temper chocolate. Tempering is a technique of raising and lowering the temperature of chocolate to make it strong and shiny. It is necessary only when molding or dipping chocolates.

What you need to remember about chocolate as a home cook is not to let it get too hot!

COFFEE AND TEA

COFFEE IS USUALLY a hot drink made from a bean that grows in the tropics. The story goes that some mountain people saw goats cavorting after eating the red berries of the coffee plant and decided to try this berry. There's no doubt people love coffee's effect on them. Names of some good-quality coffee beans are Kenya, Guatemala, and Costa Rica. The coffee beans are usually picked ripe, dried or washed and dried to remove the husks, and sorted before they are sent around the world. Good specialty coffee companies roast their own coffee. Sometimes they make their own blends.

To make a wonderful cup of coffee for breakfast or after dinner, buy freshly roasted beans from a company such as Peet's Coffee or Freed, Teller & Freed in San Francisco and grind them yourself in a grinder used just for coffee. Put the freshly ground coffee in a gold filter (rather than paper) in a drip-type coffee pot and add boiling water. No automatic coffee makers get the water hot enough to make good coffee. Freshly roasted and ground beans made with boiling hot water will give you a good cup of coffee. The kind and/or blend is up to you. The experts all agree that decaffeinating coffee reduces the flavor dramatically.

There is only one species of tea plant—it originated in Asia and is now grown in tropical regions all over the world. There are many different varieties of tea with names such as Assam, Darjeeling, Ceylon, Lapsang Souchong, jasmine, Dragon Well, and Formosa Oolong. Tea leaves are processed according to the desired result. If the leaves are steamed to halt fermentation, the result is green tea, such as Dragon Well. Partially fermented leaves result in oolongs such as Ti Kuan Yin and, traditionally, jasmine. Fully fermented leaves result in black tea, such as Assam and Darjeeling. Earl Grey is a blend of teas, as is English Breakfast. All teas, whether green, oolong, or black, are stimulating and are said to be healthful. All natural teas have some caffeine. Black tea has about one-third less caffeine than coffee. Generally, the quality of the tea is shown in the size of the leaf. The larger the leaf, the better the quality. If you open a tea bag, you will see that the tea is like powder—definitely low quality. Buy loose tea from a reputable dealer such as Freed, Teller & Freed. Keep it in a tin for no more than six months.

To make a good pot of tea, bring a kettle of cold water to a boil and pour it over loose tea leaves in a warmed teapot, using the ratio of a teaspoon of leaves for every cup (don't add a teaspoon for the pot). Let sit, covered, for no more than 5 minutes, then either remove the leaves or strain the tea into another warm pot. After 5 minutes, the tea leaves begin to release tannins, which ruin the flavor of the tea. Good tea should not be served with milk or lemon slices. I believe the reason the English started adding milk (never cream) and sugar to tea is that it was left too long in the pot. Diluting it with hot water doesn't help either. I have to admit I love black tea English style with milk and sugar. But I know better!

There are some wonderful mixtures of dried herbs offered as herbal tea in fine restaurants and supermarkets. It is better to call them tisanes, as in France, since they are not true tea. You can take almost any fresh herb or combination of fresh herbs and pour boiling water over it to make a tisane, or infusion. The water should be just below a boil, and the tisane should steep for 3 to 4 minutes. Try fresh mint and lemon verbena or a combination of the two. Offer these to your friends who insist on decaffeinated tea. Decaffeinated green or black tea is pretty bad stuff!

PANTRY

I N THIS CHAPTER are descriptions of how to make specialty ingredients called for in some of the recipes in this book. Although most can be purchased, they always taste better homemade.

The Tante Marie's Pantry

Following is a list of the ingredients that are kept on hand at all times at the cooking school:

- Lemons, oranges, onions, shallots, garlic, ginger
- Carrots, celery, leeks, parsley, potatoes
- Eggs, milk, cream, butter, Parmesan, and Gruyère
- Baguettes
- Sugar, flour, confectioners' sugar, dark brown sugar, raisins, currants, baking powder, baking soda, cornstarch, cake flour, honey, corn syrup, molasses, cocoa, semisweet chocolate, vanilla beans and vanilla extract, almond extract, instant espresso
- Almonds, hazelnuts, walnuts, sliced almonds, almond paste, red currant jelly, apricot jelly
- White wine vinegar, red wine vinegar, sherry vinegar, balsamic vinegar, French olive oil, Italian olive oil, safflower or canola oil, anchovies, capers
- Plain salt, coarse salt, black and white peppercorns, red pepper flakes
- Chicken stock, veal stock, bottled clam juice, canned tomatoes
- Coffee, tea, herb teas
- Red wine, white wine, brandy, Grand Marnier, Madeira, vermouth, kirsch

Fish Stock

*F*ish stock is used in recipes for sauces and for soups. Concentrated fish stock is called *fumet.*

2 pounds bones (fish frames) and heads from
  white-fleshed fish (not salmon), cleaned
  of all traces of blood
2 cups dry white wine
1 large onion, finely chopped
1 carrot, peeled and finely chopped
1 celery stalk, finely chopped
Bouquet garni composed of 3 sprigs
  parsley, 2 sprigs thyme, and
  1 bay leaf

Put the cleaned bones in a large stainless steel or enamel saucepan with the wine and 4 cups cold water over moderately high heat. When the mixture begins to boil, foam may rise to the top. Skim off and discard the foam and add the onion, carrot, celery, and bouquet garni. Bring to a boil, reduce to a feeble simmer, and cook gently for 30 minutes.

Strain the stock into a large container, pressing out all the liquid, and discarding the fish bones and vegetables. Taste, and if the fish flavor is not distinct, return the liquid to a clean pot and reduce by no more than half. Let cool, partially covered, in the refrigerator. Excess fish stock can be frozen for up to a year.   3 CUPS

Salmon gives fish stock a decidedly salmon flavor. It is better to make fish stock neutral so that it can be used with any fish dish. Using 30 per-
cent to 50 percent wine brings out the flavor of the fish.

The vegetables for fish stock are finely chopped because that is the best way to get the maximum flavor from the vegetables in a short cooking time.

Light Chicken Stock

*T*his stock is easy to make with ingredients *normally on hand in the kitchen. It has many uses, including soups, sauces, and chicken and other meat dishes.*

*5 pounds chicken bones (necks, backs, or
    carcasses) or one 5-pound stewing chicken*
3 onions, coarsely chopped
3 carrots, coarsely chopped
2 celery stalks, coarsely chopped
*Bouquet garni composed of 4 sprigs parsley,
    3 sprigs thyme, and 1 bay leaf*

Make sure there are no bits of liver attached to any of the bones. Put the bones in a large stockpot, cover with plenty of cold water, and bring to a boil. Carefully skim off and discard any gray scum that rises to the top. Add the vegetables and bouquet garni and return to a boil. Reduce the heat and simmer the stock gently for 3 to 4 hours, skimming from time to time and adding more water as it reduces to keep the chicken covered by an inch. Strain the stock into a clean container. Place it, partially covered, in the refrigerator. To chill it more quickly, place the container in a sink of ice water.

The stock will keep fresh for 5 days, after which it will need to be put into a pan and reboiled for 5 minutes before being stored in a clean container again. This can be repeated indefinitely, or it can be frozen.

If making the stock with whole stewing hens, remove the chicken from the stockpot when the

chicken is cooked through, after about 40 minutes. When it is cool enough to handle, remove the meat from the bones to save for chicken salad or Chicken Pot Pie with Artichokes and Shiitakes (page 192), and return the skin and bones to the stockpot for longer cooking. All the innards from the chicken except the liver can be used in the stock.

The stock may turn sour if it is stored covered in the refrigerator while still warm. That is why it is always important to add cold stock to cold stock or hot stock to hot stock. If you add hot stock to cold stock, it too may turn sour.

There is no good reason to let food come to room temperature after being cooked. Food that is left out has a higher risk of developing bacteria. Always chill food to be stored as quickly as possible. An ice bath is a good way to do this for large quantities.

It is perfectly acceptable to sneak some duck or other bones into a pot of chicken stock because duck by itself doesn't make a very flavorful stock.

Dark Veal Stock

It is important to use homemade stock for reduction sauces because prepared stocks become salty when reduced.

5 pounds veal or beef bones
5 pounds veal breast or beef shanks
1 tablespoon vegetable oil plus more for coating the pan
4 onions, peeled and quartered
4 carrots, coarsely chopped
3 celery stalks, coarsely chopped
2 tomatoes, coarsely chopped
4 mushrooms, coarsely chopped
Bouquet garni composed of 4 sprigs parsley, 3 sprigs thyme, and 1 bay leaf

To roast the bones, place them in an oiled roasting pan in a 450-degree oven, turning them from time to time until they are well browned, about an hour.

To brown the vegetables, heat them with the tablespoon of oil in a large sauté pan over moderately high heat. Cook, stirring from time to time, until brown.

To make the stock, put the bones in a large stockpot. Deglaze the roasting pan with a cup of cold water and add to the stockpot. Cover with cold water and bring to a boil over high heat. Skim off and discard any scum that rises to the top. Add the browned vegetables, tomatoes, mushrooms, and bouquet garni. Bring the stock to a boil. Lower the heat to keep the stock at a feeble simmer. Let it cook, skimming the scum that rises to the top as necessary and stirring from time to time, until all the flavor has been released from the bones and the vegetables, 5 to 6 hours. Add water as needed to keep the bones covered by an inch. Strain the stock through a large colander into a container. Chill, partially covered, in the refrigerator. To chill it more quickly, place the container in a sink of ice water.

The stock will keep fresh for 5 days, after which it will need to be put into a pan and reboiled for 5 minutes before being stored in a clean container again. This can be repeated indefinitely, or it can be frozen.

To save time and space, fill small Ziploc bags with 1½ cups cooled stock each and lay them flat on a baking pan in the freezer. When they are frozen, label them and pile them in the freezer without the baking pan. You do not have to thaw stock before adding it to your dishes.

Vegetable Stock

The only reason to use a vegetable stock instead of chicken or veal is if you are serving vegetarians. Although you can never give a dish the depth of flavor you'd get from a poultry or meat stock, this vegetable stock has plenty of flavor.

2 tablespoons vegetable oil
2 onions, coarsely chopped
1 carrot, coarsely chopped
1 celery stalk, coarsely chopped
1 leek, trimmed and coarsely chopped
1 parsnip and/or 1 rutabaga, coarsely chopped
1 ounce dried porcini (cèpe) mushrooms
6 garlic cloves, crushed
2 tablespoons tomato paste
Bouquet garni composed of 12 sprigs parsley, 6 sprigs thyme, and 2 bay leaves

To make the stock, combine the oil, onions, carrot, celery, leek, parsnip, mushrooms, and garlic in a large stockpot and cover with plenty of cold water. Bring to a boil over high heat and add the mushrooms, tomato paste, and bouquet garni. Lower the flame and simmer until all the flavor is extracted from the vegetables, about an hour. Strain the stock into a large container and discard the vegetables. Chill in the refrigerator.

Smoked Salmon

If you like smoked foods, you really ought to invest in a Little Chief Smoker. It is relatively inexpensive, easy to use, and gives food a great flavor. This smoked salmon does not slice as well as commercially smoked cold salmon, but it is delicious all the same.

One 3- to 4-pound piece of fillet of fresh salmon
¼ cup sugar
½ cup coarse salt

Remove all the bones from the salmon, leaving the skin on.

To prepare the brine, dissolve the sugar and salt in a quart of cold water in a glass baking dish. Place the salmon in the brine and refrigerate for 48 hours.

To smoke the fish, remove the salmon from the brine and pat it dry with paper towels. Put the fish on a board and angle the board in front of a home electric fan for an hour to form a skin, then put it in a cold smoker with dry wood chips. (The drying makes it easier to slice later.) Let the fish smoke for 3 to 4 hours, changing the wood chips whenever they are all black, every hour or 1½ hours. The fish is done when just firm to the touch. Chill before using.

Smoked Chicken

Y*ou can use home-smoked chicken in many ways, such as in sandwiches and salads. Although smoking was traditionally a method of preserving food, this chicken is smoked merely for flavor and will not keep for more than a week in the refrigerator.*

One 4-pound chicken
¼ cup sugar
½ cup coarse salt

Remove the innards and any fat from the cavity of the chicken. Cut the chicken into four pieces with kitchen scissors or poultry shears.

To prepare the brine, dissolve the sugar and salt in a quart of cold water in a glass baking dish. Put the chicken pieces in the brine and chill for 24 to 48 hours.

To smoke the chicken, remove the chicken from the brine, pat it dry with paper towels, and put it on a rack in a cold smoker with dry wood chips. Let the chicken smoke until it tastes smoky, 3 to 4 hours. It is important at this point to cut into the chicken to see if it is opaque down to the bone. If it's not, put it in a roasting pan in a 350-degree oven to finish the cooking.

You can add many interesting ingredients to the brine, such as fresh herbs or soy sauce.

❧

It's important to cut up chicken, duck, and turkey before smoking in a small home smoker because it takes only 4 hours at a warm temperature for foods to begin growing bacteria. That is why you want to get it out of the smoker after 4 hours and into a 350-degree oven to finish the cooking. Commercial smoking companies can smoke whole birds because they inject the birds with a saline solution.

For information on smokers, write:

Little Chief Smoker Products
c/o Luhr Jenson & Sons, Inc.
P.O. Box 297
Hood River, OR 97031
(541) 386-3811

The smoker and a box of wood chips cost about $80 and take up very little space.

Duck Confit

To make confit of duck legs is to preserve them by salting overnight, cooking, and finally storing them in their own fat. This is a tradition in southwest France, where geese and ducks are force-fed in the last few weeks of their lives to produce fattened livers called foie gras. After the geese or ducks are slaughtered, the breast (magret) can be eaten fresh and the legs preserved. The method of preserving them in vats of duck fat was developed long before refrigeration. Today, cooks make confit because it is so good to eat, not to preserve it over the winter. However, a container of duck legs cooked and preserved in fat is a great ingredient to have in the back of the refrigerator. Just pull them out, wipe off as much fat as you can, and add them to soups or casseroles. You can also wipe off the fat, coat the legs with bread crumbs, broil them, and serve them with a green salad.

One 4- to 5-pound fresh duck, quartered, skin on and excess fat removed, or 6 duck legs with thighs, disjointed
⅓ cup coarse salt
7 cups rendered duck fat
6 garlic cloves, unpeeled and smashed

To cure the duck, sprinkle both sides of the duck pieces with the salt. Put the pieces in a glass baking dish, cover with plastic wrap, and refrigerate for 24 to 48 hours. During this time the salt will draw off excess moisture from the flesh and the herbs will infuse flavor.

To make the confit, melt the fat in a large saucepan over moderately high heat. Wipe each piece of duck with paper towels and slide it into the melted fat. Add the garlic. Cook the duck in the fat over the lowest possible heat until the duck meat is fully cooked. You can tell if the duck is cooked by inserting a metal skewer or a fork in the thick part of the leg or thigh; the meat should not lift out of the fat when the skewer is lifted. Meat that is not fully cooked will lift right out. Remove the pieces of duck with tongs and put them in a plastic container. Strain the liquid fat over the duck to cover it completely. Cover and chill.

You can buy duck fat from specialty stores like Whole Foods or from a purveyor that deals in duck. Or you can save excess fat from ducks used in cooking other dishes. It takes a lot of fat to make confit. If you don't have enough duck fat, you can add pork fat from fatback. To render duck fat (or pork), heat the fat in a large saucepan with ½ cup water over low heat. The fat will melt away from any skin or tissue and become a clear liquid. When the fat is completely liquefied and clear, 20 to 30 minutes, strain it into a container and chill it. The duck fat can be used to make confit over and over as long as it is kept in the refrigerator or freezer. If the duck fat ever gets so hot that it reaches the smoking point, the flavor will change and it must be discarded.

Pork Sausages

*M*aking your own sausages can be lots of *fun, especially when done in a group. You can buy an adequate hand-crank sausage stuffer at most restaurant supply stores for about $85; it's harder to find a source for sausage casings. The best thing is to buy about 3 yards of hog casings from a butcher who makes his own sausages. You may have to order pork butt and fatback ahead. Good sausages have 25 percent fat, which helps to keep them moist when they are cooked.*

3 yards medium-size sausage casings
4 pounds fresh pork butt
2 pounds fresh fatback
2 tablespoons coarse salt
1 teaspoon freshly ground black pepper
1 cup fresh Italian parsley, coarsely chopped
½ teaspoon red pepper flakes
4 garlic cloves, minced
1 cup white wine

To prepare the casings, soak them in a small bowl of cold water while preparing the ground meat mixture. To prepare the meat, cut it into 1-inch cubes, season well with salt and pepper, and put in a bowl in the freezer until well chilled, about 1 hour.

To prepare the meat, grind it through the coarse blade of a meat grinder into a large bowl. Add the salt, pepper, parsley, pepper flakes, garlic, and white wine. Mix with a wooden spoon, not your hands. To taste, fry a small patty of this mixture over low heat in a nonstick pan without oil or butter. Add garlic, red pepper flakes, salt, and pepper to taste. Chill the mixture for at least another hour.

To prepare the casings, with your fingers, open one end of the length of casing under cold running water. Let a large bubble of water run through the entire length of the casing. This will stretch the casing and make it easier to stuff. With wet hands, thread all the casings onto the plastic attachment of the sausage stuffer.

To stuff the sausages, remove the cutting blade of the meat grinder and connect the plastic attachment to the sausage stuffer. Stuff the sausage mixture loosely into the sausage casings in one long sausage. When all the mixture has been used, adjust the size and tension of each sausage with your hands, starting at the middle and working toward the ends. Make links that are about 4 inches long. Keep twisting between links and tying the sausages with string where they are twisted. Let the sausages dry on a rack without touching each other in the refrigerator for 24 hours before cooking. They can be stored in a plastic bag in the refrigerator for up to a week or in the freezer for up to a year.

Fresh sausages are best if they ripen for a day before cooking; otherwise, they are likely to burst while cooking.

Sausage casings are the cleaned intestines from sheep, hogs, or steers. The small breakfast link

casings come from sheep; the medium casings from hogs; and the large ones for salami from steers. Often the large casings are synthetic.

If you see sausages in the meat counter that are bright red, they have been treated with a preservative known as saltpeter, Westphalia, or nitrates.

Fresh Pasta

Year after year for the past fifteen years, Giuliano Bugialli has been showing the students of Tante Marie's how to make fresh pasta. His pasta is simply delicious but hard to imitate. Here are my instructions on how to make your own fresh pasta using the hints I learned from Giuliano!

> *3 cups all-purpose flour*
> *5 large eggs*
> *2 teaspoons olive oil*
> *½ teaspoon salt*

Mound the flour on a clean counter or board. With one of the eggs make a large well about 4 inches across in the center of the flour and crack all the eggs into the well. Pretending that the well is the face of a clock, add the olive oil at 8 o'clock and the salt at 7 o'clock. With a fork, break the yolks of the eggs and mix together with the whites. Using the fork, start bringing the flour into the eggs, going around the inner circle of the well. If the walls of the well break, and the liquid egg runs out, simply bring it together with a metal dough scraper. When half the flour is incorporated, work the rest in with the dough scraper or by hand. Knead the dough with the palm of your hand until smooth and no flour remains on the outside. If there are little bits of dry dough, sieve them out and throw them away—they will never incorporate into the dough. Usually, 3 cups of flour and 5 large eggs give the right texture for this dough; however, if the dough is not very stiff, sweep additional flour under the dough and continue to knead until it is firm and smooth. It is always easier to add flour to a damp dough than to add liquid to a dry dough. If the dough seems too dry, wrap it in plastic wrap and let rest for 10 minutes. If it's the correct texture, cut the dough into four pieces and begin rolling one of the pieces in a pasta machine or by hand. (All doughs that contain flour need to be covered to prevent a crust from forming on the outside.)

To roll out the dough, press it into a ½-inch-thick patty and put it through the widest setting on the pasta machine. There should be a light dusting of flour on the counter. Flour the outside of the dough, fold it in thirds, pound it three or four times with the side of your hand to get the layers to adhere to each other, and put it through the same setting in the opposite direction. Repeat this rolling and folding at the first setting until the dough is smooth and about the size of a necktie. Continue rolling the dough at smaller and smaller settings—on most machines this is a higher number. (The idea is that the folding and rolling on the first setting will make the dough smooth and the right size. Putting it through smaller and smaller settings without folding extrudes the dough to make it thinner.) It is important to keep flour on the counter where the pasta comes out of the machine and make sure the dough gets a light dusting of flour every time it goes through the machine. Once you have put the tongue of dough into the rollers, you do not need to feed the dough continually. It

is better to catch the dough as it comes out of the machine. When you are working alone, you need to crank with one hand and feed and then catch with the other. When feeding the machine, hold the dough with the flat part of your hand up and the thumb up. If the lengths of dough get unwieldy, cut them in half.   MAKES 1½ POUNDS

They say you should roll spaghettini or fettuccine until you can see your hand through the pasta, often the next-to-last setting. For cappellacci or ravioli, roll it to the thinnest setting.

To cut the dough into spaghettini or fettuccine, simply roll the lengths of dough in the other side of the pasta machine in opposite directions through the thin or wide cutters, being sure to catch the noodles as they come out. To dry the noodles, hang them over a rack or a broom handle, being sure to separate each strand. Or toss them on a wooden counter or board with plenty of flour. Do not pile up the cut noodles; rather, spread them out to dry. They must dry at least 30 minutes before being cooked in boiling salted water.

If you want to save the pasta for another time, place the well-floured mounds of pasta that have dried for at least 30 minutes in plastic bags in the freezer. Pasta should not be thawed before being dropped in boiling salted water or the noodles will stick together. Just drop the frozen pasta in the water and separate the strands with a wooden fork.

Puff Pastry
(*Pâte Feuilletée*)

Puff pastry has many uses, including for cheese straws, palmiers, fleurons, vol-au-vents, pithiviers, napoleons, jalousies, and fruit tarts.

2 cups flour
1 teaspoon salt
2 tablespoons cold salted butter
    plus ½ pound (2 sticks) salted
    butter

To make the outer dough (*détrempe*), combine the flour and salt in a bowl. With your fingers, rub the 2 tablespoons butter into the flour until it resembles bread crumbs. Add ¾ cup cold water and mix the dough with a fork held straight up and down. Bring the mixture into a ball with the fingers of one hand with minimum kneading. Wrap in waxed paper and chill while you prepare the butter.

To make the butter pack, beat the ½ pound butter with a rolling pin or your fist until it has the same consistency as the *détrempe*. (You want butter that is malleable but not softened; otherwise it will melt into the *détrempe*.) With a pastry scraper, cut halfway into the dough in a cross so that you can pull out the four corners. Shape the butter into a 4-inch square and sprinkle it on all sides with a little flour. Place the butter square in the middle of the dough with the corners at angles to the corners of the dough.

Fold the dough over to make a smooth package.

The first rolling of this pastry is very important. To roll out the dough, pound the dough several times parallel to you and then firmly roll the dough away from you, starting at the middle. Roll it back toward yourself, again starting at the middle. Repeat until you have a strip of dough about 16 inches long. Keep lifting the dough to make sure it comes off the board or counter and always have a light coating of flour on the board, the rolling pin, and the package of dough. The important thing is that the butter rolls evenly in between the layers of the *détrempe*. Brush off any excess flour with a dry pastry brush. Fold the dough in thirds like a business letter. Make a half turn to the right, and roll it in the same manner as before, rolling away from yourself and back toward yourself, lifting to make sure the dough isn't stuck on the board. Once again, fold the dough in thirds like a business letter. This time make two marks on the dough with your fingers to indicate you have made two turns. Rewrap in the waxed paper and chill for 30 minutes.

When you remove the dough from the refrigerator, be sure the folded end is toward you so that you are always rolling in the opposite direction from the last rolling. Make two more turns as before and mark the dough with your fingers. Rewrap in the waxed paper and chill for another 30 minutes or overnight.

Make two more turns and chill, wrapped in waxed paper, until ready to use. (It is important that the dough rest between turns so that the butter stays cold and the dough does not become too elastic.) Altogether it should be turned six times. It can be stored in the refrigerator for up to 5 days or in the freezer for up to 9 months.

MAKES 1 POUND

Fresh Peach Jam

Here is a great way to preserve this wonderful fruit of summer.

5 pounds peaches, peeled, pitted, and cut in 1-inch slices
3¾ cups sugar
½ cup lemon juice

To macerate the fruit, combine the peaches and sugar in a large stainless steel or enamel saucepan. Use a potato masher to mash the mixture well. Let sit for 2 hours, stirring occasionally with a wooden spoon.

To make the jam, bring the fruit mixture to a boil, stirring constantly to prevent it from sticking. Simmer the mixture until it is thick, 30 to 40 minutes, skimming off any white foam that accumulates on the surface. When the mixture reaches 220 degrees on a candy thermometer, stir in the lemon juice. Ladle the jam into glass preserving jars, cover with new lids, and seal with the rings.

MAKES 2½ PINTS

Traditionally, there are three ways to tell when jam or jelly has reached the point when it's ready to be put into jars. It's ready when the drops run together off the side of a spoon when lifted out of the mixture; or when you put a small amount on a saucer and chill it for 5 minutes and the jam wrinkles when you push your finger across the top. The most reliable way to be sure it is ready is to wait until it reaches 9 degrees above boiling, which is 220 degrees at sea level.

❧

Of the three kinds of preserving jars, the ones with the metal rings are the best. The jars and rings can be reused, but if you want to keep preserves for a long time you need to use new lids. This is because once the seal on a lid has been broken, it may not seal properly again. To test the lids, put hot liquid jam or jelly into clean jars, screw down the rings over new lids, and the next day test the seal by pressing on the top. If it clicks when you do this, you do not have a good seal. At this point you can keep the jam or jelly in the refrigerator or start using it right away. You need to worry about a good seal on your jars only when you plan to store them for a long time. There is no way of telling whether the seal is good in glass jars with glass lids and rubber rings. In addition, I find that putting paraffin on top of jams or jellies is totally appealing.

Strawberry-Rhubarb Conserve

T*hese summer fruits marry well in a conserve to be eaten on scones or whole-grain breakfast breads.*

1 orange, both peel and pulp finely chopped
3 cups strawberries, measured after hulling
    and crushing
3 cups rhubarb, cut in ¼-inch slices
5 cups sugar
½ teaspoon plain salt
1 cup raisins
½ cup pecans or walnuts, coarsely chopped

Heat the orange with a cup of water in a large heavy saucepan. Cook until the peel is tender.

Add the strawberries, rhubarb, sugar, salt, and raisins. Stir until the mixture comes to a boil and let boil until it begins to thicken. Add the nuts and cook for another 5 minutes. Pour this hot mixture into clean jars with new lids and rings and seal tightly.

MAKES 4 PINTS

Conserves and chutneys need to be cooked only until thick; you don't have to test to see if they will set.

Spicy Apple Chutney

Chutney is a type of preserve eaten with cold meats. This is a great recipe from Susan Feniger and Mary Sue Milliken, who taught many years ago at Tante Marie's. They are great women and passionate cooks!

2 tablespoons vegetable oil
1 tablespoon mustard seeds
1 medium-size onion, finely chopped
1 red bell pepper, cored and cut in
    ¼-inch dice
1 teaspoon coarse salt
2 garlic cloves, minced
1 serrano chile, finely chopped
1 teaspoon ground ginger
1 teaspoon ground allspice
¼ cup raisins
1 cup packed dark brown sugar
¾ cup red wine vinegar
4 green apples, peeled, cored, and cut in
    ¼-inch dice

Heat the oil in a large saucepan set over high heat. When the oil is hot, add the mustard seeds, cover, and cook until the popping stops. Reduce the heat and add the onion, bell pepper, and salt. Cook the chutney, uncovered, stirring occasionally, until the onion is soft. Stir in the garlic, chile, ginger, and allspice, and cook for another minute. Add the raisins, brown sugar, vinegar, apples, and a cup of water. Cook, uncovered, over moderately high heat until the mixture is soft and aromatic, about 40 minutes. Ladle into clean jars, cover tightly, and cool.

Spicy Cranberry Chutney

This recipe was taught to us at Tante Marie's years ago by Julie Sahni, an expert in Indian cooking who lives in New York. Her knowledge of spices is fantastic! Everyone loves this recipe.

Two 12-ounce packages fresh cranberries
2 oranges, both peel and pulp finely
    chopped
½ red onion, finely chopped
4 tablespoons julienned fresh ginger
2 cinnamon sticks, broken in half
1 teaspoon coarse salt
3 cups sugar
2 teaspoons cayenne pepper
2 teaspoons dry mustard
½ cup chopped walnuts
½ cup dried Black Mission figs, tips
    removed and coarsely chopped
¼ cup dark raisins

Combine the cranberries, oranges, red onion, ginger, cinnamon, salt, sugar, cayenne, mustard, walnuts, figs, and raisins in a large enamel pan over moderate heat. Cook, stirring often, until the sugar dissolves completely and the chutney comes to a boil. Continue cooking, stirring from time to time, until the cranberries pop, about 6 minutes. Ladle the hot mixture into clean jars, cover tightly, and let cool.

To store these preserves at room temperature for up to a year, the jars must be sealed with new lids. The next day, after the preserves cool, there should be a tight seal on the jars. If there isn't, reboil the mixture and try to seal it again or simply store the preserves in the refrigerator.

Candied Orange Peel

Keep a jar of candied orange peel in the refrigerator to flavor all sorts of desserts. To use it, simply remove the peel from the syrup and cut it in the shape you need.

You can also dip both sides of the candied orange quarters in sugar and dry them overnight on a rack before cutting. Cut the peel in strips to serve after dinner.

> *1½ cups sugar*
> *6 navel oranges*
> *Grand Marnier*

To make the cooking syrup, heat the sugar with 3 cups water in a saucepan over low heat. Swirl slowly until the sugar dissolves.

Remove the peel from the oranges in four equal quarters. Use your fingers to remove these quarters of peel. Lay each peel on a board and remove as much of the white pith as possible with a spoon. Add all the peel to the sugar syrup at once and let it simmer gently until the peel is translucent. Transfer the orange peel with tongs to a glass jar. Let the syrup cool 10 minutes and then pour it over the peel. Add enough Grand Marnier to cover. Chill. The candied peel can be stored in the refrigerator for up to a year.

Rather than buy oranges only for the peel, you can eat the oranges and save the peel in the freezer until you have enough to candy.

Preserved Lemons

Preserved lemons are a traditional ingredient in North African cooking. They can be added to fish cooked with onions or lamb stew with olives, or used in a salad with fresh tomatoes.

6 lemons
2 cups coarse salt
1 cup lemon juice or water

Stand each lemon on end and make four cuts down through the rind and pulp almost to the bottom of the lemon, leaving the bottom intact. Do the same in the opposite direction. You will end up with a lemon in quarters that are still attached to each other. Put a handful of salt into each lemon and pack them into a clean glass jar. Pour in the rest of the salt with the lemon juice. Cover and refrigerate for at least a month, turning them over in the brine from time to time.

SUGGESTED
SEASONAL MENUS

Spring

Fava Bean Crostini with Pecorino *22*
Toasted Pastini with Artichokes and Hazelnuts *130*
Halibut Baked with Warm Shallot Compote *157*
Garlic Potatoes *270*
Strawberry Granita *290;*
or Strawberry Fool *290*

Herb Crêpes with Goat's Cheese Soufflé and Mesclun Salad *76*
Fillet of Salmon with Summer Vegetables and Citrus Oil *159*
Raspberry Vacherin *343*

Asparagus Salad with Fava Bean Sauce *106*
Roast Chicken with Spring Vegetables and Butter Sauce *186*
Mashed Potato Gratin (without truffle oil) *272*
Rhubarb-Strawberry Compote with Lattice *300*

Asparagus-Fontina Pizza with Truffle Oil *30;*
or Spring Vegetable Soup with Pecorino *95*
Braised Duck Legs with Lentils *208*
Gratin of Fresh Berries *296;*
or Compote of Fresh Berries with Lemon Verbena Ice Cream *295*

Vegetable Mélange of Leeks, Artichokes, and Shiitakes *57*
Braised Short Ribs with Horseradish Mashed Potatoes *249*
Buttered Green Beans *258*
Espresso–Chocolate Truffle Ice Cream *313*

Summer

Cream of Beet Soup with Cucumbers and Goat's Cheese *85*
Grilled Sea Bass with Salsa Verde *158*
Garlic Potatoes *270*
Fresh Fig and Plum Tart *331*

Yellow Gazpacho *89*
Paella *175*
Blueberries in Lemon Mousse *292*

Fresh Pea Soup with Cilantro *84*
Roast Chicken with Beans, Bacon, and Spinach *183*
Plum Sorbet in Tulipes *294*

Heirloom Tomato Galettes *59*
Grilled Skirt Steak with Roasted Potatoes and Salsa Verde *242*
Peaches with Champagne Sabayon *299*

Fig, Mozzarella, and Mizuna Salad with Basil *108*
California Choucroute Garnie *251*
Boiled new potatoes
Green Apple Sorbet with Calvados *291*

Fresh Corn Soup with Basil Butter *83*
Grilled Vegetable Brochettes and Tofu and Brown Rice Pilaf *280*
Summer Pudding *297*

Fall

White Bean Crostini with Wilted Greens   *23*
Spaghetti with Pesto, Potatoes, and Green Beans   *138*
Pacific Coast Bouillabaisse   *97*
Cold Lemon Soufflé   *310;*
or Lemon Tarts   *334*

Butternut Squash Soup   *88*
Grilled Salmon and Thai Salsa with Basmati Rice   *171;*
or Stir-Fried Chicken and Ginger-Peanut Sauce with Mixed Grain Pilaf   *201*
Tropical Fruit Tart   *337*

Charred Eggplant Dip with Pita Triangles   *24;*
or Roasted Eggplant Soup with Tomato   *86*
Chicken Sauté and Preserved Lemons and Olives with Spicy Rice   *203*
Dried Fruit Compote with Cardamom Pound Cake   *321*

Pear, Gorgonzola, and Walnut Salad   *109*
Rabbit Stew Woodland Style with Baked Cheese Polenta   *210*
Tiramisù   *317*

Molded Vegetable Risotto with Porcini Sauce   *75*
Pork Tenderloins with Onion Compote   *222*
Butternut Squash with Pecans   *255*
Hashed Brussels Sprouts with Brown Butter and Capers   *256*
Gingerbread Napoleon with Poached Pears and Caramel Sauce   *323*

Pear, Persimmon, and Pomegranate Salad with Pecans   *110;*
or Sweet Potato Risotto with Arugula and Fresh Mozzarella   *149*
Roast Pork with Dried Apricots and Prunes   *225*
Celery Root with Lemon   *259;*
and Spinach with Walnuts   *259*
Upside-Down Caramelized Apple Tart *(Tarte Tatin)*   *333;*
or Green Apple Sorbet with Calvados   *291*

Wild Mushroom Soup   *91*
Linguine with Roasted Peppers and Sausage   *139*
Artichoke and Goat's Cheese Salad   *107*
Bread Pudding with Dried Apricots and Cherries   *319*

Homemade Flour Tortillas with Avocado Salsa   *26*
Black-eyed Pea Stew Served in a Pumpkin   *277*
Caramelized Almond Tart   *336*
with Caramel Ice Cream   *307*

Winter

Avocado and Grapefruit Salad   *111*
New England Seafood Chowder   *98*
Meyer Lemon Crème Brûleé   *298*

Bistro Salad
(with Country Bacon, Garlic Croutons, and Soft-Cooked Egg)   *120*
Cabbage and Potato Soup with Duck Confit   *100*
Dried Fruit Compote with Cardamom Pound Cake   *321*

Antipasti Platter of Eggplant-Zucchini Sauté, Cauliflower with Salsa Verde,
and Red Bell Peppers with Anchovies   *50*
Seafood Risotto (with Clams, Shrimp, and Scallops)   *147*
Lemon Curd Soufflé   *302*

Artichoke and Goat's Cheese Salad   *107*
Sautéed Swordfish with Pickled Tomatoes and Couscous   *173*
Bread Pudding with Dried Apricots and Cherries   *319*

Whole Artichoke Filled with Roasted Garlic Soufflé   *55*
Chicken in Red Wine with Onions and Mushrooms   *194*
Boiled new potatoes
Chocolate Pudding Cake   *315*

Winter Vegetable Soup with Prosciutto   *96*
Crispy Chicken Breasts and Wild Mushrooms with Mashed Potatoes   *198*
Any green vegetable
Torta Regina with Chocolate and Caramel Sauces   *348*

Cream of Root Vegetable Soup with Black Truffles *94*
Magret of Duck in Cassis Sauce *205*
Carrot and Rutabaga Puree *264;*
and Root Vegetable Gratin *266*
Almond Génoise with Fresh Fruit and Raspberry Sauce *347*

Potato Galettes with Smoked Mackerel and Mesclun Salad *68*
Veal Ragoût with Olives and Homemade Spaetzle *228*
Cappuccino Brûlée *308*

French Potato Salad with Bacon Vinaigrette on Arugula *67*
Boned Leg of Lamb with Orange-Herb Stuffing *236*
Glazed Onions *261,* and Glazed Carrots *262*
Dried Apricot Soufflé *303*

Cream of Artichoke and Hazelnut Soup *92*
Pan-Fried Fillet of Beef with Red Wine Sauce and Truffle Butter *245*
Potato Gratin *271*
Green salad
Raspberry-Chocolate Crème Brûlée *316*

Celery Root, Endive, and Watercress Salad *112*
Cassoulet of White Beans, Sausage, and Duck Confit *212*
Oranges with Strawberry Sauce *293*

INDEX

Page numbers in **boldface** refer to recipes.

Metric Equivalencies

Liquid and Dry Measure Equivalencies

CUSTOMARY	METRIC
¼ teaspoon	1.25 milliliters
½ teaspoon	2.5 milliliters
1 teaspoon	5 milliliters
1 tablespoon	15 milliliters
1 fluid ounce	30 milliliters
¼ cup	60 milliliters
⅓ cup	80 milliliters
½ cup	120 milliliters
1 cup	240 milliliters
1 pint *(2 cups)*	480 milliliters
1 quart *(4 cups, 32 ounces)*	960 milliliters *(.96 liter)*
1 gallon *(4 quarts)*	3.84 liters
1 ounce *(by weight)*	28 grams
¼ pound *(4 ounces)*	114 grams
1 pound *(16 ounces)*	454 grams
2.2 pounds	1 kilogram *(1,000 grams)*